Christians and Jews in the Ottoman Empire

CHRISTIANS AND JEWS IN THE OTTOMAN EMPIRE

The Functioning of a Plural Society

EDITED BY
BENJAMIN BRAUDE
AND
BERNARD LEWIS

VOLUME II
THE ARABIC-SPEAKING LANDS

HOLMES & MEIER PUBLISHERS, INC.
NEW YORK LONDON

First published in the United States of America 1982 by
Holmes & Meier Publishers, Inc.
30 Irving Place
New York, N.Y. 10003

Great Britain:
Holmes & Meier Publishers, Ltd.
131 Trafalgar Road
Greenwich, London SE10 9TX

Library of Congress Cataloging in Publication Data
Main entry under title:

Christians and Jews in the Ottoman empire.

Papers presented at an international symposium held at Princeton University.
Bibliography: Vol. II, p. 207.
Includes index.
CONTENTS: v.1. The central lands. v. 2. The Arabic-speaking lands.
1. Christians in the Near East—Politics and government—Congresses. 2. Jews in the Near East—Politics and government—Congresses. 3. Christians in Turkey—Politics and government—Congresses.
4. Jews in Turkey—Politics and government—Congresses.
5. Minorities—Near East—Congresses. 6. Minorities—Turkey—Congresses. I. Braude, Benjamin.
II. Lewis, Bernard.
DS58.C48 1980 956.1'01 80-11337

ISBN 0-8419-0520-7 (v. 2)

Manufactured in the United States of America

Contents

VOLUME TWO: THE ARABIC-SPEAKING LANDS

Abbreviations

ABCFM	American Board of Commissioners, Foreign Missions, Cambridge, Mass.
AE	Ministère des Affaires Etrangères, Paris
Arch. Prop.	Archives of the Sacred Congregation for the Propagation of the Faith, Rome
AUB	American University of Beirut
BBA	Başbakanlık Arşivi, Istanbul
BSOAS	*Bulletin of the School of Oriental and African Studies*
CC	Correspondance Consulaire, AE
DOP	*Dumbarton Oaks Papers*
DSA	*Dahiliye Sicill-i Ahval Defterleri, BBA*
EI^2	*Encyclopedia of Islam,* second edition
FO	Foreign Office, Public Record Office Archive, London
IA	*İslâm Ansiklopedisi*
IFM	*İktisat Fakültesi Mecmuası,* Istanbul University
IJMES	*International Journal of Middle Eastern Studies*
JAOS	*Journal of the American Oriental Society*
JEEH	*Journal of European Economic History*
JEH	*Journal of Economic History*
JESHO	*Journal of the Economic and Social History of the Orient*
JQR	*Jewish Quarterly Review*
JRAS	*Journal of Royal Asiatic Society*
PRO	Public Record Office
REI	*Revue des Etudes Islamiques*
REJ	*Revue des Etudes Juives*
SA	*Sicill-i Ahval,* Hariciye Archives, Istanbul
SC	Scritture riferite nei Congressi, Arch. Prop.
SI	*Studia Islamica*
TOEM	Tarîh-i Osmânî Encümeni Mecmuası
USNA	United States National Archives

A Note on Transliteration

In view of the diversity of essays contained in these volumes, rigorous consistency has not always been possible or desirable. With certain exceptions Turkish has been transliterated according to official modern Turkish orthography and Arabic according to the system of the *Encyclopedia of Islam*. However, "ḳ" is rendered "q" and "dj" as "j". The ligatures below "ch", "dh", "gh", "kh", "sh", and "th" have been omitted.

Acknowledgments

These essays grew out of a research seminar and conference on "The *Millet* System: History and Legacy," that was conducted at Princeton University during the spring and summer of 1978. The scope of the book is somewhat narrower than that of the conference. Unfortunately considerations of space and unity of topic made it necessary to omit papers which dealt wholly or mainly with post-Ottoman or non-Ottoman topics. We gratefully acknowledge our debt to all those who participated in the seminar-conference.

A grant from the Ford Foundation to the Princeton University Program in Near Eastern Studies made possible the convening of the seminar-conference. Additional grants from both the Ford Foundation and Princeton University helped defray the costs of publication. Certain other costs were borne by the office of the Dean of the Graduate School of Arts and Sciences and the Department of History, both of Boston College.

The faculty, staff, and students of the Princeton Program and Department of Near Eastern Studies were especially helpful in the organization of the seminar-conference. Particular thanks are due Mrs. Mary Craparotta, Mrs. Grace Edelman, and Mrs. Judy Gross.

We benefited from able graduate assistance. Alan Iser, Near Eastern Languages and Civilizations at Harvard reviewed the manuscript for consistency. Alan Makovsky, Near Eastern Studies at Princeton, reviewed the bibliography. Shayndel Feuerstein, Romance Languages and Literatures at Harvard, translated portions of the text from French to English. John Feeley and James Nealon of Boston College helped correct the galleys.

A special word of appreciation is due the late Morroe Berger who, as Chairman of the Program in Near Eastern Studies, first conceived this project and gained support for it. His death came before its publication. These volumes are dedicated to his memory.

Introduction

Benjamin Braude

In 1517 Sultan Selim's conquest of Syria and Egypt expanded the territory of the Ottoman Empire to include the heartland of Islam which was also the home of the ancient Christian churches of the East and numerous, mostly Arabic-speaking, Jewish communities. Copts, Maronites, Jacobites as well as other smaller communities now entered the Ottoman domain. Consistent with their *ad hoc* policies, the conquerors were content, for the most part, to let local conditions determine the collection of taxes and relations with ecclesiastical authorities (see below chapter 1, by Amnon Cohen, and chapter 2, by Muhammad Adnan Bakhit). The conquest also brought into the empire additional communicants of the Greek Orthodox and Armenian churches. The Greek Patriarchates of Antioch, Jerusalem, and Alexandria eventually submitted to the authority of Constantinople. On the other hand, because the leadership of the Armenian church was divided between Ējmiacin, Cilicia, and Istanbul itself, local Armenian communities retained a certain freedom of action. Of all the empirewide groups, the pattern of authority of the Jewish community was the least affected by the conquest.

For nearly a millennium, these peoples of the East had lived under Islam. The Ottoman conquest merely exchanged one Muslim master for another. In the Arabic-speaking lands, the overwhelming majority of Christians and Jews had become linguistically assimilated to the Muslim population. Socially they were less obviously separated and distinctive than their coreligionists in Ottoman Europe. Concomitantly their numbers had dwindled and their influence upon society was small.

With few exceptions, the indigenous churches of the newly conquered lands were isolated from the West. They were regarded as schismatics by Roman Catholicism and, for that matter, by Greek Orthodoxy. The origins of these conflicts date from the fifth century when a number of theological disputes arose concerning the nature of Christ. Initially there were three major groups. Nestorius, who from 428 to 431 served as Patriarch of Constantinople, argued that there were two separate natures coexistent in Christ, the human and the divine. The vessel of the Godhead was Christ, a human son of Mary. In opposition to this doctrine, Cyril, Patriarch of Alexandria, argued that Christ was of a single divine nature, that is Monophysite (meaning in Greek, one nature). At the Council of Chalcedon in 451 an attempt was made, with the combined support of both the Roman and Constantinopolitan hierarchies, to formulate a doctrine which would resolve the bitter dispute between the followers of what came to be called Nestorianism and those who accepted Monophysitism. The Chalcedonian doctrine claimed that Christ had two perfect and indivisible but separate natures—effectively a compromise between those who argued for two completely separate natures and those who argued for one Divine nature. Dyophysitism, as the Chalcedonian formulation may be called, has remained the orthodox belief of the churches of Europe.

The legacy of these disputes remained in the region. The Copts in Egypt and the Jacobites in Syria were Monophysite in doctrine. Further afield, the Armenian and Ethiopian churches followed the same belief. As for the Nestorians, in the face of combined Monophysite and Dyophysite opposition, during the fifth century they withdrew from Byzantine territory and found a base to the east under Persian rule, whence they spread throughout Asia. Monothelitism—a seventh-century attempt at compromise—was branded as heretical by both Rome and Constantinople, but it found adherents among certain Christians who took refuge in Mount Lebanon and came to be known as the Maronites. Through the centuries each of these communities managed to preserve its distinct identity.

The Coptic Church, which calls itself the Coptic Orthodox Church, was the historic national church of Egypt (see below chapter 9, by Doris Behrens-Abouseif; for the Syrian Christians in Egypt see below chapter 8, by Thomas Philipp). Prior to the Arab conquests most of the country's population adhered to Coptic Monophysitism and even today, after almost fourteen centuries of Muslim rule, about ten percent of the Egyptians are Copts. Within the Arab world the Copts are the most numerous Christian community. Coptic, the liturgical language, is the last surviving vestige of Ancient Egyptian. Despite agreement on doctrine with the other Monophysite churches (Jacobite and Armenian), they have had little to do with them. The only church outside Egypt with which they have been in close and continuous contact has been the Monophysite Ethiopian Church, which they have often dominated. International commerce has been an activity of Coptic laymen—for other Christians it has also been a means of intellectual and political contact with the West—but the Coptic trading network, like the ecclesiastical network, was concentrated in Africa. Within Egypt, both before and after the Ottoman conquest, Copts maintained an almost hereditary hold on certain posts in the government bureaucracy. With the changes in administrative practice introduced by Muhammad ᶜAlı and his family and the British occupation in the nineteenth century, the Copts adapted to new circumstances, but they survived, by and large, independent of foreign influence.

In Syria the Jacobites, also known as the Syrian Orthodox or Monophysite Church, have occupied a position similar, but by no means identical, to that of the Copts in Egypt. They were called Jacobites by their opponents, the Greek Orthodox, after their sixth-century bishop, Jacob Baradaeus. Because of the survival of numerous other Christian communities in western Asia, the Jacobites, unlike the Copts, were not able to lay sole claim to the legacy of pre-Islamic Christianity in their land. Nonetheless, their early history was remarkable for its intellectual and organizational achievements. For a limited period the Church's doctrinal opposition to Byzantium earned it special recognition in the Islamic state. However, after the collapse of the Abbasid caliphate and the ensuing centuries of invasion and political instability in Syria, the Jacobites entered a period of decline from which they have never recovered. Under Ottoman rule their significance diminished.

The Nestorian Church gained adherents in Persia and its eastern neighbors. Like the Jacobites, the Nestorians had their greatest success under Islam during the early centuries of its rule. They also attained influence in the service of the Mongol invaders. After the Mongol dynasties in the Middle East were converted to Islam, the Nestorian community declined. Eastern Turkey and the adjoining areas of Iran and present-day Iraq, remote from the control of central governments, were the principal refuges of the Nestorians. Except as the object of European missionary advances, they attracted little attention under Ottoman rule.

Earlier, the Christians of Syria who accepted the Monothelite compromise came to be called Maronites. That name is derived from a semilegendary figure, Yuḥannā Mārūn, who according to the accounts of the community organized the Church in the early centuries. Although there is evidence of contact between Rome and the Maronites during the Crusades, Maronite union with Rome and abandonment of Monothelitism were not finally confirmed until the early sixteenth century. Nevertheless Maronite historians adhered to belief in their perpetual union. Whatever their earlier history, during the centuries of Ottoman rule the Maronites were indisputably Catholic. Unlike other Christian communities the Maronites thus had continuous and direct links with the West—particularly France—which made them a conduit in commercial, political, and spiritual matters. This tie was not the only distinctive characteristic of the Maronites. With their centuries of settlement in Mount Lebanon, where they constituted an important group, they cultivated a tradition of historiography which reflected their sense of community and their attachment to the land.

The Maronite union with Rome was the precursor of a development which affected every Christian church in the region. In the first flush of the Counter-Reformation, the Roman Catholic Church embarked upon a vigorous program to bring all the surviving churches of the East into its spiritual orbit. The sixteenth, seventeenth, and eighteenth centuries witnessed internal conflict within each church as those forces loyal to the established hierarchies and dogmas fought with groups won over to Rome (see below chapter 3, by Robert M. Haddad). Somewhat later, a similar process started when Protestant missionaries made inroads among these same churches (see below chapter 7, by Kamal S. Salibi). During the nineteenth century the dissident groups, with the support of the Catholic and Protestant Powers, gained recognition from the Ottoman authorities and organized their own autonomous communities.

The result was a bewildering welter of factions. For the most part the converts accepted the theology of the new church, but retained the liturgy of the old, purged, of course, of its schismatic elements. Those who followed Rome simply added Uniate or Catholic to their old church's name, e.g., Catholic Copt or Uniate Melkite.

Traditionally, dissent within the Christian churches of the East had been expressed through doctrinal disputes. In the nineteenth century dissent took a new form, ethnic-linguistic division. In the Greek Orthodox patriarchates of Jerusalem and Antioch, the hierarchy, drawn from the monastic clergy, spoke Greek, while the parish priests and the parishioners spoke Arabic. The vast majority of the Orthodox were thus excluded from positions of leadership in the Church. Recognizing the sense of powerlessness felt by the Arab Orthodox, the Russian Orthodox took their side in disputes with the Greek. Eventually under Russian protection, elements of the Arabic-speaking Orthodox community gained influence in the Patriarchate of Antioch. From the late nineteenth century onward, even after the collapse of both the Romanov and Ottoman Empires, intimate ties developed between the see of Antioch and the Russian Orthodox Church.

The Arab Orthodox were among the first to call for revival—in words which were subsequently reinterpreted as a call for the awakening of the Arab language, culture, and nation. Unlike their fellow Christians they bore a twofold psychic burden. The other Christians in the Arab provinces were inferior in status to the Muslims, but they were at least masters in their own churches. The Greek dominance of the patriarchates and the Ottoman Muslim dominance of the government denied them power and authority in both spheres. In the aftermath of the Greek War of Independence, with the gradual triumph of Hellenic ethnicity over Romaic communalism, a sense of alienation from their Greek Orthodox brethren grew. As strangers in both church and state, they, of all the communities in the Ottoman Empire, were the most in need of the new identity which nationalism offered. Not surprisingly, they were the earliest and most radical spokesmen for what became Arab nationalism.

By contrast Jewish communities in the Arab provinces were remarkably quietist. With the exception of Sabbatian messianism in the seventeenth century—a movement discussed in the introduction to the first volume—the Jews did as little as possible to attract hostile attention. Baghdad, which was first conquered by the Ottomans in 1534, during the reign of Sultan Suleyman, had probably the largest Jewish community in the region. In the nineteenth century, with the growth of steamship travel between Mesopotamia and points east, Baghdadi Jews grew prosperous from trade (see Volume I, chapter 13, by Charles Issawi). The community also enjoyed a tradition of scholarship and respected rabbinic leadership.

The Jewish communities in Egypt and Syria, the former Mamluk territories, were probably fewer in number and certainly of less importance than their coreligionists in Iraq. Their role in the economic and social life of these countries was minor; their contribution to Jewish learning and culture restricted. Even in Palestine the traditional Jewish settlement was remarkable for its poverty, piety, and lack of intellectual distinction. The period following the Ottoman conquest brought, however, some significant changes. The revival of economic activity during the early decades of Ottoman rule benefited the Jews as well as the other inhabitants of these countries. In Palestine, a substantial immigration of European Jews, both of Sefardi Jews from southern and southwestern Europe and of Ashkenazi Jews from central and eastern Europe, greatly increased the numbers and transformed the character of the Jewish community, especially in the two cities of Jerusalem and Safed, the latter of which became an important center of Jewish learning.

This tradition, however, was not maintained, and, in the centuries that followed, the Jewish community in Palestine, despite a continuing immigration from Europe, was hardly touched by the revolutionary currents of enlightenment and of secularism which had transformed Jewish life in Europe. It was only with the educational work of the Alliance Israélite Universelle and the agricultural colonies of late-nineteenth-century Zionism that these currents reached the Jews of this region.

The contrast between the non-Muslims of Anatolia and Rumelia on the one hand and those of the Arabic-speaking lands on the other is remarkable. Christians in Arab lands were few, shared the language and social culture of their Muslim neighbors (see below, chapter 7, by Dominique Chevallier) and were, with certain exceptions, deaf to the siren-calls of the West (for the results of these exceptions see below, chapters 4 and 5, by, respectively, Moshe Maᶜoz and Samir Khalaf). Christians in the Central Lands were many and restive; they retained their own languages and were more open to the Western ideas of the Enlightenment and later nationalism. Jews adopted a generally quiescent attitude toward the Ottoman authorities and regional contrasts among them were less marked but still perceptible—Salonican Jewry was clearly more advanced than that of Aleppo, for example.

The main difference between Christians from the different parts of the empire can be seen most clearly in the late and post-Ottoman period. The Balkan Christians created their own nation-states. The Armenians in Anatolia tried and failed. Christians in the Arab countries sought new roles as confessional minorities in Arab national states.

1

On the Realities of the *Millet* System: Jerusalem in the Sixteenth Century*

AMNON COHEN

I

In recent years orientalism has undergone several basic changes both in concept and methodology. Within this general framework Ottoman history has also had its own share of new approaches and techniques. One of the general works, which was initially intended to replace the fragmentary and vague material on the Ottoman Empire with an overall view, was Gibb and Bowen's monumental attempt to describe *Islamic Society and the West*. Ever since its publication it has been a focus of interest, reference, and criticism,[1] which has not, of course, detracted from its basic importance and value in the field. The topic which, unlike many others, did not have to wait for any reaction from the outside was the *millet* system: here criticism started at home. Not only was it consciously left for the last chapter in the second volume, but the authors also deemed it necessary to start this chapter—"The Dimmis"—with an apologetic remark: "We could not exclude from our survey a chapter devoted to these communities, even if it had to be based on secondary sources to a much greater extent than the other chapters."[2] Conscious of the scarcity of existing or available "firsthand materials" they indicated two possible sources which might help to overcome this deficiency: the Ottoman archives and those of the non-Muslim religious communities inhabiting or in relations with the Ottoman Empire. We do not find it difficult to agree with both the diagnosis and the treatment prescribed by Gibb and Bowen. Their chapter on the "dimmis" is disappointing in a number of ways, and it lacks

*These are preliminary findings of a wider study supported by the Israeli Academy for Science and by the Memorial Foundation for Jewish Culture. I would like to extend my thanks to both institutions for their support. Thanks are also due to the Muslim authorities in the Religious Court of Jerusalem for their permission to conduct my research in their archives, as well as to my assistant Adel Manna[c] for his help.

to a degree a sense of everyday reality. Being slightly acquainted with the Ottoman archives, we regard them as a basic element for the reconstruction of the realities of the *millet* system. Belonging to one of the "non-Muslim religious communities," we cannot, of course, be accused of ignoring or belittling the importance of sources like the Responsa literature for the Ottoman-Jewish history. Other sources (some published) known to students of Ottoman history should also be mentioned here: foreign consular reports, local Christian chronicles, and travel accounts. All of these fall within the framework of "firsthand materials" and may contribute, if properly used, to enriching our knowledge of the *millet* system. It seems to us, however, that the most valuable source both for factual evidence and appropriate conceptual appraisal of the *millet* system is the Muslim religious court archives. It is to the Islamic court records of Jerusalem, which have only recently become available to us, that we turn in an attempt to add some further dimensions to the realities of the *millet* system.

II

The term *milla* is very rare in the records and it is never used to denote any element, let alone the whole lot, of what later generations coined *millet*. When used, it is—perhaps not surprisingly—meant to single out the Muslim element of the population, as was the case in medieval Islam, as being basically different from the non-Muslim communities. Thus it was the Hanafī *qāḍī* of Jerusalem who, when explicitly asked to do so by a Jacobite Christian, agreed to conduct his marriage ceremony in accordance with the *qāḍī's* own rite, that of "the Hanafī milla" (*"wa-ṭalab kull minhuma jiriān al-aḥkām al-sharᶜīyya ᶜala wajhi al-milla al-ḥanafiyya"*).[3] The Christian element (and the Jewish, for that matter) was thus regarded as being the "non-millet." It was naturally viewed as a special group, and when referred to it was usually either a *ṭā'ifa* or *ṭawā'if*. This term was used both as a general collective noun for Christians, or to denote one of the various categories within Christianity (Frankish, Greek Orthodox, etc.).[4] But as Christians were usually referred to as one of their specific categories, a *ṭā'ifa* would be the closest possible term to what we might somewhat anachronistically call a *millet*. Within the Jewish community there were also certain subgroups, more or less distinct from one another (Karaites, Sefardi, etc.), but here the case was usually the very opposite from the Christian one: Jews were referred to collectively as belonging to one group, *ṭā'ifa*.[5] This term was, however, not always prevalent, and Jews were also quite often referred to simply as "the Jews" (*al-yahūd*), or "the *dhimmi*" (*dhimm, dhimma*), or "the Jewish *dhimmī*" (*al-dhimm al-yahūd*).[6]

III

The fact that Jews were referred to as one group, whereas Christians were usually viewed through a narrower prism, should not necessarily be regarded as implying a different degree of cohesiveness. Jewish life in Jerusalem was centered around separate synagogues, which reflected differing traditions and origins. In other urban centers (notably in Safed) the various congregations lived in separate quarters, a trait less characteristic of Jerusalem.[7] Nor can one relate Ottoman usage to the size of both communities. It is true that from the early 1560s, the Christian population in Jerusalem slightly exceeded the number of Jews, but until then the opposite was true.[8] Hence there was no logical reason for the use of different criteria, regarding the larger community as one whole, while addressing the smaller community, the Christian, according to their separate denominations. The main reason for the different approach must have had to do with the fact that the split among the Christian communities was, by far, deeper and wider than the divergent ritual customs or even the sense of distinctiveness among Jews coming from various places of origin. The official approach to them seems to have reflected both vested interests (which in the Christian case were more substantial in the form of churches and monasteries as well as in the keen interest of the relevant Christian ambassadors in Istanbul) and popular perceptions among the local population. It was not, of course, limited to formal terminology only, but found its institutionalized expression—or shall we say derived most of its relevance and weight—from the communal organization of the *millet*s.

IV

Before we turn to the communal institutions, there are some related questions: To what degree were the religious minorities as minorities conspicuous in daily life? How distinct were they from each other and the Muslim population? In actual practical terms were they indeed different? Unlike some other towns in Palestine, Jerusalem did not include a Christian or a Jewish quarter. This is, at least, what emerges from the Ottoman *taḥrīr* registers. In fact there were both Christians and Jews in various quarters. Still, among themselves they tended to live in close proximity to one another. Throughout the century there were Jewish inhabitants in three neighboring quarters (Rīsha, Maslakh, Sharaf). At the beginning of the century more than fifty percent lived in Rīsha, whereas during the second half there is a distinct tendency for the Jews to move closer to the Temple Mount, the Sharaf quarter, which encompassed over sixty percent of them.[9] Inhabiting these quarters meant, *inter alia,* that they were subject to the Muslim *shaykh al-ḥāra,* the local head of the quarter, who was held responsible for their behavior.[10] While *shaykh al-ḥāra* was an official title, we also have a list of those who were unofficially regarded as the most prominent figures, *aᶜyān,* of the various quarters. In the 1560s, when most of the Jews of Jerusalem concentrated in the Sharaf quarter (where they constituted over one quarter of the population) there was no Jew among its *aᶜyān*. There were, however, also *aᶜyān wa-akābir ṭā'ifat al-yahūd,* but there, as is clearly indicated by their title, the concept is a communal rather than a territorial one.[11] Still, the Jewish community preferred to live together, for reasons of religious practice and security. Within the official quarters they concentrated in what were, probably, narrow alleys or closely knit compounds, separated from the outside world by a gate, thereby creating an image of a quarter by itself. No wonder, therefore, that they were termed by the local population as "the Jewish street," or "quarter."[12] The same is true, to an even larger degree, with regard to the Christian communities. Some of them were living within the compounds of their respective churches (e.g., the Armenians). Others shared the "regular" quarters with the Muslims, without any specific place allocated to them. No Christian quarter *(ḥāra)* is mentioned in any of the official *taḥrīr* registers throughout the century. Still, there seems to have been a smaller unit within a quarter, termed (as was the case for the Jews) *maḥalla,* "a street." This implies a certain tendency among the Christians as well—most likely Greek Orthodox[13]—to live close to each other, though unlike the Jews, we have not come across any reference to a gate in their neighborhood. The *maḥalla* of the Christians[14] is a term which occurs several times in the records. It was situated in the Zarāᶜina quarter, thus lending its name to it.[15] There were also, however, Muslim inhabitants in the same quarter; although distinct from one another they still cooperated in the cause of their common interests.[16] As was the case with the Jews, the elders of the quarter were Muslim as was their formal head *(shaykh).*[17] This *shaykh* was in the habit of collecting certain taxes[18] from the inhabitants of the Zarāᶜina quarter, who were both Christian and Muslim. Though only a minority among those who dwelled in that quarter, the Christians used to pay two-thirds of these taxes. However, when asked by the *qāḍī,* the representatives of both elements declared that they were pleased with that arrangement and thanked their *shaykh.* If we bear in mind that the *shaykh* was in jail while the Christians expressed these sentiments, we may assume that they had no real complaints against him.

The very fact that both Christians and Jews in various ways maintained their separate religious identity implies, by definition, a certain degree of estrangement from the society as a whole. On the other hand, the authorities decreed special regulations which were aimed at distinguishing Muslims from non-Muslims by their attire. Forbidding the wearing of certain clothes did not necessarily make this distinction any easier to achieve, for there remained the problem of enforcement. There were special headgears of the Christians[19] and other items they were either required or forbidden to wear. But when it came to the test of daily life it seems to have been quite difficult to tell a Christian from a Muslim. There were several cases in which Christians were brought to trial for having behaved as if they were Muslims. The Muslim eyewitnesses testified that when seeing these Christians walking—on the Temple Mount or elsewhere—they could not tell that they were any different from themselves.[20] It is equally significant that neither in these cases nor in any others were Christians or Jews charged with having dressed in a way intended to hide their real identity; the charge was of having committed acts which they, as non-Muslims, should not have done.

In a relatively small town like Jerusalem special clothes were not needed to distinguish one person from another; for, in all likelihood, people already knew each other. Individuals frequented certain places of worship, refrained from buying certain kinds of food (especially meat), and celebrated religious holidays on certain occasions. Such information was sufficient to identify an individual's community. In some cases their living quarters also betrayed—if they tried to hide it—their origin.

If Christians or Jews engaged in a limited number of forms of economic activity, this might have further underlined their inferior status, or at least their sense of it. Contrary to certain prevailing prejudices, which this writer shared prior to the present study, there seems to be hardly any definite evidence to that effect. There were, of course, Jewish butchers as well as Christian manufacturers of candlesticks. But even at this early stage of our research increasing evidence is being accumulated on the actual involvement of members of the religious minorities in all sorts of "ordinary" trades and professions. There were Christian blacksmiths, coppersmiths, and goldsmiths, masons and carpenters, soap-producers and weavers of cotton, physicians and bakers, butchers and moneylenders. Christians engaged in trade on all levels and of different kinds. Not only were there small merchants in spices, vegetables, etc., but also there were exporters of wheat and importers of rice and sugar. In most cases they are referred to simply as "Christians," but sometimes one comes across more precise designations: Copts, Armenians, Maronites, etc. Among Jews we find high officials and physicians, blacksmiths, silversmiths, and goldsmiths, butchers and meatsellers, millers and tailors, "bankers" and moneylenders. Jews were active in trade with Egypt and Syria, as well as in the various local marketplaces *(sūq)* or even in shops situated all over the town. Unlike the Christians, there are hardly any indications as to their subcategory. In many of the above-mentioned professions there are specific references to Muslims as well. Reading through the many pages of the *sijill* gives the impression that there were no "minority" professions as such, although there might have been a specialization of one group in a certain trade. This contention may be further enhanced by the following. In August 1563, after having terminated the reparations and reconstructions in the old vegetable market *(sūq al-khuḍar),* which then became the new market *(al-sūq al-jadīd),* the intendent of the Ḥaramayn decided to lease all forty shops therein to their bidders. The long lists of names include Muslims, Christians, and Jews. Toward its end the text runs as follows: "And he [let] the [above-] mentioned shops on an equal footing among the three [groups of] the above-mentioned renters, [allotting] each group *(ṭā'ifa)* thirteen shops; still the Muslims have [got] fourteen."[21] This seems to be highly revealing not so much of the relative importance of each community (the rate, after all, may have been arbitrarily set) but rather as an indication of the perceptions among Muslims of the role of minorities in the economy in general, and in commerce in particular. To use modern terminology, here was a clear case of granting equal opportunities to Jews, Christians, and Muslims alike. Since it is difficult to divide forty into three equal parts, it is only natural that the extra one was given to a Muslim. It is this slight preferential approach in an overwhelmingly Muslim town within a Muslim empire which adds an overwhelming dimension of reality to the whole picture.

V

The most conspicuous characteristic of the minorities in Jerusalem was the institution of official heads of the different communities. Whereas the Muslim community knew only heads of quarters or professions *(shaykh ḥāra* or *shaykh ṭā'ifa),* to which members of all three religious groups were subject, Christians and Jews owed further allegiance to their respective heads. The large number of Christian sects made formal representations to the authorities through their respective heads. Greek-Orthodox, Armenians, Copts, Assyrians, and Georgians had either a patriarch *(Batrak)* or an archbishop *(Muṭrān),* while the Catholics *(Ifranj)* and the Abyssinians followed a priest of a lower rank. The Greek-Orthodox Patriarch (referred to also as Melkite) was regarded as the senior communal head[22] and he, like the others, derived his authority from a formal nomination by the local *qāḍī* upon the suggestion of the principal dignitaries of the community, both from Jerusalem and elsewhere.[23] As long as he was present and active, fulfilling his obligations toward his superiors and his congregation, he enjoyed the support—both moral and practical—of the *qāḍī*. Once he grew old and could not perform his duties he could not be replaced, unless he gave his formal consent.[24] This consent may have been only a matter of routine, but the repeated reference to it in all the cases so far available indicates that it could not be altogether disregarded. It represents one element which seems to have been as important as the other two, i.e. the approval of the *qāḍī* and the goodwill of the congregation. This last element was an important source of his authority: the ability to be "respected and obeyed"[25] by his men. Once he received the official sanction, he would be protected by the *qāḍī* from any insult to himself and his title, or against instances of disrespect and disobedience.[26] But once he ceased to please the *aᶜyān* of his community, they would withdraw their support from him and have him replaced by their new choice.[27] When complaints were submitted against the community for an alleged violation of laws or customs, it was the Greek-Orthodox Patriarch who was regarded as responsible. In very important cases he would appear in court in person.[28] It was he who was supposed to conduct all the affairs of the patriarchate and the clergymen, to deal with affairs of the personal status[29] of his community and "to be in charge of all the old fines and taxes" *(al-maghārim wa-al-ᶜawā'id).*[30] However, he was usually helped by another functionary, not necessarily a priest, also nominated by the *qāḍī* (most probably upon his recommendation) and officially called *ra'īs* or *shaykh*. In this sense he was actually in charge of the daily affairs of his community, and he was therefore also called the *mutakallim* or spokesman.[31]

In the case of the other communities, these terms usually served to designate the religious head who combined both functions (*muṭrān,* principal priest in a monastery, etc.). He was held responsible for both assets and liabilities, and was sometimes also termed as a *nāzir* of the *waqf*s of the community. There was, however, yet another prominent position, lacking any ecclesiastical status,[32] the *turjumān,* or the dragoman. These interpreters for the various Christian communities were basically, as indicated by the term, supposed to help their superiors by translating for them whenever the need presented itself—as the latter were strangers in the country and unacquainted with its language. On other occasions the *turjumān* used to accompany pilgrims coming to Jerusalem and Bethlehem. Because of their acquaintance with the issues involving their community and their experience with the Ottoman authorities (both administrative and religious), they attained a high degree of reliability and were entrusted with cases to be pleaded independently before the *qāḍī*. On one occasion, in 1588, when the Armenian *ra'īs* had to be absent from the town, he nominated the Armenian dragoman as his official delegate "to be in charge of [all] the interests of the Armenian monastery in the above-mentioned town and of all the matters [related] to it."[33] Given the large variety of matters the dragomans attended to and the intensity of their activity, we assume that this was not an exception to a rule.

The *shaykh* or *ra'īs* mainly conducted the wordly affairs of their local community, either among themselves, or vis-à-vis the local population and the authorities. One of their regular duties was the collection of the *jizya*. Since they were regarded as being responsible only for the members of their local community, they were not supposed to levy it upon those who originated elsewhere and who happened to live in Jerusalem. These people were taxed through their own *shaykh,* who had to be duly nominated.[34] The sums of *jizya* to be paid by each community were laid down in the *taḥrīr* registers, where the number (and names) of those liable to it were stated and the rate of their multiplier was fixed. Around the turn of the century they were much lower than the figures mentioned earlier. The number of tickets presented to the *ra'īs* by the *jizya* collectors was as follows: the Greek-Orthodox paid just under seventy, the Assyrians about fifteen, the Copts twelve.[35] These figures coincide with the general trend of a substantial decrease in the population of Jerusalem noted elsewhere.[36] These "tickets" were paid personally, and we may assume that had they represented an inflated number, the *shaykhs* would not have hesitated to complain.[37] Needless to say, when the very opposite was the case, there were no complaints made, though the central government tried several times to update the figures, suspecting that they were lower than they should have been. All the *shaykh* had to do was to meet his quota of *jizya* by filling in names corresponding to the exact figure demanded. He would not hesitate to claim its payment, for instance, from Christians of the empire who had been staying for some time in town, probably in order to alleviate the burden of his own people.[38] Whenever a person who annually paid this tax died, another's name was introduced onto the list, certainly implying almost beyond any doubt that the actual figure of Christians (and most probably Jews) living permanently in Jerusalem was usually higher than that of poll-taxpayers.[39] Though ostensibly levied on a personal basis, it should be viewed as a collective tax. When individuals were too poor to pay it, financial aid was extended to them by their highest religious authority.[40] The acting head of the community replaced lost taxpayers with new ones. The annual total sum was handed over collectively to the officer in charge of it by the same *shaykh.*[41]

One more concluding remark should be added here. The various Christian categories mentioned above were regarded for all practical purposes as separate entities administered internally by their respective heads. Whenever tolls, dues and extraordinary fines were levied, each had to pay its own share.[42] The *jizya* appears to have been an exception to this rule: not only was there no reference to relatively new communities such as Catholics or Maronites, but even the Armenians, regarded as an old *millet,*[43] are never mentioned as subject to this tax in Jerusalem. It was levied on the Greek-Orthodox, the Copts and the Assyrians—all of them Eastern churches. The new administration was probably following at this early stage of Ottoman rule in Palestine the old patterns which they might have come across as a result of the conquest of this part of their world.

The Jewish community—though never referred to as such—was also regarded as an old, Eastern *millet*. It paid the *jizya* at rates somewhat higher than the Orthodox,[44] but the procedure followed was identical in both cases. Institutionally speaking, it also had a *shaykh,* sometimes referred to as *mutakallim,* who was nominated by the *qāḍī* upon the recommendation of the elders of the community. The *shaykh* represented all Jews to the local authorities, dealt with all matters of public interest, levied taxes, bailed out prisoners, signed official documents, and guaranteed Jewish debts. Never referred to as a high religious authority, he may have been regarded as such by his community. He was, however, quite often involved in various private economic enterprises. Unlike the Christians the Jews, at least according to the sources examined so far, did not try to withdraw their support from an acting head and replace him with someone else. This does not necessarily indicate any major difference in the social cohesiveness of the two, and it may be pure coincidence. Still, one of the reasons may be a higher degree of readiness on the part of the Jewish *shaykh* to seek advice and support from the other prominent members of his congregation. While the Christian *ra'īs* was usually acting either on his own or helped by his *turjumān,* his Jewish counterpart was aided to a very large extent by others, who had no official capacity, but who were nonetheless highly involved in the administration of their own public affairs.

VI

Religiously speaking, both Christianity and Judaism were looked upon with disdain by the Ottoman state and its agencies. They were referred to as "their null and depraved contention" (*ᶜala zaᶜmihim al-fāsid*) or "their void rites" (*bāṭil āyyinleri*). They were regarded as different from and thus unequal to the followers of the ruling religion, basically deprived of certain rights and quite often molested and harassed. Their distinctness was consciously maintained not only out of religious considerations, but also as the best administrative means for their preservation. We have seen that the Christians went even further than that. Although the Ottomans in Palestine followed the traditional pattern of collecting the *jizya* from the Orthodox alone (thereby creating the necessary contractual conditions of *ahl al-dhimma*), the other Christian sects insisted on being regarded as distinct administrative units. They attained this recognition (involving the payment of many other dues), thus further underlining their separate character.

Still, it would be an oversimplification to state, as Gibb and Bowen have, that "The Ottoman government, by leaving the task of social unification to the religious institution, condemned the non-Moslem and heterodox Moslem groups under its control to exclusion from effective incorporation in the Ottoman structure of society."[45] Neither the Christians nor the Jews were "excluded from effective incorporation" in the Ottoman society.[45] The very opposite was the case. On both sides of the equation there were a will and many ways in which their incorporation could be and actually was effected. The heads of their religious communities (be they spiritual or temporal figures) had to share their responsibilities with others to whom members of the minority groups owed allegiance: heads of quarters and heads of professions or guilds. These were Muslims, but there is no reference to a discriminatory behavior on their part as far as the daily practice of their authority is concerned. Beyond the formal administrative dimension they actually exercised their powers when asked to do so in order to help Christians and Jews also. As for the members of the *millet,* they did not confine themselves to seeking help from the above-mentioned only. Very often they addressed the *qāḍī* himself (or his designated substitute), without any apparent preference of *madhhab*. Their involvement in the judicial system deserves a study by itself. Suffice it to say here that they were not only summoned by the court whenever Muslims sued them, but applied to it when allegedly harmed by Muslims. Christians and Jews resorted to the *Sharīᶜa* court to solve internal disputes, to render justice, to sanction economic transactions, to state legal claims and rights, and to enforce former specific decisions or the law in general. Last but not least in importance, they were economically linked with, and perhaps even interwoven in the whole system. They owned properties to be sold or bought as they wished; they were an important element in trade, industry, and agriculture; they served in various noncommunal, governmental positions and were even engaged in what we might call the liberal professions (medicine for example). All of this amounts to a complex picture in which the "religious institution" was indeed the basic, indispensable and most important factor of "social unification" (to use Gibb and Bowen's terminology). Socially and otherwise very distinct from the majority of the population, they were, however, incorporated in the Ottoman structure of society, economy, and administration.

Both Christians and Jews enjoyed a substantial degree of autonomy in Jerusalem and entertained an intensive network of links with their coreligionists in the capital and elsewhere in the empire. There is, however, no indication of any formal or even practical relationship whereby they might be held subject to any superstructure of a *millet* system in the Ottoman Empire as a whole. In the light of the Islamic court archives it appears that in Jerusalem during the entire sixteenth century, at least, the *millet* system as we know it from later times was simply nonexistent in term, form, and in what is believed to have been its overall and well-defined contents.

Notes

1. H. A. R. Gibb and Harold Bowen, *Islamic Society and the West,* London, 1950–1957, vol. 1, parts 1 and 2; R. Owen, ''The Middle East in the Eighteenth Century—an 'Islamic' society in decline?'' in *Bulletin of the British Society for Middle Eastern Studies,* 3 (1976), pp. 110–117; A. Cohen, ''Some Conventional Concepts of Ottoman Administration in the Light of a More Detailed Study—the Case of 18th Century Palestine,'' in Halil Inalcik and Osman Okyar, ed. *Turkiye' nin Sosyal ve Ekonomik Tarihi 1071–1920,* Ankara, 1980, pp. 187–192.

2. Gibb and Bowen (cited n. 1), part 2, p. 207, n. 1.

3. Islamic Court Records of Jerusalem, cited as *Sijill,* vol. 48, p. 25, dated 13 Shawwāl 972.

4. Thus, *ṭā' ifat al-Naṣārā* or *ṭawā' if al-Naṣārā* as a general term (*Sijill,* vol. 44, p. 249, and vol. 1, p. 108, respectively), and *ṭā' ifat al-ruhbān al-Naṣārā al-Franj* or *ṭā' ifat al-Rūm (Sijill,* vol. 48, p. 84 and vol. 1, p. 108, respectively).

5. *Sijill,* vol. 80, p. 17 *(ṭā' ifat al-yahūd al-qāṭinīn bi-al-Quds al-sharīf).*

6. *Sijill,* vol. 43, p. 359, vol. 44, p. 307, vol. 77, p. 387, respectively.

7. For Safed, see B. Lewis, *Notes and Documents from the Turkish Archives,* Jerusalem, 1952, p. 6. As for Jerusalem the only indication we came across was of a Karaite quarter (*Sijill,* vol. 44, p. 144), but even then it was situated within the Jewish quarter.

8. In 1525–1526 the population of Jerusalem was 21 percent Jewish and 13 percent Christian, in 1538–1539, 15 percent and 10 percent, in 1553–1554, 11 percent and 10 percent, and only in 1562, 8 percent and 10 percent respectively. Cf. A. Cohen and B. Lewis, *Population and Revenue in the Towns of Palestine in the Sixteenth Century,* Princeton, 1978, p. 94.

9. Cf. Cohen and Lewis, ibid., pp. 92–94. I further elaborated on this topic in a separate article, ''New Evidence on Demographic Change: The Jewish Community in Sixteenth Century Jerusalem,'' in R. Mantran, ed., *Memorial Ömer Lûtfi Barkan,* Paris, 1980, pp. 57–64.

10. This was explicitly mentioned in relation to the Christians (*Sijill,* vol. 10, p. 217: *wa-kafala al-Muslim wa' al-Naṣārā shaykhuhum ᶜUbayd . . . ḍamān iḥḍār*).

11. *Sijill,* vol. 44, pp. 437–438.

12. There were even two gates of this kind, an old and a new one: *bāb maḥallat al-yahūd al-qadīm* (*Sijill,* vol. 44, p. 78) and *bāb maḥallat al-yahūd* (ibid., p. 100). Both documents are from the beginning of 1563.

13. When people from the Christian quarter were supposed to testify before the *qāḍī,* he summoned some Muslims and a representative of the Greek-Orthodox community (*Sijill,* vol. 82, p. 200).

14. *Maḥallat al-Naṣārā* (*Sijill,* vol. 45, p. 307; vol. 82, p. 83).

15. *Maḥallat al-Zarāᶜina tuᶜraf bi-ḥārat al-Naṣārā* (*Sijill,* vol. 61, p. 73); *Ḥārat al-Zarāᶜina ḥārat al-Naṣārā* (vol. 46, p. 156); *Ḥārat al-Naṣārā tijāh al-maslakh al-qadīm* (vol. 46, p. 252); compare below, vol. 2, chapter 2, by Muhammad Adnan Bakhit, pp. 47–48.

16. Thus, the illicit behavior of a certain woman and her daughter caused complaints submitted to the *qāḍī* by a group of Christians and a group of Muslims (*Sijill,* vol. 67, p. 119).

17. *Ḥaḍara ᶜUbayd ibn Muḥammad shaykh maḥallat ḥārat al-Naṣārā* (*Sijill,* vol. 1, p. 394); *akābir al-maḥalla min al-Muslimīn* (*Sijill,* vol. 69, p. 23).

18. *Al-kilaf al-ᶜurfiyya,* which seems to be identical with *tekālif-i ᶜurfiye*. Upon the payment of these taxes they became exempted from various forms of enforced labor and other obligations (*Sijill,* vol. 82, p. 200).

19. *ᶜamāma min ᶜamā' im al-Naṣārā* (*Sijill,* vol. 17, p. 424).

20. *Sijill,* vol. 75, p. 65; vol. 17, p. 414.

21. *Wa-al-ḥawānīt al-mazbūra ᶜalā sabīl al-sawiyya bayna al-musta'jirīn al-mazbūrīn aᶜlāh al-thalāth likull ṭā'ifa thalātha ᶜashar ḥānūt illā al-Muslimīn fa-la-hum arbaᶜa ᶜashar ḥānūt . . . ashhada ᶜalayhi kull ṭā'ifa min al-ṭawā'if al-musta'jirīn al-madhkūrīn aᶜlāhu . . . annahā ḍāmina wa-kāfila li-ṭā'ifatihā fīmā ᶜalayhā . . . min al-ujra al-muᶜayyan aᶜlāh.* (Sijill, vol. 44, p. 462. See also p. 448.)

22. He was once even referred to as "the Patriarch of the Christians" *(Biṭrīq al-naṣārā)* (*Sijill,* vol. 46, p. 256).

23. In 1579 an application was submitted to the *qāḍī* of Jerusalem by the Patriarch of Alexandria, the Archbishop of St. Catherine (Ṭūr Sīnā), the Archbishop *(muṭrān)* of Gaza, the head of the Serbian monastery, the head of the Georgian community and others. (*Sijill,* vol. 58, p. 385.)

24. For a similar procedure undertaken by the smaller Syrian community in 1581 see *Sijill,* vol. 59, p. 346: the incumbent head came over to the *qāḍī* and declared himself in favor of an application by a group of prominent Assyrians to nominate someone else *ra'īsan wa-mutakalliman ᶜalayhim wa-ᶜalā al-ṭā'ifa al-mazbūra wa-ᶜala awqāfihim wa-maṣāliḥihim.*

25. *Sijill,* vol. 48, p. 410 *Muqām al-ḥurma masmūᶜ al-kalima.*

26. When an Assyrian priest cursed his *muṭrān* in public he was convicted by the *qāḍī,* and whipped (*Sijill,* vol. 80, p. 123).

27. Toward the end of 1535 the Abyssinian community forced their head (who was originally from Aleppo) to resign, then recommended another person who was approved by the *qāḍī* as their new *ra'īs* (*Sijill,* vol. 5, p. 308).

28. *Sijill,* vol. 77, p. 275.

29. He regulated wills and inheritances of his monks, gave his sanction to marriage documents, etc. (*Sijill,* vol. 58, p. 229; vol. 75, p. 188, respectively.)

30. *Sijill,* vol. 58, p. 385.

31. *Sijill,* vol. 59, p. 346; vol. 69, p. 69; vol. 67, p. 185.

32. The dragoman of the Greek Orthodox community in 1595–1596 was originally a soapmaker (*Sijill,* vol. 77, p. 391).

33. *Fī al-takallum fī maṣāliḥ Dayr al-Arman bi-al-madīna al-mazbūra wa-fī jamīᶜ umūrihi* (*Sijill,* vol. 67, p. 185).

34. The *Shaykh* of the Christians from Bayt Jala (*ṭā'ifat Naṣārā al-Bajājilā*) (*Sijill,* vol. 69, p. 33; vol. 62, p. 437).

35. For the year 1004/1595–1596 see *Sijill,* vol. 77, p. 358; for the year 1008/1599–1600 see *Sijill,* vol. 80, p. 183.

36. Cohen and Lewis (cited n. 8), p. 10.

37. This, in fact, was claimed under oath by the Coptic *Shaykh* in 1581 (*Sijill,* vol. 59, p. 554).

38. Thus, three Greek-Orthodox originally from Homs who had been living for three consecutive years in Jerusalem without fulfilling this obligation were sued by the Greek-Orthodox *Shaykh* at the Muslim court and forced to pay (*Sijill,* vol. 67, p. 166).

39. *Min al-ᶜāda al-qadīma anna kull man māt min al-Naṣārā yuqām shakhṣ ᶜiwaḍahū fī adā al-jizya.* (*Sijill,* vol. 82, p. 427.)

40. The Greek Orthodox Patriarchate "used to extend to each person of the Greek Orthodox living in Jerusalem twenty silver coins (*qiṭᶜa*) every year as a subsidy to them for [the payment of] their *Jizya* when it was annually due." (*Sijill,* vol. 58, p. 385.)

41. *Sijill,* vol. 59, p. 477 for the Greek-Orthodox; ibid., p. 482 for the Copts; vol. 80, p. 183 for the Assyrians.

42. *Sijill,* vol. 82, p. 377. *Min al-ᶜāda al-qadīma baynahum an . . . yusāwūn baqiyyat al-Naṣārā bi-ma yuṣraf ᶜalā duyūrihim wa-kanā'isihim min al-ᶜawā'id wa-al-kilaf wa-sā'ir al-maghārim fī al-aᶜyād wa-khidmat qudūm wa-ma-yashbuh dhālika.*

43. Recognized as a *millet* as early as 1461 according to Gibb and Bowen (cited, n. 1), part 2, p. 220, but see vol. I, chapter 3, by Benjamin Braude and chapter 4 by Kevork Bardakjian.

44. In 1596 a Christian was liable to eighty-two *pāra* while a Jew had to pay 107 *pāra*. The breakdown of these sums shows that the old rate kept the same differentiation (*Sijill,* vol. 73, p. 69). For further details see Cohen, ''New Evidence'' (cited n. 9).

45. Gibb and Bowen (cited n. 1), part 2, p. 79.

It is apparent from these surveys that the village of Ḥadath had a completely Christian population; Ṣadad was almost totally Christian, while the Christian presence in Qaryatayn was nominal.

Christians and Jews in the province of Damascus paid the poll tax (*jizya*) on the basis of eight *akche*s for each *nafar*. In 977/1569, it was raised to eighty-five *akche*s for Christians and ninety for Jews.[14] This increase reflected the fall of the value of the *akche,* a silver coin, in relation to the gold piece, which, in accordance with Islamic law, was the money of account. In case a man migrated, he would pay his poll tax at his original locality. In one of the recorded cases in the Sharᶜīa court registers of Ḥama (989/1581) the following is revealed:

A certain Ḥajjī ᶜAlī b. Ḥusayn, the Janissary, arrived at Ḥama, carrying a letter from Daoud Aghā, the official in charge of the *kharāj* in the two villages of Ṣadad and Ḥadath. He testified that he had received from Sulaymān b. Faraḥ and from each of his two sons, Yūḥannā and Ibrāhīm, from ᶜAmmār b. Yuḥannā; Yūḥanna b. Faraj Allāh, and from his brother Mūsa, from Maṭar b. Mūsā, Yūsūf b. Siwār and from the *qissīs* (priest) Jibrāᶜīl b. Manṣūr, all Christians from the village of Ḥadath and now residing in Ḥama, an amount of twelve *sulṭāni*s[15] each in payment of the poll tax for the year 988/1580. That the priest had paid the *jizya* would seem to indicate that the clergy was not exempt from the impost.[16]

Liwā' of Damascus

Nāḥiyat Qārā

As Table 2-2 shows, five cadastral registers contain demographical data about seventeen villages in this *nāḥiya*; and only seven of them had Christian populations.[17] From this point on, footnotes not in consecutive order in the text may be found in subsequent tables.

The high percentage of Christians in this plateau area is apparent. Christians in the villages of Dayr ᶜAṭiyya, Yabrūd, Salḥiyya, Sukhnah and ᶜAribista conspicuously outnumbered Muslims. In Qārā and Nabk, Christians and Muslims were almost equal in number with few variations. In all these villages the high number of Christian bachelors is striking. We can observe an increase in the number of both Muslims and Christians, which fits into the general pattern of increase followed by a decrease in the population in Ottoman Syria in the sixteenth century.[25]

During early Mamluk times this area was placed under careful surveillance. In 662/1263, a *burj* (tower) was constructed in Qārā to keep Christians there under watch, and to protect the Muslims against Frankish attacks. In 664/1265, when Sultan al-Ẓāhir Baybars al-Bunduqdārī was on his way to receive his army on its return from Sīs (Lesser Armenia), Muslims raised complaints against the Christians of Qārā. The latter were accused of kidnapping Muslims and selling them as slaves to the Franks of Ḥiṣn ᶜAkkār (Gibelacar). "The Sultan ordered that they should be plundered, which was done, and the grown men were killed while children and women were taken as captives."[26] As the registers indicate the presence of a significant Christian population after this date, it appears that this measure did not succeed in exterminating the Christians of Qārā. It appears

TABLE 2-2

	T.D. 430				*T.D. 401*				*T.D. 263*				*T.D. 543*				*T.D. 177*			
	(ca. 930/1523)				*(ca. 950/1543)*				*(955/1548)*				*(ca. 976/1568)*				*(1005/1596)*			
	h.	*b.*	*r.*	*d.*	*h.*	*b.*	*r.*	*d.*	*h.*	*b.*	*r.*	*d.*	*h.*	*b.*	*r.*	*d.*	*h.*	*b.*	*r.*	*d.*
1. Dayr ᶜAṭiyya[18]																				
M.	35	22	–	–	38	18	1	–	35	24	2	–	49	5	1	–	33	23	–	–
C.	71	28	–	–	104	26	–	–	109	62	–	–	184	16	–	–	135	64	–	–
2. Nafsi Qārā[19]																				
M.	253	12	4	–	354	55	2	–	453	34	4	–	330	174	2	–	287	92	–	–
C.	217	103	–	–	279	85	–	–	240	97	–	–	331	17	–	–	258	90	–	–
3. Yabrūd[20]																				
M.					75	7	–	–	76	23	1	–	71	28	1	–	95	30	–	–
C.					104	16	–	–	142	51	–	–	279	17	–	–	240	50	–	–
4. Nabk[21]																				
M.					155	19	1	–	124	7	2	–	115	44	1	–	131	23	–	–
C.					115	29	–	–	53	8	–	–	147	38	–	–	142	45	–	–
5. Salḥiyya[22]																				
M.					64	7	–	–					10	–	–	–	32	13	–	–
C.													54	16	–	–	55	15	–	–
6. Sukhna (?)[23]																				
M.	14	–	–	–	8	2	–	–	22	–	–	–	13	6	–	–	23	14	–	–
C.					35	11	–	–					65	5	–	–	71	–	–	–
7. ᶜAribista (?)[24]																				
M.									2	–	–	–	2	1	–	–	3	–	–	–
C.					21	–	–	–	22	–	–	–	20	15	–	–	35	–	–	–

that Qārā, Yabrūd, and Tadmur had Melkite bishoprics, but existing material about bishops holding posts in these places is very meager and less reliable.[27]

Nāḥiyat Jubbat al-ᶜAssāl

During Mamluk times, this *nāḥiya* was part of the *barr* (environs) of Damascus.[28] It was comprised of thirty-seven villages,[29] only five of which had Christian inhabitants (see Table 2-3).

TABLE 2-3

	T.D. 401				*T.D. 263*				*T.D. 474*			
	(ca. 950/1543)				*(955/1548)*				*(977/1569)*			
	h.	*b.*	*r.*	*d.*	*h.*	*b.*	*r.*	*d.*	*h.*	*b.*	*r.*	*d.*
1. Ṣaydnāya[30]												
M.	2	–	–	–	2	–	–	–	–	–	–	–
C.	167	2	–	–	183	–	–	–	230	2	–	–
2. Maᶜlūlat al- Naṣārā[31]												
M.	–	–	–	–					–	–	–	–
C.	139	67	–	–					190	130	–	–
3. ᶜAyn al- Tīna[32]												
M.	9	3	–	–					26	5	–	–
C.	138	16	–	–					170	42	–	–
4. Jubb ᶜAdīn[33]												
M.	–	–	–	–					16	–	–	–
C.	41	23	–	–					73	–	–	–
5. Maᶜarat Ṣaydnāyā[34]												
M.	1	–	–	–					–	–	–	–
C.	170	–	–	–					230	–	–	–

The Muslim presence in these five villages was rather negligible, while the Christians were increasing in number. The number of bachelors in Maᶜlūlat al-Naṣārā was very high, which may indicate that it served as a haven for young Christians from the neighboring localities. Later in the second half of the eighteenth century, Michael Breik al-Dimashqī mentions that in 1756 a new church was built in Maᶜlūla.[35] It must be pointed out here that Maᶜlūla, whose people still speak Aramaic, had its own metropolitanate in the eighteenth century.[36]

Sixteenth century sources are rather silent on Ṣaydnāyā which had the highest concentration of Christians. Shaykh Ḥasan b. Muḥammad al-Būrīnī (d. 1024/1615) relates that in the year 1021/1612 a Christian from that village, more than ten years after accepting Islam, renounced it and reembraced Christianity. The chief judge (*qāḍī al-quḍāt*) in Damascus tried to persuade him to change his mind, but he refused and the chief judge ordered that he be beheaded.[37] Again Breik, who was appointed in 1768 to look after the monastery there, states that in

1762, upon the approval of the grand *muftī* of Damascus, Shaykh ʿAlī b. Muḥammad b. Murād al-Bukhārī al-Naqshabandī (d. 1184/1770),[38] the Christians were allowed to repair the church which was destroyed three years earlier when an earthquake struck Syria.[39] It appears from Breik's account that the church suffered greatly in Ṣaydānayya due to the corruption of the clergy.[40]

Nāḥiyat al-Zabandānī

This *nāḥiya,* under the Mamluks, also constituted part of the *barr* of Damascus.[41] Four *defters*[42] supply us with the names and demography of twenty-three villages, six of which (see Table 2-4) had Christian populations.

TABLE 2-4

	T.D. 430 (ca. 930/1523)				*T.D. 401* (ca. 950/1543)				*T.D. 263* 955/1548				*T.D. 474* 977/1569			
	h.	*b.*	*r.*	*d.*	*h.*	*b.*	*r.*	*d.*	*h.*	*b.*	*r.*	*d.*	*h.*	*b.*	*r.*	*d.*
1. Zabadānī[43]																
M.	41	–	1	–	59	10	1	–	61	52	–	–	60	7	–	–
C.	–	–	–	–	13	2	–	–	15	4	–	–	10	–	–	–
2. Kafr ʿĀmir[44]																
M.	192	17	4	–	178	38	2	–	306	–	–	–	157	50	–	–
C.	50	1	–	–	52	3	–	–	77	–	–	–	71	26	–	–
3. Kafr Tuffāḥ[45]																
M.	10	–	–	–	18	–	–	–	18	5	1	–	9	4	–	–
C.	–	–	–	–	11	–	–	–	12	–	–	–				
4. Mazraʿa[46]																
M.	–	–	–	–	–	–	–	–	–	–	–	–	–	–	–	–
C.	8	–	–	–	11	–	–	–	12	–	–	–				
5. Blūdān[47]																
M.	–	–	–	–	–	–	–	–	–	–	–	–	–	–	–	–
C.	36	5	–	–	59	–	–	–	65	–	–	–	65	–	–	–
6. ʿAyn Ḥaur[48]																
M.	17	1	1	–	14	–	1	–					15	2	–	–
C.	–	–	–	–	11	1	–	–					19	1	–	–
7. Kubrā[49]																
M.	–	–	–	–	–	–	–	–	–	–	–	–	–	–	–	–
C.	36	6	–	–	51	–	–	–	43	–	–	–	42	9	–	–

It is to be noted from the above table that three villages, Mazrāʿa, Bludān, and Kubrā, were totally Christian. The village of Kafr Tuffāḥ and ʿAyn Ḥaur had about equal populations of Muslims and Christians. In Kafr ʿĀmir, the Christians were a sizable minority, but in Zabadānī itself they were a small group.

Sharīʿa court registers[50] of Damascus shed some light on the Christians of this *nāḥiya*. Two registered cases are worth mentioning because they are representative of the relationship among Christians themselves on the one hand, and between Christians and Muslims on the other.

A priest, Jirjīs b. Abī al-Khayr al-Nuṣrānī, from the village of Blūdān, received from a certain Naṣr Allāh b. ᶜĪsā b. Kassāb al-Nuṣrānī, an amount of silk to weave. The priest, however, defrauded him and sold the silk he had received. The case was brought to the attention of the Ḥanafī judge, who after listening to both, ordered the priest to pay Naṣr Allāh 25 *sulṭāni*s in compensation for the silk.[51] The second example indicates, first, that Christians did own land and second that they were able to sell such land to Muslims. In 992/1584, a certain ᶜAbd al-Razzāq Maḥmūd al-Ḥawwāṭ, from the village of Kafr Tammām, bought from Ilyās b. Rizq Allāh, a Christian from the village of Kubrā, his whole vineyard at the latter village for 520 silver pieces.[52]

Damascus

Demographical statistics for Damascus are available in three *defter*s.[53] They quote the names of *maḥalla*s (quarters) and enumerate the *zuqāq*s (narrow alleys) constituting each quarter. The religious composition of the city is shown in Table 2-5.

TABLE 2-5

	T.D. 401				*T.D. 263*				*T.D. 474*				
	(ca. 950/1543)				*(955/1548)*				*(977/1569)*				
	h.	b.	r.	d.	h.	b.	r.	d.	h.	b.	r.	d.	sh.
M.	7213	358	70	–	8119	393	136	–	7054	322	80	4	92
C.	546	31	–	–	704	96	–	–	1021	164	–	–	–
J.	512	12	–	–	516	–	–	–	546	56	–	–	–

Christians in these surveys were identified as *jamāᶜat-ı Nasārā nafs-i Shām*, and their *ḥārah*, frequently mentioned by Ibn Ṭulūn,[54] is referred to in the *Tapu Defter*s as *maḥallat-i Naṣārā der qurb-i Bāb Sharqı ve Bāb Tūmā* (Christian quarter near Bāb Sharqī and Bāb Tūmā). They lived in nineteen *zuqaq*s, one of which is identified as a Maronite[55] one. Four other *jamaᶜāt* (groups) are mentioned, but are not identified with any of the nineteen *zuqāq*s. One of them is described as *jamāᶜat-i Armanī*[56] (the Armenian group), constituting thirteen households; another is defined as that of the *Rūmyān* (Greeks).[57] Skimming through written names one encounters such names as Rizq, Ilyās, Ibrāhīm, Mūsā, Jirjīs, Mikhāᶜīl, Tūmā, Naṣr Allāh, Yūsūf, and Yaḥyā.[58] It is noticeable from these surveys that the number of Christians in the city of Damascus rose steadily, which may indicate a continuous Christian migration from the countryside to the city where stability and protection were secured.

In contrast to the local chronicles written during Mamluk times, available Arabic literature from the sixteenth century rarely mentions the Christians of

Damascus. It is amazing that this great Orthodox community did not write history. It would indeed be interesting to know what sort of relationship existed among the various Orthodox patriarchates and churches after the Orthodox world was reunited by the Ottomans. Our scanty information indicates that Aleppo, Ḥama, Ḥoms, Ḥawrān, Baʿlabakk, Tripoli, and Bānyas each had a metropolitanate in 1037/1627, while Zabadānī and Qārā each had a bishopric.[59] Neither Arabic nor Turkish material sheds light on the relationship that existed between the indigenous local clergy and the dominating Greek ecclesiastics prior to the Arabicization of the church. Nothing is known about the role of the Orthodox laity in the affairs of the church; on the other hand, the Maronite Patriarch Istifān al-Duwayhī (d. 1704) states that there was a Maronite metropolitanate in Damascus, and names the various people who were appointed to that see in the sixteenth century.[60]

It is significant that the *Ifranj* (Franks), with their own consul and their own local dragoman, were established in Damascus by the end of Mamluk times. They had their own *qaysāriyya* (hotel or caravansary), and although occasionally they were subjected to extortion, they succeeded in redressing themselves from such hardships. They participated in welcoming the Mamluk Sultan Qānṣūh al-Ghawrī on his entry into Damascus in 922/1516; it is also reported that he received the consul and his people and accepted a gift they presented to him. When Sultan Selīm I arrived in Damascus he received the consul and his retinue, while at the same time he refused audience to one of the learned men of Damascus accompanied by his students.[61] The available Arabic and Turkish sources do not provide further information on the Franks in Damascus, but it appears from the *Kanunname* of Damascus that they were engaged in a flourishing trade there. When *bahār* (spices) and *satān* (clothes) coming with the pilgrimage caravan to Damascus were sold to any Frankish merchant, he was to pay a duty amounting to 9 percent of the value of the merchandise. He was also obliged to pay 2 percent of the value of his *bahār* merchandise for storage in Damascus and seven and one-third *akche*s for each load of *bahār* on transfering it to Beirut. The detailed regulations for collecting customs in the ports of Beirut, Sidon, Acre, and Jaffa[62] indicate an active trade with Europe. This presupposes the presence of resident Frankish merchants in these places, as well as in Damascus, the main *entrepôt*. It is thus surprising that when John Sanderson of the Levant Company visited Damascus in 1601, he does not refer to any Frankish merchants there.[63]

It appears that Christians in Damascus and its environs did not suffer from persecution, though they were not free from certain restrictions. For example, in 923/1517, Christians and Jews were commanded not to ride horses, donkeys, or any other animal in the city or in its suburbs whenever there was an assembly of people.[64] When, in 968/1560, it was reported to the sultan that Christians had built houses on the site of a derelict church in the immediate vicinity of the 'Umayyad Mosque, the governor of Damascus was ordered to investigate the matter. The judge of Damascus was asked to force the Christians and Jews in the neighborhood of the mosque to sell their houses to Muslims.[65] About twenty years later, in 989/1581, the sultan commanded that Christians and Jews be prohibited from wearing turbans; they were ordered to wear the distinctive Christian headgear, the *qalansuwāt* and *kabābīs*.[66]

On the other hand, Ottoman officials also protected the Christians. When, in 926/1519, a *Rūmī* (probably an Ottoman) killed a Christian, the governor of Damascus ordered his death.[67] Again, after the governor of Damascus, Lālā Muṣṭafā Pāshā,[68] was dismissed, the sultan, in 976/1568, set up a committee comprised of the judge of Bursa, the judge of Medina, and the judge of Damascus to investigate complaints raised against him. When a certain Christian by the name of Jirjīs from Beirut claimed that Lālā Muṣṭafā Pāshā owed him 6,000 gold pieces, the sultan asked the judge of Medina to examine his claim.[69] With the exception of scattered individual cases,[70] there are no indications of massive Islamization; nor were people forced to convert to Islam in the *liwā'* of Damascus.

Sharīᶜa court registers furnish abundant material which elucidates the relationship between the various strata of the population, whether in the city or in the countryside. It is apparent in the records that Christians had to obtain the approval of the Ḥanafī judge to authenticate their marriage contracts. This arrangement was implemented with the intention of guaranteeing the collection of marriage fees, usually referred to as *resm-i ᶜarūs*.[71] Muslims sometimes acted as legal representatives (*wakīl sharᶜī*) on behalf of the bride. One of the reported cases runs as follows: In the presence of the Ḥanafī judge, a certain Christian by the name of Ibrāhīm b. Mūsā, known as Ibn Khulayf, agreed to pay his fiancée, Sukkariyya b. Yūsūf, the sum of forty silver pieces as a dowry. She received thirty-five in advance, the rest was held back as *mutaᶜakhkhir* (sum to be paid in case of divorce or death). Ḥajj Aḥmad b. Barakāt al-Ḥamawī, her legal representative, approved of this arrangement and the marriage contract was declared legal.[72]

We have cases where Christians borrowed money from Muslims, even from the treasury *(al-khazīna)*. A case dated to 991/1583 records that two Christians from the village of Maᶜrūfiyya in the *nāḥiya* of Jubbat al-ᶜAssal, had borrowed 275 gold *sultani*s from the treasury on the guarantee of al-Nāṣirī Muḥammad b. Sulaymān, who was in charge of the *muqātaᶜāt* (revenues) of the above-mentioned *nāḥiya*.[73] In another sample case from 992/1584, Ahl b. Ayyūb al-Nuṣrānī and her mother Ṭarīfa b. Mūsā al-Naṣrānī, both testified in the presence of the Ḥanafī judge that they had borrowed 250 *sultani*s from Aḥmad b. Khujā Muḥammad al-ᶜAjamī, and as a guarantee had mortgaged their house in the Subkī *zuqāq* to him.[74]

It is interesting to note that members of the military corps of Damascus used to lend money to Christians, among others. To quote but one example: A certain Faraj b. ᶜAbbūd, better known as Ibn Tamarlank, and Yūsūf b. Manṣūr, known as Ibn al-ᶜIkim, both Christians, testified that they owed the Janissary Juᶜfar b. Mūsā and his brother ᶜĪd, ninety *sulṭāni*s and that they had mortgaged their house in the Christian quarter of Damascus to these two Janissaries.[75] Recorded cases also show that Christians used to borrow wheat, barley, lentils, and many other provisions. A very common practice was to lend money in advance in return for later repayment in kind at a favorable rate. In 993/1585, for example, the *sūbāshī* of the Sulaymāniyya *tekke* in Damascus lent six *sulṭānis* to three Christians from the village of Izraᶜ in Ḥawrān for one *ghirārah* (about 200 kg.) of Ḥawrānī wheat to be handed over five months later.[76]

Transactions were carried out between Muslims and Christians. In 992/1584, a certain ᶜIsā b. Ilyās bought from Ḥajj ᶜĪsā b. Maḥmūd b. al-Dahhān his house in the Christian quarter for fifty *sulṭānis*.[77] In the same year Ahl b. Ibrāhīm bought the house of a certain Ibrāhīm b. Zayn al-ᶜĀbidīn al-Gharābīlī for 300 *sulṭānis*. This, of course, indicates that Christians were allowed to purchase real estate, though certainly not without restriction.[78]

We also find that Christians rented Muslim premises. In the year 991/1583 Nicola b. Yūhannā al-Māwardī rented a house from Ḥajj Muḥammad b. Ḥajj Taqī al-Dīn, a grocer in Damascus, for 400 silver pieces a year.[79] A more interesting case is recorded wherein in the presence of the Ḥanafī judge a certain Muḥammad b. al-ᶜUmar al-Ḥomṣī and the Christian Muqbil b. Yūḥannā b. al-Khūrī befriended each other and decided to purchase a house in Damascus jointly and to share in ownership on equal terms. Neither would have any advantage over the other; each had full freedom, in accordance with the *sharīᶜa,* to do whatever he pleased with his share of the house.[80]

Cases involving Muslims, Jews, and Christians are also numerous. In 992/1584 a certain Jew by the name of Mūsā b. Naṣr Allāh was indebted to a Muslim merchant in Damascus, Khawājā Ibrāhīm b. Shihāb al-Dīn Aḥmad al-Bukhārī, for seventy-five *sulṭanīs*. With the consent of all parties concerned and in the presence of the Ḥanafī judge, Khawājā Ibrāhīm was referred to Samᶜān b. Faraj Allāh, a Christian indebted to Mūsā, to collect his due.[81]

Similarly, Christians borrowed money from each other and carried out transactions within their community, and again there is abundant material in this connection in the court registers. Cases of differences between Christians themselves were referred to the Muslim judge. A Christian, Jabāra b. Masᶜad b. Jabāra, raised a complaint against Nicola b. Rizq Allāh and against his brother Tūmā. The two brothers had borrowed sixteen *sulṭānis* from Jabāra and did not pay him. The Ḥanafī judge, after investigating the case, ordered both to pay Jabāra the amount due.[82]

Despite continuous protests, some of them violent, Damascus continued to have taverns and *ḥashīsh* houses, courtesans, and perverts.[83] The Ottomans used to collect fees on the taverns; accruing sums (in *akche*s) as shown in Table 2-6.[84]

TABLE 2-6

T.D. 169 (ca. 930/1523)	*T.D. 401 (ca. 950/1543)*	*T.D. 423 (ca. 955/1548)*	*T.D. 263 (955/1548)*	*T.D. 474 (977/1569)*
100,000	360,000	306,000	306,000	40,000

In 972/1564 the sultan commanded that the taverns, *boza* houses, and cafés be closed, since they were regarded as dens for rascals, but it appears that this order was not scrupulously implemented.[85] Four years later in 976/1568 taxes on wine were abolished as a religious act.[86] This probably accounts for the dramatic drop in revenue at that time. By a process of elimination it would seem that wine trading and tavern keeping were largely Christian occupations.

The City of Ba^c^labakk

Five *Tapu Defters*[87] refer to Christians in Baᶜlabakk as *jamāᶜat-i Naṣārā* (the Christian community), and they were comprised of the *ṭā'ifā*s (groups) shown in Table 2-7.

The pattern of increase and decrease in the Muslim population of the city is noticeable while at the same time Christians increased steadily. It appears that Christians from the neighboring villages, e.g., Farzal and Ḥammāra, were migrating to Baᶜlabakk, which during the sixteenth century enjoyed considerable stability due to the efforts of the Shīᶜa Ḥarfūsh family.[89] Later, however, in 1033/1623 the city was looted by the army of the Druze *amir* Fakhr al-Dīn. Duwayhī states that Baᶜlabakk had two churches, one Orthodox and the second administered by a Maronite archdeacon. The Maronite church suffered heavy damage at the hands of Fakhr al-Dīn's *sekbān*s[90] (irregulars).

Bāj of *Khammāra* is among the list of the *muqāṭaᶜāt* (revenues) of Baᶜlabakk. As there were very few Jews in the city, it is most probable that trading in wine was a Christian monopoly. Collected fees (in *akches*) are shown in Table 2-9.[91] These figures show that prohibitions declared against taverns were not fully enforced.

Nāḥiyat Baᶜlabakk

The names of forty-two villages comprising this *nāḥiya* appear in five surveys,[92] but only the four shown in Table 2-10 had Christian inhabitants.

The villages of Rāis and ᶜĀqūra were totally Christian, and it should be noted that both were of considerable size. The number of Christians in Kafīla increased over that of Muslims, while the Christian element in the village of Qāᶜa was decreasing, probably due to migration to Baᶜlabakk or to ᶜĀqūra.

Nāḥiyat Karak-Nūḥ

There are forty-one villages mentioned by the accessible surveys,[97] yet only the seven villages (see Table 2–11) had Christian inhabitants:

As is reflected in these statistics, Farzal had a large Christian community which was only slightly smaller than the Muslim. In ᶜAynātā, Lammūnah, Dayr al-Aḥmar, and Ibla we find that Christians strikingly outnumbered Muslims, while Bashawāt was a totally Christian village. It is worth mentioning that this *nāḥiyat* was the haven of the Sunni Bedouin family of al-Ḥanash[105] up until 976/1568 when they were succeeded by another Sunni family, the Furaykh,[106]

TABLE 2-7

	T.D. 430				*T.D. 383*				*T.D. 401*				*T.D. 543*				*T.D. 177*			
	(ca. 930/1523)				*(ca. 937/1530)*				*(ca. 950/1543)*				*(ca. 976/1568)*				*(1005/1596)*			
	h.	*b.*	*r.*	*d.*	*h.*	*b.*	*r.*	*d.*	*h.*	*b.*	*r.*	*d.*	*h.*	*b.*	*r.*	*d.*	*h.*	*b.*	*r.*	*d.*
	125 given as a total number (of households)																			
1. Jiryis					18	8	–	–	13	3	–	–	22	–	–	–	39	–	–	–
2. Banū Shubāt					27	5	–	–	11	2	–	–	49	4	–	–	55	–	–	–
3. Ḥammāriyya					13	6	–	–	13	2	–	–	22	2	–	–	33	–	–	–
4. Majādla					18	–	–	–	15	1	–	–	23	–	–	–	45	–	–	–
5. Mawārna					28	7	–	–	23	–	–	–	38	–	–	–	55	–	–	–
6. Farāzla					39	20	–	–	52	10	–	–	62	6	–	–	79	–	–	–
7. Faraḥ (Faraj?) b. Sibāq									18	2	–	–								
8. Christians in the quarter of Shuhbān													6	–	–	–	6	–	–	–

Offering a more comprehensive view of the demography of the city, the same five *defters* provide the information shown in Table 2-8.

TABLE 2-8

		Sayyids																		
M.	1328	129	11	+3	1630	182	27	–	1445	179	13	–	1464	155	20	–	1011	249	10	–
C.	125	–	–	–	141	61	–	–	145	10	–	–	222	18	–	–	312	–	–	–
J.	30	–	–	–	23	6	–	–	30	6	–	–	23	6	–	–	50	–	–	–

TABLE 2-9

T.D. 430	*T.D. 383*	*T.D. 401*
(ca. 930/1523)	*(ca. 937/1530)*	*(ca. 950/1543)*
3,600	3,730	3,600
T.D. 423	*T.D. 543*	*T.D. 177*
(ca. 952/1545)	*(ca. 976/1568)*	*(1005/1596)*
3,730	4,000	6,000

which was eliminated in 1002/1594 when the whole area passed to the hands of Fakhr al-Dīn.

Nāḥiyat Ḥammāra

Four extant surveys[107] supply the names of twenty-three villages in this rugged area overlooking al-Biqā^c. Only two villages (see Table 2–12) had Christians:

It is obvious that ᶜAyn ᶜArab was a large, almost completely Christian village. Christians in Ḥammāra increased until they were almost equal to Muslims in numbers.

The *Tapu Defter*s do not refer to Christians in Iqlim al-Billān, Wādī al-Taym, and in Ḥawla.

Nāhiyat Iqlīm al-Zabīb

A small number of Christians resided in three villages (shown in Table 2-13) of this locality, which comprised about twenty villages.[110]

The Christian presence was very limited and the area was predominantly Muslim. In the neighboring *nāḥiyat* of Shaᶜra which had forty-four villages[114] we find Christians in only one, Biqaᶜātā,[115] which had three Christian households and two bachelors, compared to fifteen Muslim households, fifteen bachelors, and one *imām*.

Nāḥiyat Kisrawān

Out of thirty-six registered villages[116] only the sixteen shown in Table 2-14 had Christian populations.

It is of particular significance that the number of Christians in this *nāḥiya* was continuously increasing until it almost equaled the size of the Muslim population. A number of Maronite families who later played a significant role in the history of Lebanon moved to this area. By the beginning of the sixteenth century, the Maronite Shaykh Ḥubaysh and his four sons Yūsūf, Ibrāhīm, Sulaymān, and al-Zayn, moved from the village of Dayr Yānūḥ to the seat of the Turkoman family al-ᶜAssāf.[133] They served the head of the family, ᶜAssāf (d. 924/1518),

TABLE 2-10

	T.D. 430				*T.D. 383*				*T.D. 401*				*T.D. 543*				*T.D. 177*			
	(ca. 930/1523)				*(ca. 937/1530)*				*(ca. 950/1543)*				*(ca. 976/1568)*				*(1005/1596)*			
	h.	*b.*	*r.*	*d.*	*h.*	*b.*	*r.*	*d.*	*h.*	*b.*	*r.*	*d.*	*h.*	*b.*	*r.*	*d.*	*h.*	*b.*	*r.*	*d.*
1. Rāis[93]																				
M.	–	–	–	–	4	–	–	–	–	–	–	–	2	–	–	–	2	–	–	–
C.	69	13	–	–	200	–	–	–	151	12	–	–	165	30			141	45		
2. Qāᶜah[94]																				
M.					138	–	–	–	110	21	1	–	48	2	–	–	50	–	–	–
C.					105	–	–	–	56	8	–	–	30	–	–	–	4	–	–	–
3. Kafīla[95]																				
M.	33	1	1	–					40	14	1	–	81	3	–	–	64	19	–	–
C.	21	9	11	11					30	4	–	–	104	1	–	–	100	25	–	–
4. ᶜĀqūra[96]																				
M.	–	–	–	–	–	–	–	–	–	–	–	–								
C.	119	11	–	–	295	2	–	–	210	9	–	–								

TABLE 2-11

	T.D. 430				*T.D. 383*				*T.D. 401*				*T.D. 543*				*T.D. 177*			
	(ca. 930/1523)				*(ca. 937/1530)*				*(ca. 950/1543)*				*(ca. 976/1568)*				*(1005/1596)*			
	h.	*b.*	*r.*	*d.*	*h.*	*b.*	*r.*	*d.*	*h.*	*b.*	*r.*	*d.*	*h.*	*b.*	*r.*	*d.*	*h.*	*b.*	*r.*	*d.*
1. Farzal[98]				*Sayyid*																
M.	204	13	2	+1	293	34	3	–	294	62	2	–	363	47	–	–	343	56	–	–
C.	218	2	–	–	349	8	–	–	262	53	–	–	325	30	–	–	293	51	–	–
2. ᶜAynātā[99]																				
M.	8	–	1	–	20	–	1	–	22	5	–	–	18	–	–	–				
C.	43	3	–	–	67	–	–	–	61	21	–	–	72	–	–	–				
3. Lammūna[100] (?)																				
M.	9	–	1	–	10	–	1	–	33	5	–	–	8	–	–	–				
C.	36	14	–	–	34	–	–	–	80	5	–	–	20	–	–	–				
4. Dayr al-Aḥmar[101]																				
M.	–	–	–	–	8	–	–	–	6	1	–	–	8	–	–	–				
C.	16	1	–	–	16	–	–	–	23	4	–	–	21	–	–	–				
5. Bashawāt[102]																				
M.	–	–	–	–	–	–	–	–	–	–	–	–								
C.	16	3	–	–	44	5	–	–	31	11	–	–								
6. Ibla[103]																				
M.	20	1	–	–	16	2	–	–	16	1	–	–	7	1	–	–	4	3	–	–
C.	–	–	–	–	–	–	–	–	50	1	–	–	42	–	–	–	36	9	–	–
7. Bajājah[104]																				
M.	4	–	–	–	3	–	–	–	9	5	–	–								
C.	7	1	–	–	–	–	–	–	9	–	–	–								

TABLE 2-12

	T.D. 430 (*ca. 930/1523*)				*T.D. 383* (*ca. 937/1530*)				*T.D. 401* (*ca. 950/1543*)				*T.D. 474* (*977/1569*)			
	h.	*b.*	*r.*	*d.*	*h.*	*b.*	*r.*	*d.*	*h.*	*b.*	*r.*	*d.*	*h.*	*b.*	*r.*	*d.*
1. ᶜAyn ᶜArab[108]																
M.	1	–	–	–	2	–	–	–	–	–	–	–	2	–	–	–
C.	40	5	–	–	57	–	–	–	53	–	–	–	53	12	–	–
2. Ḥammāra[109]																
M.	163	20	2	–	147	22	–	–	126	2	–	–	135	40	–	–
C.	119	6	–	–	163	16	–	–	147	–	–	–	159	6	–	–

TABLE 2-13

	T.D. 430 (*ca. 930/1523*)				*T.D. 401* (*ca. 950/1543*)				*T.D. 263* (*955/1548*)				*T.D. 474* (*977/1569*)			
	h.	*b.*	*r.*	*d.*	*h.*	*b.*	*r.*	*d.*	*h.*	*b.*	*r.*	*d.*	*h.*	*b.*	*r.*	*d.*
1. Bayt Jinn[111]																
M.	55	2	–	–	121	14	1	–	186	–	1	–	103	3	1	–
C.	11	–	–	–	12	2	–	–	15	–	–	–	25	–	–	–
2. Ḥannā[112]																
M.					36	3	1	–					59	–	1	–
C.					5	1	–	–					–	–	–	–
3. Dayr[113]																
M.					9	10	1	–								
C.					6	–	–	–								

who was entrusted with the counties of Kisrawān and Jubayl. Shortly after his death the Ḥubaysh family suffered at the hands of ᶜAssāf's son Qāytbay (d. 930/1523), who died childless. The chieftainship then passed to his nephew Manṣūr b. Ḥasan; he was a recognized local chieftain for a long time, and the Ottomans very often delegated to him the tax farming of Kisrāwān, Jubayl, Baṭrūn, Bisharrī, Kūra, and Ḍinniyya. He reinstated the Ḥūbayshis, and Yūsūf and Sulaymān were his stewards.[134] They became very powerful, to such an extent that they took part, in 935/1528 and in 941/1534, in the cold-blooded elimination of two Muslim families who coveted the position of the ᶜAssāfs.[135] This, no doubt, explains why the *amīr* Manṣur gave the two brothers Yūsūf and Sulaymān a free hand to manage his affairs.[136] It is probably due to the influence of the Ḥubayshis that in 952/1545, the Maronites from the village of Jāj in the region of Jubayl moved to Kisrawān. Duwayhī names three Maronite families that relocated: the Khāzins to Bāllūna, the Jumayyils to the ridge of Bikfayyā, and the Kumayds to Ghazīr's ridge. The first later played an important role in the history of Lebanon.[137] The Ḥubayshis' help and protection for Christians was more manifest in 980/1572, when Shaykh Yūsūf, through his machinations, was able to win an exemption from a 200 *sulṭānī* tax for Dayr Qannūbīn.[138]. When he died on September 19, 1583, Shaykh Yūsūf, who was known for his vigor, was succeeded by his brother Shaykh Sulaymān as a steward *(kūkhāna)*[139] to the last ᶜAssāf *amīr,* Muḥammad. In 1591, Muḥammad was killed in obscure circumstances, near Tripoli, perhaps through the connivance of Yūsūf Pāshā Sayfā. He had no progeny, and Yūsūf Pāshā Sayfā married his widow and seized the possessions of the ᶜAssāf family. Shaykh Sulaymān Ḥubaysh and his nephew Mansūr were arrested by Yūsū Pāshā Sayfā and put to death. The possessions of the family were confiscated by him and the remaining Ḥubayshis sought refuge in Shuwayfāt.[140] When the Maᶜnids by the beginning of the seventeenth century, emerged to dominate the local political scene in Lebanon, the Ḥubayshis joined their ranks. When the Maᶜnids annexed Ghazīr, it again became the headquarters of the Ḥubayshis,[141] who were superseded later by another Maronite family, namely the Khāzins.

The Druze leader Fakhr al-Dīn took the Khāzins into his service in two capacities: as his emissaries to Europe and as his finance managers. In terms of political divisions on the local level, the Khāzins, as their lords the Maᶜnids, were Qaysis who opposed the Yamanis. Among the most influential members of the Khāzin family was a certain Abū Nādir, who held the title of *shaykh*.[142] He is described by Duwayhi as being "temperamental, courageous, decent, opposed to oppression, confidant of the Maᶜnid House."[143] While in al-Shūf in 1613 he was commissioned with others by *amīr* Yūnus, brother of Fakhr al-Dīn (who was in self-exile in Tuscany), to count the trees in al-Shūf for taxation purposes. Two years later, following *amīr* Yūnus's victory over the Sayfās in the battle of al-Nāᶜmah, Kisrawān was annexed by the Maᶜnids and Shaykh Abū Nādir was instructed to move to its seat, Ghazīr, and govern it on behalf of the Maᶜnids.[144] When Jubayl was taken in 1618 from the Sayfās it was also entrusted to Abū Nādir.[145] Not long after in 1621 Jubbat Bisharrī was amalgamated by the

TABLE 2-14

	T.D. 430 (ca. 930/1523)				*T.D. 383 (ca. 937/1530)*				*T.D. 401 (ca. 950/1543)*				*T.D. 543 (ca. 975/1568)*				*T.D. 177 (1005/1596)*			
	h.	*b.*	*r.*	*d.*	*h.*	*b.*	*r.*	*d.*	*h.*	*b.*	*r.*	*d.*	*h.*	*b.*	*r.*	*d.*	*h.*	*b.*	*r.*	*d.*
1. ᶜAjaltūn[117]																				
M.	–	–	–	–	–	–	–	–	–	–	–	–	–	–	–	–	–	–	–	–
C.	23	3	–	–	19	1	–	–	19	5	–	–	20	–	–	–	17	6	–	–
2. Bikarkiyya[118] (Bkerke?)																				
M.	–	–	–	–	–	–	–	–	–	–	–	–	–	–	–	–	–	–	–	–
C.	15	5	–	–	20	–	–	–	12	4	–	–	18	3	–	–	23	–	–	–
3. ᶜArāmūn[119]																				
M.	4	–	–	–	8	2	–	–	4	–	–	–	10	–	–	–	4	4	–	–
C.	6	2	–	–	9	1	–	–	12	4	–	–	8	2	–	–	14	6	–	–
4. ᶜAlmān[120] (Fūqā and Taḥtā)																				
M.	6	1	–	–	13	2	–	–	14	–	–	–	15	–	–	–	13	2	–	–
C.	29	6	–	–	36	–	–	–	44	7	–	–	37	–	–	–	29	10	–	–
5. ᶜAyn Jamāl[121]																				
M.	5	2	–	–	4	–	–	–	6	–	–	–	4	–	–	–	5	–	–	–
C.	8	2	–	–	13	–	–	–	10	4	–	–	14	–	–	–	12	5	–	–
6. Ghazīr[122]																				
M.	3	–	–	–	14	–	–	–	4	–	–	–	14	–	–	–	10	5	–	–
C.	16	–	–	–	21	3	–	–	20	2	–	–	26	–	–	–	28	10	–	–
7. Darᶜoūn[123]																				
M.	–	–	–	–	–	–	–	–	–	–	–	–	–	–	–	–	–	–	–	–
C.	7	3	–	–	16	1	–	–	10	3	–	–	14	–	–	–	11	5	–	–

8. Baṭḥa[124]																				
M.	–	–	–	–	–	–	–	–	–	–	–	–	–	–	–	–	–	–	–	–
C.	4	–	–	–	3	–	–	–	3	2	–	–	3	–	–	–	3	–	–	–
9. Ghousta[125]																				
M.	–	–	–	–	–	–	–	–	–	–	–	–	–	–	–	–	–	–	–	–
C.	11	–	–	–	12	1	–	–	15	1	–	–	12	–	–	–	9	5	–	–
10. ᶜAshqūt[126]																				
M.	–	–	–	–	–	–	–	–	–	–	–	–	–	–	–	–	–	–	–	–
C.	43	–	–	–	43	7	–	–	30	14	–	–	44	–	–	–	34	15	–	–
11. Abū Kaffiyyah[127] (Bikfiyya ?)																				
M.	–	–	–	–	–	–	–	–	–	–	–	–	–	–	–	–	–	–	–	–
C.	28	–	–	–	41	–	–	–	37	4	–	–	41	–	–	–	38	15	–	–
12. Muḥaydthah[128]																				
M.	–	–	–	–	–	–	–	–	–	–	–	–	–	–	–	–	–	–	–	–
C.	3	–	–	–	11	–	–	–	11	–	–	–	8	–	–	–	9	–	–	–
13. Judayda[129]																				
M.	5	–	–	–	8	3	–	–	9	–	–	–	12	–	–	–	9	3	–	–
C.	8	–	–	–	–	–	–	–	11	2	–	–	7	–	–	–	4	3	–	–
14. Ḥarīṣā[130]																				
M.	9	–	–	–																
C.	17	3	–	–																
15. Dalbat[131]																				
M.	8	3	–	–					14	–	–	–	9	1	–	–	8	2	–	–
C.	3	3	–	–					26	–	–	–	20	–	–	–	20	5	–	–
16. Bayt Shaᶜār[132]																				
M.	–	–	–	–	–	–	–	–	–	–	–	–	–	–	–	–	–	–	–	–
C.	27	–	–	–	32	–	–	–	28	2	–	–	35	2	–	–	33	15	–	–

Maᶜnids, who again invested another member of the Khāzin family, a man by the name of Abū Ṣāfī. He eliminated the Christian *muqaddam* (chief) family of Shalhūb as being partisans of the Sayfās.[146] The Khāzins joined in attacks waged by Fakhr al-Dīn against his adversaries, especially the Sayfās, and by so doing they tied their destiny to that of the Maᶜnids. When in 1633 the Ottomans decided to remove Fakhr al-Dīn from the scene, the Khāzins joined him in his escape to the cavern of Nīḥā, and later they were taken with him to Damascus. They did not accompany him to Istanbul but rather managed to return to Lebanon.[147] Christians, who had enjoyed many privileges during the time of Fakhr al-Dīn, such as being allowed to build churches, ride saddled horses, carry jeweled rifles, and receive missionaries, were subjected to many atrocities.[148] Maᶜnid and Khāzin possessions in Tripoli, Jubayl, and al-Baṭrūn were plundered by the Sayfās. Monks and clergy were arrested and humiliated in an attempt to gain information concerning the Maᶜnids and the Khazins. It was most likely due to these depredations that the Khāzins, in 1635, decided to flee to Tuscany, where they stayed for two years.[149] Similarly, the Ḥubayshis were exposed to such maltreatment that they were compelled to migrate from al-Shūf to Jubayl.[150]

When the Maᶜnids managed to recover from their misfortunes the Khāzins returned to serve them. Abū Nādir did not live long; he died in 1647, and was succeeded in the stewardship by his son Abū Nawfal. His great zeal for the Maronites is reflected by the fact that he built a church and assigned a priest to it.[151] His influence in the Maronite Church was manifested when he succeeded in appointing a certain Sarkīs b. al-Jamrī al-Hidnānī as the head of the church in Damascus.[152] A similar role was played by the Khāzin family, later in the eighteenth and nineteenth centuries. His paramount fame and prestige were no doubt boosted when the pope in 1656 honored Abū Nawfal with a golden collar. Three years later the king of France appointed him as the French consul in Beirut; he was also put in charge of the Venetian consulate in the same city. "The governors of Damascus and the Frankish consuls used to hold him in high esteem. His word had force in every place." His death in 1679 was not the end of the Khāzin family; as a paramount, recognized local power[153] it played an influential role in the Maronite Church and in the local politics of Lebanon during the Shihābī emirate. Their distinguished performance during that era merits a separate study.[154]

Nāḥiyat Shūf al-Bayāḍ

Four extant surveys[155] mention the names of twenty-one villages comprising this *nāḥiya,* but only the village of ᶜItā[156] (see Table 2–15) had a Christian population.

It is probable, as suggested by the first survey, that at first there were no Christians, and that they later began to migrate to this village on such a scale they eventually outnumbered the Muslims there. It is important to note that according to the *Tapu Defter*s the *nāḥiyā*s of Shūf Ībn Maᶜn, Jizzīn, Iqlīm al-Kharnūb, Iqlīm al-Tuffāḥ, and Iqlīm al-Shūmar did not have Christian inhabitants.

TABLE 2-15

	T.D. 430 (ca. 930/1523) h.	b.	r.	d.	*T.D. 383* (ca. 937/1530) h.	b.	r.	d.	*T.D. 401* (ca. 950/1543) h.	b.	r.	d.	*T.D. 474* (977/1569) h.	b.	r.	d.
M.	122	–	2	–	135	47	4	–	113	57	2	–	142	50	2	–
C.	–	–	–	–	184	21	–	–	197	13	–	–	174	37	–	–

The village of Majdal Maᶜaush represents an interesting case. Since 917/1511 a haven for *sufis*,[157] it was a totally Muslim village.[158] Toward the beginning of the seventeenth century feuds broke out among its Muslim inhabitants, and they agreed to sell their village and abandon it. ᶜAlī b. Fakhr al-Dīn bought it and gave it to the Christians. In 1018/1609 the Maronite patriarch visited the village, erected a church, and built himself a house there;[159] the Patriarch Istifan al-Duwayhī mentions that in 1683 he visited Majdal Maᶜaush and repaired its church.[160] Such treatment, which was in direct contravention to the *sharīᶜa,* indicates the consideration with which the Maronites were treated by the Maᶜnids.

Nāḥiyat Bayrūt (Beirut)

In the sixteenth century, this *nāḥiya* comprised the city of Beirut and its village suburb, al-Burj. Five surveys[161] supply demographical data for the city as shown in Table 2–16.

TABLE 2-16

	T.D. 430 (ca. 930/1523) h.	b.	r.	d.	*T.D. 383* (ca. 937/1530) h.	b.	r.	d.	*T.D. 401* (ca. 950/1543) h.	b.	r.	d.	*T.D. 543* (ca. 976/1568) h.	b.	r.	d.	*T.D. 177* (1005/1596) h.	b.	r.	d.
M.	610	39	16	–	809	230	17	–	847	24	3	–	773	117	11	–	865	213	5	–
C.	66	11	–	–	95	66	–	–	30	–	–	–	140	–	–	–	110	140	–	–
J.	12	–	–	–	16	–	–	–	19	–	–	–	9	–	–	–	9	–	–	–

It is clear from these surveys that Beirut was predominantly a Muslim city. Neither Shaykh Aḥmad b. Muḥammad al-Khālidī al-Ṣafadī (d. ca. 1034/1624), nor the Maronite Patriarch Istifan al-Duwayhī, indicate any significant role played by the Christians of Beirut. It appears from Duwayhī that some of the Christians were Maronites, for they had two churches there. The Muslims seized one of them in 1570 and converted it into a caravansary. The Maronites, through Shaykh Abū Manṣūr b. Ḥubaysh, reached an agreement with the Melkites to share the latter's church in the city itself in return for allowing the Melkites access to the Maronites' church outside the city.[162] In 1661, another Maronite church was taken over by Muslims; it was converted into a mosque and its endowments were confiscated.[163] It seems that by the beginning of the seventeenth century, due to the tolerant policy of Fakhr al-Dīn, more Maronites began to migrate toward Beirut and its environs. This may explain the reference in 1626 to a Maronite archbishopric in Beirut.[164]

Franks and Jews used to pass through Beirut en route to visit the holy places in Palestine. Certain fees, which were referred to as *bāj-i kefereh ḥujjāj-i naṣārā ve yahudiyyān,* were collected at the rate of fifty *akche*s per person. The total amount is reported as a lump sum equal to 2,000 *akches* yearly. Those Franks who resided in Beirut for trade were to pay an additional tax, the *bāj-i tujjār-i kuffār,* amounting to one *filūrī* (florin) for each. This tax totaled annually 1,000 *akche*s.[165] The English traveler George Sandys described Beirut in 1611 as "now stored with merchandize and much frequented by foreigners."[166] The *Kanunname* of Damascus clearly shows that there was a vigorous trade between the Ottoman Syrian provinces and Europe via Beirut and Sidon, which handled more transactions at the time of Fakhr al-Dīn.[167]

Wine was imported for the taverns of Beirut from the surrounding area, and taxes on such imports were collected on the basis of two *akche*s per *yük* (load). In ca. 976/1568, the total wine *bāj* (tax) for both wine imports and on the taverns themselves amounted to 10,000 *akche*s, rising to 12,000 *akche*s by the end of the century.[168] With so few Jewish households in the city, it may be assumed that, here also, this enterprise was in the hands of the Christians.

Reviewing the surveys of Sidon, one finds, strangely enough, reference to only three Christian households in that city, and these toward the end of the sixteenth century.[169] Perhaps, with the flourishing trade with Europe, Christians, encouraged by Fakhr al-Dīn, moved to live in Sidon and its vicinity. Duwayhī refers in 1626 to the appointment of an archbishop[170] in Sidon, which might indicate an increase in the number of Maronites. Ten years later he states that a church was built in the village of ᶜArbāniyyah[171] in the region of Sidon. In his account of this port city, George Sandys in 1611 refers to Jews and Christians who "pay for their heads two dollars a piece yearly." Concerning foreign merchants in Sidon he adds the following: "Now as for merchants who are for the most part English they are entertained with all courtesy and freedom. They may travel without the danger with purses in their hands, paying for customs but three in hundred."[172] Sidon's trade was, however, sporadically disrupted by Frankish (mostly from Malta) and Maghribi (North African) pirates.[173]

The *Qaḍā'* of Ḥawrān in the *liwā'* of Damascus consisted of seventeen *nāḥiyā*s[174] of which those in Table 2-17, 2-18, and 2-19 had Christian populations:

It may be seen that in Adhriᶜat the Christians were increasing in order to continue to outnumber the Muslims. Most probably Christians from small less-secure villages migrated to Adhriᶜat. In the *nāḥiya* of Banū Juhma,[185] which consisted of twenty-nine villages, Christians are recorded only for the village al-Bārḥa (ca. 930/1523), which had four Christian households against thirty-two Muslim households, plus one *imām*.[186] Similarly, in the *nāḥiya* of Banū

Nāḥiyat Banū Kilāb[175]

TABLE 2-17

	T.D. 401 (ca. 950/1543)				*T.D. 491* (977/1569)			
	h.	*b.*	*r.*	*d.*	*h.*	*b.*	*r.*	*d.*
1. Zubayda al-Gharbiyya[176]								
M.	11	–	–	–	20	–	–	–
C.	11	–	–	–	11	–	–	–
2. Zubayda al-Sharqiyya[177]								
M.	–	–	–	–	28	3	–	–
C.	–	–	–	–	2	–	–	–
3. Maḥajja[178]								
M.	14	1	1	–				
C.	28	1	–	–				
4. Jabab[179]								
M.	43	2	1	–	58	–	–	–
C.	6	–	–	–	7	–	–	–

Nashbah[187] the village of ᶜAmrī[188] in 976/1568 had five Christian households compared to forty-three Muslim households. In a second village, Rīm al-Khilkhāl,[189] the distribution was thirteen Muslim households and three bachelors, while the number of Christians was six households in addition to three bachelors. In the rest of the *nāḥiya* no Christian population is recorded.

The village of Riḥaba[190] in the *nāḥiya* of Banū Uᶜqba[191] had a Christian population that was a majority, as shown in Table 2-20.

Glancing at the above surveyed villages, we find that the *liwā'* of Damascus, in 977/1569, comprised five cities and 1,129 villages with a population of

Nāḥiyat Banū Muqlid[180]

TABLE 2-18

	T.D. 430 (ca. 930/1523)				*T.D. 401* (ca. 950/1543)				*T.D. 491* (977/1569)			
	h.	*b.*	*r.*	*d.*	*h.*	*b.*	*r.*	*d.*	*h.*	*b.*	*r.*	*d.*
1. Buṣra[181]												
M.	56	–	–	–	58	5	1	–	109	24	–	–
C.	–	–	–	–	14	–	–	–	23	–	–	–
2. Ṣarkhad[182]												
M.	33	–	1	–	41	6	1	–	59	–	–	–
C.	26	–	–	–	39	6	–	–	44	6	–	–
3. Saᶜā'(?)[183]												
M.	15	–	–	–	44	3	1	–	42	2	–	–
C.	–	–	–	–	–	–	–	–	6	–	–	–

Nāḥiyat Banū ᶜAbd-alla

TABLE 2-19

	T.D. 430 (ca. 930/1523)				T.D. 401 (ca. 950/1543)				T.D. 491 (977/1569)			
	h.	b.	r.	d.	h.	b.	r.	d.	h.	b.	r.	d.
1. Adhriᶜāt[184]												
M.	36	2	3	–	95	–	10	–	118	7	1	–
C.	56	3	–	–	100	3	–	–	135	–	–	–

TABLE 2-20

	T.D. 401 (ca. 950/1543)				T.D. 491 (977/1569)			
	h.	b.	r.	d.	h.	b.	r.	d.
M.	51	–	–	–	6	–	–	–
C.	19	–	–	–	46	–	–	–

Three villages out of twenty-eight reported in surveys[192] concerning Nāḥiyat Banū al-Aᶜsar, contained Christians (see Table 2-21).

TABLE 2-21

	T.D. 401 (ca. 950/1543)				T.D. 491 (977/1569)			
	h.	b.	r.	d.	h.	b.	r.	d.
1. Ṣakhra[193]								
M.	45	–	1	–	55	–	–	–
C.	17	–	–	–	18	–	–	–
2. ᶜIbbīn[194]								
M.	25	2	1	–	34	–	–	–
C.	15	–	–	–	15	–	–	–
3. Iᶜbillīn[195]								
M.	11	–	1	–	13	–	–	–
C.	16	–	–	–	4	–	–	–

57,110 households, 8,348 bachelors, plus 287 religious functionaries. The number of *zuᶜamā'*, *aghā*s and other officials totaled fifty-one. Added to this, the number of the *sipāhī*s was 399.[196] If we take the number of Christians, we find that they constituted a marginal segment of the total population.

TABLE 2-22

	T.D. 970 (ca. 955/1548?)				T.D. 185 (1005/1596)			
	h.	*b.*	*r.*	*d.*	*h.*	*b.*	*r.*	*d.*
1. ᶜAjlūn[200]								
M.	195	11	9	–	330	30	2	–
C.	9	–	–	–	23	–	–	–

Liwā' of ᶜAjlūn[197]

At the beginning of the century Christians in this *liwā'* paid the poll tax at the rate of eighty *akche*s for the *nafar,*[198] rising to 85.[199] Most references to this tax are termed as *maqṭū'* (lump sum). The city of ᶜAjlūn had a small Christian population, as shown in Tables 2-22, 2-23, and 2-24.

Note the high number of Christians in Būrmah. The poll tax accruing from the village of Rabaḍ (1,080 *akche*s) was part of the endowments of Khalīl al-Raḥmān

Nāḥiyat Banū ᶜUlwān

TABLE 2-23

1. Dibbīn[201]								
M.	–	–	–	–	–	–	–	–
C.	48	–	–	–	75	–	–	–
2. Marj Shaykh[202]								
M.	5	–	–	–	8	–	–	–
C.	17	–	–	–	11	–	–	–
3. Manṣūra[203]								
M.	31	–	1	–	48	2	–	–
C.	5	–	–	–	8	–	–	–
4. Rāᶜā[204]								
M.	13	1	–	–	6	1	–	–
c.	19	–	–	–	8	2	–	–
5. Muṣallā[205]								
M.	35	1	–	–	44	5	–	–
C.	6	–	–	–	7	–	–	–
6. Wādī Ṣūf[206]								
M.	71	4	2	–	75	5	–	–
C.	8	–	–	–	10	–	–	–
7. Buqayyᶜat al-Naṣārā[207]								
M.	–	–	–	–	4	–	–	–
C.	29	–	–	–	19	1	–	–
8. Naqqiyya al-Suflā[208]								
M.	46	1	–	–	34	–	–	–
C.	4	–	–	–	9	–	–	–
9. ᶜAyn Najrā[209]								
M.					17	3	–	–
C.					3	–	–	–

Nāḥiyat Kūrā

TABLE 2-24

	T.D. 970				*T.D. 185*			
	(ca. 955/1548?)				*(1005/1596)*			
	h.	*b.*	*r.*	*d.*	*h.*	*b.*	*r.*	*d.*
1. Zūbiyya[210]								
M.					14	6	–	–
C.					7	–	–	–
2. ᶜAnjara[211]								
M.	32	4	1	–	28	4	–	–
C.	19	–	–	–	13	1	–	–
3. ᶜAyn Janna[212]								
M.	49	4	1	–	42	3	–	–
C.	21	–	–	–	12	3	–	–
4. Rabaḍ[213]								
M.					26	–	–	–
C.					12	–	–	–
5. Būrma al-Suflā[214]								
M.	26	3	–	–				
C.	58	–	–	–				

(Hebron). The number of Christians in 986/1578 was nine *nafar*s, and the supervision of the endowment was entrusted to the *Sūfī* Samādī family.[215]

The town of Salṭ[216] was comprised of two *maḥalla*s as shown in Tables 2-25 and 2-26.

It is worth noting that the town of Karak was mainly Christian. The number of Christians in Shawbak, however, was very small; this is not in agreement with available Mamluk literature which emphasizes the Christian dominance among the inhabitants.[223] Fortunately, the puzzle is resolved by the Gaza surveys, which show Christians from Shawbak and Wādī Mūsā living in Gaza. Most likely, the vulnerability of Shawbak and its adjacent areas to Bedouin attacks forced Christians to move to more secure places like Gaza where official authorities could protect them.

TABLE 2-25

	T.D. 970				*T.D. 185*			
	(ca. 955/1548?)				*(1005/1596)*			
	h.	*b.*	*r.*	*d.*	*h.*	*b.*	*r.*	*d.*
1. Maḥallat ᶜAwāmala								
M.	83	22	–	–	26	4	1	–
C.	–	–	–	–	4	–	–	–
2. Maḥallat Akrād								
M.	65	8	2	–	13	1	–	–
C.	10	–	–	–	21	–	–	–

Nāhiyat Karak

TABLE 2-26

	T.D. 970 *(ca. 955/1548?)*				*T.D. 185* *(1005/1596)*			
	h.	*b.*	*r.*	*b.*	*h.*	*b.*	*r.*	*d.*
1. Nafsi Karak[217]								
M.	64	2	–	–	78	2	–	–
C.	117	–	–	–	103	8	–	–
2. Kafr Rabba[218]								
M.	110	1	–	–	16	–	–	–
C.	5	–	–	–	3	–	–	–
3. ᶜAyn Shabīb[219]								
M.	66	1	–	–	19	–	–	–
C.	7	–	–	–	3	–	–	–
4. Ḥarfa[220]								
M.	214	5	–	–				
C.	12	–	–					
5. Khunayzīra[221]								
M.	60	2	–	–				
C.	2	–	–	–				
6. Shawbak[222]								
M.	145	16	2	–	65	–	–	–
C.	11	–	–	–	5	–	–	–

Palestine in the sixteenth century consisted of the *liwā*'s of Ṣafad, Lajjūn, Nablus, Jerusalem, and Gaza.

Liwā' of Ṣafad

This *liwā'*, consisting of 282 villages embracing 14,884 households, 1,921 bachelors, plus 307 religious functionaries and disabled,[224] had only six villages with a Christian presence, in all cases minor as shown in Table 2-27.

One would expect to find more Christians dwelling in Nazareth.[231] It should be remembered that Sultan al-Ẓāhir Baybars, in 661/1263, ordered the destruction of the town's main church, which was razed.[232] This is perhaps indicative of the reasons for this nominal Christian presence. George Sandys, who visited the town in 1611, states, "Now at Nazareth no Christian is suffered to dwell by the Moors that inhabit it."[233] Christians in this *liwā'* paid the poll tax at the rate of eighty *akche*s for each *nafar,* and in the second half of the century the impost was raised to eighty-five *akches;* this was collected, it seems, as a lump sum.[234]

Liwā' of Nāblus

Similar to the *liwā'* of Ṣafad, this one was highly populated[235] in comparison to other *liwa*'s in Syria, yet Christians are scarcely discernible in the six places shown in Table 2-28.

TABLE 2-27

	T.D. 427 (*ca. 932/1523*)				*T.D. 1038* (*ca. 940/1533*)				*T.D. 72* (*955/1548*)				*T.D. 300* (*963/1555*)				*T.D. 686* (*1005/1596*)			
	h.	*b.*	*r.*	*d.*	*h.*	*b.*	*r.*	*d.*	*h.*	*b.*	*r.*	*d.*	*h.*	*b.*	*r.*	*d.*	*h.*	*b.*	*r.*	*d.*
1. Rayna[225]																				
M.	32	–	–	–					28	6	1	–	25	10	–	–				
C.	8	–	–	–					6	–	–	–	10	–	–	–				
2. Yarūn al-Naṣārā[226]																				
M.					35	20	1	–	35	20	–	2	50	10	–	1	34	15	–	–
C.					21	9	–	–	38	11	–	–	46	10	–	–	33	20	–	–
3. Baᶜna[227]																				
M.									44	1	–	–	41	7	–	–	18	4	–	–
C.									15	–	–	–	15	–	–	–	5	–	–	–
4. Nazareth[228]																				
M.	43	–	–	–	95	1	–	–	254	29	–	–	200	11	3	4				
C.	–	–	–	–	8	–	–	–	17	3	–	–	17	–	–	–				
J.	6	–	–	–																
5. Iklīl (?)[229]																				
M.	6	–	–	–	6	–	–	–					14	6	–	–				
C.													3	–	–	–				
6. Kafr Bukāt[230](?)																				
M.									22	2	–	–								
C.									3	–	–	–								

TABLE 2-28

	T.D. 1038				*T.D. 258*				*T.D. 546*				*T.D. 100*			
	(ca. 940/1533)				*(955/1548)*				*(no date)*				*(1005/1596)*			
	h.	*b.*	*r.*	*d.*	*h.*	*b.*	*r.*	*d.*	*h.*	*b.*	*r.*	*d.*	*h.*	*b.*	*r.*	*d.*
1. Nāblus[236]																
M.	984	43	17	5	717	109	13	6					796	10	–	–
S.	29	4	–	–	34	–	–	–					20	–	–	–
J.	71	–	–	–	37	4	–	–					15	–	–	–
C.	7	–	–	–	16	–	–	–	17	1	–	–	18	–	–	–
2. Kafr Ḥāmid[237]																
M.	57	2	1	–												
C.	7	–	–	–												
3. ʿAskar[238]																
M.	25	–	–	–												
C.	15	–	–	–					7	–	–	–				
4. Marjayn[239]																
M.					7	5	–	–					30	–	–	–
C.					11	1	–	–	17	–	–	–	36	–	–	–
5. Zayta[240]																
M.									83	8	–	–	82	9	–	–
C.									7	–	–	–	7	–	–	–
6. Rafīdiyya[241]																
M.													9	6	–	–
C.													85	–	–	–

The poll tax collected at this *liwā'* constituted part of the revenues of Khalīl al-Raḥmān.[242] Christians and Jews coming from abroad (Europe) and passing through Nāblus for the purpose of visiting Jerusalem and other holy places paid a toll tax *(bāj)* amounting to 20,000 *akche*s in ca. 940/1533, and to 23,000 *akche*s in 1005/1596.[243] In 1601 John Sanderson, escorted by a Jewish guide, passed through Nāblus. They went to visit the grave of Joshua at the village of Tibneh which was "kept by the Moores as the others are. . . . This we did very well discerne. The Jewes at all pay pole pence, some more some lesse to the Moores, before they be permitted to say thier ceremonies."[244]

Liwā' of Jerusalem

The total population of the *liwā'* of Jerusalem in 955/1548–1549 (for details for other years see Table 2-29) was 7,365 households, 516 bachelors, and 1,254 tax-exempt individuals.[263] The number of Christians, according to T.D. 298 (ca. 974/1566) was 1,003 households, fifty-eight bachelors, and three disabled persons. It is worthy of note that in the city of Jerusalem, persons belonging to the various Christian confessional groups resided either in their own narrow alleys or in their own monasteries.[264] John Sanderson, visiting the city in 1601, gives the following antagonistic account:

> Many idolatrus Christians have thier alters, every sort apart; to say, an altar for the Romanists; for the Greks; for the Cufties [Copts] of Cairo; Georgians about the Black Sea; Armenians of Persia; Abbasies [Abyssinians] of Ethiopia; Nestorians of Baghdatt; Jacobites of Alepo, Merdi [Mardin] and Babilon; Maronit[es] of Mount Libanus, Shemsi in Sirria [Syria] and Celisia (a kind of familie of love). In the Sepulchre, thes sorts of Christians have their lamps continually burninge to the nomber (as say the Greke friers) of 66 and alike have their superstitious Crosses apart.[265]

George Sandys, visiting Jerusalem one decade later, describes the followers of the various churches in the city and gives a brief sketch of their history. He mentions the Latins, Greeks, Armenians, Copts, Abyssinians, Georgians, Maronites, and Nestorians. He notices their various religious celebrations in Jerusalem on Easter. Talking about the Abyssinians he states:

> To conclude they joyn with the Copties for the most part in substance of religion and ceremony, one Priest here serving both: an Ethiopian poore and accompanyed with few of his nation, who fanatically clad, doth dance in their processions with a skipping motion, and distortion of his body not unlike to our Antiques. To which musick is answerable; the instruments no other than snappers, gingles and round bottom'd drums, born upon the back of one, and beaten upon by the followers.[266]

Christian pilgrims from Georgia and Abyssinia, as well as from Europe, came to visit the holy places in Palestine. At times, pilgrims from Abyssinia arrived in particularly large numbers. For example, in 922/1516, about eight hundred people escorted by a special guide *(khāṣṣakī)* arrived in Jerusalem. Muslims were infuriated when these pilgrims displayed the cross in the streets; fighting broke out, and there were casualties on both sides.[267] Such incidents as this one, which occurred just prior to the fall of the Mamluks, are not reported during the later sixteenth century in Palestine.

Fees described as *maḥṣūl-i resmi Dār al-Qumāma* were collected from pilgrims at the rate of eight *asper*s from Christians and six from Jews.[268] Abū ᶜAbd Allāh Muḥammad b. ᶜAbd Allāh b. Ibrāhīm b. Baṭūṭah (d. 779/1377), visiting Jerusalem in 726/1325, states that each Christian pilgrim visiting the Church of the Holy Sepulcher had to pay a fixed tax.[269] The recorded amount accruing in ca. 934/1527 was 40,000 *akche*s,[270] rising to 120,000 *akche*s in 970/1562,[271] which indicates an increasing traffic of pilgrims through the city. Complying with the wishes of Sultan Sulayman the Magnificent, this money was spent on the reciters of the Holy Quran in the sanctuary of the Dome of the Rock.[272] Extra fees were extorted under various titles, such as the *ḥaqq-i ṭarīq* (toll tax), *ghafāra* (protection money), or *muhr akchesi* (seal money). In 959/1552, the sultan ordered: "The pilgrims must not be forced to pay more taxes than was customary in the past and as is laid down in the Cadastral Registers. The protection-fee is to be abolished altogether."[273] The accounts of John Sanderson[274] and George Sandys,[275] however, reveal that pilgrims continued to be the target of excessive extortions on the part of the officials and Arab Bedouin *Shaykh*s.

Our *Tapu Defters* show that some Christians in Jerusalem were identified according to their places of birth or origin, e.g., Bethlehem, Bayt Jālā, etc., indicating Christian migration from these places to Jerusalem. All indigenous Christians in the *liwā'* of Jerusalem paid the poll tax which was collected at the rate of eighty *akches* per *nafar,* rising later to ninety *akches*. In some villages, however, the rate varied between sixty to seventy *akches*. The poll tax accruing from Bethlehem and Bayt Jālā constituted part of the revenues of *al-ᶜAmāra al-ᶜĀmira* (the Sultan's Charitable Foundation), founded in 1552 by Roxelana, wife of Sultan Sulayman the Magnificent.[276] The poll tax collected from the Christians of Bayt Rīma and ᶜAyn ᶜArīk was earmarked as part of the income of the Dome of the Rock[277] while the poll tax of Christians from Majdalat Fuḍayl and Rāmallāh was reserved for the Khalīl al-Raḥmān Mosque. The remaining collected *jizya* constituted part of the incomes of timar holders, according to the specific stipulations of the *Tapu Defters*.[278]

The historian Mujīr al-Dīn al-ᶜUlaymī al-Ḥanbalī (d. 927/1520), a native of Jerusalem, records that there were about twenty churches and monasteries in Jerusalem. The Church of the Holy Sepulcher, the Ṣahyūn (Zion) Church belonging to the Franks, the Mar Yaᶜqūb Church belonging to the Armenians, and the Cross Church (Muṣallabiyya) belonging to the Georgians were the most important four according to al-ᶜUlaymī.[279] During the second half of the fifteenth century, Christian churches in Jerusalem were the targets of attacks by Muslims. In 856/1452, new additions to the Church of the Holy Sepulcher, Zion Church, and the Church of Bethlehem were destroyed. The wooden banisters of the Holy Sepulcher Church were removed and taken to be fixed in the Aqṣā Mosque. In addition, the supervision of David's Tomb was removed from Christian hands and entrusted to Muslims.[280] Christians, generally, were the subject of harassment. Similarly, when in 863/1458, Christians succeeded in bribing the Mamluk governor of Jerusalem and the Ḥanafī judge so they could restore a church dome destroyed by an earthquake, the Ḥanbalī judge was able to obtain the support of the sultan and demolished not only the restored section, but part of the old building as well.[281] The same Ḥanbalī judge of Jerusalem issued a *fatwā* (responsum) according to which orphan Christian infants were to be counted as Muslims.[282] Such attitudes help to explain why Christians frequently sought the protection of influential people among the senior Mamluk officials. It was in such a climate that in 880/1475 a Christian was beheaded for reviling ᶜAlī b. Abī Ṭālib and his wife Fāṭima, the Prophet's daughter.[283] The tense relationship existing between Christians and Muslims reached its highest point during the years 894–896/1488–1490, in the dispute over a restored church near the Church of Zion. ᶜUlaymī claims that monks at Zion, in 894/1488, constructed a church near their monastery. Christians were also able to get a *marsūm sharīf* (an exalted order) from the chief Mamluk *amīr* Özbek allowing Christians to take back the Tomb of David. But the *ᶜulamā'* and the judge refused to comply with that order. Their consensus was that David's Tomb had long had a *miḥrāb* (a prayer niche) and consequently must be counted as a Muslim shrine. Under these circumstances the sultan sent a *khāṣṣakī* (special envoy) to investigate the matter.

After long consultation with the *ᶜulamāʾ* and investigation of the site of the church, it was agreed that the Christians had built a new church, and that David's Tomb should remain in Muslim custody. On Sunday 3 Rajab 895/12 February 1490, the church was demolished by a great multitude of Muslims. Finally, in 896/1587, the sultan gave his orders to destroy the remaining parts of the church, which accordingly were razed.[284]

Moving into the Ottoman period, we note that in 956/1549, Sultan Sulayman ordered that the Frankish monks be evacuated from Zion Monastery and moved inside the city.[285] The monastery, with its gardens and the surrounding area, was given to the grand *Sufi Shaykh* Shihāb Aḥmad b. ᶜAlī b. Yāsīn al-Dajānī[286] (d. 969/1561) and his disciples; the cemetery in the proximity of the monastery was left in the hands of the monks.[287]

Muslims and Christians in the second half of the sixteenth century had a dispute regarding a church built on the site of a derelict mosque in the neighborhood of the Cross Church. Complaints were sent to the sultan, to whom the judge of Jerusalem had reported that he had investigated the place and had found no trace of a derelict mosque on that site.[288] The sultan, perhaps not satisfied with the findings of the judge of Jerusalem, commanded the chief judge of Damascus, Jayzade, and the chief *Muftī* in Damascus, Fawzi Efendī to travel to Jerusalem and investigate the case. They left Damascus on Monday 18 Shaᶜbān 978/5 January 1571, and on Ramaḍān, 23 January, accompanied by the *ᶜulamāʾ* and a multitude of people, examined the newly built church.[289] They found traces of an old mosque on the site so the new church was immediately demolished. The mosque was later rebuilt and ᶜaṣr prayers were held there.[290]

With the approval of the judge, Christians could repair their churches. In 1613 the monks of Mar Sābā were allowed to repair their monastery, provided that they should not expand it.[291] Muslims and Christians were not allowed to interfere with the Armenians, as was demonstrated by the case of the repair of al-Ṭūr Monastery to the east of Jerusalem.[292] Christians were also permitted to make donations and establish endowments to their churches. In 982/1574 the Armenian metropolitan Andiryās b. Ibrāhīm endowed his nephews and their descendants with a small garden in the neighborhood of the Armenian Monastery. The place was planted with vine trees, figs, olives, and pomegranates and had five wells. In case their line would come to an end the endowment would go to the Armenian community, and in case the latter should vanish, it would go to Khalīl al-Raḥmān.[293]

Available literature shows that conflicts existed among the various churches and groups in Jerusalem. When, in 985/1577, the Georgians complained to the sultan that the Franks and the Armenians had taken over a holy site entrusted to them, the sultan commanded officials there to investigate the case and give each community custody of exactly the same areas it previously controlled.[294] In 1561 the Copts seized the Maronite Church after a fatal accident there. The Maronites preferred not to dispute the matter with the Copts, and the conflict was resolved when the Latins volunteered to allow the Maronites to share their church.[295]

Liwā' of Gaza

Contrary to what one might expect, a sizable Christian population used to live in the *liwā* of Gaza, which as a whole had (ca. 940/1533) 7,826 households and 707 bachelors, in addition to 256 persons in various religious capacities.[296] For the city of Gaza, four surveys[297] supply the data shown in Table 2-30.

We notice that all groups underwent an increase in population followed by a decrease. The number of Christians in Gaza runs rather high. It is observable from the table of names that Christians from Shawbak and Wādī Mūsā in Transjordan, Copts from Egypt, and Christians from Hebron and Jerusalem migrated to Gaza. This probably indicates a high degree of stability prevailing in the city. The Ottoman Shāhin[298] family, which was entrusted with the government of Gaza in the sixteenth and first half of the seventeenth centuries, provided a great deal more security than prevailed elsewhere in Palestine; this in turn enhanced the commercial prosperity of the city which was a meeting point on the highway to Egypt, Hijaz, and Syria. Glancing through the tables of Christians, one notices a high number of names common among the Bedouins, e.g., Ghunaym, Makhlūf, and Tuᶜma and others which were religiously oriented, such as 'Ilyās, Jirjīs, ᶜĪsā, and Mūsār.

Five villages in the *liwā'* of Gaza had Christian populations (see Table 2-31).

All these villages had a high Christian population. The poll tax accruing from Ramla and Lydda was assigned as an endowment to the Holy Dome of the Rock.[304]

George Sandys, traveling via Gaza to Jerusalem, relates that he and his companions were guided by a certain Attala "a Greek of Rama and Drugardman to the Pater-guardian: paying seven sultanis a piece for his mules, his labour and discharge of Caphar [ghafar]." They paid two dollars each to the *shaykh* of the Arabs near Gaza, "but the Zanziack [Sanjak, i.e., the sanjak governor] of Gaza had sent unto him that should be remitted," while "The subassée [Subashi] of Rāma besides had two Madines upon every camell."[305]

Among the numerous endowments *(awqāf)* recorded for this period, there are a few indications that Christians could establish such endowments, but to legalize them, they had to be registered with the office of the chief judge. One concerns a certain Mikhāᶜīl b. Mikā'īl and Ibrāhīm b. Mannā, both Christians from Ramla, who in 955/1548 endowed their offspring with a piece of land.[306] It also seems that in the early sixteenth century, Christians owned a limited amount of land. A case in 912/1506 reports that three Christian brothers owned a tract in Ramla.[307]

In concluding we should note several general points of considerable importance for the study of the *millet* communities under Ottoman rule. First, the *Tapu Defters* indicate that, at least in the sixteenth century, the Christian population of the province of Damascus was significantly smaller than the literary sources have led scholars to believe.[308] And secondly, the *sharīᶜa* court registers seem to indicate that, with the exception of the sensitive city of Jerusalem, the Christian population did not suffer from any official policy or program of what could properly be termed persecution. Discrimination, implicit

TABLE 2-29

	T.D. 427				*T.D. 1015*				*T.D. 516*				*T.D. 298*				*T.D. 178*			
	(ca. 932/1525)				*(ca. 940/1533)*				*(970/1562)*				*(ca. 974/1566)*				*(1005/1596)*			
	h.	*b.*	*r.*	*d.*	*h.*	*b.*	*r.*	*d.*	*h.*	*b.*	*r.*	*d.*	*h.*	*b.*	*r.*	*d.*	*h.*	*b.*	*r.*	*d.*
1. Quds[245]																				
M.	635	2	1	–	937	55	20	–	1627	91	109	4	1985	143	12	2	1271	73	–	–
C.	129	–	–	–	164	26	–	1	387	–	–	–	388	25	–	3				
a. Melkites	96	–	–	–	85	20	–	1	198	–	–	–	184	17	–	3	42	–	–	–
b. Jacobites (Armenians)	15	–	–	–	–	–	–	–	34	–	–	–	54	–	–	–	missing			
c. Assyrians	8	–	–	–	13	–	–	–	24	–	–	–	22	4	–	–	missing			
d. Monks in various monasteries					–	40	–	–	–	70	–	–	–	85			missing			
e. Copts					26	6	–	–	61	–	–	–	43	4	–	–	missing			
J.	199	–	–	–	224	19	–	–	270	–	–	–	321	13	–	1	missing			
2. Bethlehem[246]																				
M.	39	–	–	–	46	–	1	–	106	1	–	–	152	10	–	–	missing			
C.	61	–	–	–	82	2	–	–	144	5	–	–	152	12	–	–	287	–	–	–
3. Bayt Jālā[247]																				
M.	–	–	–	–	–	–	–	–	2	–	–	–	–	–	–	–	–	–	–	–
C.	129	–	–	–	151	6	–	–	171	47	–	–	292	21	–	1	239	–	–	–
4. Bayt Sāḥūr[248]																				
M.	–	–	–	–	–	–	–	–	17	–	–	–	21	–	–	–	15	–	–	–
C.	7	–	–	–	–	–	–	–	9	–	–	–	13	–	–	–	8	–	–	–
5. Faqou^ca[249]																				
M.	25	2	–	–					91	14	–	–	115	–	–	–	66	–	–	–
C.	55	–	–	–					5	–	–	–	14	–	–	–	5	–	–	–

6. Ṭayyibat al-Isim[250]																				
M.	–	–	–	–	–	–	–	–												
C.	98	–	–	–	100	–	–	–												
7. Bayt Rīma[251]																				
M.	–	–	–	–	30	1	1	–	56	–	–	–	63	–	–	–	54	–	–	–
C.	–	–	–	–	6	–	–	–	13	1	–	–	11	–	–	–	14	–	–	–
8. Hebron[252]																				
M.					914	127	30	–												
C.					7	–	–	–												
J.					20	1	–	–												
9. Yabrūd[253]																				
M.									23	–	–	–					24	–	–	–
C.									3	–	–	–					4	–	–	–
10. Naḥālīn[254]																				
M.									24	–	–	–	27	–	–	–	40	–	–	–
C.									7	–	–	–	7	–	–	–	16	–	–	–
11. Darabān[255]																				
M.									23	–	–	–	32	–	–	–	23	–	–	–
C.									23	–	–	–	22	–	–	–	23	–	–	–
12. Rāmallāh[256]																				
M.									10	–	–	–					9	–	–	–
C.									63	8	–	–					71	–	–	–
13. ᶜAyn ᶜArīk[257]																				
M.									11	3	–	–					14	–	–	–
C.									10	–	–	–					10	–	–	–
14. Ḥattūba(?)[258]																				
M.									19	2	–	–	21	–	–	–	15	–	–	–
C.									6	–	–	–	6	–	–	–	7	–	–	–

TABLE 2-29 (cont.)

	T.D. 427 (*ca.* 932/1525)				*T.D. 1015* (*ca.* 940/1533)				*T.D. 516* (970/1562)				*T.D. 298* (*ca.* 974/1566)				*T.D. 178* (1005/1596)			
	h.	*b.*	*r.*	*d.*	*h.*	*b.*	*r.*	*d.*	*h.*	*b.*	*r.*	*d.*	*h.*	*b.*	*r.*	*d.*	*h.*	*b.*	*r.*	*d.*
15. Jafnat al-Naṣārā[259]																				
M.									–	–	–	–					–	–	–	–
C.									31	–	–	–					31	–	–	–
16. Arṭās[260]																				
M.													61	4	–	–				
C.													7	–	–	–				
17. Majdal Fuḍayl[261]																				
M.													–	–	–	–				
C.													91	–	–	–				
18. Jayb[262]																				
M.																	–	–	–	–
C.																	103	–	–	–

TABLE 2-30

	T.D. 427				*T.D. 1015*				*T.D. 304*				*T.D. 192*			
	(ca. 932/1525)				*(ca. 940/1533)*				*(963/1555)*				*(1005/1596)*			
	h.	*b.*	*r.*	*d.*	*h.*	*b.*	*r.*	*d.*	*h.*	*b.*	*r.*	*d.*	*h.*	*b.*	*r.*	*d.*
1. Gaza																
M.	528	14	25	–	1428	114	37	1	1655	–	59	20	697	113	34	19
J.	95	–	–	–	98	–	–	–	78	–	–	–	70	–	–	–
S.	25	–	–	–	15	–	–	–	18	–	–	–	8	–	–	–
C.	233	–	–	–	271	–	–	–	331	–	–	2	272	–	–	7
C. in detail																
a. Maḥallat Naṣārā	82	–	–	–	115	–	–	–	98	–	–	–	94	–	–	1
b. Jamāᶜat Rizq Allāh	35	–	–	–	35	–	–	–	38	–	–	–	35	–	–	–
c. Jamāᶜat Wādī Mūṣā	–	–	–	–	–	–	–	–	26	–	–	–	–	–	–	–
d. Jamāᶜat Shawbak	28	–	–	–	26	–	–	–	43	–	–	2	31	–	–	–
e. Jamāᶜat Jabāriyyah	25	–	–	–	27	–	–	–	51	–	–	–	38	–	–	6
f. Jamāᶜat Taqāᶜina from Jerusalem	–	–	–	–	6	–	–	–	–	–	–	–	9	–	–	–
g. Jamāᶜat Wādah	16	–	–	–	19	–	–	–								
h. Jamāᶜat Khalīl	23	–	–	–												
i. Naṣārā Ṣakhrah	19	–	–	–	36	–	–	–	75	–	–	–	65	–	–	–
j. Copts	5	–	–	–	7	–	–	–								

in any legal system embodying the principle of inequality among various groups, did indeed occur, but the court records point to the conclusion that this did not prevent Christians from playing an active role in society or compel their total isolation from the Muslim population. Their treatment seems to have depended more on local considerations (e.g., political) than on any imperial canon; and in any case, their numbers would not seem to have been large enough to cause them to be regarded as a significant threat. Here again, Jerusalem stands out as an exceptional case.

As alluded to above, much of the material available in the official Ottoman documents contradicts the testimony of the literary sources. The issue cannot be settled conclusively here, but it points to the pressing need for further research and study in the Ottoman archival materials, and in the field of Ottoman

TABLE 2-31

	T.D. 427				*T.D. 1015*				*T.D. 304*				*T.D. 192*			
	(ca. 932/1525)				*(ca. 940/1533)*				*(963/1555)*				*(1005/1596)*			
	h.	*b.*	*r.*	*d.*	*h.*	*b.*	*r.*	*d.*	*h.*	*b.*	*r.*	*d.*	*h.*	*b.*	*r.*	*d.*
1. Dayr al-Dārūm[299]																
M.	82	1	2	–	180	14	2	–	180	–	–	–	175	–	–	–
C.	56	–	–	–	55	8	–	–	114	11	–	–	125	–	–	–
2. Sawāfīr al-Khalīl[300]																
M.					76	–	–	–	91	–	–	–	71	–	–	–
C.					34	–	–	–	41	–	–	–	41	–	–	–
3. Ramla[301]																
M.	311	15	5	–	289	13	26	–	478	54	24	7	216	23	7	1
C.	26	–	–	–	33	–	–	–	75	–	–	–	40	–	–	–
4. Lydda[302]																
M.	197	33	–	–	256	11	4	–	245	30	–	–	237	14	1	3
C.	129	11	–	–	150	–	–	–	245	–	–	–	233	–	–	–
5. ᶜAbbūd(?)[303]																
M.									16	–	–	–	16	–	–	–
C.									19	–	–	–	19	–	–	–

historiography as a whole. So far as the Christians of Syria are concerned, the picture will become clearer once we have more precise information on the other two Syrian provinces, Aleppo and Tripoli. For other religious communities, including the various Islamic sects, the Ottoman archives are potentially as informative as they prove to have been for the Christians.

Abbreviations

b.	Bachelor
C.	Christian
d.	Disabled
h.	Household
J.	Jew
M.	Muslim
M.D.	*Muhimme Defteri,* Başbakanlık Arşivi, Istanbul
r.	Religious functionary
S.	Samaritan
Sh.	*Sherif*
T.D.	*Tapu Defter*

Notes

1. For further details on this rebellion, see Shams al-Dīn Muḥammad b. Ṭūlūn (d. 953/1546), *Mufākahat al-khillān fī ḥawādith al-zamān,* ed. Muḥammad Muṣṭafā, Cairo, 1962–1964, vol. 2, pp. 122–124, ibid., *Iᶜlām al-Warā biman wulliya min al-atrāk bi-Dimashq al-Shām al-kubrā,* ed. Muḥammad Aḥmad Duhmān, Damascus, 1964, pp. 231–237; Najm al-Dīn al-Ghazzī (d. 1061/1650), *Al-kawākib al-sā'irah fī aᶜyān al-mi'a al-ᶜāshira,* ed. J. Jabbur, Beirut, 1945–1959, vol. 1, pp. 168–71; and M. A. Bakhit, "The Ottoman Province of Damascus in the Sixteenth Century," Ph.D. dissertation, University of London, School of Oriental and African Studies, 1972, pp. 34–42.

2. For the administrative divisions of Syria during the sixteenth century, see Bakhit (cited n. 1), pp. 44–94.

3. Ibn Ṭūlūn (cited n. 1), vol. 2, p. 31.

4. For further information on the *Tapu Defter*s see Midhat Sertoglu, *Muhteva bakımından Başvekalet Arşivi,* Ankara, 1955; Bernard Lewis, "The Ottoman Archives as a Source for the History of the Arab Lands," *JRAS,* 1951, pp. 139–55; ibid., *Notes and Documents from the Turkish Archives,* Jerusalem, 1952; *ibid.*, "Studies in the Ottoman Archives," *BSOAS,* 16 (1954), pp. 469–501; *ibid.*, "Daftar" *E.I.*², vol. 2, pp. 77–81; and Ö. L. Barkan, "Daftar-i Khaḳāni," *E.I.*², vol. 2, pp. 81–83.

5. The following *Tapu Defters* (T.D. 127, 131, 132, 169, 192, 219, 258, 263, 275, 289, 295, 296, 300, 304, 312, 313, 342, 346, 383, 393, 401, 423, 427, 430, 491, 522, 543, 559, 602, 621, 656, 686, 710, 950, 962, 964, 970, 1015, 1025, 1034, 1038, and 1039) are preserved at the Prime Minister's Archives, Istanbul, and they were consulted for this study. For this collection, see Bernard Lewis, "Başvekalet Arşivi," *E.I.*², vol. 1, pp. 1089–1091 and further references mentioned therein.

6. The following *defters* (T.D. 72, 99, 100, 112, 177, 178, 181, 185, 192, 195, 283, 312, 319, 320, 539, 546, and 581) are to be found in the Tapu ve kadastro Arşivi in Ankara. For seven *defters* from this department pertaining to the province of Damascus in 1005/1596, see Wolf-Dieter Hütteroth and Kamal Abdulfattah, *Historical Geography of Palestine, Transjordan and Southern Syria in the Late Sixteenth Century,* Erlangen, 1977, pp. 1–16.

7. For these divisions, see U. Heyd's introduction to *Ottoman Documents on Palestine, 1552–1615,* Oxford, 1960, pp. 40–41; and Bakhit, (cited, n. 1), p. 96.

8. See Ö. L. Barkan, *XV ve XVIıncı asırlarda Osmanlı imparatorluğunda zirai ekonominin hukuki ve mali esasları, Kanunlar,* Istanbul, 1943, pp. 226–227; and Hütterroth and Abdulfattah (cited n. 6), pp. 37–38.

9. For these special groups, see Hütteroth and Abdulfattah (cited n. 6), pp. 38–42; see also Claude Cahen, "Dhimma," *E.I.*², vol. 2, pp. 227–230; and G. Vajda, "Ahl al-Kitāb," *E.I.*², vol. 1, pp. 264–266.

10. For a general outline of the history of the *jizya* tax, see Claude Cahen, "Djizya," *E.I.*², vol. 2, pp. 559–562; Halil Inalcik, "Djizya—Ottoman," *E.I.*², vol. 2, pp. 562–566; "Djawālī," *E.I.*², vol. 2, p. 490; and Ḥabīb al-Zayyāt, "Al-jawālī," *Machriq,* 41 (1941), pp. 1–12.

11. T.D. 430, p. 144; T.D. 401, p. 19; T.D. 263, pp. 362–364; T.D. 491, pp. 444–447.

12. T.D. 430, p. 147; T.D. 401, p. 20; T.D. 263, p. 365; T.D. 491, pp. 465–466.

13. T.D. 430, p. 158; T.D. 401, p. 16; T.D. 263, p. 4; T.D. 491, p. 461.

14. See T.D. 263, p. 7; T.D. 474, p. 21; Barkan (cited n. 8), p. 262.

15. The *sultani,* minted of gold, appears to have been a continuation of the old Mamluk currency. It generally equaled the value of eight silver *shāhi*s. See Damascus Court *Sijill,* vol. 1, case no. 136, 992/1584, pp. 157–158. For the value of the various currencies in the sixteenth century Ottoman Empire, see H. A. R. Gibb and Harold Bowen, *Islamic Society and the West,* London, 1950–57, vol. 1, part 2, pp. 49–59. See also U. Heyd, *Studies in Old Ottoman Criminal Law,* ed. V. L. Menage, Oxford, 1973, pp. 46–53.

16. Ḥama Court *Sijill,* case no. 63, year 989/1581, p. 13. For the records of Ḥama, see J. E. Mandaville, "The Ottoman Court Records of Syria and Jordan," *JAOS,* 86 (1966), PP. 311–319; and Abd al-Wadūd Muḥammad Yūsūf, "Liwā' Ḥamā fī al-qarn al-sādis ^{c}ashar," M.A. thesis, ^{c}Ayn Shams University, Cairo, 1970.

17. See T.D. 430, pp. 7–20; T.D. 401, pp. 144–163; T.D. 263, pp. 358–396; T.D. 543, pp. 6–31, pp. 494–510; T.D. 177, pp. 3–13, 221–229.

18. T.D. 430, pp. 17–18; T.D. 401, p. 160; T.D. 263, pp. 358–361; T.D. 543, p. 6; T.D. 177, pp. 3–4.

19. T.D. 430, pp. 7–8; T.D. 401, pp. 154–155; T.D. 263, pp. 375–387; T.D. 543, pp. 11–18; T.D. 177, pp. 6–10.

20. T.D. 401, p. 149–150; T.D. 263, pp. 388–392; T.D. 543, pp. 25–27; T.D. 177, pp. 10–11.

21. T.D. 401, pp. 151–152; T.D. 263; T.D. 543, pp. 494–499; T.D. 177, pp. 221–222.

22. T.D. 401, p. 163; T.D. 543, pp. 500–501; T.D. 177, pp. 223–224.

23. T.D. 430, p. 20; T.D. 401, p. 161; T.D. 263, p. 388; T.D. 543, pp. 506–507; T.D. 177, pp. 226–227.

24. T.D. 401, p. 160; T.D. 263, p. 388; T.D. 543, pp. 509–510; T.D. 177, p. 228.

25. See Bakhit (cited n. 1), pp. 44–94.

26. Muḥyī al-Dīn b. ^{c}Abd al-Ẓāhir (d. 692/1292), *Al-rawḍ al-ẓāhir fī sīrat al-malik al-ẓāhir,* ed. and trans. Fatima Sadeque, Dacca, 1956, p. 100 of the Arabic text, p. 212 of the English translation. See also Nāsir al-Dīn Muḥammad b. ^{c}Abd al-Raḥmān b. al-Furāt, *Tārīkh al-duwal wa-al-mulūk,* ed. and trans. U. and M. C. Lyons, Cambridge, 1971, vol. 1, pp. 126, 187, of the Arabic text, pp. 99–100 of the English text; also Aḥmad b. ^{c}Alī al-Maqrīzī (d. 854/1450), *Al-sulūk li-ma^{c}rifat duwal al-mulūk,* ed. Muḥammad Ziadeh, Cairo, 1936, vol. 1, part 2, p. 511, 522–523. Both Ziadeh and Sadaque read Ḥiṣn ^{c}Akkār as Ḥiṣh ^{c}Akka, which is obviously incorrect.

27. See P. Cyrille Charon, "Silsilat asāqifat al-Rūm al-malkāniyyīh fī Qārā wa-Yabrūd wa-Tadmur wa-Zaḥla wa-al-Zabadānī," *Machriq,* 13 (1910), pp. 328–338.

28. Shihāb al-Dīn Aḥmad b. Faḍl Allāl al-^{c}Umarī (d. 742/1341), *Al-ta^{c}rīf bi-al-musṭalaḥ al-sharīf* (Cairo, 1312/1894), p. 177; and Aḥmad b. ^{c}Alī al-Qalqashandī (d. 821/1418), *Ṣubḥ al-a^{c}shā fī ṣinā^{c}at al-inshā',* Cairo, 1913–1919, vol. 4, p. 97.

29. T.D. 401, pp. 115–138; T.D. 263, pp. 308–312; T.D. 474, pp. 265–276, 584–632.

30. T.D. 401, p. 115; T.D. 263, pp. 308–310; T.D. 474, pp. 617–621.

31. T.D. 401, p. 119; T.D. 474, pp. 602–607.

32. T.D. 401, p. 120; T.D. 474, pp. 592–595.

33. T.D. 401, p. 138; T.D. 474, pp. 610–611.

34. T.D. 401, p. 116; T.D. 474, pp. 624–625.

35. Michael Breik al-Dimashqī, *Tārīkh al-Shām, 1720–1782,* ed. Qustanṭīn al-Bāshā, Harīṣā, 1930, pp. 33–34.

36. Ibid., p. 28.

37. Shaykh Ḥasan b. Muḥammad al-Būrīnī (d. 1024/1615), *Tarājim al-a^{c}yān min abnā' al-zamān,* Vienna Cod. Arab. 1190 Mixt. 346, fols. 155b–156a (this section is as yet unpublished).

38. For his biography, see Muḥammad Khalīl b. ^{c}Alī al-Murādī (d. 1206/1791), *Silk al-durar fī a^{c}yān al-qarn al-thānī ^{c}ashar,* Baghdad, n.d., vol. 3, pp. 219–228.

39. Breik (cited n. 35), pp. 69, 74.

40. Ibid., pp. 92–93.

41. al-^{c}Umarī (cited n. 28), p. 117; Qalqashandī, (cited n. 28), vol. 4, p. 97.

42. T.D. 430, pp. 451–465; T.D. 401, pp. 304–325; T.D. 263, pp. 324–346; T.D. 474, pp. 287–295.

43. T.D. 430, p. 451; T.D. 401, p. 304; T.D. 263, pp. 337–339; T.D. 474, pp. 656–657.

44. T.D. 430, p. 452; T.D. 401, pp. 305–306; T.D. 263, pp. 329–334; T.D. 474, pp. 653–655.

45. T.D. 430, p. 458; T.D. 401, p. 306; T.D. 263, pp. 343–344; T.D. 474, p. 293.

46. T.D. 430, p. 462; T.D. 401, p. 312; T.D. 263, p. 329.

47. T.D. 430, p. 463; T.D. 401, p. 310; T.D. 263, pp. 327–328; T.D. 474, p. 644.

48. T.D. 430, p. 455; T.D. 401, p. 315; T.D. 474, p. 644.

49. T.D. 430, p. 463; T.D. 401, p. 309; T.D. 263, pp. 326–327; T.D. 474, p. 644.

50. For these records see ᶜAbdul-Karīm Rāfeq, "The Law-Court Registers of Damascus with Special Reference to Craft-Corporations during the First Half of the Eighteenth Century," in *Les Arabes par leurs archives (XVIᵉ-XX siècles),* ed. Jacques Berque and Dominique Chevallier, Paris, 1976, pp. 141–159.

51. Court-*Sijill* for the year 992/1584, case number 227, p. 205.

52. Ibid., case number 200, pp. 190–191.

53. T.D. 401, pp. 2–51; T.D. 263, pp. 11–174; T.D. 474, pp. 28–201.

54. Ibn Ṭūlūn (cited n. 1), vol. 1, p. 173.

55. T.D. 474, pp. 188–189.

56. T.D. 474, p. 191; for a general assessment of the Armenians in Ottoman Syria, see Avedis K. Sanjian, *The Armenian Communities in Syria under Ottoman Dominion,* Cambridge, 1965.

57. T.D. 474, p. 191.

58. T.D. 263, pp. 156–166.

59. Cf. the manuscript numbered miscellaneous 1571, Library of the Orthodox Patriarchate, Damascus (comprising 373 pages, copied in 1839), pp. 92–93. For an appreciative review of the Christians' role in Syria, see Robert M. Haddad's monograph, *Syrian Christians in Muslim Society, An Interpretation,* Princeton, 1970.

60. Istifan al-Duwayhī, *Tārīkh al-azmina,* ed. Ferdinand Taoutal, Beirut, 1951, pp. 244, 247–248, 264–265, 274.

61. Ibn Ṭūlūn (cited n. 1), vol. 1, pp. 94, 112, 120–121, 169, 215; vol. 2, pp. 16, 20, 32, 111, 120.

62. Barkan (cited n. 8), pp. 221–226.

63. *The Travels of John Sanderson in the Levant 1584–1602,* ed. William Foster, London, 1931, pp. 95–96, 116–117. For the role of John Sanderson in the Levant Company, see A. C. Wood, *A History of the Levant Company,* second edition, London, 1964, pp. 22, 23, 24, 27, 28.

64. Ibn Ṭūlūn (cited n. 1), vol. 2, p. 66.

65. M.D. III, *ḥukum* numbers 1556, 1557, Muḥarram 968/1560, p. 527.

66. Sharaf al-Dīn Mūsā b. Jamāl al-Dīn Ibn Ayyūb al-Anṣārī (d. ca. 1000/1592), *Al-tadhkira al-ayyūbiyya,* Ẓāhiriyya Library Ms. No. 7814, f° 82b.

67. Ibn Ṭūlūn (cited n. 1), vol. 2, p. 121.

68. For the biography of Lālā' Muṣṭafā Pāshā (d. 988/1580), see Ghazzī (cited n. 1), vol. 3, p. 207; see also Muḥammad b. Jamaᶜa al-Maqqār (d. ca. 1156/1743), *Kitāb al-bashāt wa-al quḍāt,* ed. Ṣalāḥ al-Dīn al-Munnajid in a collection of texts entitled *Wūlāt Dimashq fi al-ᶜahd al-ᶜuthmānī,* Damascus, 1949, pp. 15; see also Muḥammad Süreyya, *Sicill-i Osmani,* Istanbul, 1897/8, vol. 4, p. 377, Bekir Kütükoglu, "Muṣṭafā Pāshā," *I.A.*, vol. 8, pp. 732–736.

69. M.D. vii, No. 2035, 2038, 15 Rabiᶜ I 976/27 June 1568, pp. 743–744.

70. Ibn Jumaᶜa al-Maqqār (cited n. 68), p. 55.

71. For this tax, see B. Lewis, "ᶜArūs Resmi," *E.I.*², vol. 1, p. 679.

72. Damascus Court-*Sijill,* 993/1585, p. 200.

73. Damascus Court-*Sijill,* 991/1583, case no. 31, p. 23.

74. Damascus Court-*Sijill,* 992/1584, case no. 264, p. 225.

75. Damascus Court-*Sijill,* 993/1585, pp. 306–307.

76. Ibid., pp. 259–260.

77. Damascus, Court-*Sijill,* 992/1584, case 145, p. 162.

78. Ibid., case 265, pp. 225–226.

79. Damascus Court-*Sijill,* 991/1583, case 5, p. 3.

80. Damascus Court-*Sijill,* 993/1585, case 21, p. 240.

81. Damascus, Court-*Sijill,* 992/1584, case 164, p. 173.

82. Damascus, Court-*Sijill,* 993/1585, p. 273.

83. Ibn Ṭūlūn (cited n. 1), vol. 1, pp. 21, 30, 32, 84, 139, 153–154, 158, 205, 210, 230, 288, 303, 313; Ghazzī (cited n. 1), vol. 1, pp. 245–246. See also the anthology of Muḥammad b. Aḥmad Māmāī al-Rūmī (d. 987/1579), *Rawḍat al-mushtāq wa-bahjat al-ᶜushshāq,* The Arab Academy Library, Damascus, Ms. no. 124, f° 101a, 129a; this text includes a number of poems professing the author's love for a certain Christian boy.

84. T.D. 169, p. 1; T.D. 401, p. 52; T.D. 423, p. 5; T.D. 263, p. 175; T.D. 474, p. 202.

85. M.D. VI, no. 1363, 972/1564, p. 620.

86. Bakhit (cited n. 1), p. 158.

87. T.D. 430, p. 34; T.D. 383, pp. 31–35; T.D. 401, pp. 176–177; T.D. 543, pp. 64–68; T.D. 177, pp. 25–27.

88. T.D. 430, pp. 22–34; T.D. 383, pp. 6–35; T.D. 401, pp. 168–179; T.D. 543, pp. 36–69; T.D. 177, pp. 16–28.

89. Concerning the role of this family as an indigenous power group in the sixteenth century, see Bakhit (cited n. 1), pp. 200–204.

90. Duwayhī (cited n. 60), pp. 318–319.

91. T.D. 430, p. 34; T.D. 383, p. 35; T.D. 401, p. 178; T.D. 423, p. 36; T.D. 543, p. 69; T.D. 177, p. 28.

92. T.D. 430, pp. 34–79; T.D. 383, pp. 39–111; T.D. 401, pp. 177–215; T.D. 543, pp. 112–155, 514–531; T.D. 177, pp. 30–53, 231–238.

93. T.D. 430, p. 59; T.D. 383, pp. 92–95; T.D. 401, p. 179; T.D. 543, pp. 112–115; T.D. 177, pp. 47–48.

94. T.D. 383, pp. 102–105; T.D. 401, p. 186; T.D. 543, pp. 122–123; T.D. 177, p. 53.

95. T.D. 430, p. 44; T.D. 401, p. 202; T.D. 543, pp. 415–418; T.D. 177, pp. 231–233.

96. T.D. 430, pp. 75–76; T.D. 383, pp. 107–111; T.D. 401, p. 186.

97. T.D. 430, pp. 82–119; T.D. 383, pp. 113–177; T.D. 401, pp. 215–245; T.D. 543, pp. 155–171, 534–561; T.D. 177, pp. 239–253.

98. T.D. 430, pp. 86–88; T.D. 383, pp. 125–136; T.D. 401, pp. 219–222; T.D. 543, pp. 539–551; T.D. 177, pp. 242–247.

99. T.D. 430, p. 100; T.D. 383, pp. 173–175; T.D. 401, p. 226; T.D. 543, pp. 155–156.

100. T.D. 430, pp. 97–98; T.D. 383, pp. 175–176; T.D. 401, p. 241; T.D. 543, pp. 171–172.

101. T.D. 430, p. 108; T.D. 383, p. 171; T.D. 401, p. 225; T.D. 543, p. 165.

102. T.D. 430, p. 99; T.D. 383, pp. 172–173; T.D. 401, p. 232.

103. T.D. 430, p. 114; T.D. 383, p. 583; T.D. 401, p. 237; T.D. 543, pp. 560–561; T.D. 177, pp. 250–251.

104. T.D. 430, p. 102; T.D. 383, p. 176; T.D. 401, p. 236.

105. For the history of this family, see Francis Hour and Kamal Salibi, "Muḥammad Ibn al-Hannas Muqaddam de la Biqāᶜ, 1499–1518," *Mélange de l'Université Saint-Joseph,* 42 (1968), pp. 3–23.

106. For this family, see Bakhit (cited n. 1), p. 192.

107. T.D. 430, pp. 160–177; T.D. 383, pp. 234–252, 612–623; T.D. 401, pp. 290–303; T.D. 474, pp. 353–364.

108. T.D. 430, p. 161; T.D. 383, p. 246; T.D. 401, p. 294; T.D. 474, p. 357.

109. T.D. 430, pp. 167–169; T.D. 383, pp. 239–242; T.D. 401, p. 292; T.D. 474, pp. 350–353.

110. T.D. 430, pp. 421–431; T.D. 401, pp. 354–365; T.D. 263, pp. 251–272; T.D. 474, pp. 452–474, 765–772.

111. T.D. 430, pp. 430–431; T.D. 401, p. 358; T.D. 263, pp. 251–254; T.D. 474, p. 461.

112. T.D. 401, p. 354; T.D. 474, p. 766.

113. T.D. 401, p. 254.

114. T.D. 430, pp. 405–420; T.D. 401, pp. 531–549; T.D. 263, pp. 400–417; T.D. 474, pp. 437–452.

115. T.D. 401, p. 535.

116. T.D. 430, pp. 226–244; T.D. 383, pp. 353–388; T.D. 401, pp. 385–401, T.D. 543, pp. 178–236; T.D. 177, pp. 74–89.

117. T.D. 430, p. 227; T.D. 383, p. 367; T.D. 401, p. 386; T.D. 543, p. 192; T.D. 177, p. 80.

118. T.D. 430, p. 227; T.D. 383, p. 355B; T.D. 401, p. 386; T.D. 543, p. 180; T.D. 177, p. 75.

119. T.D. 430, p. 228; T.D. 383, p. 362; T.D. 401, p. 386; T.D. 543, p. 186; T.D. 177, p. 78.

120. T.D. 430, p. 230; T.D. 383, p. 356B–357B; T.D. 401, pp. 387–388; T.D. 543, p. 181–182; T.D. 177, pp. 75–76.

121. T.D. 430, p. 230; T.D. 383, p. 359B; T.D. 401, p. 388; T.D. 543, p. 183; T.D. 177, p. 76.

122. T.D. 430, p. 231; T.D. 383, p. 360B; T.D. 401, p. 388; T.D. 543, pp. 184–185; T.D. 177, p. 77.

123. T.D. 430, p. 233; T.D. 383, p. 379; T.D. 401, pp. 389–390; T.D. 543, p. 190; T.D. 177, pp. 79–80.

124. T.D. 430, p. 234; T.D. 383, p. 365; T.D. 401, p. 390; T.D. 543, p. 192; T.D. 177, p. 79.

125. T.D. 430, p. 234; T.D. 383, pp. 364–365; T.D. 401, p. 390; T.D. 543, p. 180; T.D. 177, p. 79.

126. T.D. 430, p. 235; T.D. 383, pp. 366–367; T.D. 401, p. 391; T.D. 543, pp. 190–191; T.D. 177, p. 80.

127. T.D. 430, p. 236; T.D. 383, p. 386; T.D. 401, p. 392; T.D. 543, pp. 208–209; T.D. 177, p. 88.

128. T.D. 430, p. 237; T.D. 383, p. 386; T.D. 401, p. 391; T.D. 543, p. 210; T.D. 177, pp. 88–89.

129. T.D. 430, p. 244; T.D. 383, p. 361B; T.D. 401, p. 394; T.D. 543, p. 185; T.D. 177, p. 77.

130. T.D. 430, p. 235.

131. T.D. 430, p. 228; T.D. 401, p. 386; T.D. 543, p. 187; T.D. 177, p. 87.

132. T.D. 430, p. 237; T.D. 383, p. 384; T.D. 401, p. 392; T.D. 543, pp. 206–207; T.D. 177, p. 87.

133. Duwayhī (cited n. 60), p. 236, Shaykh Ṭannūs al-Shidyāq (d. 1859), *Akhbar al-aᶜyān fī Jabal Lubnān,* ed. Fouad Afrām al-Bustānī, Beirut, 1970, vol. 1, pp. 76–82; for the ᶜAssāf family, consult Kamal Salibi, "Northern Lebanon Under the Dominance of Gazīr, 1517–1591," *Arabica,* 14 (1967), pp. 144–166.

134. Duwayhī (cited n. 60), pp. 238–239, 244.

135. Ibid., pp. 247–248, 250–251.

136. Ibid., p. 251.

137. Ibid., p. 257.

138. Ibid., pp. 271–272.

139. Ibid., p. 283.

140. Ibid., p. 288.

141. Shidyāq (cited n. 133), vol. 1, pp. 76–82, 100–102; vol. 2, pp. 313–314.

142. On the role of the Khāzin family, see Shaykh Aḥmad b. Muḥammad al-Khālidī al-Ṣafadī (d. ca. 1034/1624), *Tārikh al-Amīr Fakhr al-Dīn,* ed. al-Bustānī, Beirut, 1969, pp. 53, 116–117; Duwayhī (cited n. 60), p. 305; Shidyāq (cited n. 133), vol. 1, pp. 61–75.

143. Duwayhī (cited no. 60), p. 305.

144. Ibid., pp. 307–308.

145. Ibid., p. 311.

146. Ibid., p. 315.

147. Ibid., pp. 327–328.

148. Ibid., p. 329.

149. Ibid., pp. 331–333.

150. Ibid., p. 337.

151. Ibid., pp. 345–346.

152. Ibid., p. 355.

153. Ibid., p. 355, 373, 381.

154. For the role of the family during the Shihābī period, see Iliya F. Harik, *Politics and Change in a Traditional Society, Lebanon, 1711–1845,* Princeton, 1968, pp. 20, 21, 32, 46, 47, 50, 80, 82, 84, 87–93.

155. T.D. 430, pp. 179–205; T.D. 383, pp. 197–222, 635–641; T.D. 401, pp. 277–289; T.D. 474, pp. 329–347.

156. T.D. 430, pp. 181–183; T.D. 383, pp. 199–204; T.D. 401, pp. 272–274; T.D. 474, pp. 323–329.

157. al-Ghazzī (cited n. 1), vol. 1, pp. 51, 62, 63, 276–278, 283; vol. 2, p. 184, 189.

158. The population of Majd al-Naᶜaush was as follows:

T.D. 430		*T.D. 383*		*T.D. 401*		*T.D. 543*		*T.D. 177*	
h.	*b.*	*h.*	*b.*	*h.*	*b.*	*h.*	*b.*	*h.*	*b.*
45	5	69	11	53	10	145	—	100	45

See T.D. 430, p. 248; T.D. 383, p. 341; T.D. 401, p. 415; T.D. 543, pp. 270–272; T.D. 177, pp. 114–115.

159. Duwayhī (cited n. 60), p. 301.

160. Ibid., p. 375.

161. T.D. 430, pp. 248–250, 253–255; T.D. 383, pp. 253–276; T.D. 401, pp. 403–407, 410–411; T.D. 543, pp. 218–234; T.D. 177, pp. 91–102.

162. Duwayhī (cited n. 60), p. 270.

163. Ibid., p. 359.

164. Ibid., pp. 323, 378.

165. T.D. 169, p. 25; T.D. 430, p. 251; T.D. 383, p. 269; T.D. 401, p. 408.

166. George Sandys, *A Relation of a Journey,* London, 1652, p. 163.

167. Al-Khālidī al-Ṣafadī (cited n. 142), pp. 127–190.

168. T.D. 543, p. 236; T.D. 177, p. 98.

169. T.D. 430, pp. 332–334; T.D. 383, pp. 395–406; T.D. 401, pp. 474–478; T.D. 543, pp. 339–351; T.D. 177, pp. 144–150.

170. Duwayhī (cited n. 60), pp. 323, 344, 346, 365, 374, 375.

171. Ibid., p. 334.

172. Sandys (cited n. 166), p. 165.
173. Al-Khālidī al-Ṣafadī (cited, n. 142), pp. 109–110, 126–127, 132.
174. See Hütteroth and Abdulfattah (cited n. 6), pp. 195–220; and Bakhit (cited n. 1), pp. 85–92.
175. T.D. 430, pp. 525–537; T.D. 401, pp. 587–599; T.D. 491, pp. 88–102.
176. T.D. 401, p. 592; T.D. 491, pp. 98–99.
177. T.D. 491, pp. 101–102.
178. T.D. 401, p. 595.
179. T.D. 401, p. 592; T.D. 491, p. 88.
180. T.D. 430, pp. 546–562; T.D. 401, pp. 666–683; T.D. 491, pp. 329–331, 384–385.
181. T.D. 430, p. 550; T.D. 401, p. 667; T.D. 491, pp. 329–331.
182. T.D. 430, p. 553; T.D. 401, p. 670; T.D. 491, pp. 288–289.
183. T.D. 430, p. 547; T.D. 401, p. 681; T.D. 491, pp. 384–385.
184. T.D. 430, pp. 569–570; T.D. 401, p. 690; T.D. 491, pp. 362–366.
185. T.D. 430, pp. 584–589; T.D. 401, pp. 600–608.
186. T.D. 430, p. 584; T.D. 401, p. 606.
187. T.D. 430, pp. 538–542; T.D. 401, pp. 642–649; T.D. 491, pp. 329–340.
188. T.D. 401, p. 647; T.D. 491, pp. 334–335.
189. T.D. 491, pp. 339–340.
190. T.D. 401, p. 663; T.D. 491, p. 216.
191. T.D. 430, pp. 584–591; T.D. 401, pp. 661–664; T.D. 491, p. 216.
192. T.D. 430, pp. 591–596; T.D. 401, pp. 661–664; T.D. 491, pp. 221–241.
193. T.D. 401, p. 651; T.D. 491, pp. 239–241.
194. T.D. 401, p. 653; T.D. 491, pp. 221–222.
195. T.D. 401, p. 654; T.D. 491, pp. 231–232.
196. T.D. 474, p. 2.
197. For this *liwā'*, see T.D. 970 and T.D. 185.
198. T.D. 970, p. 2.
199. T.D. 185, p. 2.
200. T.D. 970, pp. 3–4; T.D. 185, pp. 5–7.
201. T.D. 970, p. 7; T.D. 185, pp. 30–31.
202. T.D. 970, p. 7; T.D. 185, p. 31.
203. T.D. 970, p. 10; T.D. 185, p. 33.
204. T.D. 970, p. 10; T.D. 185, p. 35.
205. T.D. 970, p. 17; T.D. 185, p. 35.
206. T.D. 970, p. 19; T.D. 185, p. 36.
207. T.D. 970, p. 15; T.D. 185, p. 49.
208. T.D. 970, p. 8; T.D. 185, p. 30.
209. T.D. 185, p. 38.
210. T.D. 185, p. 15.
211. T.D. 970, p. 8; T.D. 185, p. 22.
212. T.D. 970, p. 10; T.D. 185, p. 22.
213. T.D. 185, p. 28.
214. T.D. 970, pp. 33–34.
215. Damascus Court-*Sijill*, vol. 1, 993/1585, pp. 314–315.
216. T.D. 970, p. 23; T.D. 185, pp. 17–18.

217. T.D. 970, p. 46; T.D. 185, pp. 78–79. For the history of Karak during the Mamluk period, see my study *Mamlakat al-Karak fī al-ᶜahd al-mamlūkī*, Amman, 1976.

218. T.D. 970, p. 48; T.D. 185, p. 82.

219. T.D. 970, pp. 50–51; T.D. 185, p. 89.

220. T.D. 970, pp. 51–52.

221. T.D. 970, p. 50.

222. T.D. 970, p. 55; T.D. 185, p. 91.

223. Bakhit (cited n. 217), pp. 27–28.

224. T.D. 72, p. A. See also Lewis, ''Studies'' (cited n. 4), pp. 476–477.

225. T.D. 427, p. 142; T.D. 72, pp. 232–233; T.D. 300, pp. 329–330.

226. T.D. 1038, p. 19; T.D. 72, pp. 93–95; T.D. 300, pp. 79–80; T.D. 686, pp. 83–85.

227. T.D. 72, pp. 169–170; T.D. 300, pp. 169–170; T.D. 686, pp. 181–182.

228. T.D. 427, pp. 234–238; T.D. 1038, pp. 132–133; T.D. 72, pp. 234–238; T.D. 300, pp. 247–248.

229. T.D. 427, p. 372; T.D. 1038, p. 105; T.D. 300, p. 372.

230. T.D. 72, p. 256.

231. See Bernard Lewis, ''Nazareth in the Sixteenth Century according to the Ottoman Tapu Registers,'' in *Arabic and Islamic Studies in Honour of Hamilton A. R. Gibb,* Leiden, 1965, pp. 416–425.

232. Ibn al-Furāt (cited n. 26), English text, vol. 2, pp. 56–57, 59; Arabic text, vol. 1, p. 69; Maqrīzī (cited n. 26), vol. 1, part 2, p. 487.

233. Sandys (cited n. 166), p. 158.

234. T.D. 72, p. 180, p. 234; T.D. 581 (1005/1596), p. 189; T.D. 686, p. 85.

235. The population of this *liwā'* was as follows:

932/1525-6				*961-4/1533-7*			
h.	*b.*	*r.*	*d.*	*h.*	*b.*	*r.*	*d.*
5,463	360	86	—	14,884	1,921	307	—

See Lewis, ''Studies'' (cited n. 4), pp. 474–475; Hütteroth and Abdulfattah (cited n. 6), pp. 125–141.

236. T.D. 1038, pp. 146–156; T.D. 258, pp. 7–23; T.D. 546, p. 1; T.D. 100, pp. 1–8.

237. T.D. 1038, pp. 158–159.

238. T.D. 1038, p. 181; T.D. 546, p. 7.

239. T.D. 258, p. 145; T.D. 546, p. 4; T.D. 100, p. 81.

240. T.D. 546, p. 11; T.D. 100, pp. 43–44.

241. T.D. 100, p. 98.

242. T.D. 258, p. 145; T.D. 100, pp. A, 44, 81; T.D. 581, p. 118.

243. T.D. 1038, p. 156; T.D. 100, p. 10. According to T.D. 269 (n.d.), p. 1, it was 22,000 *akche*s.

244. Sanderson (cited n. 63), p. 99.

245. T.D. 427, pp. 262–269; T.D. 1015, pp. 180–189; T.D. 516, pp. 5–17, T.D. 298, pp. 6–48; T.D. 178, pp. 4–15.

246. T.D. 427, pp. 273–274; T.D. 1015, pp. 198–199; T.D. 516, pp. 64–65; T.D. 298, pp. 72–74; T.D. 178, pp. 72–74.

247. T.D. 427, pp. 274–275; T.D. 1015, pp. 196–197; T.D. 516, pp. 65–66; T.D. 298, pp. 75–80; T.D. 178, pp. 74–75.

248. T.D. 427, p. 298; T.D. 516, p. 34; T.D. 298, pp. 109–110; T.D. 178, p. 36.

249. T.D. 427, p. 300; T.D. 516, pp. 33–34; T.D. 298, pp. 131–132; T.D. 178, p. 32.

250. T.D. 427, p. 302; T.D. 1015, p. 215.

251. T.D. 1015, p. 265; T.D. 516, p. 63; T.D. 298, p. 173; T.D. 178, p. 70.

252. T.D. 1015, pp. 265–277.

253. T.D. 516, p. 36; T.D. 178, p. 38.

254. T.D. 516, p. 51; T.D. 298, p. 153; T.D. 178, p. 56.

255. T.D. 516, p. 55; T.D. 298, p. 115; T.D. 178, p. 60.

256. T.D. 516, p. 80; T.D. 178, p. 68.

257. T.D. 516, p. 64; T.D. 178, p. 71.

258. T.D. 516, p. 36; T.D. 298, p. 144; T.D. 178, p. 37.

259. T.D. 516, p. 31; T.D. 178, p. 29.

260. T.D. 298, pp. 79–80.

261. T.D. 298, pp. 222–223.

262. T.D. 178, pp. 72–78.

263. B. Lewis, "Studies" (cited n. 4), p. 474; also on Jerusalem and Gaza see Amnon Cohen and Bernard Lewis, *Population and Revenue in the Towns of Palestine in the Sixteenth Century*, Princeton, 1978.

264. Compare above, Volume II, chapter 1, by Amnon Cohen, section IV, pp. 9–10.

265. Sanderson (cited n. 63), p. 108.

266. Sandys (cited n. 166), p. 133.

267. Ibn Ṭūlūn (cited, n. 1), vol. 1, p. 5. See also Mujir al-Din al-^{c}Ulaymī, (d. 927/1520), *Al-uns al-jalīl bi-tārīkh al-Quds wa-al-Khalīl*, al-Najaf, 1968, vol. 2, pp. 51, 97–98, 300–304, 312–314, 317–318, 326, 345–346, 347–352, 359–360.

268. Heyd (cited n. 7), pp. 182–183.

269. Muḥammad b. ^{c}Abd Allāh b. Ibrāhīm b. Baṭūṭa, *Tuḥfat al-nuẓẓār fi gharā'ib al-amṣār wa-^{c}ajā'ib al-asfār*, ed. C. Defremery and B. R. Sanguinetti, Paris, 1853–1855, vol. 1, p. 124.

270. T.D. 427, p. 270.

271. T.D. 518, p. 18; T.D. 298, p. 48.

272. Heyd (cited n. 7), pp. 175, 183, no. 5.

273. Ibid., pp. 182–183.

274. Sanderson (cited n. 63), pp. 122–123.

275. Sandys (cited n. 166), pp. 119–120.

276. T.D. 516, pp. 64–66; T.D. 343, p. 4; Heyd (cited n. 7), pp. 139, 143–144.

277. T.D. 516, pp. 63–64; T.D. 298, p. 222; T.D. 178, p. 68.

278. T.D. 178, p. 60; T.D. 346, p. 34.

279. al-^{c}Ulaymī (cited n. 267), vol. 2, p. 51.

280. Ibid., vol. 2, pp. 97–98.

281. Ibid., vol. 2, pp. 263–265.

282. Ibid., vol. 2, p. 265.

283. Ibid., vol. 2, p. 317.

284. Ibid., vol. 2, pp. 345–352, 359–360.

285. Heyd (cited n. 7), pp. 149, 178–179.

286. For his biography, see Ghazzī (cited n. 1), vol. 3, pp. 120–121.

287. Heyd (cited n. 7), p. 179.

288. Ibid., p. 176.

289. Muḥibb al-Dīn Muḥammad b. Dā'ōud al-Ḥamawī (d. 1016/1608), *Bawādī al-dumū^{c} al-^{c}andamiyya bī wādī al-diyār al-rūmiyya*, ms. ^{c}Atif Efendi (Istanbul) no. 2030, f° 2a, 6b–7a.

290. Ibid. Heyd (cited n. 7), p. 177.

291. Heyd (cited n. 7), p. 179.

292. Ibid., pp. 180–181.

293. T.D. 581, p. 186.

294. Heyd (cited n. 7), pp. 181–182.

295. Duwayhī (cited n. 60), p. 262.

296. See Bernard Lewis, ''Studies'' (cited n. 4), p. 474.

297. T.D. 427, pp. 161–169; T.D. 1015, pp. 2–17; T.D. 304, pp. 4–52; T.D. 192, pp. 2–16.

298. For the history of this family see Quṭb al-Dīn Muḥammad b. Aḥmad al-Nahralwālī (d. 990/1582), *Al-barq al-yamānī fī al-fatḥ al-ᶜuthmānī*, ed. Ḥamīd al-Jāsir, Riyāḍ, 1967, pp. 86, 93, 123, 137; al-Būrīnī (cited n. 37), vol. 1, pp. 191–192; Muḥammad al-Muḥūbbī, *Khulāṣat al-athār fī aᶜyān al-qarn al-ḥādī ᶜashar,* Cairo, 1284/1867, vol. 1, p. 187. al-Khālidī al-Ṣafadī (cited n. 142), pp. 121, 160.

299. T.D. 427, pp. 176–177; T.D. 1015, pp. 59–60; T.D. 304, pp. 115–116; T.D. 192, pp. 49–50.

300. T.D. 1015, pp. 119–120; T.D. 304, pp. 221–222; T.D. 192, pp. 109–110.

301. T.D. 427, pp. 234–235; T.D. 1015, pp. 125–128; T.D. 304, pp. 229–244; T.D. 192, pp. 119–120.

302. T.D. 427, pp. 246–247; T.D. 1015, pp. 137–139; T.D. 304, pp. 299–305; T.D. 192, pp. 144–148.

303. T.D. 304, p. 320; T.D. 192, p. 157.

304. T.D. 542, pp. 25–26; T.D. 427, pp. 246–247.

305. Sandys (cited n. 166), p. 119.

306. T.D. 312, p. 111.

307. T.D. 312, p. 131.

308. Cf., for example, Haddad (cited n. 59), p. 10.

3

On Melkite Passage to the Unia: The Case of Patriarch Cyril al-Za^{c}īm (1672–1720)

ROBERT M. HADDAD

The Melkites of the Patriarchate of Antioch, by the Muslim centuries shorn of numbers and vitality, dwelt at the margin of Ottoman society. Men thus precariously positioned tend to evolve an acute sensitivity to impending shifts in power that promise danger or, conversely, an added measure of political security and material advantage. The distant rumbling of those forces fated to crumble the old and foster the new are heard first by the marginal community. Seen in this light, the tale of Melkite passage to the Unia and of Cyril al-Za^{c}īm's own odyssey westward provides an index to the faltering of Ottoman power and the eastward extension of the European hegemony.

When in 1716 Cyril al-Za^{c}īm, Melkite Patriarch of Antioch (1672–1720), entered haltingly upon the road to Rome, his way had been under preparation for some one hundred years. During that period the interests of the papacy and Catholic France had converged in Aleppo and Sidon, two of the three most important Melkite centers in Syria. The Latin missionaries had been propelled eastward in the early seventeenth century as the Counter-Reformation lent fresh urgency to the recurring dream of Christian unity under the auspices of the Fisherman's western see. From the outset the missionaries fell under the diplomatic protection of France. The merchants of France, for their part, were drawn to Aleppo as the great entrepôt of Syria and to Sidon as the bustling port for Damascus. The existence of a resident French consul in Aleppo as well as Sidon testified to the extent of French commercial interests in those cities and to France's incipient political interest in all of Syria.

By the end of the seventeenth century, then, the Melkites of Aleppo and Sidon found themselves enmeshed in the religious concerns of Rome and in the commercial and political interests of France. For as the lassitude of Ottoman officialdom, Muslim and Christian, helped fructify the labors of the missionaries, and as considerations of trade bound Melkite economic interests to the French factories and consular protection, Uniate majorities emerged in Aleppo and Sidon, presided over by prelates who had, however surreptitiously, made formal submission to Rome.[1] A Franciscan protégé, the Damascene Athanasius al-Dabbās, had bowed to the papacy in 1686,[2] contested briefly the patriarchate with Cyril al-Zaᶜīm and, since 1687, had governed the Aleppine faithful as antipatriarch and arch foe of the Patriarch Cyril. Yet another scion of a Damascene clan, Euthymius al-Ṣayfī, in communion with Rome since 1683,[3] ruled as Metropolitan of Sidon. Enjoying the support of their respective flocks, the protection of the consuls and, at least in al-Ṣayfī's case, the Lebanese *amīr*s as well,[4] and encountering only sporadic Ottoman opposition, both Athanasius and Euthymius stood beyond the disciplinary power of Cyril al-Zaᶜīm, the man recognized by the Orthodox Melkites, the Ecumenical Patriarch and the Ottoman Sultan as canonical Patriarch of Antioch.

Damascus, seat of the patriarchate, hosted a phalanx of active Latin missionaries—largely Franciscan and under the not too remote protection of the French king's consul in Sidon. Because the City of Praise housed neither French consul nor factory, however, its Melkites had escaped the full force of the Franco-papal combination.[5] As a corollary, Damascus had also been free of any papal zeal on the part of Patriarch Cyril al-Zaᶜīm. But while the Damascene Melkite community in the second decade of the eighteenth century could still boast a clear Orthodox majority, that majority was being eroded together with Cyril's Orthodox commitment. Missionary success—virtually complete in Aleppo and Sidon, impressive in Damascus, and expanding elsewhere within the patriarchate—was not lost on Cyril. The sensitivity of a growing Melkite trading class to the pleasures of French consular protection—particularly as the toll taken on non-Uniate shipping by the Latin Christian corsairs mounted—provided the patriarch with yet another nudge toward Rome. (It need hardly be stated that the price of consular protection was entry into the Unia.[6]) Rome also beckoned to the degree that Ottoman Istanbul and Greek Constantinople faltered. The failure of the Porte and the Great Church consistently to counter Latin penetration rankled Cyril. So did the signs of Phanariot ambitions to substitute a Greek for a Syrian hierarchy in the see of Antioch. *Wālī*s marching less firmly to Istanbul's step, semiautonomous Lebanese amīrs and influential French consuls all loomed as prophets of the new localism that had already helped to spawn and sustain the Uniates and would seriously qualify Ottoman authority in eighteenth- and early nineteenth-century Syria. Doubtless too the patriarch was beginning to understand that the debilitation of the Ottoman authority of which he was part was inseparable from the expansive strength of Western Europe. It is not irrelevant that Cyril's reign sprawled over the period during which the Ottoman state yielded the balance of power to Christian Europe. In the second decade of the eighteenth century Cyril's long contest with the Latins and their Syrian neophytes appeared to promise diminishing returns.

As early as 1713 Euthymius al-Ṣayfī sensed Cyril's equivocation. In one of his periodic communications to the Sacred Congregation for the Propagation of the Faith, the agency founded in 1622 to coordinate Latin missionary efforts throughout the world, the Uniate Metropolitan of Sidon wrote of his ecclesiastical superior:

> He is a man lacking in learning but possessing intelligence and judgement. He has had a great hatred for the [Roman] Church but is now in the middle, awaiting the impossible: when the Patriarchs of Constantinople and Alexandria submit, he will submit.[7]

Al-Ṣayfī was yet unaware that half the "impossible" had come to pass: on June 6, 1712 Samuel, Pope and Patriarch of Alexandria, had made his obeisance to Rome.[8] So it was that when Cyril's own assessment of the realities of power was complemented by the persistent pressures of the French consuls,[9] the Latin missionaries[10] and the Uniate Melkites, and crowned finally by an invitation from the vicar himself,[11] the patriarch's resolve of some fifty years fell finally from him. The aged prelate turned toward Rome and submission, or so at least it seemed. For if we cannot see the Syrian hierarch raging against his journey westward, we may nonetheless detect the muffled regret of an infirm and old man whose world, the Ottoman world with its peculiar modalities—limited, limiting but comfortable and comprehensible—had cracked and broken.

Cyril's letter of August 20, 1716,[12] apparently his first to Pope Clement XI, is a long discursive document wherein the Syrian's pride struggles with some success against the obsequiousness he suspects is demanded and the historical fact mingles easily with more obvious myth. Yet Cyril's epistle is useful for determining the patriarch's understanding of the ecclesiology at issue as well as the probable repercussions of declaring openly for Rome. To begin with, the document, as a Uniate profession of faith, is clearly imperfect. Cyril cleaves unabashedly to the faith of the Seven Councils:

> We believe firmly and certainly that the Church of Rome is of the Seven Great Holy Councils and of the smaller councils, and we defend Her status as Mother of the churches of the world. We acknowledge and confess one Church and one baptism and we sanction that which these [Councils] sanction and forbid that which they forbid.

The pope—"the most holy brother," "the eldest brother," "the brother in Christ"—remains for Cyril Bishop and Patriarch of Rome, first among equals and scarcely the ecclesiastical monarch possessing jurisdiction over the whole Church of Christ. The Union of Florence, "the eighth council," looms as a light that glimmered and died, albeit as a consequence of Greek rather than Syrian or Latin perversity: ". . . all that for which Pope Eugenius toiled . . . the Greeks ruined." Indeed, the patriarch's anti-Greek bias, born perhaps of two depositions at the instance of the Great Church[13] and nurtured by his mounting suspicion of Phanariot designs, merits special notice. For it will be sounded again and again in the future not merely by Cyril but by others at Antioch and elsewhere in an Ottoman Empire whose polyglot Orthodox Christian populations, in blatant contradiction to their historic ecclesiology, were fast slipping under the hegemony of the Phanariot-dominated see of Constantinople.[14] The jurisdictional pretensions of the Great Church, then, had not a little to do with Cyril's westward turning.

The Syrian hierarch also attempts to make clear to Clement the price that could be exacted from the prelate possessed of temerity sufficient to embrace publicly his "eldest brother". He may become marked a "Frank"—a branding which, Cyril implies, tells of political no less than religious disloyalty, of treason as well as schism. Those submitting to Rome have sometimes been seen by the sultan's officials as yielding to an alien power which, insofar as it truly held power, had of necessity to be temporal as well as religious. The attitude of France toward the Uniates and that of the Uniates toward their patroness, over the succeeding two hundred years, would demonstrate that such an Ottoman reading was anything but naive. An Ottoman Christian's submission to an ecclesiastical authority standing outside the civil and political control of the Muslim Empire would prove to be scarcely more assimilable than a Muslim's apostasy.[15] At all events, for Cyril or any Ottoman subject flirting with Rome there had to exist a countervailing political force to shield the evolving Uniate from the possible reaction of the Muslim state and the non-Uniate community he was in the process of abandoning. Hence Cyril's insistence that the energetic efforts of the Catholic consuls be forthcoming. Cyril no doubt viewed protection by the French consuls in Aleppo and particularly in Sidon as a perfect complement to the solicitude of those heterodox Muslim *amīr*s of the Lebanon who served so well the Maronites and such Uniate Melkite pioneers as Euthymius al-Ṣayfī.

Cyril also heatedly remarks on the social dislocations occasioned by the Latinization of rite and canon law by those Maronites and Melkites who have yielded unreservedly to Rome:

> . . . we are become naked among the nations and the heretics as one Christian fasts while another breaks fast, as one Christian marries outside the seven degrees [of consanguinity] while another marries outside three. . . . All this becomes a source of division . . . and when the untutored see . . . they turn away . . . and doubts occur.

Western canons bearing upon marriage had (and continue to have) an attraction for Orthodox Melkites caught between their communion's extremely restrictive marital laws and the quite different standards of a clan- and family-oriented society dominated by Arab Muslims. Marriage between first cousins, to take an obvious example, a marriage strictly proscribed under Melkite canon law, was encouraged by Arab social values and countenanced by Muslim law. Thus the patriarch's tirade against the Uniate plunge into Latin law and ritual, and his oft-expressed hostility toward the substitution of Western for Eastern canons in matters as universal as marriage and fasting, reflected Cyril's immediate problems with Melkites who passed to the Unia that otherwise forbidden nuptials be blessed or that the duration and severity of fasting be lessened.[16] The patriarch was also aware that such substitution, when sanctioned by Rome, made a mockery of the ideal of unity among Churches with usages of equal legitimacy and threatened to activate, among the various Eastern Christian communities, that immemorial hostility which the Latin missionaries, however inadvertently, had already done so much to arouse.

Finally no analysis of the forces urging Cyril westward is complete without allusion to the patriarch's concern over the European corsairs who persisted in disinclination to distinguish between Muslim and Christian shipping. Unmentioned in Cyril's letter to Clement, this concern is expressed forcefully in his instructions to Biaggio dà Salamanca, the Franciscan vicar in Damascus, who with Seraphim Ṭānās, Uniate Melkite priest and nephew of the redoubtable Euthymius al-Ṣayfī, was charged with delivering the patriarchal missive to the pope's hand. The friar was enjoined, among other things, to impress Clement with the urgency of protecting Syrian Christian vessels from plunder by Latin pirates.[17]

Cyril's letter of August 20, 1716 reached Rome but not as his only word on the subject of union. For the patriarch had confided this letter, and another addressed to the Sacred Congregation for the Propagation of the Faith, unsealed to the hand of Seraphim Ṭānās that the latter's uncle as well as Poullard, consul of France in Sidon, might peruse them before dispatching them to Rome.[18] After all, it had been through al-Ṣayfī's agency that Ṭānās, in company with dà Salamanca and a Uniate deacon, had carried the pope's initial communication to Cyril, "in great secrecy with no one seeing it, neither the missionaries nor the native sons."[19] The patriarch's reply to that letter, now duly examined in Sidon by Euthymius, received the metropolitan's endorsement. In his own epistle to Clement, Euthymius termed Cyril's letters to pope and Propaganda satisfactory.[20] Any doubts concerning Cyril's sincerity—and the long history of the relations of the often refractory metropolitan with his patriarch would suggest that doubt was not lacking—al-Ṣayfī left unspoken, informed perhaps by a honed episcopal instinct that unequivocal acceptance of Cyril's equivocal profession of faith might serve to render it real or, in any case, make easier the path of him who would succeed the ailing patriarch. And in that role Euthymius had already cast himself. Hence, we may surmise, that colorful exhortation with which al-Ṣayfī concluded his covering letter to the man he acknowledged as the Vicar of Christ:

> For Jesus' sake, my Lord, embrace him without reservation. For he is the son of a dynasty, long on the stove and, to all the notables and officials, well-cooked in his leadership; his word pierces the East. When from you he sees perfect love, he will perhaps restore in his own day something gone now for many generations.[21]

Not so the reaction of the consul of France upon reading Cyril's communications to pope and Propaganda. This Latin layman, who appears to have understood nothing of the ecclesiology informing Cyril, stood aghast at the patriarch's reference to the pope as "brother" and at the presumption of the prelate who "speaks of himself as patriarch of Antioch and all the East" in conferring his benediction upon the cardinals of the Propaganda. Poullard made haste gently to notify Cyril of the impropriety of his missives and to cajole and pressure him into revisions acceptable to the papal powers.[22] But let the singular Poullard speak for himself:

> The virtues of this Patriarch had more and more induced me to cultivate relations with him so that, after having employed secret means and measures to bring him to submit to the Holy See, I had eight days ago the sweet pleasure of receiving from him letters by which he shows me that he has come to my persuasion. . . . I replied that I have seen with joy the happy resolution he has taken but that I have learned with pain that these two letters were not in form suitable to send to the Pope and the Sacred Congregation. . . . For . . . his letter to His Holiness began with "our very dear brother" . . . while he began [his letter] to the Sacred Congregation by giving it his benediction. This did not seem to me in the rules or befitting a Patriarch submitting sincerely to the true successor to St. Peter. I joined to my . . . proddings a model which this Patriarch so well appreciated that with his reply of 19th September he directed to me two letters conforming entirely to the said model. . . . These two letters . . . will be no doubt more agreeable to the Pope.[23]

Cyril's second letter to Clement carries the date September 8, 1716 and must have adhered strictly to the "model" sent by Poullard. In stark contrast to Cyril's earlier communication, it lacks utterly the stamp of the patriarch's self-esteem and agonized equivocation. "I accept," wrote Cyril al-Zaᶜīm with all the passion of the catechal response,

> all of the Seven holy councils . . . [and] especially the Florentine Council and the verities established therein. They are, first, that the Roman See has primacy over all the sees and that its occupant—that is, the Roman Pope—is successor to Peter and the vicar of our Lord Jesus Christ.

The occupant of the other throne of Petrine foundation proceeded listlessly to state his acceptance of the *filioque* and "all that in which the Roman Church believes." Cyril dispatched his pastoral staff "as a perfect sign of union with Your Holiness."[24]

Of the few in Syria privy to these developments (carried through, it must be noted, with a circumspection bordering on the conspiratorial) none was more jubilant than the consul of France in Sidon. The more knowing missionaries and Uniates, including Euthymius al-Ṣayfī, could never free themselves of certain misgivings. Had the shrewdness and tenacity of Cyril—those qualities which had enabled him to survive the tumult of a half-century on the throne of Antioch—really come finally to rest in the service of Rome? What would be the consequences should Cyril's submission become generally known among his predominantly non-Uniate Damascene flock? And, perhaps the chief concern, how would the Great Church and the Ottoman central government react to news that the Syrian patriarch had bent at last to the bishop of Rome?[25] Poullard, on the other hand, driven perhaps by a desire to magnify his role in a consummation so long and so devoutly wished, fell easy prey to an enthusiasm which carried him beyond Cyril and Damascus to embrace all Syria (including Jerusalem) and thence Alexandria and the ecumenical see itself:

> . . . the Greeks of Damascus, of whom there is a Catholic party, will follow the example of their chief, as have the Bishops of Beirut and Ṣaydnāyā . . . these Bishops having also sent to the Holy Father their profession of faith . . . the Patriarch of the Greeks of Aleppo [Athanasius al-Dabbās] is a good Catholic; he of Alexandria sent his profession of faith to Rome three years ago, and Mgr. Cyril [now] comes to play this happy part; with time the Patriarchs of Jerusalem and Constantinople will be able to emulate them and reenter the bosom of the Roman Church. . . .[26]

The rather muted response of Rome, as well as French diplomats outside Syria, to Cyril's submission may perhaps be gauged by the content of an exchange which took place late in 1716 or early the next year between a Cardinal of the Propaganda and the French ambassador in Rome. Aware that unless the patriarch were certain of the capacity of Rome and France to shield him against the possible wrath of the Phanar and Porte, Cyril could not be held, the cardinal asked the ambassador to recommend anew to the French ambassador in Istanbul and to the French consuls in Syria that the patriarch receive special protection against anticipated molestation at the hands of the Turks. The Latin prelate also saw this as the opportune time to have the king's ambassador in Istanbul seek, through application of appropriate pressure to the Patriarch of Jerusalem, the restoration of the Sea of Acre to the jurisdiction of Antioch, the cardinal observing that Acre had been "usurped" by Jerusalem some ninety years ago but failing to remark Euthymius al-Ṣayfī's ambition that the throne of a restored Acre devolve upon his own Seraphim Ṭānās. Sensitive to the role played by the European corsairs in inspiring the patriarch's negotiations with Rome, the Latin hierarch also called upon "His Christian Majesty" to stand between the Uniates of Syria and the pirates of Latin Christendom, particularly those Frenchmen who sailed habitually under the colors of non-French Christian princes. Finally, moved by high presumption and an even higher estimate of French influence at the Porte, the cardinal requested that the French monarch "permit" his ambassador in Istanbul to obtain from the Ottoman government an order banning the appointment of ethnic Greeks over "the Arab Melkites." This, the Latin prelate remarked, to facilitate the conversion of the "schismatics."[27] Curiously the cardinal, while appreciating the Syrian susceptibility to Rome, apparently failed to comprehend that it was often born of Syrian fear of direct Greek rule over Antioch.

To the cardinal's solicitations the French ambassador in Rome replied that he would with utmost pleasure embrace every opportunity to favor and protect Cyril, though it was hoped that the patriarch would conduct himself with "prudent zeal" while serving as model for his flock's return to "their true shepherd." The ambassador did not see this as the time to press the issue of Acre's return to Antioch but he assured the cardinal that action awaited only the propitious moment. On the subject of the corsairs, the Frenchman avoided any intimation of direct French responsibility, contenting himself with the observation that corsairs active along the Syrian coast, whether flying the colors of Malta or those of any Christian prince, should, upon receipt of their patents, be reminded that plunder of the Catholics of Syria constituted no part of their mandate. The cardinal's desire to mitigate Phanariot power over Antioch evoked from the ambassador only the response that France would do all she could to bring about the nomination of Arab Melkite bishops.[28]

While the cardinal and the ambassador stood engaged in their diplomatic exercise, and Consul Poullard saw the imminent "reversion" of the entire Christian East, voices could be heard from Syria which revealed that Cyril's submission had failed to weld into an effective unity even those Latins and Uniates who were privy to it. On this count a letter, almost certainly of Franciscan authorship though addressed to Clement XI "by the Catholics of the Antiochian Patriarchate," is most revealing.[29] Something of an extended apology for the activity of the friars in Syria, this document reviews the chain of events initiated by Cyril's succession in 1672 and, reflecting always the characteristic Franciscan bias in favor of Athanasius al-Dabbās ("an exemplar of the Catholic truth"), culminates in a discussion of the circumstances surrounding Cyril's recent declaration in favor of Rome, a declaration inspired by "the holy persuasions" of the Franciscans, notably those of Padre Biaggio dà Salamanca, the friars' vicar in Damascus. It is dà Salamanca's erstwhile traveling companion, Seraphim Ṭānās, who endures the brunt of the Franciscan attack as the friars argue that his and his uncle's indiscretion threatens the hard-won papal position in Syria. The negotiations leading to Cyril's submission, the letter would have us believe, had been conducted by the Franciscans alone (neither the role of the French consul in Sidon nor that of Euthymius al-Ṣayfī is acknowledged) and the friars had proceeded "with the greatest secrecy possible." Secrecy, Clement is informed, continues to be imperative. For awkwardness inheres in recognizing Cyril as legitimate patriarch after decades of according that distinction to Athanasius al-Dabbās. Ottoman reaction, particularly in this time of war against Europeans, "could place in jeopardy the lives of Monsig. Cyril and the many Catholics and [Franciscan] religious . . . in Damascus" and either eliminate the friars' control over the holy places in Palestine or force them "to pay the Turkish government some avania of many pieces of eight." "The so very dangerous source . . . of publicity" threatening to precipitate these calamities is no other than Seraphim Ṭānās, whom Cyril's want of discernment had brought to Rome in company with the impeccable dà Salamanca. (It is of course probable, despite Cyril's later regrets over treating with Rome through Ṭānās, that a truer measure of the patriarch's discernment lay precisely in his decision to commission two quite different men as checks one upon the other. For the Franciscan affinity for Athanasius al-Dabbās—for Cyril a most tender concern—would likely be offset in Rome by the nephew of the man who, in a letter to the Propaganda, had said of Athanasius: ". . . known among you as a Catholic and known to me as a hypocrite."[30] Then too Poullard, who seems to have trusted Ṭānās rather more than he did the largely non-French friars, had firmly urged Cyril to name the youthful Uniate as envoy.[31])

Moreover, the Franciscan missive continues, Ṭānās "is biased and a close relative of a certain prelate . . . who wished the Franciscans to induce Monsig. Athanasius to renounce [his claim], then, expelling Monsig. Cyril, establish himself in the patriarchate. . . ." Ṭānās also stands accused by the Franciscans of arriving in Rome and undertaking "to inspire by diverse means distrust of . . . P. Biaggio." Ṭānās, in addition, is said to have assumed "arbitrarily the title 'Agent of Monsig. Cyril' . . . posing as [the Patriarch's] defender . . . as though the Franciscans were hostile to him." The Uniate then had himself "painted in the habit of a bishop" and submitted

> a petition in the name of Monsig. Cyril, without commission from him and offensive to the Greek Patriarch of Jerusalem, claiming that the Bishopric of Ptolemais [Acre] (with hope of [obtaining] which he caused himself to be painted in the manner aforesaid) does not belong to [Jerusalem] but to Antioch.

Because the friars, as "Custodians of the Holy Land," wished no upset in their relations with the Patriarch of Jerusalem they opposed Ṭānās's petition, "whereupon his indignation towards the Franciscans rose" and he fell to "accusing them of intrigues and machinations in the Levant, which have no bases even in his own mind." Seraphim stands guilty too of remaining

> studiously silent about [Athanasius al-Dabbās'] zeal for the Catholic religion, which the Holy See holds proven, and expressing only, without evidence or foundation, that which denigrates his ascension to the patriarchate and the legitimate interventions and Catholic zeal interposed in his favor by the Padres of the Holy Land.

Thus, in the Franciscan view, to pluck Cyril was not to abandon Athanasius. At once trumpeting their role in Cyril's submission and attempting to persuade Athanasius to surrender his claims to the patriarchate, the padres knew well the fragility of Cyril's health. Upon his demise, sooner rather than later, the patriarchate in his fullness would fall at last to the long-time "canonical" patriarch, their protégé Athanasius. The friars sensed—rightly as the events would demonstrate—that Euthymius al-Ṣayfī aspired to the patriarchal succession, and that this nephew saw as intrinsic to his mission in Rome the elimination of the Propaganda's vestigial support for the antipatriarchate of Athanasius al-Dabbās. Ṭānās' perversity, insist the Franciscans with no lack of acuity,

> can serve only to provoke new discord between Cyril and Athanasius and to deter the latter . . . from renunciation in favor of the former. Because Seraphim is not unaware of the extreme damage that such behavior may inflict upon Monsig. Cyril, one must infer that he persists in his intent to convey . . . the patriarchate to the other prelate [Euthymius al-Ṣayfi]. . . .

The friars conclude this remarkable document with the request that Pope Clement permit Padre Biaggio to return immediately to Syria "so that upon his arrival the Franciscans, seconding the will of the Holy See, may be able to complement Her union with . . . Monsig. Cyril . . ."

This baroque Franciscan brief affords a precious glimpse of some of the forces contending within the see of Antioch and in Syria generally. The tripartite ambitions surrounding the patriarchal throne, and the Franciscans' not-yet-relinquished enthusiasm for Athanasius al-Dabbās, are sharply delineated. The document contains instructive allusion to Seraphim's and his uncle's plans for Acre—plans which, the friars feared, would galvanize the Phanariot establishment against not only the Unia but the "Holy Custodianship" itself. The antipathy separating the Franciscans (in Syria at least comprised largely of Spaniards and Italians) from the representatives of the Most Christian King of France is everywhere implicit. More than implicit is the friars' and Cyril's fear of Ottoman reaction to the latest papal advance, particularly in time of war between the sultan and his European foes. Finally, the Franciscans make clear that unity of action and method among the Latin and Uniate principals at Antioch appears to have been all but absent.

While the Franciscans and Ṭanās pressed their various suits upon pope and Propaganda, in Syria Uniate doubts over the sincerity of Cyril's submission continued to grow. In February 1717 Isṭifān ᶜAṭāllāh, abbot of the Uniate Monastery of the Savior (Dayr al-Mukhalliṣ), lamented to the pope that during four months in Damascus

> I failed to find in the Patriarch . . . anything of the appearance or nature of Catholics. All his actions [stem] from fear over the headship. . . . Have utterly no faith in him. His concerns are the world and the confirmation and perfection of his headship.[32]

"For Cyril . . ." our Uniate commentator insists, "marches with the majority" and when the Orthodox have the advantage "he tramples [us] without mercy." Seemingly willing, however, to work with the poor stuff of which Cyril was made, ᶜAṭāllāh urged Pope Clement as well as the cardinals of the Propaganda to heed the patriarch's request and "ask the sultan of France to extract from the sultan of the Muslims an order to all [Ottoman] authorities forbidding them to honor any complaint against any Christian who prays with the Franks"[33] or "who wishes to learn the teaching and religion of the Franks."[34] Such an order, obviously tantamount to winning the Muslim sultan's blessing upon Latin proselytizing among Ottoman Christians, might, suggests ᶜAṭāllāh, "make firm [Cyril's] adherence."[35] ᶜAṭāllāh's reservations no doubt duly noted, Rome pursued her Syrian prize. And in charging the Uniate priest Jabrā'īl Fīnān with the responsibility of carrying to Syria, for Cyril's signature, the standard profession of faith formulated for Eastern prelates by Urban VIII, the Propaganda had awarded the palm to Seraphim Ṭanās and his maternal uncle rather than to their Franciscan antagonists. For Fīnān had been spawned by the Monastery of the Saviour and would never lose his affinity for that institution's founder, Euthymius al-Ṣayfī. In any case we have Consul Poullard's testimony that it was "Don Gabriel" Fīnān who brought to him from Rome on the fourth of October 1717 the Propaganda's "consignments" to Cyril.[36] For a period thereafter, Poullard and members of al-Ṣayfī's entourage are the central figures in Rome's negotiations with Cyril al-Zaᶜīm.

"I imitate my Patron St. Peter," exulted Pierre Poullard on the fifth of October

1717, "and cast my nets to lure to the Bosom of the Roman Church a Patriarch. . . ." Undeflected by the mutterings of those who "decry [Cyril's earlier] profession of faith because it had not passed through their channels," the French consul dispatched the "consignments" of the Propaganda to Damascus and Cyril. His courier was Seraphim Ṭānās.[37] It fell to Ṭānās then to prod the patriarch into taking that final formal step demanded by Rome. We have Cyril's admission that

> I have terminated the affair . . . and have sent . . . Urban's profession of faith to the hands of my faithful friend and confidant the Consul. I have sealed it with my seal . . . and signed it with my hand.[38]

An earlier version of Urban's profession went unsigned, the patriarch remarked without distress, "because it was not in our language and because I know Greek not at all, it being reasonable not to sign that which one does not understand."[39] Ten days later, on November 15, 1717, Poullard announced to his superiors a continent away that he had already sent to Rome, in the care of "Don Gabriel," the patriarch's profession of faith "signed and sealed with his seal according to the form, in Latin and Arabic, required of Eastern prelates by Pope Urban VIII."[40] And if Cyril's subscription to Urban's formulae failed to metamorphose the Patriarch of Great Antioch into a convinced Uniate, Rome could nonetheless boast that the Uniate line of Melkite Patriarchs, rid now of the canonical ambiguity imparted by the status of Athanasius al-Dabbās, had been formerly "reinstituted" after a lapse of centuries. For Orthodox Melkites of course it was a question of "institution" rather than "reinstitution." Neither term, however, could afford them comfort.

It would be more than a year before Fīnān returned to his homeland, disembarking at Sidon in company with the inevitable Seraphim Ṭānās on the ninth of December 1718. There the two priests remained until a patriarchal summons, sounded during the Eastern Holy Week of 1719, called them to Damascus.[41] Poullard would have us believe that the summons was issued at his behest, for the consul was eager to obtain a faithful account of Cyril's conduct, that doubt concerning the patriarch's intentions, abiding yet in Rome as well as in Syria, be allayed.[42] The times must have appeared to Poullard propitious. The events culminating in the Peace of Passarowitz (1718) provided France, a nonbelligerent, a certain leverage with the defeated sultan, and the Uniates an added measure of confidence, a confidence inspired not only by the sturdier position of their European patroness in dealing with the sultan but by the Syrian Christians' pride in the Austrian victory.[43] Understandably, however, caution qualified the optimism of the consul as well as the Uniates. Poullard, in explaining why a chest intended as a papal gift to Cyril remained still in the consulate, insisted that ". . . it is inappropriate to do things with show in a land where the Catholic Christians have many enemies ever prepared upon the slightest pretext to devour them." Yet in the same communiqué the consul could relate with pleasure that before ᶜUthmān Pāshā Abū Ṭawq departed Sidon to assume the crucial governorship of Damascus, the Pāshā had ordered his private "symphonie" to entertain his Frankish friend in the audience chamber and on the terrace of the French consulate.[44] And Poullard, in considering the local advantages currently enjoyed by the papists, might well have added to the name of the sympathetic Abū Ṭawq that of Manṣūr al-Ṣayfī, staunch Uniate, cousin to Euthymius, and tailor to Abū Ṭawq. It was thus to the congenial Damascus of ᶜUthmān Pāshā Abū Ṭawq that Seraphim Ṭānās and Jabrā'īl Fīnān repaired in the fullness of the Syrian spring. The two were invited to dwell with their patriarch.[45]

In Fīnān's ensuing report to Cardinal Caraffa of the Propaganda[46] we are afforded a rare, if jaundiced, view of Cyril al-Zaᶜīm in that twilight between his embrace of Urban VIII and his death. Fīnān spoke often to Cyril about the faith; sometimes, the Uniate informs us, "he disputed with me mildly." It became plain, however, that the aged patriarch, whose ignorance of peculiarly Latin doctrine Fīnān thought perfect, had little interest in theological debate. Exercising the virtue of consistency—his approach to Rome after all had never displayed taste for theological nicety—Cyril preferred to fault Rome for failure, among other things, to eliminate the depredations of the corsairs. When Fīnān countered by calling him to task for lack of public candor about the Catholic truths, Cyril offered the familiar response that "we are under the government of the Turk," a defense which Fīnān saw as euphemism for the patriarch's fear of his Greek brothers on the thrones of Constantinople and Jerusalem. Fīnān echoed Iṣṭifān ᶜAṭāllāh's summation of two years before:

> His correspondence with Rome notwithstanding, he coveted wordly things . . . [and acted] out of fear lest the Catholics within his see trouble the throne. . . . Were not the Turks defeated now by the Christians, and the heretical Greeks as limp as the Turks, he would have worked a persecution in this land more vicious than the one he had earlier perpetrated.

Cyril's progress toward Rome appeared to keep pace with the march of European armies into the Ottoman Balkans.

Fīnān gives vent also to Melkite suspicions of Phanariot designs upon the Patriarchate of Antioch, although he tends to see them as engendered by the deepening Greek unease over Uniate penetration at Antioch, rather than as merely a concomitant of the Phanariot drive for direct Greek jurisdiction over all the Orthodox Christian subjects of the sultan. Fīnān charges that, shortly before his arrival in Damascus, Cyril, at the instance of the patriarchs of Constantinople and Jerusalem, had consecrated a "heretical" Greek bishop over the see of Bāyās. The same hierarchs, according to Fīnān, have obtained a *firman* designating the newly consecrated to succeed Cyril upon his death. That they may "eliminate the Catholic faith from the see" the Greek Patriarchs intend to have no "Arab" follow Cyril on the throne of Antioch. The consecration of yet another "heretic" to the vacant see of Ḥimṣ is, Fīnān asserts, imminent. And even as the pall of heresy overspreads Bāyās and Ḥimṣ, and the Phanariots menace all of Antioch, Athanasius al-Dabbās, "the former Patriarch," reveals himself as "more savage" than Cyril in deceiving the Roman Church. Cyril,

Fīnān concludes, should be shown the carrot (Rome ought to discipline the corsairs) as well as the stick ("a mild threat" of deposition). "Because of his fear he would be reconciled, not inwardly [but] for us the appearance suffices." So in Jabrā'īl Fīnān's report to Caraffa some few aspects of the next phase of the struggle may be discerned, most notably of course the waxing hostility of the Phanar toward Latin penetration in Syria and, not unrelated to it, the new posture of Athanasius al-Dabbās. "The former Patriarch" had clearly rejected the supporting role assigned to him by Rome.

Predictably, Seraphim Ṭānās's assessment of his patriarch's commitment to Rome stood even lower than that advanced by his fellow-guest in the patriarchal palace. The nephew of Euthymius al-Ṣayfī wrote of Cyril:

> A Catholic approaches him and he speaks as a Catholic; a schismatic approaches and he speaks as [a schismatic]. . . . Upon my conscience this Patriarch hardly deserves confirmation by the Holy See. . . . If, during his years in Damascus, more than thirty thousand souls have become Catholic it is only because the Patriarch has remained silent, speaking neither good nor evil against either Catholics or schismatics. . . . Five months have I been in Damascus and each day urged him to reply to the Sacred Congregation and to the Pope. . . . Finally he wrote three letters, less out of obligation than shame.[47]

Cyril, whether out of obligation or shame, wrote to Cardinal Sacripanti on September 1, 1719 in an attempt to dispel the cloud which had come to hedge his submission. The cardinal received the patriarch's assurance that none but Uniates comprise "the make-up of my house and entourage." As for allowing Melkites to receive the Eucharist from Latin priests, the patriarch, in a characteristically Eastern appeal to tradition as the arbiter of legitimacy, dismissed the usage as recent, nor ancient. Latinization, the Syrian patriarch implied, is unnecessary, for the twenty thousand Melkites of Damascus, of whom "only a few remain unreconciled," have twenty-five of their own priests to administer the Catholic sacraments. And Rome need not be concerned about the indoctrination of the young, for "long since" had Cyril designated certain of his own priests as well as some of the Latin missionaries to accomplish that end. Nor is Cyril able to restrain himself from pressing Sacripanti to take action against the corsairs, asserting, with perhaps a thrust at Euthymius al-Ṣayfī, metropolitan and shipowner of Sidon, that he owns no vessel but is stirred by the plight of those "Catholics" who do. And the incumbent of the Fisherman's eastern see, in a remark that speaks authoritatively of the traditional Melkite Orthodox attitude toward the Ottoman temporal power, protests: "They mention to me the prayer made for the soldiers of Islam; no doubt it was made but I did not think it contrary to the faith."[48] The scholar here tempted to shrug lightly and murmur "Byzance après Byzance" must also remind himself that the Uniates who took umbrage at the prayer—"they" probably denotes Fīnān and Ṭānās—represented a different generation of Syrian Christians whose very entry into the Unia was part symptom, part cause of a significant shift in loyalties. The transfer of religious allegiance to an authority dwelling where no Muslim writ could run, and represented with progressively greater effect on the Ottoman scene by the men of the French monarch, implied a complementary transfer of political allegiance. If the old patriarch—every inch the product of an age in which no such option was feasible—could not wholly assimilate this moral, men of the cut of Euthymius al-Ṣayfī and the young who followed him had little difficulty doing so.

Cyril's letter to Sacripanti found its way to Rome with another of the same date addressed to Pope Clement XI and bearing down heavily upon the wreckage wrought by the Latin Christian corsairs. In tones even bolder than those of his first letter to the Roman pontiff in August 1716 and altogether reminiscent of the man whose "word pierces the East," Cyril asks how he is to reply to the chide of other "nations" (*umam*) that the corsairs—who have gone from the plunder of Christian shipping to the desecration of monasteries and the murder of monks—"are sons of your own faith." Two years after his union with Rome, Cyril reminded the Western hierarch, "not one of the goals towards which we asked [your aid] has been attained."[49] In this, apparently the last of Cyril's letters to Clement, the pope is again reduced to Eastern dimensions, to bishop and patriarch of Rome, first among equals, the brother in Christ, who, alas, has failed to keep his part of the bargain. But while Cyril's disenchantment with Rome deepened, so did that of al-Ṣayfī's partisans with their patriarch.[50] For when Cyril barbed and dispatched his complaints to cardinal and pope, he already stood accused by the metropolitan and his minions of having connived with the Greek patriarchs in the excommunication of the metropolitan himself.

Anathema appears to have been hurled at Euthymius al-Ṣayfī late in 1718 although we first hear of it on April 29, 1719 when Poullard noted that the patriarchs of Constantinople, Jerusalem, and Alexandria had informed Cyril of Euthymius's excommunication at their hands. Poullard's immediate response was to write to the ambassador in Istanbul, "commending" al-Ṣayfī.[51]

Cyril, upon receipt of this luminous example of Greek jurisdictional trespass against the see of Antioch, notified Euthymius of his fall from Pharnariot grace but refrained from so informing the faithful. Enjoined by Cyril, the Franciscan dà Salamanca relates, to "give some satisfaction to the schismatics, *pro bono pacis* . . . Euthymius scorned the excommunication and made jest of it." It was probably late in the summer of 1719 that there

> came new letters from the schismatic Patriarchs to Lord Cyril . . . charging him with partiality toward the Lord Bishop of Sidon and toward His Holiness; for which reasons, and because the said Lord Bishop had not only disobeyed but insulted him, he resolved to reveal the excommunication.

The Franciscan vicar continues:

> Don Seraphim, . . . through the agency of the Pasha's tailor, further provoked him. [The tailor], after slandering [Cyril] in words unworthy . . . of the vilest Christian, caused him to disburse 45 Venetian gold pieces. Under these circumstances—now goaded [by Ṭānās], now incensed by the Lord Bishop of Sidon, now fearful of the schismatics—[Cyril] decided (unjustly) to publish the excommunication everywhere in the patriarchate save Damascus and Sidon where he did not publish it, more out of fear of the Catholics than for want of desire.[52]

Even Consul Poullard's optimism over the progress of the Unia, not to mention his faith in Cyril's Catholic commitment, seems to have been shaken by the action of the Great Church and Cyril's apparent response to it, and he wrote quickly to the Syrian prelate for the truth as seen from the patriarchal palace. In Cyril al-Zaᶜīm's reply to Poullard, set down in November 1719, the patriarch's rancor toward his refractory metropolitan—for years untouchable because of the unqualified support of his Sidonese flock, the solicitude of the King's consuls and the succor of the *amīr*s of the Lebanon—quite simply erupted, and in that pungent colloquial Arabic which "orientalists," until recently, assured us was never written. From the patriarchal perspective, Euthymius al-Ṣayfī loomed as the hierarch whose independent, often uncanonical behavior, had tended to undermine hierarchy throughout Antioch:

> . . . we have been unable to drive out of him a single cent [*miṣrīya*], receiving from him annually, at most, saltwater fish or forty chunks of Cyprus cheese worth two piastres. . . . [When] . . . we forbade him [to bless an uncanonical marriage], he went back to the [petitioner] . . . swallowed her mouthful and married her. . . . It is because of him that . . . [our] Bishops come to us saying: "Why does not the Metropolitan of Sidon pay you the patriarchal dues? And while you remain silent . . . he blesses many marriages forbidden by our faith."[53]

Cyril cites too Euthymius's vaulting ambitions which, pending a vacancy at Antioch, stretched northward to Beirut and southward to Acre—territory situated, not accidentally, within the area embraced by the political aspirations of the *amīr*s:

> After the recent death of the Metropolitan of Beirut, he urged Amīr Ḥaydar [al-Shihābī] to join [the sees of] Beirut and Sidon that he might assume [over both] the metropolitan dignity. He . . . gave [the amīr] money. We went then to inform the amīr that this was uncanonical and without precedent. He gave us satisfaction but only God knows how much we spent in thwarting [Euthymius].[54]

That Amīr Ḥaydar even contemplated al-Ṣayfī's scheme perhaps testifies to his own interest in securing the loyalty of an ecclesiastical prince who governed much of the trading class of Syria's major port, whose alliance with the French monarch might be turned to advantage, and whose status in Ottoman eyes was as suspect and irregular as his own. Al-Ṣayfī's long and profitable association with the Mountain chieftains may also be seen as an example of the regrouping of Syrian society around local foci of authority.

On the other hand, the Greek ecclesiastics, whose interests would lie for yet another century with the Ottoman central government, were less enthusiastic about Euthymius's machinations, specifically those over the see of Acre. At the center of the Greek Patriarchs' condemnation of al-Ṣayfī on seven counts of uncanonical behavior stood the charge of jurisdictional trespass against the Greek controlled Patriarchate of Jerusalem. "For this," Cyril insists, "did the Patriarchs . . . excommunicate him and strip him of the degrees of priesthood":

> They also solicited a firman decreeing his exile. . . . Although we took the firman and returned it . . . arguing that it was unnecessary, we resolved immediately to send to Euthymius a copy of his excommunication.[55]

Cyril, while informing al-Ṣayfī of his excommunication, claims to have informed no one else for seven months. Learning of this, his Greek colleagues wrote, "rebuking us . . . [and] pressuring us . . . to publish in all the dioceses . . . the text of excommunication." But the strength of al-Ṣayfī's position rested so much on his Uniate status that excommunication by Greeks was nothing compared to an imperial threat of exile. And in the cabal inspired by Ṭānās and his tailor-cousin, to which dà Salamanca alludes, the issue of Cyril's publication of Euthymius's excommunication ranked a distant second to the question of the whereabouts of the firman of exile:

> [Seraphim] marked us to *al-Tarzī Bāshī* [Manṣūr al-Ṣayfī] who then denounced us to the *wazīr* (may God protect him). [He] in turn summoned us. . . . We told him that we had indeed received [the] firman but had returned it to its senders and had washed our hands of it. . . . We ended by paying [him] 100 piastres in addition to 30 piastres . . . to the Porte. This has [Seraphim] done to us.[56]

Not only had Seraphim aroused to avania the *wazīr* of Damascus, ᶜUthmān Pāshā Abū Ṭawq, but he had "wounded us" during his visits to Rome, while his hunger for Acre had helped send the patriarch of Jerusalem scurrying to the Great Church to shake at last the lethargy which had formerly marked Her attitude toward Uniate inroads in Syria.

For in the year 1718 the ecumenical see indeed stirred, and in a manner that illustrates the utterly subordinate status of the Patriarchate of Antioch within the *millet* of the *Rūm*. According to Cyril's own recitation of events, he, the canonical superior of Euthymius, played no part in the deliberations that led to his metropolitan's excommunication. The patriarch was left only the task of spreading abroad the fact of his subordinate's fall and calling upon the Ottoman governor to enforce the firman decreeing the Uniate's exile, a firman elicited by Constantinople probably without the foreknowledge, much less the consent, of her sister Antioch. That Cyril's letter to Poullard betrays no resentment toward the Greek initiative is perhaps as attributable to his conditioned acceptance of status secondary to that of "the chiefs among the Patriarchs" as to his covert delight that their initiative promised to bring to heel that prelate who had been least susceptible to the patriarchal discipline. Cyril, in deference to Rome and Poullard, may indeed have refused to register the firman with the *wālī* of Damascus but he gives every sign of having published with something like pleasure the text of excommunication and of concurring enthusiastically in its indictment, particularly since the text spared Cyril the embarrassment of explicit allusion to al-Ṣayfī's Catholicism.[57] As for the ecumenical see's careful silence on the subject of al-Ṣayfī's devotion to Rome, of which the Great Church must have been abundantly aware, it no doubt reflected the hope that, by removing the metropolitan ostensibly on other grounds, the patriarch of Constantinople might avoid an open confrontation with the French ambassador to the Porte.

The text of excommunication published, dá Salamanca relates:

> There ensued great dissension between Catholics and schismatics . . . in a manner that passed beyond communal hatred into private feud. Ruin spread, and the Devil

> applied his every skill. All murmured but none spoke of a remedy for so grievous an infirmity until . . . Thomas Diaz Campaya . . . a missionary in the hospice of the Franciscans in Damascus, having consulted with his superiors and brethren, undertook to resolve the disagreement between these two princes of the Church. . . . Receiving the permission and thanks of Lord Cyril, [Thomas] travelled to Sidon where . . . his plan was accepted immediately by Lord Bishop Euthymius.[58]

Initially, dà Salamanca confides, Consul Poullard had been kept from the talks between the Spanish Franciscan and the Syrian Uniate largely because the friar was persuaded that the Frenchman would view his mission as ". . . too great an engagement for a single religious [and] more proper for a Consul than for a missionary." But a Uniate prelate whose solemn excommunication by the Great Church had received its temporal complement in an imperial ferman decreeing his exile had little interest in alienating the French consul who had served faithfully and well the spiritual and material interests of the coastal and Damascene Uniates. At the urging of Euthymius, therefore, Poullard was apprised and, despite an abrasive encounter with the friar, appears to have accepted di Campaya's plan to have al-Ṣayfī journey to Damascus and there acknowledge Cyril as his lawful superior ("which until now he has not done"), in return for which submission Cyril would "dispatch patriarchal letters annulling the excommunication. . . ."[59] In sum, a rift between two of the three most consequential Uniate Melkite hierarchs was not to be contemplated with equanimity either by Rome or Versailles. The mutual disdain which often, and certainly in this instance, separated the agents of pope and Catholic monarch in Syria was secondary to their mutuality of interest.

And so Poullard wrote urging Cyril al-Zaᶜīm to receive the metropolitan of Tyre and Sidon,[60] the while applying, we may assume, appropriate pressure upon Euthymius to accept as sincere Cyril's submission to Rome and, acting accordingly, to seek reconciliation with his canonical superior. Concurrently, the formidable friar Thomas di Campaya ("Padre Tūmā" to the Syrians) assured the metropolitan that failure to appear in Damascus would earn him the enmity of all the Franciscans in Syria.[61] So it was that on the fifth of December 1719 Cyril wrote informing Poullard that Euthymius, in company with Padre Tūmā, had arrived; that the metropolitan sojourned now in the patriarchal residence "in all honor and respect"; and that he, Cyril, had written in Euthymius's behalf to Constantinople.[62]

Dà Salamanca too alluded to the benign reception ("well received and by the Lord Patriarch well lodged"), adding that, the patriarch's "repugnance toward the Lord Bishop" notwithstanding, Cyril had opened the way toward settlement by sending to five of his bishops letters voiding Euthymius's excommunication. But, the Franciscan superior continued, "no sooner had he sent the letters than Euthymius sent . . . evil." For dà Salamanca, not to mention di Campaya, believed firmly that the man who appeared recently before the governor of Damascus to accuse the patriarch of having solemnized the union of a Melkite to a Muslim woman had acted in collusion with Euthymius al-Ṣayfī. "Cyril," wrote the friar, "extricated himself by paying six purses [but] felt keenly this cruel ingratitude of the bishop. . . ." The Franciscan added that the patriarch of Antioch felt keenly too the gangrene advancing through his left leg.[63]

On the 31st of January 1720 Euthymius recounted his side of truth. Obedient to their instructions, the metropolitan assured the cardinals of the Propaganda, he had tried to monitor the patriarch's activities that the depth of his Catholic convictions be measured. Unable however to leave his flock he had assigned his nephew Seraphim Ṭānās and Jabrā'īl Fīnān to observe closely while partaking of the patriarchal hospitality:

> And twice they wrote to us that all his conduct is deception. And we are shamed by his fraud against God, against your eminences and against our wretched self, particularly after we received word that he was writing against us to the Patriarchs of Jerusalem and Constantinople. And after a time the words became manifest in the deed and they twice extracted from the Sultan an order calling for our arrest and exile to Anatolia. . . . They [also] . . . decreed our excommunication and sent [the decree] to Cyril who made copies and distributed them throughout the land. . . . Then, because of the . . . disgrace in which the people held him for the offense given us, he implored Padre Tūmā . . . to run . . . to Sidon and bring us to him that he might make peace with us before strife against him multiplied. When we refused to go the Padre threatened us saying: "Should you not journey with me to Damascus you shall see what befalls you as I and all my monks stand against you."

Thus persuaded by the friar's promise, the reluctant prelate crossed the winter-hard Mountain to Canossa-on-Barada.

> [Cyril] welcomed us with fine words and after three days sent documents to Ḥāṣbāyā, Acre, Beirut, and Tripoli, asserting that he had blessed us. We told him: "These papers would benefit us but two or three months before [the Greek Patriarchs] send others; what we desire is that you hand over the Sultan's firman against us." He replied, through Padre Tūmā, that he wished us to retire to the Mountain, to al-Shūf, and not to enter . . . [Sidon], for if we entered the city we would not be safe from their injury. . . . We gained nothing but his words: "Go hide on the Mountain; God bless you." . . . Meanwhile a Muslim made a false charge against Cyril which cost him seven [*sic*] purses. . . . Then [Padre Tūmā] made the rounds of the houses and shops of the city, saying: "Euthymius inspired an avania against the Patriarch and caused him to lose this loss."

Here Euthymius al-Ṣayfī, with apparently perfect equanimity, intrudes these words: "I inform your eminences that the Patriarch developed gangrenous sores in his legs and died."[64]

Thus, on the authority of Euthymius al-Ṣayfī, the last days of Cyril al-Zaᶜīm and the tale of the final fracture and "reconciliation" between the patriarch and his less-than-obedient metropolitan. Euthymius now must have been utterly convinced that Cyril's submission to Rome had been induced by nothing more than opportunism and fear of Uniate and Latin power. Al-Ṣayfī saw as certain, too, the patriarch's complicity in eliciting his excommunication and the firman that promised him arrest and exile. The metropolitan's first point was well taken—only considerations of power beckoned Cyril westward—and Euthymius may not have been wrong in claiming collusion between Damascus and Constantinople. On the other hand, dà Salamanca echoes the patriarch's insistence that the Greeks had acted unilaterally and that Cyril had returned the firman to its senders. Certainly there is no evidence—indeed there is not even Euthymius's testimony—that Cyril ever sought enforcement of the imperial order by registering it with the Ottoman authorities in Damascus. It is of course conceivable that the patriarch neither registered nor returned the firman, preferring, as al-Ṣayfī intimates, to retain it as the device with which to intimidate Sidon's hierarch. Nor is it possible to determine the veracity of the metropolitan's, as opposed to the patriarch's, account of the avania visited upon the latter. Here too, however, al-Ṣayfī's word contradicts dà Salamanca's as well as di Campaya's; and while al-Ṣayfī may be said to have possessed some semblance of motive, he equips his Muslim author of Cyril's humiliation with nothing more than anonymity.

Cyril al-Zaᶜīm's wretched death (from diabetes?) ended but a phase of the protracted struggle between Christendom East and West—a microcosm of the duel between the Muslim East and a less and less Christian West. Even before Cyril took his place in the Cemetery of the Patriarchs on St. George's Hill in Damascus, Euthymius al-Ṣayfī is said to have declared in the presence of Seraphim Ṭānās and Padre Thomas di Campaya his right to the vacant throne of Antioch. Reportedly, Padre Tūmā then "turned to Seraphim and said to him: why not put your uncle straight for I believe he is delirious."[65] In the event, it was Athanasius al-Dabbās who succeeded one old rival and shattered the pretensions of another. Despite the recent antipapal mutterings which spoke his resentment over Rome's negotiations with Cyril, Athanasius had managed to retain Franciscan support as well as the loyalty of the largely Uniate Aleppine Melkites. He had also retained, without fanfare, the bulls of three sovereign popes confirming him as Uniate Patriarch. Euthymius, on the other hand, bore the weakness of his papal proclivities. Under ban of the Greek Patriarchs and under order of exile by the Ottoman sultan, he lacked wide support in Damascus for genuine Uniates there were in the minority and many among them were hostile to Euthymius's uninhibited policy of Latinizing Melkite rite and canon law.[66] In addition, of course, his and Ṭānās's maneuvers over the see of Acre had earned them both the profound bitterness of the Franciscans. In wealth and numbers al-Ṣayfī's devoted Sidonese flock was no match for either the Damascene or Aleppine community, much less the two combined. Whatever influence he carried with the *wālī* of Damascus, ᶜUthmān Pāshā Abū Ṭawq, appears to have been mitigated by the countervailing influence of Consul Poullard who, in acknowledgment of the three bulls, threw his support to the prelate from Aleppo.[67] The consensus held that Euthymius's succession would have constituted an invitation to disorder and avania. The long-awaited prize would best be bestowed upon Athanasius al-Dabbās, whose political dexterity had preserved him in full communion with the Second Rome long after he had submitted to the First. He had adhered more or less faithfully to Eastern usage—thus echoing papal, though not always missionary, policy and doing little to grate the Greek sensibility. He had confined himself to the see of Aleppo and, in contrast to

Euthymius, appeared to threaten no specifically Greek jurisdiction. If the Great Church had been unprepared to cite as cause of excommunication al-Ṣayfī's thirty-five years of ostentatious obedience to Rome, She could scarcely have been expected at this juncture to exploit Athanasius's thirty-four years of studiously silent submission. In 1720 the extent of the Melkite dichotomy demanded the perfect ambiguity of Athanasius rather than the unclouded commitment of Euthymius. Al-Ṣayfī understood something of his predicament. "Ponder," he urged the cardinals of the Propaganda, ". . . and praise God for these strange and miraculous doings":

> Because we fled the oppression of the Greeks we fell into oppression from our own people. . . . Oh, what a land, what remorselessness, what lack of shame and fear of God. I risk my blood, my meager bread and wealth for the victory of the Catholic faith. I have scorned my own Church and upheld the dignity of the Roman Church. I have broadened the path of the missionaries, and the missionaries have sided with the false and visited evil upon us. And what I relate to Your Eminences is but a small part of the large.[68]

Death unburdened Euthymius al-Ṣayfī in November 1723 and dispatched Athanasius al-Dabbās seven months later. Euthymius did not survive to see the Cyrilian and Athanasian ambivalence destroyed by its inner contradictions, by the Uniate and Latin militancy which swelled as Ottoman power ebbed, and by the Phanariot-Ottoman reaction—now firm, now uncertain, and never more than partially successful. Nor would Euthymius witness his nephew inaugurate, soon after the death of Athanasius, the line of unambiguously Uniate patriarchs, even as the Orthodox Melkite throne fell from Syrian control into the Greek hands from whose "oppression" the self-consciously Syrian Euthymius had fled. In this deepening of the Melkite dichotomy into formal schism, one may see reflected the fresh forces reshaping Syrian society in the eighteenth century. Increasingly, Ottoman Istanbul and Greek Constantinople would be compelled to share control over Melkite events and actors not only with refractory *amīr*s and pāshās, symbols of the localism that rose to fill the void left by the retreat of the Ottoman central authority, but with the representatives of Rome and Versailles, heralds of the impending Western hegemony. The emergence of a distinct Uniate Melkite Church, nurtured by indigenous Syrian and extra-Ottoman forces, offers a graphic example of the substitution of new loyalties for those that had informed the classical Ottoman age.

The Melkite schism, too, helps make intelligible the special role played by Orthodox Melkites in eastern Arab affairs since the late nineteenth century—a role which, at the death of Cyril al-Zaʿīm, seemed destined for Uniate players. The Syrian-Arab consciousness evinced in the early eighteenth century by Euthymius al-Ṣayfī and many of his cohorts grew dim among their spiritual progeny. Even before sympathetic Syrian pāshās were swept away by the post-1840 Ottoman restoration, the dependence of Uniate Melkites upon the European and specifically Lebanese connections had deepened. Their leadership, lay and clerical, sought to ease the burden of marginality by abstracting themselves from the Greater Syrian and pan-Arab contexts, in which a Muslim majority had to be assumed, and availing themselves of the protection apparently proffered by Paris, Rome, and a Maronite-dominated Lebanon.

The crystallization of schism subsequent to the era of Cyril al-Za^{c}īm set the Orthodox Melkites down a different road. Counting themselves among the earliest victims of the European intrusion into Ottoman society, the Orthodox faithful would seek their secular salvation less as the political clients of Europeans (Holy Russia's entry into Syria was tardy and her stay brief) than as advocates of European political concepts seemingly fated to govern the Greater Syrian or pan-Arab nation promised by the bright brave future. Compelled early to acknowledge the more obvious implications of Muslim numerical preponderance, the Orthodox Melkites sought an end to marginality itself by urging the creation of polities in which the Islamic definitions would be superseded by others, spun of secular strands and free of confessional distinctions. A nineteenth-century proponent of this position was As^{c}ad Khayyāṭ, an Orthodox Melkite of no influence but of prophetic voice. Among its twentieth-century advocates stand the Orthodox Melkites: Anṭūn Sa^{c}āda, the principal ideologue of Syrian nationalism; and Michel ^{c}Aflaq, chief theorist and cofounder of the pan-Arab Ba^{c}th Party. Their religious background is not incidental to their political persuasions.[69]

Notes

1. On this evolution, see Robert M. Haddad, *Syrian Christians in Muslim Society* Princeton, 1970, pp. 29–49 particularly.

2. The original Arabic version of Athanasius's profession of Uniate faith rests in l'Archivio della S. Congregazione di Propaganda Fide [henceforth cited as Arch. Prop.], Scritture riferite nei Congressi [henceforth cited as SC], vol. 4, fol. 4 (Ital. trans., fols. 5–8). A French translation may be found in A. Rabbath, ed., *Documents inédits pour servir à l'histoire du christianisme en orient,* Paris, 1905–1921, vol. 2, p. 107.

3. The text of Euthymius's profession of Uniate faith may be found in Qusṭanṭīn al-Bāshā, *Ta'rīkh* ṭā'ifat al-Rūm al-malakiyyīn, Sidon vol. 1, 1938, pp. 105–106.

4. On al-Ṣayfī's relations with the *amīrs,* see L. Shaykhū, "Aftimiyūs Ṣayfī, Muṭrān Ṣaydā, munshi' al-rahbāniyyat al-mukhalliṣiyyat," *Al-Machriq,* 14, 1911, 647–648; Haddad, pp. 37–38 and n. 49; al-Bāshā (cited n. 3), vol. 1, pp. 210–247; below p. 81.

5. On the probable connections between the Melkites of Damascus and those of Sidon, see Haddad (cited n. 1) p. 47, n. 62.

6. On which, see ibid., pp. 40–46.

7. Arch. Prop., Le Scritture originali riferite nelle Congregazioni Generali [henceforth cited as SOCG], vol. 585, fol. 328 (manuscript), fol. 330 (printed), Euthymius to S. Congregation, Sidon, 9/15/1713, in Arabic (Ital. trans., fols. 325–329); edited version in al-Bāshā (cited n. 3), vol. 1, pp. 272–276.

8. Joseph Hajjar, *Les chrétiens uniates du Proche-Orient,* Paris, 1962, pp. 243–44. See also below, p. 73 and Qusṭanṭīn al-Bāshā, *Muḥaḍara fī ta'rīkh ṭa'ifat al-Rūm al-kāthūlīk fī Miṣr* Ḥarīṣā, Lebanon, n.d., pp. 21–22.

9. France. Archives Nationales. Ministère des affaires étrangères [henceforth cited as A.E.], B[1]1020, fol. 82, Poullard au Conseil de Marine, Sidon, 10/4/1716; ibid., fol. 274, Poullard au Conseil de Marine, Sidon, 11/15/1717; Arch. Prop., SC, vol. I, fol. 303, Poullard à Mgr. Macario, Seyde, 10/5/1717, in French.

10. Ibid., fols. 183–188, Fra Lorenzo to Cyril, Jerusalem, 3/10/1714, in Italian; ibid., fols. 30–33, "Alla . . . Clemente P.P. XI . . . per li cattolici del Patriarcato Antiocheno in Oriente," n.p., n.d., in Italian. Of all the Latins, the Franciscans in Damascus and Jerusalem appear to have exerted the greatest influence upon Cyril in this period.

11. I have been unable to find the letter itself but Cyril several times alludes to it [Arch. Prop., SOCG, vol. 608, fols. 98, 100, Cyril to Clement XI, Damascus, 8/20/1716, in Arabic (Ital. trans., fols. 109–111); ibid., fol. 304, Cyril to Clement XI, Damascus, 9/8/1716, in Arabic; ibid., fol. 368, Cyril to S. Congregation, Damascus, 9/8/1716, in Arabic (Ital. trans., fol. 113)] as does Euthymius al-Ṣayfī [ibid., fol. 117, Euthymius to Clement XI, Dayr al-Mukhalliṣ, 9/20/1716, in Arabic (Ital. trans., fol. 115)] and Consul Poullard (A.E., B[1]1020, fol. 82, Poullard au Conseil de Marine, Sidon, 10/4/1716), among others.

12. Arch. Prop., SOCG, vol. 608, fols. 98, 100, Cyril to Clement XI, Damascus, 8/20/1716, in Arabic (Ital. trans., fols. 109–111). This letter has been inaccurately edited by al-Bāshā (cited n. 3), vol. 1, pp. 309–314, apparently in the interests of portraying Cyril as a firm Uniate.

13. In 1676, during his struggle against a Greek patriarchal claimant, Neophytus the Chiot, and again in 1686, during his brief contest with Athanasius al-Dabbās.

14. By this time, of course, every Orthodox Christian patriarchate within the Ottoman Empire, save the Antiochian, either had been suppressed by the Ecumenical Patriarchate or was governed by Greek prelates dependent upon the Great Church.

15. The Maronites would seem to have been the exception, but it is to be remembered that, while their adherence to Rome dated from the time of the Crusades, it was but recently that Rome found herself able to exert much influence over them. The Maronites, moreover, remained concentrated largely in the Lebanon, an area which the Ottomans were rarely able to govern directly.

16. It would appear that, in these matters, the Maronites had come to adhere to Western rather than Eastern canons.

17. Cyril instructed the friar to make clear to the pope: that Syrian Christian vessels must be protected from the corsairs; that Latins are not to administer communion to Melkites (this, Cyril insisted correctly, in conformity to a decision of the Council of Florence); and that the canons governing marriage derive from the Seven Councils and forbid marriage within the third and fourth degree of consanguinity as well as the ordination of the twice-married (Arch. Prop., SOCG, vol. 608, fol. 149, Cyril to Biaggio [Damascus], 8/20/1716, in Arabic; Ital. trans., fol. 148).

18. Arch. Prop., SOCG, vol. 608, fol. 117, Euthymius to Clement XI, Dayr al-Mukhalliṣ, 9/20/1716, in Arabic (Ital. trans., fol. 115); ibid., fol. 105, Poullard to Monseigneur, Sidon, 10/3/1716, in French; ibid., fols. 138–139, Poullard to Clement XI, Sidon, 10/3/1716, in French (a copy of the same letter is also to be found in A.E., B[1]1020, fol. 86); Arch. Prop., SC, vol. 1, fols. 254–255, Poullard to di Cavaglieri, Sidon, 10/6/1716, in Italian; A.E., B[1]1020, fol. 66, Poullard au Conseil de Marine, Sidon, 8/28/1716.

19. Arch. Prop., SOCG, vol. 608, fol. 117, Euthymius to Clement XI, Dayr al-Mukhalliṣ, 9/20/1716, in Arabic (Ital. trans., fol. 115).

20. Ibid.

21. Ibid.

22. A.E., B[1]1020, fols. 81–84, Poullard au Conseil de Marine, Sidon, 10/4/1716; Arch. Prop., SOCG, vol. 608, fol. 138, Poullard to Clement XI, Sidon, 10/3/1716, in French.

23. A.E., B[1]1020, fols. 82–83, Poullard au Conseil de Marine, Sidon, 10/4/1716.

24. Arch. Prop., SOCG, vol. 608, fol. 304, Cyril to Clement XI, Damascus, 9/8/1716, in Arabic.

25. On the doubts expressed concerning Cyril's submission, see below, pp. 76, 78–79.

26. A.E., B[1]1020, fols. 83–84, Poullard au Conseil de Marine, Sidon, 10/4/1716.

27. Arch. Prop., SC, vol. 1, fols. 259–260, n.p., n.d., in Italian. This document represents a summary of the exchange between the ambassador and cardinal, rather than the texts of the exchange themselves. The document's substance suggests that the exchange took place in late 1716 or early 1717.

28. Ibid.

29. Unless otherwise indicated, quotations used in the following discussion of the letter are drawn from the letter itself (ibid., fols. 30–33, "Alla . . . Clemente P. P. XI . . . per li cattolici del Patriarcato Antiocheno in Orienté," n.p., n.d., in Italian).

30. See document cited n. 7.

31. The phrase actually used by Cyril is "you compelled us" [Arch. Prop., SOCG, vol. 625, fol. 444, Cyril to Poullard, Damascus, 11/?/1719, in Arabic (Ital. trans., fols. 440–442); al-Bāshā (cited n. 3), vol. 1, 403–408, provides a poorly edited version of this document.]

32. Arch. Prop., SOCG, vol. 609, fol. 594, Isṭifān ᶜAṭāllāh to S. Congregation, Damascus, 2/15/1717, in Arabic (Ital. trans., fol. 596); edited version in al-Bāshā (cited n. 3), vol. 1, 397.

33. Arch. Prop., SOCG, vol. 609, fol. 593, ᶜAṭāllāh to Clement XI, Damascus, 2/15/1717, in Arabic (Ital. trans., fol. 595); edited version in al-Bāshā (cited n. 3), vol. 1, 396.

34. See document cited n. 32.

35. Ibid.

36. A.E., B[1]1020, fol. 274, Poullard au Conseil de Marine, Sidon, 11/15/1717.

37. Arch. Prop., SC, vol. 1., fol. 303, Poullard à Mgr. Macario, Sidon, 10/5/1717, in French.

38. A.E., B[1]1020, fol. 278, "Copie d'une lettre de M. Cyrille . . . envoyée le 5 Novembre 1717 au Consul de Seyde pour la S. Congrégation." There is no sign of the original Arabic from which this document is a French translation.

39. Ibid.

40. A.E., B[1]1020, fol. 274, Poullard au Conseil de Marine, Seyde, 11/15/1717.

41. Arch. Prop., SOCG, vol. 625, fol. 495, Jabrā'īl Fīnān to M. Caraffa, Secretary of the S. Congregation, n.p.; 7/11/1719 (Julian), in Arabic (Ital. trans., fols. 463–464); edited version in al-Bāshā (cited n. 3), vol. 1, pp. 398–400.

42. Arch. Prop., SC, vol. I, fol. 341, "Articles d'une lettre du Consul de France. . . .," Sidon, 4/29/1719, in French.

43. This is distinctly the impression conveyed by Fīnān; see his letter cited n. 41.

44. See document cited n. 42.

45. See document cited n. 41.

46. Ibid.

47. Arch. Prop., SC, vol. I, fol. 358, Seraphim Ṭānās to S. Congregation [Damascus?], 10/1/1719, in Italian trans.

48. Arch. Prop., SOCG, vol. 625, fol. 481, Cyril to Cardinal Sacripanti, Damascus, 9/1/1719, in Arabic (Ital. trans., fols. 479–480).

49. Ibid., fol. 486, Cyril to Clement XI [Damascus], 9/1/1719, in Arabic (Ital. trans., fols. 484, 487). Cyril's allusion to "the desecration of monasteries and the murder of monks" concerns the corsairs' pillage, in March 1717, of Dayr Nāṭūr, located above Tripoli. In the attack, one aged monk was killed. See A.E., B[1]1020, fol. 158, Fakhr to Jalabī, 3/17/1717, in Arabic (French trans., fols. 159–160).

50. Ibid., vol. 622, fol. 479, ᶜAṭāllāh to S. Congregation, Dayr al-Mukhalliṣ, 9/15/1719, in Arabic (Ital. trans., fols. 476–477); edited version in al-Bāshā (cited n. 3) vol. 1, pp. 400–402.

51. Arch. Prop., SC, vol. I, fol. 341, "Articles d'une lettre du Consul de France," Sidon, 4/29/1719, in French.

52. Ibid., fol. 384, "Breve e veridico ragguaglio del succeduto in Damasco . . . dall'Aprile 1719 all'Aprile 1720," by dà Salamanca, Damascus, 4/28/1720, in Italian.

53. Arch. Prop., SOCG, vol. 625, fol. 444, Cyril to Poullard, Damascus, 11/?/1719, in Arabic (Ital. trans., fols. 440–442); al-Bāshā (cited n. 3), vol. 1, pp. 403–408, provides a poorly edited version of this document.

54. Ibid.

55. Ibid.

56. Ibid.

57. Both Cyril and dà Salamanca attest to the absence, in the document of excommunication, of any reference to Euthymius's submission to Rome (ibid.; fol. 384 of document cited n. 52).

58. Ibid., fols. 384–385.

59. Ibid., fol. 385.

60. We know of this letter only through Cyril's reply to it (n. 62).

61. Below, p. 84.

62. Arch. Prop., SOCG, vol. 625, fol. 456, Cyril to Poullard [Damascus], 12/5/1719, in Arabic (Ital. trans., fol. 455).

63. Document cited n. 52, fols. 385–386.

64. Arch. Prop., SOCG, vol. 625, fol. 453, Euthymius to S. Congregation [Damascus?], 1/31/1720, in Arabic (Ital. trans., fols. 451–452); edited version in al-Bāshā (cited n. 3), vol. 1, pp. 408–412.

65. Document cited n. 52, fol. 386.

66. Even Euthymius appears to admit Damascene receptivity to the argument that his departures from Eastern custom made him unfit for the patriarchate. See document cited n. 64; also Haddad (cited n. 1), pp. 54–57 and n. 71; Arch. Prop., SOCG, vol. 636, fol. 137, Athanasius to S. Congregation, Aleppo. 9/23/1721, in Arabic (Ital. trans., fols. 134, 139).

67. Ibid., vol. 624, fol. 266, Poullard à Caraffa, Sidon, 2/20/1720, in French (Ital. trans. fol. 270).

68. Document cited n. 64.

69. For a fuller discussion of these themes, see Haddad (cited n. 1), especially pp. 49ff; compare below, Volume II, chapter 6, by Kamal S. Salibi.

4

Communal Conflicts in Ottoman Syria during the Reform Era: The Role of Political And Economic Factors*

MOSHE MA^cOZ

Introduction

The intercommunal relations in the Syrian *eyalets* of the Ottoman Empire underwent a substantial transformation during the *Tanzimat* period. Although the *Tanzimat* regime aimed at creating a new pattern of intergroup accommodation and fraternity among all Ottoman subjects, in Syria it served in effect to aggravate and further polarize the intercommunal relationships particularly between Muslims and Christians as well as between Christians and Jews. The relations between Muslims and Christians, which for generations were shaped by tolerable coexistence under Muslim dictates, became highly antagonistic under the reforms: the traditional Muslim attitudes of contempt for and humiliation of *ahl al-dhimma* turned into deep hatred for Christians but not for Jews. Similarly, while traditional Muslim-Jewish relations hardly changed, and in part even improved during the *Tanzimat* era, the age-old Christian-Jewish conflict sharpened and became worse than ever before under Ottoman rule.

Simultaneously, relations between Muslim heterodox sects, notably the Druzes, on the one hand, and *ahl al-dhimma,* particularly Christian Maronites, on the other hand, turned violent during the middle of the nineteenth century;

*My chapter is based on research into the role of religious and ethnic minorities in the modern history of Syria, in which I am presently engaged. A shorter version has appeared as ''Intercommunal Relations in Ottoman Syria during the Tanzimat Era: Social and Economic Factors,'' Osman Okyar and Halil Inalcik, eds. *Social and Economic History of Turkey (1071–1920),* Ankara, 1980, pp. 205–210.

while the traditional hostile feelings between the Sunnis and the *rawāfid,* as those among the various Christian sects, did not by any means abate in the course of the *Tanzimat* period. A British observer who spent several years in Syria during the early 1870s described these intersectarian feelings as follows:

> They hate one another. The Sunnites excommunicate the Shiahs and both hate the Druzes; all detest the Ansariyyehs; the Maronites do not love anybody but themselves and are duly abhorred by all; the Greek orthodox abominate the Greek Catholics and the Latins, all despise the Jews.[1]

These animosities were periodically manifested in great physical violence which resulted in heavy loss of life, breach of human honor, and destruction of property. The most violent and best known, or rather notorious, cases were the Druze-Maronite civil war in Lebanon between 1840 and 1860, the 1840 Damascus "blood libel" by Christians against Jews, and the Muslim riots against the Christians of Aleppo and Damascus in 1850 and 1860 respectively. It is evident that the major factors which led to this Muslim-Christian intercommunal polarization were religio-political in their nature. The bulk of the Muslim population in the Syrian provinces objected to the freedom of worship and to the equal political status granted to *ahl al-dhimma* by the Egyptian regime in the 1830s and subsequently by *Tanzimat* edicts, in 1839 and 1856. Many Muslims, particularly in the ranks of the *ʿulamā'* and notables, feared that the equal status granted to Christians would in all likelihood damage the Islamic character of the state and endanger their own dominant positions in government institutions and in the political community of the Ottoman-Muslim regime.

Yet, although religio-political causes, and motives of self-preservation, played a dominant role in shaping the newly emerging Muslim-Christian conflict, social, and economic forces (as well as cultural, psychological, and other factors) were also interwoven into that complex fabric of intergroup relations. These forces, predominant in Christian-Jewish rivalry, had indeed a marked impact also on the scope and depth of the Muslim-Christian conflict in Ottoman Syria. In this paper a preliminary attempt will be made to examine the relative weight and impact of these various factors and motives on the triangular intergroup relationship between Muslims, Christians, and Jews in the Syrian provinces (excluding Lebanon) during the *Tanzimat* period.

The Prereform Period

As a background note it should be pointed out that during the prereform period economic and social factors constituted a major source of conflict between Muslims and non-Muslims in the Syrian *eyalet*s. For the *dhimmī* population, although small in number (particularly Jews), had a large share in the country's economic activities, such as trade and commerce, banking and moneylending, gold and silver work, and the like. In addition, a considerable number of Christians and Jews were accepted into government service because of their higher education, and served as advisers to the pashas, treasury officials, accountants, and clerks; some of them occupied senior positions in the provincial administration. Naturally, the economic gains and the public status acquired by members of *ahl al-dhimma* produced feelings of envy and greediness on the part of various sections of the Muslim population. But those Muslims who actually managed to satisfy their lust for the *dhimmī*'s wealth were, by and large, local governors, notables, and military officers. These individuals would use, or rather misuse, their powers in order to extract large sums of money in various ways from wealthy non-Muslims, as well as from certain Jewish communities or Christian convents as "loans" and "donations," "protection" or "ransom" money, "special taxes," or "gifts."[2] In contrast, the Muslim common people had only few opportunities to squeeze money from the *dhimmī*s, partly because this was normally the "protected monopoly" of the governors, notables, and officers, partly because the Muslim masses themselves were oppressed and exploited by those functionaries, and partly because the *dhimmī*s were careful not to provoke the Muslims' jealousy and greed.

The main area of conflict between the Muslim common people and *ahl al-dhimma* was, in effect, socioreligious. Muslims would occasionally force Christians and Jews to abide by the discriminatory religious and social rules, which had stemmed from the covenant of ᶜUmar, regarding restrictions on public worship and behavior. These included obligation to wear clothing only of certain colors as well as the prohibition to ride on horseback in towns or to walk alongside Muslims in the streets.[3] In order to remind the *dhimmī*s of their inferior status, Muslims would periodically maltreat and humiliate them, particularly those who transgressed the traditional discriminatory regulations.

The *dhimmī*s, on their part, in an attempt to avoid conflict with Muslims, would normally dress inconspicuously, reside in humble houses, and engage in their internal affairs within the *millet* system. This approach, together with the fact that the Christians and Jews also acquiesced in their inferior legal-political status in the country served to mitigate Muslim antagonism toward the *dhimmī*s, and helped to maintain the traditional structure of tolerable intergroup coexistence between Muslims and non-Muslims.

The Emergence of the Muslim-Christian Conflict: Religio-political Factors

The traditional fabric of intercommunal coexistence was torn in the Syrian provinces during the reform era which commenced under Egyptian rule in the 1830s and continued throughout the *Tanzimat* period up to the reign of Sultan ᶜAbdülhamid II. The newly emerging pattern of relations between Muslims and Christians was characterized by strong feelings of hatred mixed with fear. These feelings found their outlet in widespread aggression, and, for the first time in centuries, in several bloody massacres of Christians.

Indeed, for the first time in their history Muslims throughout Syria faced the shocking sight of public Christian cross processions and heard the alarming sound of church bells. Muslim religious and political leaders were, furthermore, stunned by the official Ottoman proclamations which abolished the *jizya* on the non-Muslim subjects in 1855 and granted them equal political rights by the *Hatt-i Hümayun* of 1856. Syrian Muslims joined their brethren throughout the Ottoman Empire in protest. As Cevdet describes it: "Today we have lost our sacred national rights which our ancestors gained with their blood; while the nation used to be the ruling nation it is now bereft of this sacred right. This is a day of tears and mourning for the Muslim brethren."[4]

Yet these religio-political grievances, however deep and widespread, could not alone motivate all Syrian Muslims into transforming their feelings of animosity into acts of physical violence against their Christian neighbors.

In fact the extent of Muslim anti-Christian aggression, like the intensity of Muslim hatred of Christians, varied in different places and periods, being determined to a considerable degree by additional factors.

Obviously, the positions taken by the Ottoman authorities, particularly the local governors, regarding, on the one hand, the implementation of equal rights for Christians and, on the other, the checking of Muslim violence, greatly influenced the degree of Muslim aggression toward Christians. Thus in places where Ottoman pashas overlooked or even supported—from weakness or identification with—local Muslim opposition to Christians, the level of Muslim violence against Christians was naturally higher than in areas where pashas endeavored to protect their Christian subjects and secure their new rights. It should be pointed out, in this connection, that even strong and liberal pashas—let alone weak or conservative ones—made no special effort to implement measures concerning Christian political equality,[5] nor would pashas of this category be eager to or capable of efficiently defending their Christian subjects under all circumstances. Such situations occurred when Christian behavior was particularly provocative in the eyes of the Muslims and/or was regarded as defying government orders. Thus, for example, the Aleppo riot of 1850 and the Damascus massacre of 1860 were both influenced, to a certain degree, by acts such as: "The Greek Catholic Patriarch Maximus is accused of having excited the ill will of the Mussulmans by a sort of triumphant entry which he made not long since into Aleppo with much pomp and great display of costly church ornaments"[6] or "a large bell lately placed in the Maronite church gave great umbrage" to the Muslims of Damascus, as did the opening of wineshops in the town marketplaces[7] or the refusal of Damascus Christians to pay the compulsory *bedel* to the government.[8] To be sure, in the Aleppo event the Ottoman *vali,* Mustafa Zarif Paşa, was unable, for other reasons as well, to stop the riot while in the Damascus case the *vali,* Aḥmad Paşa, adopted various steps which in fact encouraged the Muslim rioters.[9] Ottoman pashas were especially unable or unwilling to check outbursts of local anti-Christian sentiment at times of Christian-European attacks or threats against the Ottoman Empire. On such occasions these pashas would tend to identify and sympathize with the local Muslims' belief that the "European powers are hostile to the Turkish authorities in Syria . . . and in union with the Christians they wish to overset it."[10]

Indeed, it should be emphasized that the Syrian Muslims' anger at, and/or fear of, external European threat to Islam, the Ottoman state, and to their own destiny constituted perhaps the deepest and most lasting result of the newly emerging Muslim-Christian antagonism. This factor had already developed during the prereform era. In 1799 when the Napoleonic troops invaded Palestine from Egypt, Muslims in Damascus rioted against their Christian neighbors;[11] and in 1821 when the Greek revolt broke out, Christians were attacked by Muslims in many parts of Syria and Palestine.[12] During the reform era, Muslim suspicions of the local Christians' association with European powers grew stronger in reaction to both the widespread expansion of European activities within Syria and the mounting military pressures of European powers on the borders of the Ottoman Empire. Thus the wars waged by Czarist Russia against the Ottoman Empire in remote places such as the Crimea in 1853–1855, Central Asia and the Balkans in 1868–1873 and 1876–1877 triggered anti-Christian outbursts among Syrian Muslims.[13] During the Russo-Turkish War of 1876–1877, for example, Muslims in several Syrian towns claimed that their Christian neighbors "caused the war,"[14] or "insisted on having from the *mufti* a *fetva* declaring it lawful to kill Christians,"[15] and then set upon them. In attacking their Christian fellow countrymen the Muslims did not make a distinction between those affiliated with Russia or with other European powers, nor did Syrian Muslims clear the Western powers—France and England—the veteran allies of the Ottomans, from suspicion. To be sure these powers engaged in periodic actions which, in Syrian Muslim eyes, affected *dar al-Islam* as well as the integrity of Ottoman and Syrian territory. Such actions were, for example, the French occupation of Algeria (1830) and Tunisia (1881) and the landing of French troops in Lebanon in August 1860. The British were likewise blamed for putting down the Muslim rebellion in India (1857) and for the occupation of Cyprus (1878) and Egypt (1882). In addition, British and French warships patrolled the Syrian coast at times of intercommunal tension and once, in 1858, shelled the port of Jidda after their consuls were murdered by local mobs. Simultaneously during the nineteenth century the French and British, as well as the Russians, established vast networks of political, economic, and cultural links with the Christian communities throughout the Syrian provinces, thus intensifying the Muslims' suspicions and anxieties regarding the dangerous association between the European powers and local Christians. Consequently almost any hostile action undertaken by the European powers against Muslim dominions, let alone Ottoman Syria, would provoke Muslim ill feeling and aggressive acts against their Christian neighbors: the most conspicuous cases of this sort were the Russian offensive in the Crimea, the French landing in Lebanon in 1860,[16] and the ᶜUrabi Egyptian revolt against the British in 1882.[17]

In summary, it should be pointed out that the European activities, whatever their extent, obviously served to undermine or retard the efforts made, particularly after the bloody events of 1860, to establish a common basis of intercommunal coexistence and accommodation in Ottoman Syria. This was not only due to the direct military pressures and political intervention of the big powers in Ottoman dominions, but also to the indirect impact of European economic activities in the Syrian provinces during the reform era.

The Impact of Socioeconomic Factors

Broadly speaking, the development of Muslim antagonism toward Christians during the reform era was linked to new socioeconomic changes in Syrian towns. On the one hand there was the remarkable and conspicuous economic prosperity of many Syrian Christians and their rapid emancipation from the old restrictions on their public conduct. On the other hand there developed a growing economic gap between Christians from upper and middle classes and Muslims from the middle and lower classes; the latter, as well as some rich Muslims, also suffered from the new economic and political developments. For example, the expansion of Syrian foreign trade, notably imports from Europe, following the Egyptian occupation, helped especially to enrich local Christian merchants who acted as agents and brokers for European firms, whereas most Muslim merchants hardly benefited from this economic development. In contrast, the great influx of European goods, which were sold cheaply (under the capitulations agreements) contributed to the destruction of the traditional local industry particularly in Damascus and Aleppo. As Baedeker witnessed in the 1870s: "European industry chiefly introduced by Christians has almost extinguished the native manufacturers."[18] This process, consequently, undermined the livelihood of many Muslim craftsmen, artisans, and traders, the backbone of the Muslim urban middle class.[19]

Simultaneously, the establishment of a strong government and a modern administration, as well as a network of European consulates in the Syrian provinces after 1831, provided the Christians with a guarantee for their socioeconomic ascendancy and enabled many of them to utilize their higher education in order to occupy various positions in the expanding government and consular administration.[20] By contrast this government was able to deprive some Muslim notables of certain financial benefits they formerly enjoyed; it also managed to levy regular taxes and recruits from the Muslim masses, thus bringing hardship and poverty to many families.[21] Related to this development was the growing socioeconomic cleavage and credibility gap between wealthy Muslim notables and the *'ulama* on the one hand, and, on the other hand, the lower classes of the population who were exploited as a result of a tacit understanding between local notables and Ottoman pashas.[22] Due to all these socioeconomic changes, there developed among the different classes of Muslims antagonistic and hostile attitudes toward Christian economic prosperity, social ascendancy, and cultural superiority. To quote a contemporary source: "Their growth in wealth, and the appointment of their prominent men had kindled fires of fanatical hatred and preparations were made for the destruction of their Christian vassals. . . ."[23] It is not inconceivable that not a few Muslims were concerned lest the Christians "should take advantage of the power which their financial resources give them to encompass the destruction of the Moslem either by corrupting or impoverishing him."[24]

These feelings were particularly strong in Damascus and Aleppo where Muslims were greatly hurt by the new economic trends, notably by Christian competition, and where Christians' behavior was regarded by Muslims as highly provocative. In Damascus, for example, "The splendid houses built by the rich class of Christians excited jealousy and their general prosperity tended to create in the Mussulmans feelings of envy. The persons who managed the affairs of the pashalik were Christian, they kept the public accounts and grew richer in the employment. The Christian traders were more prosperous than the Mussulmans."[25] Some of the Christian government employees were tax collectors and custom officers who levied taxes and duties from Muslims, sometimes at allegedly high rates; while Christian (and Jewish) moneylenders would also lend money to Muslims at exorbitant interest.[26]

With regard to public behavior, some Christians in Damascus occasionally dressed like Muslims, sometimes even in green colors; wealthy individuals employed Muslim male and female slaves, while Christian businessmen opened wineshops in the markets.[27] All this occurred in addition to the erection of new Christian establishments, the ringing of church bells, and the carrying of crosses in street processions.[28]

The Muslim reaction in Damascus was not late in coming. By the early 1840s Muslim merchants and craftsmen, who had been affected by the new economic trends, were already endeavoring to undermine the livelihood of their Christian colleagues by restricting their production or forcing them to employ only Muslim workers.[29]

Muslim common people, hurt by the new government measures, envious of Christian economic prosperity, and provoked by Christian public conduct, would insult, maltreat, and physically attack Christians when the opportunity arose. Muslim notables and *ᶜulamā'*, who were greatly upset by the new religious and political privileges granted to the Christians, and were perhaps trying to divert Muslim popular grievances against themselves toward the Christians, chose, with certain exceptions, to incite the Muslim masses against their Christian neighbors. Consequently, this combination of feelings and reactions which had been building up since the early 1830s finally burst out in 1860 in the massacre of Christians in the city of Damascus.[30]

As in Damascus, socioeconomic factors in Aleppo played an important role in shaping the Muslim-Christian conflict during the early reform period, and in precipitating the attack against Christians by Muslims in 1850. Here again the forces at work were the government decision to abolish the opulent *itizams* and demand heavy arrears from ᶜAbdulla Babilsi, the wealthy and powerful local leader,[31] and the new measures of conscription and personal taxation *(ferde)* which threatened to undermine the livelihood of many Muslim families. Various sections of the Muslim population were also antagonized by "the increasing prosperity and ascendancy" of local Christians, the employment of Muslim slaves in Christian houses, and the public manifestations of Christian religious worship, such as "A Greek [Catholic] bishop . . . unwisely ostentatious in his sacerdotal pomp and retinue; gold-embroidered saddle-cloth on the episcopal mule [which] was too much for Islam to bear . . . worst of all a rich Christian had dared to refuse a loan to a needy [Muslim] notable."[32]

To sum up this analysis of the role of socioeconomic grievances in the Muslim-Christian conflict, it is worthwhile indicating that whereas Muslim notables were those mainly responsible for instigating the Aleppo and Damascus pogroms, the riots themselves were executed largely by the local mobs enforced with groups of neighboring nomads and Druzes. The chief common aims of these rioters were to loot and rape.[33] The few Christians who had managed to buy off the rioters prior to the riots were able to save their lives.[34]

If the cases of Aleppo and Damascus point to the significant role of economic and social forces in sharpening Muslim antagonism toward Christians, there is evidence to suggest that certain social and economic factors had, conversely, also a moderating effect on the Muslim-Christian religio-political conflict during the reform period. Thus in places like Beirut and Jerusalem where both communities enjoyed economic prosperity, Muslim attitudes toward Christians were relatively milder and more tolerant. As the local English consuls reported in 1853 and 1856 respectively: "Thirteen years of peace, commercial emulation and industry had contributed to soften down the intolerance and hatred which the Mussulmen in Beyrout were wont to exhibit towards their Christian countrymen. . . ."[35] Regarding Jerusalem we are told that "all communities are advancing . . . from wealth"[36] and "that the Muslems subsist upon the means of livelihood afforded in various ways by the Christians"[37] while "old prejudices are abating and liberality of sentiment greatly increased . . . inasmuch as the Moslems live by the trade created by pilgrimage and by letting houses to Europeans" and by also obtaining monies from the Christian convents.[38] Thus, "a combination of the Moslems against Christians in this district has been improbable for first the Jerusalem Effendis are likely from pecuniary motives to disapprove of insurrection."[39]

It also seems that in such towns Muslims had been long accustomed to the public appearance and religious activities of their Christian neighbors and were thus not easily provoked by Christian publik conduct; or it is likely that Christians in such towns, being aware of their limits and their proper place in the country, were careful not to antagonize the Muslims, and consequently contributed to the avoidance of intercommunal conflicts.

Muslim-Jewish Relationship: The Traditional Pattern Continues

If some Christians were careful not to antagonize their Muslim neighbors this was also, by and large, true of the Jewish communities in the Muslim Syrian environment throughout the period of reform. This, along with other reasons, explains why Jews were much less exposed than Christians to Muslim animosity and attacks in Syrian towns, notably Aleppo and Damascus, where during the anti-Christian riots Jews were not hurt at all.

It is true that more than a few Jews, particularly in Damascus and Aleppo, enjoyed during the *Tanzimat* era—as during the prereform period—economic prosperity and some social status as merchants, bankers, moneylenders, and as officials in the provincial government administration. In these positions and functions they occasionally affected the interests, and aroused the envy of various Muslim groups such as notables, traders, moneyborrowers as well as mobs. Consequently, from time to time Jews were intimidated, blackmailed, maltreated, or killed by Muslims who were motivated by economic and/or socioreligious incentives. Such cases occurred comparatively more frequently in Palestinian towns where the Jews were largely foreign subjects, and the government control was fairly lax.[40]

Basically, however, the Muslim attitude to Jews was not different now from what it had been before the reforms. It manifested the traditional contemptuous toleration of an inferior class of *ahl al-dhimma,* but was devoid of the hatred which Muslims had developed for Christians. The major reason for this Muslim-Jewish accommodation was that the Jewish private self-image and public conduct remained essentially unchanged under the *Tanzimat* regime. As Ubicini described the Ottoman Jews in the 1840s ". . . this tranquility under Ottoman rule so opposite to the agitations and convulsions of other raiahs . . . is explained partly by the peaceable habits and disposition of the Jews, which cause no umbrage to the porte . . . patient industrious and resigned to their fate, they wear without apparent sense of humiliation the coloured benish (Jehoudane) which the ancient sumptuary laws of the empire enjoined as a mark to distinguish them from the Mussulman."[41] Indeed, the Jews in the Syrian provinces continued to conduct their religious affairs and social behavior in a modest manner. Unlike the Christians they normally did not erect magnificent synagogues nor worship publicly. They were the first to discharge their Muslim slaves when requested and the last to dress like Muslims when permitted.[42] Jews also continued to pay local Muslim notables and leaders sums of money as a kind of "insurance fee" in order to guarantee or protect the lives and property of their communities against assaults and encroachments by both these leaders and by mobs. In certain places these fees were paid to Muslim leaders, or rather taken by them, in a regular manner. The local leader of Hebron, Shaykh ᶜAbd al-Raḥmān, for example, "has had himself enrolled on the books of the Jewish Treasury as a pensioner for 100 piasters a month, and always sends for his pension two days before the day of due."[43] Likewise a Muslim member of the Jerusalem council "declared his right derived from time immemorial in his family to enter Jewish houses and take toll and contributions at any time without giving account."[44]

Although these payments did not always save Jews from further exactions, they certainly contributed to saving many Jewish lives. Indeed, during the Aleppo and Damascus riots the local Jewish communities were not harmed at all, largely thanks to great sums of money which they paid or had paid to Muslim leaders prior to the events.[45]

Yet it must be pointed out that the Jews of Aleppo and Damascus were saved not only because they managed to neutralize or satisfy the financial grudge or greed of their Muslim neighbors. In the first place, the Jews of Syria remained relatively secure because they were careful not to stir up or attract the Muslims' political hostility—a factor which constituted the chief cause of Muslim antagonism and violence toward Christians. In summing up the factors which shaped the pattern of Muslim-Jewish coexistence in contrast to the Muslim-Christian conflict[46] it should be emphasized that most Syrian Jews, unlike many local Christians, remained apolitical during the reform era in spite of the political equality officially granted to them under the *Tanzimat* edicts. They were content with the religious privileges and economic opportunities afforded to them and did not insist on obtaining full political rights as they realized that this was infeasible. At the same time, the Jews of Syria also continued their prolonged efforts to win the goodwill and sympathy of the Muslims also by demonstrating their loyalty to the Ottoman state and by siding with Muslims at times of Muslim-Christian tensions. Thus, for example, like their brethren in Turkey who had joined Muslims in attacking Christians during the Greek revolt,[47] Jews in Syria either actively aided or passively sided with Muslims, who attacked Christians during both the Crimean War and the Damascus riot. As for the former event, Syrian Jews, apart from donating money to the Crimean War effort, were accused by Christians of having paraded in the streets, hoisting a cross tied to a shoe and yelling *"Allahu yanṣur al-Sulṭān, Allahu yalᶜab al-Kuffār."* During the 1860 incident Damascus Jews allegedly "put at the gates of their houses sugared ice water to give the rioters to drink."[48]

The Christian-Jewish Conflict: Economic and Religious Factors

These actions of Syrian Jews were not only directed at improving Muslim-Jewish relations; they were also taken in reaction to Christian hostility against Jews, notably in the form of "blood libels" and in order to secure Muslim support in the fierce Christian-Jewish conflict in Syria which had persisted for ages and had been aggravated during the reform era.

Intense economic rivalry, colored by religious antagonism, had taken place for generations between Jews and Christians for positions in commerce and in government administration in the Syrian provinces (as elsewhere in the Ottoman Empire). During the latter part of the eighteenth century and the beginning of the nineteenth century, for example, Jews in several towns, led by the Farḥi family in Damascus and Acre, and the Picciotto family in Aleppo, had the upper hand in this economic competition. This was mainly due to the senior positions held by the Farḥis in the financial and administrative affairs of the Damascus and Sidon *eyalet*s. One member of the family, Ḥayim Farḥi, who served under Jezzar Aḥmed Pasha (1775–1804) and Sulaymān Pasha (1804–1818) was described with certain exaggeration by a contemporary Christian historian as follows: "Ḥayim the Jew has been holding all reins of government and has been doing whatever he wishes. It is said that a Jewish person dominates the Muslims and the Christians, the great and the small, the near and the far—without any restriction."[49]

But when in 1820 Ḥayim Farḥi was executed and his property confiscated by ᶜAbdullah Pasha of Sidon (1819–1831), the position of the Jews was declining both in Acre and Damascus. Simultaneously a Christian (Greek Catholic) rival family, the Baḥris, began its rise from junior secretarial functions in the provincial administration. During the Egyptian occupation a member of the family, Ḥanna Baḥri, was appointed by Ibrāhīm Pasha as chief accountant (*mubāshir*) of all of Syria and president of the new central advisory council in Damascus. The Baḥris endeavored to further undermine the economic and public positions of the Farḥis by staffing the new administration with Christian officials. And at the same time other Christians in Damascus were apparently determined to destroy their Jewish rivals once and for all. Taking advantage of the sympathetic attitudes of both the Egyptian authorities and the French consul in Damascus, and relying on the anti-Jewish prejudices of both Christian and Muslim masses, Christian leaders instigated the notorious 1840 "blood libel" of Damascus.

The employment of the blood libel weapon by Christians against Jews had already started in Ottoman Syria at the beginning of the nineteenth century and gradually replaced the traditional instruments of Christian-Jewish struggle, i.e., the financial and political use of influence, intercession, and subversion. These blood accusations which appeared sporadically in Syria from 1810 on[50] took place more regularly during the reform period.[51] This occurred not only because Christian-Jewish economic competition expanded with the growth of both economic activities and government administration, but also, particularly after 1840 when the incidence of such accusations increased, presumably because the growing Muslim animosity to the Christians induced the latter to try by this means to divert the hatred from themselves to the Jews—thereby providing Muslims and Christians with a common scapegoat. By accusing the Jews of such crimes the Christians aimed at discrediting and delegitimizing the Jews in the eyes of Muslims, thus undermining the moral basis for their existence and justifying their physical destruction. This practice, however, proved useful only under the pro-Christian Egyptian regime in Syria and also sporadically during the *Tanzimat* period, when Muslims would join Christians in attacking Jews, or would individually initiate blood accusations against Jews in order to extort money from them.[52] Yet, by and large, not only were the Christian blood libels eventually refuted, but essentially they did not serve to decrease Muslim animosity and violence towards the Christians themselves. Furthermore, Syrian Muslims generally tended to side with Jews in their disputes with Christians,[53] and Jews would naturally utilize these Muslim attitudes to take revenge on their Christian enemies and/or gain an advantage in their economic competition.[54]

This pattern of intercommunal relationships remained basically unchanged until late in the nineteenth century, with two parallel continuing conflicts—Muslim-Christian and Christian-Jewish—influenced to a certain degree by an uneven and fluctuant Muslim-Jewish coalition. Thus the Christian-Jewish conflict developed during the century with further Christian blood accusations, both oral and written, against Jews,[55] usually countered by apologetic Jewish self-defense and occasionally by acts of revenge.[56] Simultaneously, Muslim-Christian antagonism persisted, although Muslim aggression toward Christians decreased for a while after the 1860 events in Damascus and the subsequent punishment inflicted on both Muslim rioters and ringleaders. However, at a later date it revived and periodically burst out in physical violence, particularly at times of European threats against Islamic dominion, and in places where Muslims were conscripted and impoverished, while Christians were conspicuously prospering.[57]

Epilogue

A gradual decrease in Muslim antagonism toward Christians started only at the turn of the century, alongside a newly developing Muslim hostility toward Jews. These changes in the triangular intercommunal relationship occurred against the background of both the appearance of political Zionism in Palestine and the emergence of Arab national sentiments in the Syrian provinces. David Yellin, a local Jewish leader in Jerusalem, expressed these changes in 1911 as follows: "Fifteen years ago the Muslims hated the Christians, while their attitude to the Jews was one of contempt. Now their attitude to the Christians has changed for the better and to the Jews for the worse."[58] In order to complement this observation it is interesting to compare it with a comment made half a century previously by another Jew of Jerusalem. He wrote (with some exaggeration) in the very midst of the reform era (1859): "The Ishmaelites [i.e., Muslims] and the Jews do not hate each other; on the contrary, they love each other; but towards the uncircumcised [Christians] the Muslims are filled with hate."[59]

It should, however, be noted that during the period of reform there were, as in the past, cases of friendship between individual Muslims, Christians, and Jews in Palestine and Syria. Sporadically there also appeared instances of intercommunal solidarity in facing a common misfortune, such as a drought which moved Muslims, Christians, and Jews in Jerusalem to simultaneously, but separately, pray for rain;[60] or a peasants' attack on Haifa against which "The Christians and Moslems fought side by side in defending their town."[61] Aside from these isolated cases on the popular level, certain steps were also taken, particularly after 1860, by a few Ottoman governors and Christian intellectuals alike to bring about an accommodation and coexistence among the various communities. For example, several pashas, notably Midhat Paşa, initiated the establishment of schools and hospitals "open alike to Christians and Mussulmen considering that such institutions would do much to lessen the mutual ill-feeling now existing between the two sects."[62]

More systematic efforts to the same end were made during the 1860s and 1870s by Christian intellectuals in several cultural and social organizations or societies, as well as in a few literary journals, all of which were spreading ideas of common Ottoman-Syrian patriotism and Arab cultural affinity among the various Syrian communities and sects.[63] And in the late 1870s it was even reported "that secret committees in Syria were composed of Mahommedans and Christians alike and that their object was to bring about a movement to free the province from the misgovernment of the Porte and establish some kind of Arab autonomy."[64]

Nevertheless, as is well known, all these various examples of intercommunal solidarity or common patriotism were either isolated, sporadic, or premature. Among the common people the sociocommunal compartmentalization and self-orientation continued to be deep-rooted and rigid. As it was recorded during the mid-nineteenth century: "Moslem boys do not generally play with Christians and even the Christian children are divided amongst themselves."[65] "There is not a man in the country whether Turk or Arab, Mohammedan or Christian who would give a para to save the Empire from ruin. . . . The patriotism of the Syrian is confined to the four walls of his own house, anything beyond them does not concern him."[66] Even at the beginning of the twentieth century there was not much change in these age-old religio-communal allegiances, as well as in the powerful religio-political and/or socioeconomic conflicts among the Syrian population. At least two Western resident-observers reported at that time that "Religious differences are still as powerful as ever to effect a cleavage among neighbours and fellow citizens."[67] "The Moslems are ever conscious that theirs is the religion of the race that conquered Syria. The Christians can never forget that theirs is the faith that was conquered. On the one side are found hatred, arrogance and contempt; on the other hatred, fear and suspicion."[68] This testimony could be complemented by the words of Yusuf al-Ḥakim, a contemporary Syrian Christian intellectual, who stated early in the present century that "The patriotic bond (*irṭibāt waṭani*) is weak and is felt by only a few members of the upper class."[69]

Notes

1. I. Burton, *The Inner Life of Syria,* London, 1875, pp. 105–106.

2. M. Maᶜoz, *Ottoman Reform in Syria and Palestine,* Oxford, 1968, p. 10n.; H. L. Bodman, *Political Factions in Aleppo, Chapel Hill, 1963, p. 98.*

3. *(Anon.), Ḥasr al-litham ᶜan nakabāt al-Shām,* Egypt, 1890, pp. 37, 43; F. Taoutel, ed., *Wathā'iq ta'rīkhiyya ᶜan Ḥalab,* Aleppo, 1958–1962, vol. 1, p. 97; A. Y. Kayat, *A Voice from Lebanon,* London, 1847, pp. 52–53.

4. Ahmed Cevdet, *Tezakir,* ed. C. Baysun, Ankara, 1953–1960, vol. 1, pp. 67–68; English translation by Şerif Mardin, *The Genesis of Young Ottoman Thought,* Princeton, 1962, p. 18.

5. See Maᶜoz (cited n. 2), pp. 222–225.

6. Great Britain, Public Record Office: F. O. 78/836, Beirut, 5 November 1850.

7. F.O. 78/1520, Damascus, 6 September 1860.

8. *Kitāb al-aḥzān fī ta'rīkh al-Shām wa-jabal Lubnān,* MS No. 956.9 K 62 KA, AUB; Muḥammad Abū Saᶜud al-Ḥaṣībī, *Ḥadithat al-sittin,* MS No. (4) 4668 Zahiriyya Library, Damascus.

9. See Maᶜoz (cited n. 2), pp. 235–237; M. Maᶜoz, "Syrian Urban Politics in the Tanzimat Period," *BSOAS,* 29 (1966), pp. 295 ff.

10. F. O. 195/1945, Beirut, 21 March 1842.

11. Mikha'il al-Dimashqī, *Ta'rīkh hawādith al-Shām wa-Lubnān,* Beirut, 1912; *Kitāb al-aḥzān* (cited n. 8), pp. 48–50.

12. Mikha'il Mishāqa, *Al-jawāb ʿalā iqtirāḥ al-aḥbāb,* MS. No. 956.9 M 39 JA, AUB, pp. 170–171; Monk Neophytus of Cyprus, *Annals of Palestine 1821–1841,* ed. S. N. Spyridon, Jerusalem, 1938, pp. 18–29.

13. See, for example, F. O. 78/2282, Damascus, 23 July 1873; F. O. 195/944, Beirut, 11 January 1871.

14. F.O. 78/2494, 20 November 1876.

15. F.O. 226/190, Aleppo, 19 February 1877.

16. F.O. 78/1519, Caiffa, 29 August 1860.

17. F.O. 195/1410, Aleih, 2 July 1882.

18. K. Baedeker, *Palestine and Syria, Handbook for Travellers,* Leipzig, 1876, p. 467.

19. Maʿoz (cited n. 2), pp. 178–180; Charles Issawi, *The Economic History of the Middle East,* Chicago, 1960, pp. 223 ff.

20. See for example PRO F.O. 78/2242, Aleppo, 18 January 1872; (Anon.), *Aḥwāl al-naṣārā baʿd al-ḥarb al-Qirim,* M. No. 66 AUB, pp. 27–28.

21. See Maʿoz (cited n. 2), pp. 182–183; F.O. 226/197 No. 5, Damascus, 27 March 1878; F.O. 195/207, Aleppo, 14 February 1846.

22. See M. Maʿoz (cited n. 9), pp. 277 ff.

23. H. H. Jessup, *Fifty-three Years in Syria,* New York, 1910, vol. 1, p. 165; cf. *Aḥwāl* (cited n. 20), pp. 27–28; *Ḥasr al-litham* (cited n. 3), p. 223.

24. L. Oliphant, *The Land of Gilead,* New York, 1880, p. 497.

25. F.O. 78/1520, No. 17. Damascus, 6 September 1860, cf. Mishāqa (cited n. 12), p. 350.

26. Maʿoz (cited n. 2), p. 193 & n.

27. Qusṭanṭīn al-Bāsha, ed., *Mudhakkirāt Ta'rikhīyya,* Lebanon, n.d., pp. 236–238; F. O. 195/226, Damascus, 8 July 1846.

28. Maʿoz (cited n. 2), p. 190.

29. F.O. 78/499, No. 45, Damascus, 12 July 1842.

30. Maʿoz (cited n. 2), pp. 235 ff.

31. Kāmil al-Ghazī, *Nahr al-dhahab fī ta'rīkh Ḥalab,* Aleppo, 1342–1345/1723–1726, vol. 2, pp. 370–372; F.O. 195/302, Aleppo, 24 October 1856, Başbakanlik Arşivi, *Irade Daḥiliye,* 13493, 8 Safar 1267/1850.

32. [Consul Skene], *Rambles in the Desert of Syria,* London, 1864, p. 241.

33. F.O. 78/836, Aleppo, 19 October 1850; Jamīl al-Shattī, *Rawd al-bashar fī aʿyān Dimashq,* Damascus, 1946, p. 42.

34. *Ḥasr al-litham* (cited n. 3), p. 237; Taoutel (cited n. 3), vol. 2, p. 69.

35. F.O. 78/958, No. 12, Beirut, 29 June 1853.

36. F.O. 78/1454, Jerusalem, 1 January 1859.

37. F.O. 78/962, No. 8, Beirut, 29 June 1853.

38. F.O. 78/1217, No. 1, Jerusalem, 7 January 1856.

39. F.O. 78/1521, Jerusalem, 31 July 1860.

40. Maʿoz (cited n. 2), pp. 205–207.

41. M.A. Ubicini, *Letters on Turkey,* London, 1856, vol. 2, p. 346.

42. F.O. 195/196, No. 46, Damascus, 15 June 1842.

43. F.O. 78/839, Jerusalem, 27 September 1850; J. Finn, *Stirring Times,* London, 1878, vol. 1, pp. 118–119, 392.

44. F.O. 78/1383, Jerusalem, 8 July 1858.

45. Anṭūn Ḍāhir al-ᶜAqīqī, *Thawra wa-fitna fī Lubnān,* Beirut, 1938, p. 117; F. Walpole, *The Ansayrii and the Assassins,* London, 1851, vol. 3, p. 218; Yūsuf Qara'lī, ed., *Ahamm hawādith Ḥalab,* Egypt, n.d., p. 81.

46. For a detailed study on the subject see M. Maᶜoz, "Changes in the Position of the Jewish Communities of Palestine and Syria in the Mid-Nineteenth Century," in M. Maᶜoz, ed., *Studies on Palestine during the Ottoman Period,* Jerusalem, 1975, pp. 142 ff.

47. Ubicini (cited n. 41), p. 350.

48. See respectively *Kītab al-aḥzān* (cited n. 8), p. 125, Mishāqa (cited n. 12), p. 357.

49. Ibrāhim al-'Awra, *Ta'rikh wilāyat Sulaymān Bāsha al-ᶜAdil,* Sidon, 1936, p. 477.

50. ᶜAbd al-'Atī Jallāl, ed., *Al-dhabā'iḥ al-bashariyya al-talmūdiyya,* Cairo, 1902, pp. 116–120.

51. "This accusation is annually revived at Easter at different parts of the Empire . . ." F.O. 78/1219, No. 33, Beirut, 14 July 1856.

52. Ibid.; London Church Missionary Society (CMS), CM/028 from Gobat, 2 August 1841; F.O. 78/714, No. 5, Damascus, 30 April 1847.

53. Maᶜoz (cited n. 46), pp. 160–161.

54. Ibid., pp. 151–152.

55. *Al-Jinān* (Beirut), 2 (1870), pp. 42–43; 6 (1870), pp. 176–177.

56. Taoutel (cited n. 3), vol. 4, p. 81.

57. S. Shamir, "The Modernization of Syria," in W. R. Polk and R. L. Chambers, eds., *Beginnings of Modernization in the Middle East,* Chicago, 1968, p. 379.

58. Y. Ro'i, "The Zionist Attitude to the Arabs 1908–1914" in *Middle Eastern Studies,* 10 (1968), no. 1, p. 227.

59. A. Yaᶜari, *Masaᶜot Shliaḥ Zfat,* Jerusalem, 5704/1944, p. 19.

60. Finn (cited n. 43), vol. 2, pp. 404–405.

61. F.O. 78/1120, Sidon, 29 September 1855.

62. F.O. 78/1586, Damascus, 10 January 1861.

63. See for example *Nafīr Sūriyya* (Beirut), 25 October 1860; *Al-Jinān,* 22 (1870), p. 674; 11 (1870), pp. 340–342. For more details see Maᶜoz (cited n. 2) pp. 241–243.

64. F.O. 429/91, No. 31, Therapia, 20 October 1879.

65. M. E. Rogers, *Domestic Life in Palestine,* London, 1863, p. 190.

66. J. Murray, *A Handbook for Travellers in Syria and Palestine,* London, 1858, p. XLVI.

67. F.O. 195/2255, Jerusalem, 10 August 1907.

68. F. J. Bliss, *The Religions of Modern Syria and Palestine,* New York, 1912, p. 29.

69. Yūsuf al-Ḥakīm, *Sūriyya wa-al-ahd al-ᶜUthmānī,* Beirut, 1966, vol. 1, p. 84.

5

Communal Conflict in Nineteenth-Century Lebanon

SAMIR KHALAF

Introduction

The social and political history of Lebanon has experienced successive outbursts of civil strife and political violence. Dramatic episodes such as the peasant uprisings of 1820, 1840, and 1857; the repeated outbreaks of sectarian hostilities in 1841, 1845, 1860, 1958; and the protracted civil war of 1975 to the present, reveal the fragility of Lebanon's precarious democracy, its deficient civility, and perpetual grievances of dominant groups within society.

Typical of small, communal, and highly factionalized societies, much of the earlier violence took the form of internal strife between factions and feuding families. Little of it assumed an open confessional conflict. At least until 1840 the bulk of violence was more in the nature of intermittent feuds, personal and factional rivalry between bickering feudal chieftains and rival families vying for a greater share of power and privilege in society. Nineteenth-century travelers and local chroniclers all uniformly commented on the spirit of amity that had characterized confessional relations at the time.

During the two decades following the Egyptian occupation, from 1840–1860, civil unrest and communal conflict began to assume a more confessional form. Excluding, perhaps, the current civil war, they were also the most turbulent and violent decades Lebanon had experienced. One civil disturbance provoked another until the unrest culminated in the massacres of 1860. What brought about such conflict? More specifically, what transformed the earlier nonsectarian, factional rivalries and peasant seditions into confessional hostilities?

This is not an idle question. It reflects, among other things, the survival of sectarian sentiments and the deficiency of civic and secular ties. In earlier, as in more recent, episodes of communal conflict social and "class" issues have always been transformed or deflected into confessional hostility. One might easily argue that had the earlier class conflicts succeeded in eroding confessional, feudal, and communal loyalties, Lebanon might have been spared much of its subsequent turmoil. It would have also become more of a nation-state and less of a mosaic of pluralistic and fragmented communities. Within such a context, it is meaningful to reexamine a few of these episodes to find out why they failed to bring about such a transformation.

It is no exaggeration to say that no episodes in the social and political history of Lebanon have been chronicled as much as the events surrounding the civil disturbances of 1860. Some of the chroniclers trace major events to trivial and inconsequential origins. Accordingly, an incidence of trespassing, a Maronite shooting a partridge on a Druze property, or a petty affray between a Druze and Maronite boy are often singled out as the immediate causes for the outbreak of confessional hostilities.[1]

There were, of course, deeper and more profound causes for the conflict. Despite the confessional character of the tension, it was neither motivated nor sustained by purely religious sentiments. There were socioeconomic disparities underlying the confessional enmity. Furthermore, these disparities did not just unfold shortly before the outbreak of hostilities. Christians in general had had a head start over other groups in cultural and material advancements. Throughout the seventeenth and eighteenth centuries they were able to maintain close cultural, commercial, and political contacts with Europe and had, as a result, grown disproportionately richer and more influential. Political and socioeconomic developments early in the nineteenth century reinforced these imbalances.

More specifically, I will argue in this essay that Christians, on the whole, were the main beneficiaries of the socioeconomic changes generated by the Egyptians' presence. Two more decades of Ottoman reforms with the concomitant improvements in civil and social liberties—limited as they were—accentuated the disparities further. To understand, then, the nature and pattern of communal conflict we must consider some of the changes during the Egyptian occupation and the period of Ottoman reforms.

The Egyptian Occupation of Mount Lebanon (1831–1841)

The circumstances that culminated in the Egyptian occupation of Syria are multiple and diverse. They range from Muḥammad ᶜAlī's ambitious expansionist designs and development projects, which necessitated an intensive exploitation of Syrian resources (particularly timber, tobacco, and Lebanese silk as an exportable cash crop) and easier access to Egyptian-Syrian trade routes, to the growing hostility of Europe to a weakened Ottoman Empire and Muḥammad ᶜAlī's eagerness to pose as the protector of Christian minorities in Syria. These and other such contributing factors have been documented by several historians.[2] What concerns us here is not so much the motives and events surrounding Muḥammad ᶜAlī's expedition as the impact and consequences of a decade of Egyptian rule for accentuating socioeconomic disparities and communal conflict.

For several historians Ibrāhīm Paşa's ten-year interlude in Lebanon continues to be perceived as the beginning of the "modern" period; a dawn of a new era of change marked by the disintegration of feudal society and the so-called "opening" up of the country to foreign influence.[3] The reforms introduced by Ibrāhīm Paşa are seen as "bold" and "profound" changes which transformed "almost every aspect of the old life."[4] Others speak of a "brief golden age which set in motion certain trends and movements which were to influence profoundly the future course of Middle Eastern history."[5]

Can one not advance a more realistic appraisal of the modernizing impact of the Egyptian occupation? A view which recognizes the transformations generated by the Egyptian presence, but one which also recognizes the disruptive impact of such changes on communal conflict.

The kind of political regime Muḥammad ᶜAlī envisaged for Mount Lebanon, which would permit a more efficient exploitation of the country's resources and maintain law and order, required a greater degree of government control. This was apparent in the measures undertaken by the Egyptians to promote public security and safeguard the freedom of movement of both goods and people. In some respects, the significant developments associated with the Egyptian presence in Mount Lebanon—economic development, religious equality, conscription, disarmament, and tax innovations—were a by-product of Ibrāhīm Paşa's concern with public security.

The Egyptians had every reason to be concerned. The people of Mount Lebanon, with their tradition of feudal autonomy and spirit of independence, had not been very hospitable to any system of centralized control. The rugged mountainous terrain and the isolation of villages rendered certain areas beyond the effective reach of any government authority. Bedouin tribes, encamped in the Biqāᶜ valley, derived much of their income from pillaging trade caravans and imposing "protection money" and "brotherhood" tributes upon villages.[6] Many villages and towns levied their own tolls and duties while cities prevented the entry and restricted the mobility of certain religious minorities. Even Beirut, "by all odds the most open of the cities of the Levant, was under restraints. On the eve of the Egyptian invasion, none of the numerous family of Shihāb was allowed to enter without special permission."[7]

These, and other forms of public insecurity, restricted the flow of goods and people, handicapped commercial transactions, and prevented easier access to the country's natural resources. Accordingly, early in the occupation the Egyptian government determined to take the necessary steps to assuage the adverse effects of such conditions. Hence, it resorted to such measures as conscription, disarmament, and the imposition of a more regular system of exactions. Such enforcements were not only extremely unpopular; they proved to be damaging in inciting confessional jealousy and discord. This was particularly so since the measures were not uniformly applied. Eager to win European goodwill, the Egyptians allowed Christians differential treatment by exempting them from many of the impositions levied on Muslims and Druzes. It is instructive to note that the first major act of Ibrāhīm Paşa's government was the declaration he made before the fall of Acre in November 1831, in which he ordered the notables of Jerusalem to cease levying extra taxes on native Christians, places of worship and pilgrims.[8] Likewise, in the imposition of personal or head taxes *(farda)* there is evidence that Muslims were paying higher rates than Christians.[9] They were also exempted from conscription and disarmament, permitted to hold responsible positions in government, appear in public on horseback, and wear a white turban—all exclusively Muslim privileges.[10]

Indeed, so privileged had the Christian community become as a result of these and other socioeconomic benefits that the conversion to Christianity witnessed at the time may be attributed to the disproportionate rights and advantages they enjoyed under the Egyptians. Writing from Beirut in December of 1835, Eli Smith, the American missionary, observed: ". . . the Christian community apparently escaped all of the fears of sudden arrest and conscription experienced by Muslims and Druzes. Indeed, there was a certain amount of conversion by the latter to escape conscription."[11]

It is the central argument of this essay that this growing disparity between the religious groups, a feature which has had a lasting impact on Lebanese society, was one of the by-products of the Egyptian occupation. To understand how this disparity emerged we must consider some of the transformations which occurred during that eventful decade.

The most visible changes were in the economic sphere. This was to be expected. Economic motives, after all, loomed high in Muḥammad ᶜAlī's justification for occupying Mount Lebanon. The Egyptians were eager to reform the fiscal and economic organization to permit a more efficient utilization of the country's resources.

One of the initial changes in the tax structure was the lifting of taxes levied upon pilgrimage groups and religious establishments. This did not mean, however, that Christians had become entirely free of exemptions. A portion of the poll tax *(jizya)* was earmarked as a "toleration tax" which the Christians of Mount Lebanon were compelled to pay. The *farda,* as a personal or head tax, was retained. The same was true of the conventional yearly tribute (*mīrī*). So were the other impositions and fines levied on public baths, animals, customs, and monopolies.[12] The system of *corvée,* which took the form of a direct tax on the community, continued to drain the resources of the peasants. Henri Guys cites an instance in 1837 when Bashīr drafted some two hundred peasants to work in the government-controlled coal mines of Qurnayil in the Maṭn and were paid only three piasters daily. Since this was hardly adequate to support their families, the villages from which the laborers were drawn were compelled to contribute five piasters further to each person.[13]

Conscious of the apprehensive and restive mood of Mount Lebanon and eager to woo the populace, Ibrāhīm Paşa exercised initial moderation in his tax collection and other exactions. The moderation, however, did not survive for too long. By 1835, acting on stern instructions from his father, Ibrāhīm Paşa raised taxes to about three times their size, extended state monopolies over silk, soap, and other necessities and insisted on disarmament and conscription. The last two were the source of much outrage and bitter resentment.

Altogether, then, the tax structure during the Egyptian period may not have had sufficient time to develop into a coherent system. The same inconsistencies, local variations, and deficiencies which characterized the fiscal system at the turn of the century continued to exist. Without these changes the administration was still able to "regularize, to an extent before unknown, the system of exactions and to squeeze out of the population money, men, and goods on a scale quite out of line with previous experience."[14] The point to be underscored here is that, on the whole, Christians were favorably treated. Despite the stringent exactions and tighter controls they somehow found more circumstances to escape them than Muslims and Druzes.

Of the extensive economic changes introduced during the Egyptian period no factor had as significant an impact on the local economy as the change in the scale and pattern of foreign trade. This, too, had its effect on widening disparities among the religious communities.

Prior to the Egyptian invasion the little international trade that did exist was predominantly an Asian trade. Beirut, still confined to its medieval walls, was just emerging as a major entrepôt for the hinterland. Until then, and because of the traditional "caravan navigation," the main cities of Syria such as Damascus and Aleppo, were inland cities oriented toward the desert. Ports on the Syrian and Lebanese coast were, by comparison, relatively small towns. Beirut's population before the Egyptian occupation barely reached ten thousand. The rise of Beirut, as Dominique Chevallier among others has argued, is linked with the shift of trade from the interior to the Mediterranean.[15] This shift would not have occurred without the revolution in shipping and the introduction of steam navigation lines into the eastern Mediterranean. Vessels with deeper drafts for mass cargos were established first by the British in 1835. Shortly thereafter, competition from French and Austrian lines increased the number of vessels operating in the Mediterranean. Beirut's harbor was naturally more endowed to accommodate deeper vessels and began to attract the bulk of growing traffic. Other coastal cities, without such natural advantages, like Sidon, Tripoli, and Tyre, began to witness a decline.[16]

Beirut's prominence as a trade center was more than an accident of geography and natural harbor facilities. Muḥammad ᶜAlī took a keen interest in encouraging and stimulating trade. Commercial treaties, intended as a compromise between the provisions of the old capitulatory privileges and modern requirements, were introduced to regularize custom duties and facilitate the circulation of goods.[17] The opening of Damascus to Europeans, the transshipment of Western goods to the interior, growing public security and safety in the transport of goods and travels, growth of a foreign community and the freedom granted to missionaries to expand their activities, all aided in Beirut's development as a major Mediterranean seaport. During the decade of Egyptian occupation Beirut's population rose rapidly from ten to nearly fifteen thousand and tax returns for the same period increased fourfold.[18]

The growth of Beirut did not mean draining the hinterland of people and resources. The noticeable growth in public safety and revival of security in villages encouraged the movement of capital from urban to rural areas. Direct measures were taken to encourage agriculture by urging people to settle and invest in land and by introducing new crops and extending areas under cultivation. Government monopolies over items such as timber, which Egypt needed for her growing fleet, animal hides, coal, iron, wool for army uniforms, and olives were introduced.[19] Other commodities, such as wines and liquor, though not made into state monopolies, received much encouragement as exportable items to Egypt. And, of course, Egypt was in urgent need of Lebanon's silk as an exportable cash crop. In fact, Muḥammad ᶜAlī had hoped to impose a state monopoly over the entire silk crop of Mount Lebanon. European opposition, however, and the difficulty of controlling such a widely diffused crop prompted him to abandon his plans.[20] Planting of mulberry trees, nonetheless, continued to receive encouragement and government support. So widespread was silk cultivation that it almost became a national pastime, like apple growing was to become more than a century later. Lured by the growing demand for silk, villagers started converting their farm lands to mulberry trees and "city dwellers began to buy or rent lands and to make arrangements to share the crops with peasant laborers. Land devoted to mulberries increased from 25 to 50 per cent; in addition to thirty-seven thousand planted along the coast under government auspices, others were privately planted in every part where its growth presents a probability of success."[21]

These new forces of regeneration—introduction of order and security, revival of foreign trade, easing of restrictions from which Christians had previously suffered, opening up the hinterland by extending agriculture and stimulating economic activity—had compelling social implications. Some of the most visible consequences were the changes in tastes and life-styles. Travelers in the late 1830s and early 1840s were already describing Beirut as the "Paris of the East." As the seat of diplomacy, residence for consul-generals, headquarters for French, American, and British missions and a growing center of trade and industry, Beirut was "rapidly increasing in wealth, population and dimensions. . . . Stupendous new mansions, the property of opulent merchants, were daily being built; beautiful country houses, summer residences of the wealthy; hotels and billiard rooms and cafes, elegantly fitted. . . . Everywhere utility was blended with magnificence."[22] Travelers, particularly those coming to Beirut after visiting other towns and cities in Syria and Palestine, were all struck by how "European" the character and amenities of the city had become. The British traveler Frederick Neale, like several others, was almost rhapsodic when describing the stylish lounging bars and Italian locandas "with the latest European journals and French papers."[23] Others were more impressed by the freedom of movement and the new liberties people were beginning to enjoy in their dress and appearance in public places.[24]

The economic and technological changes, particularly the upsurge in foreign trade and the consequential growth of Beirut, had other less favorable implications. To begin with, the stimulation and growth of commercial exchange with the more advanced industrial countries of Europe—France and England in particular—began to generate a chronic deficit in the balance of trade. In 1833, for example, Beirut's imports were nearly twice the value of its exports. The deficit declined in subsequent years but continued to provoke a "grave monetary hemorrhage" throughout the 1830s and 1840s.[25] In fact, it was not until 1854 that Beirut had a surplus in its balance of trade.[26] Both the French and British consuls of the period repeatedly noted the gravity of the trade deficit and its consequences for draining the country of its currency and precious metal. One of Consul Bouree's dispatches of 1842, quoted by Chevallier, is a poignant summary of this situation:

> This state of affairs [the deficit in the balance of trade with Europe and the decline of Syrian production] has already exhausted the country to the point that all silver and gold coins whose intrinsic value approximates their face value have flowed out. Those that are still found do not have the intrinsic worth of their quoted value and, for this reason, are not exported. Anyway, these coins have the indelible sign of their origin for they are all pierced, that is, they come from necklaces or from other women's ornaments which had to be parted with. They are jewels which misery transformed into coins and thus returned to their intended purpose.[27]

Along with this loss of precious metals, the country was gripped by a general inflation characterized by a rapid rise in the cost of living, value of urban property, rent, and food prices.[28]

More important than the trade deficit and inflation were the growing disparities in the relative positions of the various religious groups. The first symptoms of the uneven distribution of wealth and privilege—a feature which became endemic to Lebanese society ever since—were becoming more visible. This was particularly noticeable in Beirut where a small segment of the population enjoyed a disproportionate share of prosperity. A new mercantile middle class—mostly Christian merchants and agents for European traders and firms—emerged as the most prosperous group. Foreign travellers who were so impressed by the conspicuous consumption, lavish display of wealth and Parisian life-styles in Beirut at the time must have been observing the changes within this rather exclusive community. Other groups were largely excluded from these manifestations of prospertiy. The most prominent Druze feudal families—such as the Jānbulāṭs, Abū Nakads, and ᶜImāds—were dispossessed and exiled by Amīr Bashīr, and the bulk of the middle and lower classes did not fully participate in the new economic opportunities.

By virtue of their European predispositions and contacts and the security and privileges they were enjoying, Christian capitalists ventured in commercial speculations and dominated the bourgeoning free enterprise activities. Colonel Charles Churchill had this to say about the growing disparity between Christians and Druzes during the Egyptian occupation:

> . . . Christians were admitted into the local councils. Their evidence, before mixed tribunals of Christian and Mussulman, was valid. All distinction of dress was abolished. As secretaries, as local governors, even as military officers, in all departments of the State their services were accepted and rewarded. Numbers, who had for years been hiding themselves up in the mountains amongst the Druzes, to escape the tyrannous exactions of Djezzar and of Abdallah Pasha, returned to the

> sea-coast towns, and recommenced their commercial business. A brisk trade with European merchants was quickly opened, and the harbour of Beyrout, in particular, soon became thronged with the shipping of London and Marseilles.[29]

This disproportionate prosperity of Christians was in part achieved at the expense of other groups, particularly the Druze feudal lords. Indeed, we are told that it is possible to observe Christians "in the 1820's as serfs of such Druze shaikhs as the Abū Nakad and at the end of the Egyptian period as the chief moneylenders to the same shaikhs."[30] Furthermore, Christians in general appear to have benefited considerably from the improvements of public health as evidenced by their growing numbers relative to other religious groups.[31]

Manifestations of the economic prosperity of Christians during the Egyptian period were not confined to Beirut. The town of Dayr al-Qamar, which at the beginning of the eighteenth century was no more than a "small straggling village inhabited by Druzes,"[32] rose under the patronage of Amīr Bashīr and from a reputable silk trade to a major town of nearly eight thousand composed mostly of Maronites and Greek Catholics. Once again, Colonel Churchill commented:

> Its merchants built spacious houses, with marble courts and fountains, and furnished in a style of costly luxury. All the Druze landed property in the neighborhood passed into their hands. Thus they finally attained a position of wealth and affluence which excited the jealousy and cupidity of their feudal superiors, the Druze sheiks of the family of Abou Nakad. . . . Released from the restraints which had hitherto weighted upon them from being placed under a Turkish governor, the Christians of Deir-el-Kamar enjoyed the full and unimpeded development of commercial activity. Their leading men amassed riches; they kept studs; their wives and daughters were apparelled in silks and satins, and blazed with jewelry, gold, and pearls, and diamonds. The few Druzes who still inhabited the town were reduced to absolute insignificance, were always obliged to be on their good behavior, and, to use their own expression, often repeated in the bitterness of their hearts, had become to the Christians as "hewers of wood and drawers of water."[33]

The same is true of other towns like Zaḥla and Ḥasbaya. Zaḥla, which formed a kind of federal alliance with the Christians of Dayr al-Qamar for the general protection of Christian interests, had also risen "with astounding rapidity to a state of affluence and consideration."[34] Its predominantly Greek Catholic population of about twelve thousand carried on a large trade with inland Syria and farmed the fertile land of the Biqāᶜ.[35]

By disrupting the delicate balance between the various communities, these growing disparities deepened confessional antagonisms between Christian and Druze and renewed hostilities between peasants and feudal lords. The economic transformations had also helped generate a group of commercial capitalists potentially able to threaten the wealth, power, and prestige of the traditional elite.

The change in the pattern of trade produced further dislocations within the rural economy. The village was no longer a self-contained economic community. The peasant and village craftsman became increasingly dependent on urban creditors and entrepreneurs, and their economic well-being was now linked to fluctuations in the world market. The primitive methods of local production could not face competition from European products. Even silk, Lebanon's major cash crop, suffered from native reeling methods. It was not until the end of the Egyptian period that steam-powered silk reeling was introduced and the output was more suitable for European factories. Furthermore, some of the new laws were not to the advantage of the villagers or the products of their labor. The commercial treaties of 1838 were designed to favor foreign trade. Accordingly, these treaties stipulated that local products be taxed when circulating within the Ottoman Empire while foreign trade merchandise required duty only upon entrance or exit from Ottoman territory.[36]

During the last few years of the Egyptian occupation conditions became progressively worse. Some of the favorable aspects of the Egyptian presence wore off, and the population—both Christian and Druze—grew increasingly restless. Disenchantment with the despised measures of conscription, *corvée* and stringent taxation was more widespread. As early as 1834, there were uprisings in Palestine, Tripoli, and Lattakia against the imposition of such measures, and in each case, Ibrāhīm Paşa was successful in subduing the insurrections with the assistance of Amīr Bashīr. He then turned to Mount Lebanon and requested from Bashir the conscription of sixteen hundred Druzes to serve for the regular fifteen-year term in the Egyptian army.

Of all the measures associated with the Egyptians, conscription was by far the most odious and widely feared. Since it involved permanent absence from a village or town it imposed a serious drain on the economic resources or livelihood of Mount Lebanon. It meant a prolonged isolation from kinship and other primordial ties which are the source of personal reinforcement and support in village society. Indeed, it was so despised that potential conscripts would do their utmost to avoid its terrors. Beiruti Muslims—and their coreligionists in Sidon and Tripoli—were known to seek refuge in European consulates and foreign residences, hide in caverns and excavations or take to the sea in a vain effort to flee from the pursuit of Egyptian officers. Druzes sought immunity in baptism or conversion and there were cases of mutilation and emigration. Subjects suspected of concealing or aiding fugitives suffered severe punishment and the humiliation of a public *bastinado*.[37] Little wonder that the horrors of conscription should finally provoke armed rebellion.

The initial success of the major Druze insurrection of Ḥawrān in 1838, in opposition to conscription, encouraged their coreligionists in Mount Lebanon to take up their arms in support of the same cause. Through French and European consular intervention, Christians had gained a temporary respite from conscription. They were, however, dragged into the confrontation in a more damaging and pernicious manner. Ibrāhīm Paşa requested Bashīr to recruit some four thousand Christian mountaineers to assist in subduing the Druze rebels. The request was unprecedented in the history of Mount Lebanon. So far the "tradition of asylum" and the sort of peaceful confederacy that evolved between the various communities prevented any direct clash between them.[38] For generations Lebanon was torn by internal strife, but it was the strife of factions and feuding families. Little of it took the form of religious rivalry. The Ḥawrān episode, by pitting Christian against Druze, was bound to provoke bitter confessional hostility.

In appreciation of their assistance in suppressing the Druze uprising, the Maronites were allowed to keep possession of their arms; they were also promised no additional tax increases.[39] In 1840, however, Muḥammad ᶜAlī reversed his decision and insisted on disarming all Christians of Mount Lebanon, which was a step toward general conscription. He even drafted some of the Lebanese students enrolled at the medical school in Cairo.[40] By then Bashīr II had been reduced to a mere instrument of his Egyptian masters and had no recourse, despite his initial reluctance, but to obey their orders. Accordingly, in May 1840 he summoned the Druzes and Christians of Dayr al-Qamar to surrender their arms. The outcry was total. First in Dayr al-Qamar and then in other towns and villages, armed resistance spread. Christians, Druzes, Sunni Muslims, and Shiᶜites temporarily ignored their differences and acted collectively to resist Bashīr's orders.

Reminiscent of the *ᶜammiyya* uprising of 1820, the insurgents held a conference at Intilias on June 8, 1840, drew up a covenant outlining their grievances, expressed firm determination to resist the oppressive injustices of Egyptian rule and pledged "to fight to restore their independence or die."[41] Initiative and leadership was, once again, assumed by Maronite peasants. After promises from Bashir to make them masters of the Maronite district of Kisrawān, the Druze withdrew their support. Some of the feudal *shaykh*s and *aᶜyān,* however, saw in the insurrection a chance to reclaim part of their lost privileges, and offered their support. So did the higher clergy. After some initial reluctance, the patriarch came out openly in support of the rebellion, and the clergy took an active part in encouraging the rebels.[42]

Apart from specific grievances with regard to conscription, disarmament, *corvée,* and taxation, the expressed objectives of the revolt were similar in form and substance to those of 1820. For example, the same confessional and class consciousness was manifested by the leaders in a letter to the patriarch: "We have come together in a real Christian unity free from [personal] purposes and from spite, made rather for the welfare of the common folk *(jumhūr)* of the community."[43]

Similarly, the rebels of 1840 were calling for the end of foreign rule and the restoration of Mount Lebanon's autonomy and independence. "The rebels made it clear that they were not against the Amīr himself nor against the Shihabi dynasty and its prerogatives, but against the foreign power, the Egyptians, who were tyrannizing over both the Amīr and the people."[44] They were also demanding the reorganization of the administration by forming a new administrative council representing the various communities to assist the Amīr in governing the public affairs of Mount Lebanon.

Like the *ᶜammiyya* uprising of 1820, the civic and public consciousness articulated by Maronite peasants did not find much support among the Druze.

Once again, in other words, a genuine civic revolt was muted and became predominantly parochial.

The first phase of the revolt—roughly between mid-May and the end of July 1840—ended with failure. The rebels were dispersed and their leaders captured and exiled. By then, however, the Eastern Question was already attracting the attention of European powers. Reinforced by the terms of the London Treaty of July 1840, in which they had agreed to expel the Egyptians from Syria, each of the five powers sought to intervene on behalf of their chosen protégés. Turkey, who had all along desired to undermine the autonomy and privileged status of the Shihābī Emirate, seized this opportunity to support the rebels. Along with Britain the Turks supplied the insurgents with armaments and other provisions and urged them not to yield. Russia stepped in to reclaim her position as protector of the Greek Orthodox. France was in the delicate and embarrassing position of, on the one hand, supporting the Egyptians, but on the other being eager not to alienate her traditional protégés in Lebanon—i.e., the Maronites and Catholics. Austria took advantage of France's diplomatic predicament and sought to replace her as the protector of Lebanese Catholics.[45]

When Muḥammad ᶜAlī refused to accept the terms of the London Treaty an Anglo-Austrian-Turkish fleet landed troops at the Bay of Junieh, reinforced the Lebanese insurgents and bombarded Beirut. Within two weeks the allies occupied the main towns and cities and by early November, the Egyptians withdrew their demoralized and decimated forces from Syria. The defeat of Ibrāhīm Paşa carried with it the humiliating downfall of Bashīr's illustrious reign of over half a century. He had steadfastly supported the Egyptians and had no recourse but to deliver himself up for exile.

By the end of the so-called "brief golden age," Mount Lebanon was in a less enviable position. The growth of public security, reforms in the fiscal system, rationalization of land tenure, growth in foreign trade, movement of capital, and the opening up of village society etc. produced a shift in the relative socioeconomic and political position of the various religious groups. The delicate balance which held the society together was disrupted. Civil crisis and confessional rivalry, so far kept in abeyance, had become imminent.

The Ottoman Reforms of 1839 and 1856

The end of the Egyptian affair and the consequent collapse of the Shihābī Emirate mark a significant turning point in the political history of Lebanon: the traditional Lebanese privilege of autonomy under hereditary rule was seriously challenged. The Egyptian threat and the growing recognition of Western superiority prompted the Ottomans to advance a new ideology of reform. The traditional system of Ottoman reforms, it must be recalled, had recognized the autonomy and importance of various *millet* communities. Accordingly, the scope of the reforms was limited to military and administrative changes. Matters such as health, education, social security, communications, and the promotion of industry, trade, and agriculture remained within the scope of local religious authorities.[46] Care was taken, in other words, to preserve the old institutions even when they were being superseded by new ones.

The edicts of 1839 and 1856 mark a fundamental departure from the traditional system: rather than sustaining the autonomy of the *millet*s they sought to introduce new institutions and to extend the scope of the central government. This also necessitated increasing measures of autocracy and centralization. More important, the secular tones of the edicts—particularly in their promises of religious equality—generated as we shall see considerable tension and hostility. A brief review of the events and circumstances that led to the outbreak of conflict is in order.

Foremost among these was the residue of ill-feeling and resentment the Druze continued to bear against Bashīr for undermining their feudal authority and privileges. Not only were they dispossessed and forced into exile, but Bashir had assisted Ibrāhīm Paşa in suppressing the Druze uprising in Ḥawrān. During the Egyptian interlude the Druzes enjoyed none of the preferential treatment accorded to Christians. At least they could not escape as readily from some of the hardships of conscription and disarmament. Returning from exile, they were embittered further by the heightened prestige and prosperity of Christians and the comparative destitution of their own communities. Much of their property was now held by Christians, and all their traditional rights and prerogatives—collection of taxes, maintenance of law and order, and judicial authority—had been absorbed by the Shihābī Emirate.

The political vacuum generated by Bashīr's exile doubtless played a part in encouraging such hostility. Until the end of his reign Bashīr remained master of the internal politics of Lebanon and managed to keep the sectarian and partisan divisions under control. Furthermore, during the 1840 insurrection, common hostility toward his tenacious allegiance to Egyptian presence brought the contending groups—Maronites and Druzes, peasants and feudal lords—together. With Bashīr out of the way there was no common force or cause to keep the various factions united.[47]

The downfall of Bashīr II and the appointment of his incompetent cousin, Bashīr III, as his successor gave the Ottomans a welcome opportunity to undermine the local autonomy of Lebanon's feudal chiefs. Upon the insistence of the Ottoman authorities, Bashīr III organized a council or *dīwān* of twelve men (two from each of the dominant sects; Maronites, Druzes, Greek Orthodox, Greek Catholics, Sunnī Muslims, and Shiᶜites) to assist him in the administration of justice. Both Druze and Christian feudal shaykhs saw in this an encroachment on their traditional authority and refused to cooperate in this arrangement. Druze *shaykh*s in particular, especially the Jānbulāṭs, Arslans, and Talḥuqs, who were eager to restore the rights and privileges they lost during Bashīr II's reign were not prepared to suffer further usurpations. More provocative was the circular issued by Patriarch Yusūf Ḥubaysh, and signed by leading Maronite families, calling on their coreligionists in the Druze districts to assume the judicial authority traditionally held by the feudal chiefs. "This was tantamount to an assertion by the Patriarch of the power to withdraw authority from the Druze *shaykh*s."[48]

Following a dispute in October 1841 over the distribution of taxes, a party of Druzes led by the Abū Nakad *shaykh*s attacked Dayr al-Qamar, set the town on fire, pillaged Christian homes and besieged Bashīr III. The incident touched off other sectarian clashes throughout the Shūf, Bīqā^c and Zaḥla. This was the first sectarian outburst and it left a staggering toll: a loss of about three hundred people, the destruction of half a million dollars of property;[49] the dismissal of Bashīr III under humiliating conditions, the end of the Shihābī Emirate; a large residue of ill-feeling and mutual suspicion.[50] The animosity was further aggravated by the complicity of the Ottoman authorities. Eager to undermine the autonomy of Mount Lebanon the Ottomans supported the Druzes in an effort to disrupt or discredit the Shihābī Emirate. Not only were they suspected of having been involved in the initial Druze plot against the Christians,[51] there were also instances in which Ottoman troops participated in the acts of plundering. Such instances gave rise to the saying common then among Christians: "We would sooner be plundered by Druzes than protected by Turks."[52]

By 1842 it was becoming apparent that an irreparable breach was drawing the religious communities further apart. The Maronite-Druze confederacy, which had sustained Lebanon's autonomy for so long, suffered its first serious setback. The Ottomans were eager to step in and impose direct rule over Mount Lebanon. They declared the end of the Shihābī Emirate and appointed ^{c}Umar Paşa *al-Nimsāwī* (the Austrian) as governor. The Druze, already jealous of Christian ascendancy in power and prosperity, greeted the downfall of the Shihābs with enthusiasm without realizing that the introduction of Ottoman centralized rule would ultimately have adverse effects on their own community. The Christians, naturally, refused to recognize the new arrangement and insisted on a restoration of the emirate which could only be achieved with Druze cooperation.[53]

^{c}Umar Paşa's main concern was to gain support for his efforts to establish direct Ottoman rule. He turned first to the Druze and Maronite feudal *shaykh*s who had been dispossessed by the Shihābs. By restoring their estates and traditional prerogatives and appointing several of them as his advisors and agents, he won their support for the new regime. Second, he was eager to demonstrate to European powers that direct Ottoman rule enjoyed wide support in Lebanon. To this end, agents were hired to circulate petitions and secure signatures—a sort of plebiscite by coercion—in favor of direct Ottoman rule. He resorted to bribery, entreaties, false promises, threats, intimidation, blackmail, and "every species of personal indignity"[54] to procure the necessary signatures. So flagrant were the extortionist pressures that European consuls in Beirut collectively protested against the use of such measures and declared the petitions to be "completely unrepresentative of true Lebanese opinion."[55]

In the meantime, internal alignments within Lebanon were being swiftly redefined. The petitions had hardly been circulated when the Druze had serious afterthoughts about direct Ottoman administration and their place within it. They considered themselves responsible for the collapse of the Shihābī Emirate and the establishment of Ottoman rule and were therefore reluctant to assume a subservient position and accept the arbitrary dictates of Ottoman officials. Confronted with such Druze pretentions, and in desperation, ᶜUmar Paşa turned to the Maronites for support and started his policy of ingratiation to win their favors. This only aroused the suspicion of the Maronites and the bitter resentment of the Druzes. So intense was Druze opposition that ᶜUmar Paşa was forced to arrest seven of their prominent *shaykh*s. The outrage was instantaneous. An open Druze rebellion was declared demanding the immediate dismissal of ᶜUmar Paşa, immunity from conscription and disarmament, and exemption from taxes for a three-year period.[56] Despite strong resistance a joint Turkish-Albanian troop forced the surrender of Druze leaders.

The rebellion, nonetheless, was a clear indication that direct Ottoman control was disagreeable to both Druzes and Maronites. Efforts for a new Druze-Maronite coalition had failed, but the insurgents enjoyed the moral support of Maronite leaders.[57] Druze feudal *shaykh*s were resentful of the loss of the traditional prerogatives and the arbitrary arrests and imprisonment they were subjected to under the autocratic control of ᶜUmar Paşa. The Maronites were equally appalled by the demise of the Shihābī dynasty and, with it, the frustration of their hopes for establishing an autonomous Christian Emirate.[58] In the face of such opposition, the Ottomans were forced to dismiss ᶜUmar Paşa before he completed his first year in office. So ended this brief interlude with direct Ottoman rule. But more important, this interlude had intensified the enmity between the religious communities. The desperate efforts of the Ottomans to assert their direct authority over Lebanon prompted them to resort to their time-worn ploys of inciting sectarian suspicions and hostility:

> Such is the way in which the Turks ever maintained their power. Not by vindicating their authority, as a legitimate government ought to do, but by exciting and playing upon the worst passions of human nature; by setting sect against sect; subdividing again, by corruption and intrigue, these sects amongst themselves; by bribing the worthless to betray their relations, their religion, and their country; and by dissolving all the ties which create confidence and happiness amongst mankind.[59]

European intervention—particularly on behalf of France and Britain—prevented the Ottoman government from imposing direct control over Lebanon but failed to reconcile the Druzes and Maronites. Consequently, the five powers and the Porte agreed in 1843 to a scheme of partitioning Lebanon into two administrative districts: a northern district under a Christian *qa'imaqām* (sub-governor), and a southern under a Druze *qa'imaqām,* each to rule over his coreligionists and both responsible to the local Ottoman governor residing in Beirut. The Beirut-Damascus road was used as an arbitrary line of demarcation. The partition scheme was a compromise plan—advanced by Prince Metternich—between the French and Ottoman proposals. The French—supported by the Austrians—continued to hope for a restoration of the Shihābī Emirate while the Ottomans—backed by the Russians—insisted on the complete integration of Lebanon in the Ottoman Empire and opposed any reinstatement of Lebanese autonomy.

The double *qa'imaqāmiyya* was an ill-fated plan from the day of its inception. The partition was an artificial political division which aggravated rather than assuaged religious cleavages. In the words of a contemporary observer, "it was the formal organization of civil war in the country."[60] According to the scheme each *qa'imaqām* was to exercise authority over his own coreligionists. The religious composition, however, of the two districts was far from homogeneous. This created the problem of how to treat those who belonged to one religious community but happened to be living under the political authority of another, especially in areas like the Shūf, Gharb, and Maṭn.

To overcome the jurisdictional problems created by the mixed districts, the Porte decided to limit the authority of each *qa'imaqām* to his own territory, thus denying Christians in the Druze districts the right of appealing to a Christian authority in judicial and tax matters.[61] As usual, European powers intervened on behalf of their protégés. France, as the protector of Maronite and Catholic interests, opposed the Ottoman plan and encouraged the church to remove Maronites from the jurisdiction of the Druze *qa'imaqām* and to place them directly under the Christian one. Britain, eager to safeguard the prerogatives of the Druze feudal *shaykh*s, approved of the revised scheme. In the meantime, Russia maintained that the 28,500 Greek-Orthodox community was populous enough to justify the creation of a special *qa'imaqāmiyya*.[62] In the face of such conflicting expectations, an arrangement was arrived at whereby in each of the mixed districts, a Christian and Druze agent *(wakīl)* would be chosen, each with judicial authority over his coreligionists and responsible to the *qa'imaqām* of his sect. Mixed cases, involving Christians and Druzes, would be heard jointly by the two *wakīl*s. The *wakīl*s were also empowered to collect taxes, each from his own sect, on behalf of the feudal chief.[63]

A fresh outbreak of hostilities in the spring of 1845 finally convinced the Ottomans of the inadequacies inherent in the double *qa'imaqāmiyya*. Nevertheless, the Ottomans opted not to resort to a thorough reorganization of Mount Lebanon. Instead, they modified the existing arrangement by settling the jurisdictional problems of Christians living in Druze districts. A review of the articles and provisions of the Reglement Shakib Efendi, as the plan is identified by historians, reveals that altogether it reinforced rather than undermined the prevailing social and political power of the feudal families.[64] In the words of Shakib Efendi, the Ottoman foreign minister who was dispatched to Beirut in September 1845 to implement the revised plan, "the goal of my mission is to apply fully and completely the arrangements and the more recent enactments on local administration while preserving the particular privileges granted by the Sultan . . ."[65] Accordingly, the *qa'imaqām* was to be appointed from the princely families (Arslans in the case of the Druzes and Abillama in the case of the Maronites) after consultations with the *aᶜyān* and clergy. An elected council of twelve members (two from each of the major six religious communities) was to be selected at large from the people without restriction to birth and status, yet the Christian clergy had the strongest voice in determining the election while the Muslim members were appointed by the *walī* of Sidon.[66] Furthermore, in the event that any vacancies were to arise in the council, the heads of the religious sects were to appoint the new members.

Feudal families throughout Lebanon had recognized Shakib Efendi's Reglement as a direct threat to their status and traditional privileges and did their utmost to resist its application. Shortly after the departure of Shakib Efendi both Christian and Druze feudal *shaykh*s began "to resort to the old ways and to revive old fiscal abuses, much to the distress of the peasants."[67] For example, the enforcement of many of the provisions envisaged by the Reglement required carrying out cadastral surveys and a census to ascertain land ownership and population estimates. Both these measures were perceived by the feudal *shaykh*s as an encroachment on their feudal privileges, and the projects were abandoned in 1847 because of feudal opposition.[68]

It is within this context that the Ottoman reforms should be viewed and interpreted: growing social and political unrest generated by the perennial problems of taxation; feudal authority; disarmament and conscription; the rather fluid state of affairs existing after the expulsion of the Egyptians and the demise of the Shihābs; growing disparities between religious communities; increasing foreign intervention in the internal affairs of Lebanon; and the eagerness of the Ottomans to impose direct rule on Mount Lebanon and to undermine all vestiges of its local autonomy.

In their general and overall conception, the *Tanzimat* essentially involved a series of Western-inspired reforms directed towards a radical transformation of all aspects of Ottoman society.[69] The basic drive behind the movement was to "revitalize the empire through measures of domestic reorganization which should include the adoption or adaptation of some western ideas and institutions"[70] involving practically every dimension of the social structure: military, economic, social, intellectual, legal, and political. The earlier phase of such reforms—roughly covering the era of Mahmud II (1809–1839)—was very limited in scope and involved predominantly military and administrative changes. Historians are in agreement that most of the earlier efforts, generally sporadic attempts to eliminate certain administrative abuses, were largely unsuccessful. They were almost always foiled by powerful local resistance to change.[71] At least in Mount Lebanon the early reforms had little effect on controlling the powerful feudal chiefs. Autonomous life and communal loyalties continued unabated in a population which had little faith in the power of a central government.

It is not within the scope of this essay to elucidate the underlying objectives, ideology and specific circumstances which led to the promulgation of the two edicts. It is sufficient to note that they were both inspired by the belief in the need to treat with equality people of all creeds within the empire. They were also motivated by the desire to introduce order into government, to enhance the role of ministers and to safeguard the bureaucracy against the arbitrary whims of the sultans.[72]

The edict of 1839, the *Hatt-ı Şerif* of Gülhane (Noble Rescript), was explicit in its promises. It espoused three major guarantees to ensure: "1) . . . perfect security for life, honor, and fortune. 2) A regular system of assessing and levying taxes. 3) An equally regular system for levying of troops and the duration of their service." In addition, other provisions were made regarding the compilation of a penal code which would apply to all irrespective of "rank, position or influence"; payment of suitable salaries to public servants; and legislation against the "traffic of favoritism and bribery."[73] There was nothing novel or outstanding about the edict. To a considerable extent, it was echoing the eighteenth century principles of "life, liberty, and property" of the American and French revolutions as a charter of civil liberties.[74]

The general reaction in the empire was mixed. The promises of security, life, and property, of tax and conscription reforms drew favorable reactions, but the promise of "equality without distinction as to religion and sect"—which was to become a sort of *leitmotif* of the entire *Tanzimat* period—was met with strong opposition, particularly among Muslims.[75]

The large measure of toleration and autonomy the non-Muslim communities were granted within the Ottoman Empire was predicated on the assumption that the tolerated communities or *millet*s were separate and inferior. "The Muslim could claim that he assigned to his inferiors a position of reasonable comfort and security; he could moreover claim that his discrimination related not to an accident of birth but to a conscious choice on the most fundamental questions of human existence. Infidel and true believer were different and separate; to equalize them and to mix them was an offence against both religion and common sense."[76] In this sense, the call for religious equality represented the most radical breach within traditional Islamic practice. Little wonder that it was met with strong resistance.

The principle of equality of all Ottomans, Christians, and Muslims, was implicit in the adoption of mixed tribunals, secular education, and Western law. But these efforts were for foreign consumption—to win the goodwill of Western powers or to stave off European intervention—and did not reflect a genuine desire for reform. Indeed, the implementation of many such schemes was never put into effect. The fundamental changes, for example, promised in the conduct of courts, provincial administration, the assessment and collection of taxes, and the terms of military service were never wholly executed.[77] Muslims, likewise, could not bring themselves to accept Christians as officers, and Christians were reluctant to serve in the army, preferring to pay the traditional exemption tax.[78]

Altogether the outcome of the reforms generated by the edict of 1839 were disappointingly few. The edict of 1856 did not fare any better. Like the edict of 1839, the *Hatt-ı Hümayun* had something for everybody. It confirmed the promises of 1839 but went further in identifying the specific changes to be made. Since the edict was designed to weaken Russian claims to the right of protecting Greek Orthodox Christians in the empire (a claim which, incidentally, had been one of the major causes of the Crimean War), it once again promised to take "energetic measures to insure to each sect, whatever the number of its adherents, entire freedom in the exercise of its religion. Every distinction or designation pending to make any class whatever of the subjects of my empire inferior to another class, on account of their religion, language, or race, shall be forever effaced from administrative protocol."[79]

The edict made further guarantees that all subjects, without distinction to sect or nationality, should have access to military and civil schools, should be admitted to public employment, and be qualified to fill them according to their capacity and merit. Mixed tribunals were called for to hear commercial, correctional, and criminal suits involving Christians and Muslims. It reiterated the same concern for introducing administrative reforms in the system of taxation (a system of direct collection was to replace the abuses of tax farming), recruitment and exemption from military duty and constitutional reforms in provincial and communal councils. More than the edict of 1839, the *Hatt-ı Hümayun* expressed concern for works of public utility, monetary and financial reforms, and encouragement of commerce and agriculture.[80]

Like its predecessor, the edict of 1856 "left nothing to be desired but its execution."[81] At least in Lebanon the effect of the reforms on the social order was negligible. None of the three general objectives professed by the two edicts—the imposition of direct centralized rule; improving social and economic conditions, and the promotion of equality between religious communities—was adequately realized. Effective provisions for implementing the reforms were deficient, and the secularizing and sweeping tone of the edicts, particularly the second *Hat,* seemed too threatening to some of the vested traditional interests. A word about each is in order.

To undermine the local autonomy inherent in *iqtāᶜa* society and to impose direct rule on Mount Lebanon, the Ottomans had to resort to the detested measures of conscription and disarmament. They also attempted to introduce a system of direct taxation to replace the quasifeudal system responsible for perpetuating the power of the feudal *shaykh*s. The earlier experience of the Lebanese with such instances of direct rule and tight controls under Ibrāhīm Paşa did not leave much room for the expectation that the Ottomans would succeed where the Egyptians had failed. The same outcome accompanied Ottoman efforts to organize local councils (*majlis* or *dīwān*). Both Christian and Druze feudal *shaykh*s perceived such arrangements as an attempt to undermine their local autonomy and refused to participate.[82]

The impact of the *Tanzimat* on social and economic conditions was even more negligible. The reforms, by the admission of several historians, had failed to bring about any significant change in rural areas. Reports and accounts of consuls, missionaries, and travelers repeat the same theme: "Life and property in the country were becoming daily more insecure."[83] Peasants continued to be subjected to the high interest rates demanded by urban creditors and other exploitations. The high incidence of mass migration during the 1840s and 1850s was a by-product of the peasants' state of impoverishment and dispossession.[84]

Works on public utilities such as roads, bridges, canals, post and telegraph services, port facilities, and the like—which had a direct impact on the state of agriculture and commerce—were also generally neglected. This neglect was all the more flagrant because the Ottomans during the same period displayed little reluctance in lavishing disproportionate sums of public expenditure on military barracks, forts and guardhouses, government buildings, and ostentatious palaces for their resident pashas which had no bearing on enhancing general welfare.

The prosperity and private initiative the local economy was able to generate were further depleted by the instability of the Ottoman monetary system. Inflationary practices and the debasement of the currency, measures frequently resorted to by the Ottomans, inflicted drastic hardships on the population. The first bank in Syria, a branch of the Ottoman Bank, was established in 1856 in Beirut but was unable to regulate the monetary system, guarantee securities, and advance the needed credit.[85] Nearly all the monetary affairs were in the hands of bankers who monopolized the currency and charged exorbitant rates of interest.

The socioeconomic changes observed during this period did not affect the various elements of the population equally. Once again, the burgeoning urban middle class—mostly Christian merchants and agents for European traders—continued to prosper. The rest of the society, particularly craftsmen, artisans, peasants, and small traders, were adversely affected by the growing dependence of the Lebanese economy on European production and trade. The new trading patterns deprived a large portion of the rural society of its traditional sources of livelihood and rendered the economy sensitive to external circumstances. Any disturbance in the European economy had its reverberations within Lebanon. The French consul general in Beirut noted that the French financial crisis of 1857–1858 had "disastrous consequences for Syrian business. Numerous and important bankruptcies, an extraordinary financial uneasiness felt until the end of 1859, loss of credit everywhere, and all this added to two years of poor harvest."[86] Furthermore, in violation of the Anglo-Turkish Commercial Treaty of 1838, which established the principle of free trade and laissez-faire, the Ottomans imposed a tax on silk cocoons at the place where they were raised, an act which contributed to the consequent ruin of many of the local reeling factories.[87]

More damaging than the socioeconomic disparities were the widening religious cleavages and confessional hostility. The two edicts, which espoused the principle of equality between Christians and Muslims, did in fact achieve just the opposite: a complete rift between the two dominant groups which ultimately provoked the massacres of 1861. It is instructive that the two decades of widespread turmoil and bitter civil and confessional unrest in Lebanon's history should have also coincided with the epoch of Ottoman reforms. The coincidence could not be dismissed as accidental. The liberal policy of Ibrāhīm Paşa, the egalitarian provisions of the edict of 1856 and the efforts of the Ottomans to subject Lebanon to more intensive centralized rule generated a large residue of confessional hostility. Muslims, on the whole, found the secularism inherent in the reforms too repugnant. This was apparent in the educational and judicial reforms introduced by the Ottomans which undermined rather than reinforced existing traditional systems.[88] They were also jealous of the religious liberties and economic prosperity the Christians were generally enjoying. Christians were the main beneficiaries of the socioeconomic changes generated by the Egyptian presence. The *Tanzimat* accentuated the religious disparities. Initially, Christians in Lebanon, as elsewhere in the Ottoman Empire, welcomed the egalitarian provisions of 1856 with much exuberance. Church bells were sounded in the countryside, and in some instance the French flag was hoisted above churches and monasteries and religious processions were held in public, often in open defiance of Muslims and Druzes.[89] Gradually, however, Christians began to doubt the motives behind the reforms and continued to perceive Ottoman presence as an instrument to reinforce the predominance of Islam.

Factional, Class, and Confessional Conflict

Around the middle of the nineteenth century Mount Lebanon had all the ingredients of a feuding and fractured social order: factional conflict between rival feudal chiefs; family rivalry between factions of the same extended kinship group; a bit of class conflict between a feudal aristocracy eager to preserve its eroding power and privilege; an emerging Maronite clergy; and the mass of exploited peasantry determined to challenge the social and political supremacy of feudal authority. This intricate network of competing and shifting loyalties was reinforced, often deliberately incited, by Ottoman paşas playing one faction against another or the intervention of Western powers each eager to protect or promote the interest of its own protégé.

The interplay of all these forces was apparent in the early phases of the conflict. The Khāzins, as feudal masters of Kisrawān, were outraged by the appointment of an Abillama (Bashīr Aḥmad) as Christian *qa'imaqām* of the north. They were reluctant to recognize the Abillamas as social superiors and were incensed by the encroachment on the aristocratic rights and feudal privileges they enjoyed for ages. To cope with the growing challenge and displeasure of the feudal families, the *qa'imaqām* turned to the Maronite clergy and peasants for support. Encouraged by the French and Austrians, he posed as the champion of Roman Catholics. He also incited a number of intersectarian conflicts between Maronites and Greek Orthodox Christians. The British, aware of the support of the French and Austrian consulates, threw their weight on the side of another Abillama (Bashīr Assaf) who was making a bid for the *qa'imaqāmıyyah*. This persuaded other feudal families, particularly Khāzin and Ḥubaysh, to support Bashīr Assaf. With this in mind, the townsmen of Zaḥla were encouraged to form a village council and elect a *shaykh shabab* (a village strongman) to manage the public affairs of the town. Such a move was an open defiance of the authority of the *qa'imaqām*. It set the pattern for townsmen elsewhere to establish similar defiant and rebellious movements. In some of the towns of Kisrawān and Maṭn the uprisings, which first took the form of mass agitations and public rallies, openly challenged the supremacy of feudal families. Petitions were drafted and public assemblies were organized to articulate the grievances of commoners against feudal injustices and oppression.

In short by the spring of 1858 the Christians districts in the north were in a state of total disorder bordering on anarchy. At both ends of the social hierarchy, there were growing signs of unrest. Feudal families, jealous of their feudal privileges and kinship consciousness, were challenging the authority of the *qa'imaqām*. Their rebellion succeeded in destroying his power over their districts. The peasant movement, as a protest against feudal abuses, was also beginning to gain considerable momentum.

It was, however, the peasant movement which proved instrumental in shaping the course of events in the years preceding the outbreak of confessional hostilities. Peasant agitation in the north can be understood when viewed within the context of the economic transformations, particularly the expansion of European trade and the consequent emergence of a new urban bourgeoisie which weakened the stability of the feudal economy. Feudal families tried to curtail their growing indebtedness and recoup their losses by intensifying the forced exactions and taxation on peasants. Others ceded or sold portions of their land to villagers and then tried to reclaim them forcibly through their armed retainers.

Much of the protracted civil disturbances of the middle decades of the nineteenth century—which took the form of bitter political struggle over control of land, the power of taxation and the rights and privileges of feudal families—were provoked by such arbitrary impositions and exploitation the peasants were subjected to. These issues were apparent in the demands of the peasants in Kisrawān in their revolt against the Khāzin *shaykh*s. Among other things they were demanding an equalized distribution of the land tax, an end to the exactions of gifts, dues, and the imposition of forced labor services, an abolition of contrived taxes on land sold by the *shaykh*s to peasants, and the abolition of the right to authorize marriages.

Peasant agitation began gradually to assume violent forms. In one village after another, *shaykh shabab*s organized village councils, usurped power, and demanded further concessions from their feudal lords. The reluctance of the notables to grant these concessions—such as the abolition of feudal impositions and the vesting of feudal authority in only three members of the Khāzin family—only provoked added bitterness among the peasants. Leadership also passed into more radical hands. For example, the relatively moderate Ṣaliḥ Sfeir (the *shaykh shabab* of Ajaltun) was replaced by the intemperate, arrogant, and ambitious Ṭaniyūs Shāhīn of Rayfun.

The transfer of leadership to Shāhīn, the illiterate farrier who had "little to recommend him other than his tall and muscular frame and violent temper,"[90] was a turning point. Almost overnight Ṭaniyūs Shāhīn became a legendary folk hero, the avowed and undisputed spokesman of peasants and their redeemer from feudal tutelage.

> He seemed to the people to be their redeemer, bringing forth all that they required of whatever sort. He gave them rest from the sheikhs as they desired; he toured from place to place and received the highest acclaim from everyone. In every village he entered, the people would prepare a grand reception for him amid joy and celebration and continuous firing of rifles, as if it were the visit of a ruler to his subjects.[91]

Shāhīn was not acting alone. It is rare for uprisings of this sort to be inspired and sustained by local initiative alone. The peasant movement enjoyed the moral encouragement of the Ottoman authorities and the French consulate in Beirut. As in earlier instances, the Maronite clergy also offered its blessings, although it remained suspicious of Shāhīn's character and personal ambitions.

By the spring of 1859 the peasant insurrection became a full-fledged social revolution, at least in the Christian districts of the north. The Khāzins and other feudal families were evicted from their homes and stripped of their possessions following scenes of violence and bloodshed. Feudal property, household provisions, and ammunition were parceled out among the peasants, and Ṭaniyūs Shāhīn was issuing his commands with the authority of a "republican government," or the self-appointed dictator of the so-called "peasant commonwealth."[92]

Successful as the peasant revolt in Kisrawān had been in raising the hopes of other peasants throughout Lebanon, the movement remained predominantly a local upheaval. Druze peasants were apprehensive about taking similar action against their own feudal *shaykh*s. They were distrustful of their Christian neighbors and were counseled by their *ᶜuqqāl* (religious elite) to avoid sedition. As in earlier peasant uprisings, the enthusiasm for class struggle and public consciousness among Christian peasants in the north found little appeal among their counterparts in the Druze districts. The lapse of forty years since the 1820 revolt, in other words, had done little in transforming the loyalties and attachments of the peasants. Confessional, local, and feudal allegiances continued to supersede other civic and class interests.

Indeed, the peasant movement in the Druze districts assumed a sectarian rather than a "class" conflict. Druze *shaykh*s were successful in muting and deflecting the grievances and discontent of their own peasants by provoking sectarian rivalry particularly in the religiously mixed communities of the Shūf and Maṭn. The communities were already seething with confessional enmity and required little provocation. After the first clash of 1841 both Druzes and Maronites continued to rearm themselves. The supply of arms and ammunition which cleared Beirut customs in the years preceding the war was quite voluminous.[93] The two communities had also been preparing for the confrontation, although Christians went about it much more openly, and with greater deliberation and boasting, often taunting their adversaries. Several of the Christian villages, for example, were in a state close to actual mobilization. Units of armed men, with special uniforms, led by a *shaykh shabab,* were organized in each of the villages. In turn, these small units were placed under the command of higher officers. In Beirut, the Maronite bishop himself organized and headed such an armed group while wealthy Maronites competed with one another in raising subscriptions for the purchase of arms and ammunition.[94]

In short, the fray between the two boys, the shooting of a partridge, or the collision of two pack-animals—often cited as sources of provocation—were no more than a spark that set ablaze an already explosive situation. Once ignited, agitation and violence became widespread. With every renewed confrontation the ferocity of the fighting was intensified. So was the magnitude of damage to life and property. Although the Maronites, with an estimated fifty thousand men, were expecting to overwhelm the twelve thousand Druzes (indeed, they often boasted of exterminating their adversaries) early in the struggle, the Druzes manifested superiority in fighting effectiveness. In one battle after another they defeated and humbled the Maronites.

So sweeping was the Druze victory that historians talk with amazement about the "flagrant temerity of the Druzes . . . and the seemingly inexplicable Christian cowardice."[95] The Druze forces were better organized, disciplined, and fought more fiercely and menacingly while Christians suffered from inept and bickering leadership.[96] The magnitude and intensity of the violence was more astonishing.

Sometimes within hours entire villages and towns would fall, often with little resistance. Townsmen, seized with panic, would abandon their destroyed villages and homes and seek refuge in Christian strongholds. Other fugitives on their way to Beirut or Sidon were often overtaken, robbed, and killed indiscriminately by their assailants. Even the Christian strongholds were not spared. In fact, it was in these towns that the worst atrocities were perpetrated. First in ᶜAyn Dara, then in Babda, Jazzine, Ḥasbayya, Rashayya, Zaḥla, and Dayr al-Qamar the same atrocious pattern of violence repeated itself with added intensity. The Ottoman garrison commander would offer the Christians asylum in the local *saray,* request the surrender of their arms, and then stand idly by watching the carnage.

In the short span of four weeks—from mid-May until June 20—an estimate of twelve thousand Christians lost their lives, four thousand perished in destitution, 100,000 became homeless, and property damage amounted to nearly £4,000,000.[97] Added to this devastation of life and property was the legacy of confessional bitterness and suspicion the civil war generated. Lebanon was clearly in urgent need of swift and sweeping measures to pacify, rehabilitate, and reconstruct the fabric of a dismembered society. It was also clear that more than a mere restoration of order and tranquility was needed. The political reorganization of Mount Lebanon became imminent. Once again the future of Lebanon was at the mercy of foreign powers.

Concluding Remarks

During the short span of twenty years Lebanon witnessed at least five major episodes of civil strife and communal conflict. Not only did the scale and intensity of political violence increase during this period, it also assumed a new form. Until the end of the Egyptian occupation civil strife was largely nonsectarian. Feuding families and bickering feudal chiefs fought one another and, on two occasions, peasants revolted against their overlords. All such alignments were sustained by partisan, feudal, or class rivalry but rarely took the form of outright confessional hostility. Travelers and observers continued to be impressed by the spirit of amity and harmony which characterized relations between the various religious communities. As late as 1840, Maronites and Druzes were still signing joint declarations in opposition to Ibrāhīm Paşa's repressive measures.

An attempt was made in this essay to identify some of the internal and external sources of change which disrupted the balance of forces between the various religious communities. Factors such as the demise of the Shihābī dynasty, efforts to undermine local autonomy and traditional authority of feudal *shaykh*s, Maronite involvement in crushing the Druze uprising in Ḥawrān and the divisive consequences of the partition scheme all contributed to the intensification of confessional hostility.

The great power rivalry and the consequent internationalization of Lebanese politics also left their toll. Foreign powers, eager to gain inroads into the Middle East and win protégés, sought to pit one religious community against another. Added to this was the new centralized policy of the Ottomans directed at undermining the privileged status of Mount Lebanon and the local authority of feudal chiefs.

More important in this regard were the consequences of the liberal policies of Ibrāhīm Paşa and the egalitarian provisions of the two Ottoman edicts. A decade of Egyptian rule opened up the village society of Mount Lebanon to all sorts of societal changes and secular reforms but also generated a pronounced shift in the relative socioeconomic and political positions of the religious communities. The precarious balance which held society together and sustained confessional harmony was disrupted. The Ottoman *Tanzimat* did little to assuage these dislocations. On the contrary, the secular and innovative tones of the reforms were a threat to the vested interests of traditional Muslims, and the egalitarian provisions of the second edict provoked further hostility between the sects.

What general inferences, if any, can be made about the nature and consequences of communal conflict in pluralistic societies like Lebanon?

In some obvious respects, Lebanon then and now, had all the features of a fragmented political culture. Sharp divisions, sustained by striking differences in religious beliefs, communal, and regional allegiances continued to split the society and reinforce segmental and parochial loyalties. Superimposed on these traditional divisive forces were new forms of socioeconomic differentiation generated by the asymmetrical growth Lebanon witnessed during the nineteenth century. In short, there were both vertical and horizontal divisions which pulled the society apart and threatened the delicate balance of power. Accordingly, much of the (communal) conflict—factional, class, and confessional—Lebanon has repeatedly experienced might very well be an expression of its fragmented political culture and deficient civility.

That a fragmented and pluralistic society of this sort should display a high propensity for conflict is not unusual. What is unusual is the frequency, intensity and form of conflict or violence. The recurrence of violence suggests that the resort to violence has had little effect so far on redressing the gaps and imbalances in society or in transforming its communal and confessional loyalties and institutions into more secular and civic entities typical of a nation-state. Indeed, the very persistence of conflict means that something is not changing.

The persistence and changing form of conflict also reveals another curious feature of Lebanon's pluralism. The exposure of a growing portion of the population to secular forms of social control, the extension of state services, and the spread of market economy did little to weaken the intensity of communal loyalties. Confessional, kinship, and regional attachments continued to serve as viable sources of communal solidarity. They inspired local and personal initiative and accounted for much of the proverbial resourcefulness of the Lebanese at the time. However they also undermined civic consciousness and commitment to Lebanon as a political entity. Expressed more poignantly: the forces which motivated and sustained prosperity, harmony, and balance were also the very forces which on occasion pulled the society apart and contributed to conflict, tension, and civil disorder.

Notes

1. See, for example, Philip Hitti, *Lebanon in History,* London, 1957, p. 434; Kamal Salibi, *The Modern History of Lebanon,* London, 1956, p. 44.

2. For a detailed and factual description of the events and circumstances surrounding the Egyptian occupation of Syria, see Ṭannūs al-Shidyāq, *Akhbār al-aᶜyān fī Jabal Lubnān,* ed., Munir al-Khāzin, Beirut, 1954; Asad Rustum, "Ṣafḥa jadīda fī ta'rīkh al-thawra al-Durziyya: 1834–1838," *Al-Mashriq,* 35 (1937); William Polk, *The Opening of South Lebanon,* 1788–1840, Cambridge, MA, 1963.

3. Among others, this view is particularly advanced by William Polk (cited n. 2), Moshe Maᶜoz, *Ottoman Reform in Syria and Palestine* 1840–1841, Oxford, 1968, pp. 12–19; Charles Issawi, "British Consular Views on Syria's Economy in the 1850's–1860's," *American University of Beirut Festival Book* (Festschrift), F. Sarruf and S. Tamim, eds. Beirut, 1967, pp. 103–120.

4. Maᶜoz (cited n. 3), p. 12.

5. Polk (cited n. 2), p. 226.

6. Ibid., p. 109.

7. Ibid., p. 112.

8. For a full text of this historic document, see Haydar Shihāb, *Lubnān fī ᶜahd al-umarā' al-shihābīyyin,* Beirut, 1933, vol. 2, pp. 825–826.

9. Polk (cited n. 2), p. 135; Maᶜoz (cited n. 3), pp. 16–18.

10. Hitti (cited n. 1), p. 423.

11. As quoted by Polk (cited n. 2), p. 131.

12. For further details, see Polk (cited n. 2) pp. 153–157.

13. Henri Guys, *Beyrout et le Liban,* Paris, 1850, vol. 2, pp. 131–132.

14. Polk (cited n. 2), p. 159.

15. Dominique Chevallier, "Western Development and Eastern Crisis in the Mid-Nineteenth Century: Syria Confronted with the European Economy," in Polk and Chambers, eds., *Beginnings of Modernization in the Middle East,* Chicago, 1968, pp. 205–222.

16. For evidence of the increase in the number of ships visiting Beirut's harbor and for the consequent rise in the value of imports, see John Bowring, *Report on the Commercial Statistics of Syria,* London, 1840, p. 167; F.A. Neale, *Eight Years in Syria, Palestine and Asia Minor,* 2d edition, London, 1852, vol. 1, p. 247; Dominique Chevallier (cited n. 15), p. 214.

17. Chevallier, ibid., p. 208.

18. Bowring (cited n. 16), p. 167.

19. Polk (cited n. 2), pp. 167–168.

20. Ibid., p. 271.

21. Ibid., p. 171.

22. Neale (cited n. 16), vol. 1, p. 209.

23. Ibid., pp. 235–236.

24. Hester Stanhope, *Memoirs of the Lady Hester Stanhope,* second edition, London, 1846, vol. 1, pp. 216–217.

25. See Chevallier (cited n. 15), p. 210.

26. For further details see ibid., p. 214.

27. Ibid., pp. 211–212.

28. Polk (cited n. 2), p. 173.

29. Charles H. Churchill, *The Druzes and Maronites under the Turkish Rule,* London, 1862, pp. 29–30.

30. Polk (cited n. 2), p. 137.

31. For population estimates, see Guys (cited n. 13), pp. 275–277.

32. Churchill (cited n. 29), p. 104.

33. Ibid., pp. 104–105.

34. Ibid., p. 107.

35. For other pertinent details regarding the growing gulf between Christians and Druzes and their implications for inciting the confessional hostilities of the 1840s and 1850s, see ibid., pp. 95–131.

36. Chevallier (cited n. 15), p. 218.

37. For further details see William M. Thomson, *Lebanon, Damascus and Beyond Jordan,* London, 1886, p. 110; Stanhope (cited n. 24), vol. 2, pp. 102–112; Hitti (cited n. 1), p. 424; Polk (cited n. 1), p. 117.

38. For an elaboration of this notion of "asylum" and its implications for confessional coexistence, see Albert Hourani, *Syria and Lebanon,* London, 1946, pp. 129–130.

39. Hitti (cited n. 1), p. 424.

40. Salibi (cited n. 1), p. 38.

41. Hitti (cited n. 1), p. 424. For a full text of this remarkable revolutionary tract, see Asad Rustum (ed.), *Al-usūl al-ᶜArabiyya li-tarīkh Suriyya fī 'ahd Muḥammad ᶜAli Pasha,* Beirut, 1934, vol. 5, pp. 102–103.

42. See Iliya Harik, *Politics and Change in a Traditional Society, Lebanon, 1711–1845,* Princeton, 1968, p. 246.

43. As quoted ibid., p. 248.

44. Ibid., p. 249.

45. See Salibi (cited n. 1), p. 42.

46. Stanford Shaw, "Some Aspects of the Aims and Achievements of the 19th Century Ottoman Reformers," in Polk and Chambers (cited n. 15), pp. 32–33.

47. Salibi (cited n. 2), p. 44.

48. Malcolm Kerr, ed. and trans., *Lebanon in the Last Years of Feudalism,* Beirut, 1959, p. 4. For further details, see also Salibi (cited n. 1), pp. 47–48.

49. Churchill (cited n. 29), pp. 63–64.

50. For further details, see ibid., pp. 46–62; Hitti (cited n. 1), pp. 434–435.

51. See Salibi (cited n. 1), p. 50; Hitti (cited n. 1), pp. 434–435.

52. Churchill (cited n. 29), p. 52.

53. See Salibi (cited n. 1), p. 53.

54. Churchill (cited n. 29), pp. 66–75.

55. Salibi (cited n. 1), p. 55.

56. Ibid., p. 62.

57. See Kerr (cited n. 48), pp. 5–6; Churchill (cited n. 29), pp. 64–79.

58. See Harik (cited n. 42), p. 268.

59. Churchill (cited n. 29), pp. 76–77.

60. As quoted by Salibi (cited n. 1), p. 64.

61. See Kerr (cited n. 48), pp. 6–7.

62. For further details, see Salibi (cited n. 1), pp. 63–66.

63. For further details, see Kerr (cited n. 48), pp. 8–9; Salibi (cited n. 1), pp. 66–67.

64. For an excellent and thorough analysis of the whole question of the double *qa'imaqāmiyya* and the Reglement Shakib Effendi, see M. Jouplain (pseudonym of Bulus Nujaim), *La Question du Liban; Etude d'histoire diplomatique et de droit international,* Paris, 1908, pp. 297–353; see also D. Chevallier, *La Societe du Mont Liban a l'epoque de la revolution industrielle en Europe,* Paris, 1971, pp. 174–179; Eugene Poujade, *Le Liban et la Syrie;* 1845–1860, Paris, 1867, pp. 34–35.

65. For an English translation of the full text of the Reglement, see J. C. Hurewitz, *Diplomacy in the Near and Middle East,* Princeton, 1956, pp. 132–135.

66. Harik (cited n. 42), p. 273.

67. Salibi (cited n. 1), p. 73.

68. Ibid., p. 73.

69. See Moshe Maᶜoz, "The Impact of Modernization on Syrian Politics and Society during the Early *Tanzimat* Period" in Polk and Chambers (cited n. 15), p. 333.

70. Roderic Davison, *Reform in the Ottoman Empire, 1856–1876,* Princeton, 1963, p. 7.

71. For a critical treatment of these and earlier military reforms, see ibid., pp. 21–31; Bernard Lewis, *The Emergence of Modern Turkey,* London, 1968, pp. 74–103; Şerif Mardin, *The Genesis of Young Ottoman Thought,* Princeton, 1962, pp. 133–155.

72. See Davison (cited n. 70), p. 37.

73. For a full English translation of the edict, see Hurewitz (cited n. 65), vol. 1, pp. 113–116.

74. Davison (cited n. 70), p. 41.

75. It is of interest to note that Rashid Pasha, the architect of the edict, was labeled by his reactionary opponents as *gavur* (infidel). See Maᶜoz (cited n. 3), p. 25.

76. Lewis (cited n. 65), p. 107.

77. See Hurewitz (cited n. 65), vol. 1, p. 113; Maᶜoz (cited n. 3), pp. 25–26.

78. Davison (cited n. 70), p. 45.

79. Hurewitz (cited n. 65), vol. 1, p. 151.

80. For an English translation of the full text of the edict, see ibid., pp. 149–153.

81. Hitti (cited n. 1), p. 430.

82. For further details, see R.H. Davison, "Turkish Attitudes Concerning Christian Muslim

Equality in the 19th Century,'' *American Historical Review,* vol. 59 (1954), p. 848; Ma^{c}oz (cited n. 3), pp. 81–84; Al-Shidyaq (cited n. 2), vol. 2, p. 345.

83. See Ma^{c}oz (cited n. 3), pp. 151–152.

84. For further elaboration of this point of view, see I.M. Smilianskaya, ''The Disintegration of Feudal Relations in Syria and Lebanon in the Middle of the Nineteenth Century,'' in Charles Issawi, ed., *The Economic History of the Middle East, 1800–1914,* Chicago, 1966, pp. 234–235.

85. See J. Lewis Farley, *Two Years in Syria,* London, 1858, p. 36.

86. As quoted by Chevallier (cited n. 15), p. 219.

87. See Charles Issawi (cited n. 3), p. 115; see also Chevallier (cited n. 15), p. 218.

88. For a convincing exposition of this form of ''dualism'' in the *Tanzimat*–i.e., a ''Pretence of maintaining two parallel systems, officially in harmony but actually in deadly conflict'' see, A.L. Tibawi, *A Modern History of Syria,* London, 1969, pp. 132–134.

89. See Ma^{c}oz (cited n. 3), p. 203.

90. Salibi (cited n. 1), p. 85.

91. Kerr (cited n. 48), p. 49.

92. Ibid., p. 53; Churchill (cited n. 29), pp. 111–112.

93. Tibawi (cited n. 88), p. 123.

94. Henry H. Jessup, *Fifty-Three Years in Syria,* 1910, vol. 1, pp. 165–166.

95. Salibi (cited n. 1), p. 93.

96. Churchill (cited n. 29), pp. 142–143.

97. For these and other estimates, see Churchill, ibid., p. 132; Hitti (cited n. 1), p. 438; Salibi (cited n. 1) p. 106.

6

The Two Worlds of Assaad Y. Kayat

KAMAL S. SALIBI

As a Beirut Christian of the nineteenth century, the handsome, urbane, perceptive, and articulate businessman and physician, conversing freely in no less than eight languages, was undoubtedly ahead of his times. A well-traveled man, highly informed, versatile, of liberal views, and of a vision unobstructed by prejudice, he understood the power of the emerging industrial world of his day as few of his Arab contemporaries did and accepted its impact on the traditional society of Ottoman Syria with complete openness of mind. Yet, in his own times, Assaad Y. Kayat (Asᶜad Yaᶜqūb al-Khayyāṭ) does not appear to have made much of an impression on his compatriots. In an age when other thoughtful Christians in his native city, mainly under the influence of American Protestant missionaries, were seeking—in some cases genially, in others somewhat pedantically—to resolve the problem of their cultural identity at the intellectual level by placing themselves at the head of an Arab humanist revival of Western liberal inspiration, the particular Greek Orthodox moneychanger and trader whose career is presently under review was seen to be no more than a freewheeling businessman with an unusual gift for languages and a facility to get along with foreigners which often aroused suspicion. Heedless of social censure, the man had no qualms about breaking ties with a native culture to which he was never profoundly attached, ultimately to become a British subject and spend the last seventeen or eighteen years of his life in the consular service of the British Crown.

Had Kayat not written the story of his own life, his name would hardly have been remembered in the annals of his native land. His career, indeed, would scarcely have warranted more than a marginal digression in the history of the British consular service in the Levant—which is what it rightly received in A. L. Tibawi's *British Interests in Palestine, 1800–1901.*[1] In fact, even his autobiography, *A Voice from Lebanon,* was not meant for his own folk to read. Written in English and published in London in 1847 by Madden & Co. of Leadenhall-Street, it was addressed to his "British friends," in the hope that it would "not be unacceptable to the British public."[2] Little wonder that it remained unread—and virtually unknown—in his own country until a carefully expurgated and inadequate translation of it into Arabic was published in Beirut under the auspices of the Catholic Press in 1957. As a document of the period, the book is nevertheless of special importance. In an engaging style of Victorian flavor highlighted by exotic Arabic idioms, it relates the story of a man whose career coincided with the opening of the Levant to large-scale European economic penetration, and with the growth of Beirut from a small, walled coastal town into the leading seaport of Ottoman Syria. It also reveals a man with an agile mind who came to grips with problems faced by other Syrians of his age, and resolved them to his own satisfaction, though not, perhaps, to the satisfaction of his society.

Assaad Kayat himself was blissfully unaware of the little impression he made on his Syrian contemporaries. To his British readers, he depicted himself as the bold leader of a movement of social reform, and the unwavering champion of the cause of modernism (notably of modern education and woman's liberation) among his people. The Arabic literature of the period does not, however, bear out these claims on his part; nor does the contemporary Protestant missionary literature endorse his pretensions, although he was among the first natives of Syria to associate with the Protestant missions. It was probably in an unconscious attempt to atone for the readiness with which he abandoned many native ways that Kayat never opted for Protestantism, but remained a faithful follower of the Greek Orthodox Church throughout his life. Those among his Christian countrymen who abandoned the native churches found in their conversion to Protestantism an avenue for intellectual liberation within the context of their own culture, and were thus able to remain Arab—and in some cases eminently so—while accepting the fundamental tenets of Western liberalism. The influence of the missionaries—particularly the broad humanism of such American scholar-preachers as Eli Smith and Cornelius Van Dyck—sharpened their perceptions and widened their horizons, but it encouraged them at the same time to deepen their appreciation of their own Arab heritage and seek to infuse it with a new vitality. Thus they were able to develop their minds, so to speak, without losing their souls. In the case of Kayat, the situation was different. While he remained to the end a defender of what he called "Eastern Orthodoxy" against the Protestant missionaries, he turned his back to the rest of his heritage—of which his understanding was in any case superficial—to become the prototype of the Syrian Levantine.

Assaad Kayat was born in Beirut in 1811. His father, Ya^cqūb, was apparently a well-to-do trader who "spoke well the modern Greek, Turkish, and Albanian languages, but did not write them."[3] One uncle, Attalla (ᶜAṭāllāh), who died when Assaad was still a child, could understand Italian; in 1799, when a British naval squadron arrived in Syria to help Aḥmad Jazzār Paşa defend Acre against Napoleon Bonaparte, this Attalla had acted as interpreter to the squadron commander, Commodore Sir Sidney Smith, and had also accompanied him on a tour of Mount Lebanon.[4] Another uncle, Yoosef (Yūsuf)—apparently a celibate, who lived in Yaᶜqūb's house—was "a scholar and a good man" who read the Bible regularly, and who was "almost [the] first friend" of the first American missionaries to come to Beirut.[5] Thus young Assaad, who was the second of two sons, grew up in a family which had already had contacts with foreigners. He was still a child when his father set him to learn Greek, in addition to Arabic, and before he was ten the boy began to frequent the port and offer his services as interpreter and market guide to the Greek sea captains who stopped in Beirut:

> The trade of the Mediterranean was carried on by Ionian or Greek ships under the British flag, and also by French and Italians, Austrians and Sclavonians. The Arab and Turkish vessels were frequently stopped by the Greeks, who were the chief traders. These men employed me cheerfully as their interpreter and broker, for I was satisfied with whatever they gave me. They gave me a commission on the goods they sold, and the natives who purchased of, or sold them, did the same. I have been seen leading ten captains at a time through the market at Beyrout. I did not allow the common sailors to escape me, but also interpreted for them. I bought oil, meat, & c., for the ships . . . and my income often amounted to three hundred piastres a day. . . .[6]

Kayat, indeed, had already acquired considerable experience in the money market and in trade before he began to do business with the Greek sea captains:

> When I was about eight years of age, I began to think seriously on my future life, and I broke the jar in which I had saved all my pocket-money, amounting to 1000 piastres, or about £10 English. . . . I took part of my little fortune in my pocket, and went from shop to shop . . . and collected all the old paras I could, giving other currency in exchange. These old paras I . . . separated according to their weight: the heaviest I sold to the silversmith, who put them into the crucible, and I thus gained from ten to twenty percent. . . . The Turkish current money is in piastres: forty paras make one piastre. . . . But the paras of the old sultans were of nearly pure silver; so that a para of Sultan Mustapha, or Sultan Mohammad, is worth ten paras of the present day. In other regions, paras and all coins were struck at a much lower standard, but all paras passed as such, whatever their intrinsic value; and this was the great secret of money-making, known to all silversmiths, moneychangers, and merchants in Syria. . . . In one year, my capital augmented from 1000 to 6000 piastres, or from £10 to £60. Finding myself so rich, I came to the resolution no longer to be a burden on my father, which of course delighted him, and he made me a present of a donkey which had been previously employed by a man named Shaheen [Shāhīn], in carrying on a little trade about Lebanon. I retained this man and the donkey to convey goods such as calico, handkerchiefs, & c., from Beyrout to the valley [of the Biqāᶜ] between Lebanon and Anti-Lebanon, exchanging them for butter, eggs, etc. . . . In this way I gained about forty piastres each journey he made.[7]

The leading *ṣarrāf* (moneychanger) in Beirut at the time was a man called Abū ᶜAwn, and Kayat found it prudent to cooperate with him: "He did the great business, and I the minor: he waited on the great merchants, and I went to the shopkeepers and collected all the valuable coins. This secured for me the favour of the retail dealers, and I used to gain about 100 piastres a day."[8] Learning how to accommodate the venality of the local police chief was the next step. "Finding that I was moving among the rich Moslem merchants . . . [he] determined to squeeze me. . . . I went on in this manner, squeezing the coins, and being occasionally squeezed myself; yet I grew fat in gold."[9]

By cultivating the acquaintance of the muleteers (*mukāriya,* sing. *mukārī*) who carried goods between Beirut and other parts of Syria, Kayat gained expert knowledge of the value of coins in different towns. In Jerusalem, gold currency was cheaper than in Beirut, and silver more expensive. This resolved young Kayat to combine business enterprise with filial piety and religious zeal by taking his mother on a pilgrimage to the Holy City. The account of his commercial undertakings on the occasion is disarmingly frank:

> I cannot say that I employed all my time in devotion. . . . I felt that my pilgrimage would not be the less valid if I did a little business, and made money to cover our expenses. I began, therefore, to frequent the society of pilgrims, and I bought up all sorts of old coins, silver plates, & c., which they bring both for their expenses and their offerings.[10]

Kayat does not say what was the net profit that accrued to him from his lucrative visit to Jerusalem. He reports, however, the accidental loss of 500 gold pieces on one occasion, which were subsequently recovered to his delight.[11] Clearly, his total profits must have exceeded this amount.

It was some years before he undertook his pilgrimage to Jerusalem that Kayat made his first acquaintance with the American Protestant missionaries who began to arrive in Beirut in the early 1820s. The boy, at the time, was anxious to learn Italian, as he "was desirous of being employed . . . by the Sclavonian traders" who spoke that language.[12] A certain Padre Modesto, from the local Italian Capuchin convent, was willing to give him the required instruction. Before long, however, the padre began to exert pressure on the boy to convert to Roman Catholicism, and the lessons were subsequently dropped. It was then that his Uncle Yoosef introduced him to Isaac Bird and William Goodell of the American Mission Board, who had only recently arrived in the city. "At once I began Italian with dear Mr. Bird . . . and I was the first pupil of that mission. In a short time, I acquired so much Italian that I was appointed teacher in the school, when other Syrian boys were attracted there. . . ."[13] In addition to Italian, young Kayat studied English with another American missionary, Pliny Fisk, who lived with William Goodell. When Fisk died soon after, he continued his English studies with Goodell and also with Mrs. John W. Farren. The latter was a British lady who was staying with the American missionaries in Beirut, while her husband—who later became the first British consul-general in Syria—was traveling around the country. For the moment, Kayat "left the money-making business with the sea captains" and contented himself with the allowance of "five-dollars, or £1 per month" which he received from the missionaries in return for his teaching services.[14] Meanwhile, he learned "to read Armenian and Turkish, from Mr. Carabet and Mr. Stephan, two Armenian converts to Protestantism."[15]

For a time, young Kayat actually lived with the missionaries. His parents and family friends, however, fearing that he might be converted to Protestantism, intervened and prevailed on him to return home and maintain only a casual relationship with his American friends. The conversion to Protestantism of a certain Asᶜad al-Shidyāq—a young Maronite who taught Arabic in the American missionary school—had recently provoked a scandal in the country, and the Kayats were anxious not to have the scandal repeated in their own family. As it happened, Assaad Kayat, unlike his Shidyāq namesake, was more interested "in the business of the world" than in fine points of theology: "many errors might prevail amongst our people, but I thought they did not concern me."[16] He therefore resolved to stop working for the missionaries, although he continued to visit them and attend their Scripture-reading meetings. Shortly after, he became a business associate of "two rich Swiss merchants," M. Brelaz and Gauthey, who arrived to establish themselves in Beirut:

> Their business was very extensive, and, as they did not understand Arabic, they engaged me as interpreter and storekeeper at ten dollars per month, and a certain percentage. This was a very responsible situation, and by it I was initiated to the secrets of commerce. I copied their French letters, and thus from them I learnt French, so that we no longer wanted Italian as the medium of conversation between us.[17]

The association between Kayat and M. Brelaz and Gauthey came to a sudden end in 1827, when the European naval intervention at the battle of Navarino, on behalf of the cause of Greek independence, precipitated an acute crisis in the relations between the Ottoman Empire and the European powers. Suddenly, "every hat left our shores"[18]—the hat, at the time, being the distinctive mark of the European or American. It was then that Kayat, deprived of his "rich and worthy employers," decided to go into business on his own, and, as already mentioned, proceeded to take his mother on the pilgrimage to Jerusalem, his first truly independent commercial venture.

Encouraged by his success in Jerusalem, Kayat, who was now barely nineteen years old, decided to expand his commercial activities. He therefore entered into partnership with a certain Hājj ᶜAbdallāh—a "most respectable" Muslim merchant of Beirut—and set out on a prolonged business trip which took him to Damascus, Homs, Hama, and Tripoli. "There cannot be more honorable men of business than these Moslem merchants"[19]—such was Kayat's judgment with respect to his association with Ḥājj ᶜAbdallāh.

On his way to Damascus, Kayat—by a fortunate accident—formed a useful connection with a Damascene "Aga," or grandee:

> At that time, alas! the Christian at Damascus, "who had no back," as they term it, was in a very awkward position. . . . The Aga seemed pleased at my sitting in his presence with proper respect. He happened to want some letters written: I offered my services, and wrote them for him. . . . He told me I might seek his protection at Damascus, and that as his protegé I should have nothing to fear in that great city. . . . At that time [Damascus] was only a fit habitation for Moslems, both

> Christians and Jews being exposed to the greatest indignities. They were not allowed to ride at all, not even a donkey, nor to wear any dress but black. Even European travellers with a firman from the Sultan were compelled to alight from their horses on arriving at the city gate, and to wear the Eastern dress. . . . The Mohammadans exercise the utmost power over the "infidels," as they term all who do not hold to their faith.[20]

As a Greek Orthodox Christian, albeit with some Protestant views, Kayat had already experienced the usefulness of the religious connection with members of his own community when he visited Palestine. Wherever he traveled in Syria, Greek Orthodox Christians—both clergy and laity—received him with the cordial spirit of religious fraternity. Upon reaching Damascus, he went to stay in the house of a Greek Orthodox priest in the Christian quarter, and lost no time before going dutifully to pay his respects to "his Eminence Methodius, patriarch of Antioch," who resided in the city close by. "The sight of this venerable patriarch was to me a testimony for the truth."[21] He was deeply impressed by the "perseverance" of the Damascene Christians in their faith through the centuries of Muslim domination, and noted the fact with a glow of pride:

> On entering the church at Damascus, I could not help reflecting, that the many hundred years of persecution had not been able to extirpate the followers of the Cross. . . . I was much struck by the devotion of some of the Christians. . . . The Christians of Damascus, in common with others of Syria, cannot but be the descendants of the primitive Christians of the time of our Lord and his Apostles and their immediate successors; for Syria was the first country conquered by the Moslems in the seventh century, and as the Mohammedan law forbids, on pain of decapitation, any convert being made to Christianity, or to any other religion except their own, so it must be evident that no converts were made after Islamism prevailed in Syria. Thus, the present Christians must be the descendants of those whom . . . the [Muslim] conquerors of Damascus . . . found it good policy to tolerate. This, no doubt, was directed by the finger of God, as an evidence of the truth of Christianity, for we learn much by the perseverance of these Christians. They show us the original foundation of the Church nineteen centuries ago.[22]

Turning to more worldly matters, Kayat was quick to observe the enterprise of the merchants of Damascus—Muslims, Christians, and Jews alike. He also noted the unscrupulous voracity of the European businessmen who envied the commercial success of the emerging Syrian entrepreneurial class and (as he was convinced) sought its destruction:

> The Moslems [among the Damascene merchants] are very rich: they carry their trade all over Syria, Turkey, Egypt, Bagdad, and across the desert to Persia and India. One of these merchants, named Pashagi, whom I knew intimately, made, it is said, a fortune of £400,000 by his commerical skill. Both Jews and Christians of Damascus have carried on commerce with Bengal and England, importing their indigo from Bengal, and their shirtings and calicoes from Liverpool and Manchester.

Turning to the merchants of Syria in general, he continues:

> Some of them, such as Barbir and Farajalah of Beyrout, Hanhourie of Damascus, Hashém of Aleppo, and others, desirous of extending their commerce, embarked for Europe, and established houses in Marseilles, Leghorn, Geneva, Trieste. This kind of enterprise excited the jealousy of some foreign merchants, also trading to those parts of the world, who pretended that if these nations were enlightened, they might follow the steps of their ancestors, the Phoenicians, and take the whole commerce of the Levant into their own hands. This jealousy, without any regard to conscience, has caused great efforts to be made to crush them; and false reports were raised against Jews, Christians, and Moslems, however honest. Would to God that His Highness the Sultan knew the spirit of enterprise among his people, and that his government would extend to them the same privileges as to other nations! then he would see what a flourishing band of merchants he would have![23]

The irony was that the author of this eloquent expression of mercantilist patriotism was to end his career as an agent—and indeed a prominent agent—of foreign commercial expansion in his own native land; more so, that he never became aware of the irony of his own position, considering that the above was written by him long after his first association with the British consular service in Syria had been established!

From Damascus, Kayat set out for Homs with a letter of introduction from Patriarch Methodius to the bishop of the city. Here, as in Damascus, he was warmly received by the local members of his community. The same cordiality and assistance were accorded to him by the Greek Orthodox Christians of Hama. Next he proceeded to Tripoli, whose staunchly Greek Orthodox Christians were "the most liberal . . . in Syria":

> [They are] Christians of the Eastern Church, among whom the Pope's agent has never succeeded in making a schism.[24] . . . They pay their ladies due homage; and the lady, though veiled when she goes out with fifteen yards of bleached calico, presides at home as the lady of the house, receives her visitors in the presence of her husband, and converses with them, provided they are Christians. They have been accused by other Syrians of ruling their husbands.[25]

From Tripoli, Kayat returned to Beirut laden with profit and settled accounts with his Muslim partner. The year was 1830, the question of Greek independence from the Ottoman Empire had finally been settled, and the British government had just appointed John W. Farren as the first British consul-general in Syria; the place assigned for his residence was to be Damascus. Arriving first in Beirut, Farren appointed a certain N. (Niqūlā?) Misk, "an elderly gentleman who spoke Italian,"[26] to be first dragoman to the consulate-general. He then summoned Kayat, who had once studied English with Mrs. Farren, to assume the position of second dragoman, an appointment which "made many friends rejoice, and caused many enemies to weep."[27] Like other native dragomans in the service of European consuls, Kayat was permitted to carry on with his personal business. The immunities he enjoyed as a consular employee were eminently useful to him in this respect, and he soon became involved in complex trading operations in money and commodities, with agents in Jerusalem, Jaffa, and Egypt. The circumstances of the war, which broke out shortly after between Muḥammad ᶜAlī Paşa of Egypt and the Ottoman sultan, and which ended in 1832 with the Egyptian occupation of Syria (1832–1840), favored Kayat's speculations and secured for him considerable profits. Shortly after the Egyptians took Damascus, the first dragoman Misk "departed this life"[28] and Kayat was promoted to assume his position. It was then that Consul-General Farren, accompanied by his first dragoman, was finally able to enter the city on horseback (he refused to enter the city otherwise) and establish himself there.

As a man mainly interested in business, Kayat did not understand the complex power politics of his time, and his political judgments were generally shallow. For example, his comments on the Lebanese revolt of 1840—a revolt which ended with the expulsion of Ibrāhīm Paşa, Muḥammad ᶜAlī's son, from Syria, and the departure of the Lebanese Emir Bashīr Shihāb II into exile—show that he was either unaware of the British complicity in the revolt, or else that he was echoing the British minority opinion of the period (and that of local merchants and European residents) which was favorable to continued Egyptian rule in Syria:

> What was the object of this war? It was to drive Ibrahim Pasha out of Syria. It was to drive out the best government the country had had for many years. Syria was wretchedly governed before him, and it was he who gave liberty to Christians and Jews. He entered Syria with a great army in 1831, and was welcomed by the whole Syrian population of all sects [*sic.*]. He wisely secured the cooperation of the Emir Bashir, the best governor that ever ruled the people of Lebanon and the mountainous district. . . . [Ibrahim] gained the love of the people by making all equal before the law, Mohammedan, Christian, Jew, Druse, Matwali, Anzeir [Nuṣayrī], etc. . . . He allowed both Christians and Jews to wear any color they pleased; and he granted them full liberty to ride horses in the streets, which vexed the bigots. He at last began a conscription, which was levied amongst the people of every sect except the Christians, he took the idle and the bad, and made soldiers of them. This roused the bitterness of the Mohammedan population, and their report of some acts of injustice resounded through Europe. The Sultan's army, the agitation in Europe, and other difficulties so absorbed his thoughts, that he could not look into the internal affairs of the country. The Druses revolted in Hooran [Ḥawrān]; also some of the people of Lebanon and some self-interested agitators, half Levantines, half Europeans, were hired to spread the report that England and other European powers were about to take upon themselves to arrange the affairs of Syria. This unsettled state of things continued from 1836 to 1839 and gave the Pasha much trouble. The disturbance in Lebanon was put a stop to by Emir Bashir, though the country generally continued in a state of excitement. I was at this time in the mountains, and can testify that the Pasha's troops behaved in the most becoming manner, and I believe the whole country might then have been restored to tranquility, and the question might have been settled by diplomatic agency.[29]

While Kayat was unable to understand the machinations of his British friends in Syria at the political level, he certainly understood what their interests in the country were at the more concrete economic level. His summary of the career of Consul-General Farren is highly informed and full of insight, although he attributes to him mainly humane and Christian motives:

> Mr. Farren filled his office most ably. By him, the route, the interior, and commerce were opened to Englishmen and Europeans in general; and he was without doubt, the only Christian that had been seen in Damascus on horseback for 1100 years. He first started the post from Beyrout to Damascus and Bagdad for India. He did the highest honour to the nation he represented; and we, as Syrians, ought to be thankful to him for the Dispensary he established at Damascus, at his own expense. His having done this for the love he bore to the Christians, increased his influence in the right channel, and broke down the prejudices of many of the natives of Damascus. I wish I was able to do justice to this very talented and benevolent man, and his truly Christian lady. . . . This gentleman had, during his travels in the country some years before, penetrated into the different cities, and acquired the Arabic language, together with much influence over the minds of some of the grandees of Damascus. . . . In order to promote British commerce, [he] himself [as consul-general] introduced in the bazaars of Damascus the beautiful goods of Manchester, Glasgow, Sheffield, and Birmingham, encountering all the difficulties and losses, by paving the way for regular merchants. . . . His first act, within a month of his arrival, was to establish a post for letters between Damascus and Beyrout twice a week, and ultimately the distance was performed in twelve hours. . . . He spared not his own horses, and made his own janissaries [*sic.*] take the post by turns, going the distance at full gallop. . . . This enterprising and active Consul next undertook to establish a similar mail across the desert for Bagdad, and thus to forward the British mail via Bassara [Baṣra] for Bombay. At first there was great difficulty; but, having invited the chiefs of the Bedouins to his house, by means of coffee, kindness and dollars, with firmness and reasonable explanations, he prevailed upon the Sheikhs to assist; and one of them, Jaed by name, engaged to convey the mail to Bagdad by dromedaries. The journey was performed in twelve days, and afterwards in nine! . . . In a very short time, the British commercial houses of Todd, Black, Christie, and Tubie, Ionians and Judaeans, all in their hats, established themselves at Damascus; and under the security of Ibrahim Pasha's government the city became full of Europeans, Persians, Hindoos, Greeks, and other foreigners, and commerce flourished beyond measure. . . . Not a single tax was imposed on British goods beyond the tariff. . . . When the expedition up the Euphrates, under . . . Colonel Chesey, arrived at Sevedia [Suwaydiyya, the port of Antioch], Mr. Farren obtained an order . . . to afford it every assistance.[30]

Kayat was full of praise for the "wonderful change" that was "occasioned" in Syria by the arrival of Consul-General Farren.[31] His own "unexpected appointment" as a dragoman to Farren established him as a man of privilege. Among other things, it "made a great revolution in [his] dress":

> Christians at the time were only allowed to wear black turbans and red shoes. I now had to change my black turban, the sign of humiliation, for a white one, the sign of liberty; my red shoes for yellow ones; my poor sash for a cashmere shawl; and I was mounted on horseback instead of walking on foot. This style was required to maintain the dignity of the office, and must be kept up for the sake of influence.[32]

It was while Kayat was established in Damascus as first dragoman to Consul-General Farren that three princes of the Persian royal house arrived in the city, in 1835, on their way to visit England. Kayat "had the honour of waiting" on these illustrious travelers, and made such a favorable impression on them with his linguistic versatility that they urgently requested Farren to permit him to accompany them on the rest of the journey. Setting out from Beirut in the British steamer *Africane,* the royal party, attended to by Kayat, stopped at Alexandria, then at Malta, proceeding from there to Cadiz, and finally to Falmouth, on H. M. S. *Spitfire*. On the way, Kayat picked up a speaking knowledge of Persian, which he later found occasion to develop:

> I ought to mention, for the encouragement of those who wish to acquire a foreign language, that perseverance and determination carry one through beautifully. I admit that my Arabic was of great use to me in the study of Persian, for an Arabic scholar can learn any Eastern language with ease; with this help I learnt Persian in three months, and I used to spend hours with Prince Wali discussing religious subjects, and defending Christianity as the truth. His highness was most reasonable. No fear now of my head being taken off! Indeed, they were all most gracious and condescending Princes, and it was a great honor to be in their company. Our conversations were most interesting.[33]

The first impressions which England made on Kayat were mixed. On the surface at least, there was much to admire:

> The splendid residences of the nobility and gentry, with the wealth displayed in the shops, astonished us greatly. . . . There is a vast difference between one, who, making wealth by his industry, can shew the possession of it by the splendor of his establishment, and bequeath it to his children and grandchildren; and one who must wear rags out of doors, lest he should be suspected of having money, and lose his head in consequence. We could not help but remark the unostentatious appearance of the ministers of state, contrasted with the petty dignity assumed by those in office in parts of the East, where a Pasha with two tails has more pride about him than the prime minister of Great Britain. . . . Here the government borrows money, and must pay interest; and a man of the highest rank cannot touch the person of the meanest peasant. . . . By observing these contrasts, we may learn the benefits arising from civilisation, and hope that they will soon be extended to other parts of the globe; and this may be expected by steam communication affording the means of rapid intercourse. . . . The perfect liberty of London is very agreeable, a man may go anywhere, at any time, and do what he likes, provided he does not disturb the public peace, and nobody cares or thinks about him. . . . English merchants and bankers observe the highest honour in their dealings. . . . With all the disadvantages of climate, and the dearness of living, a man in no part of the world can enjoy greater liberty and comfort than in England; and, taking it altogether, it is indeed a most happy country. The constitution is divine! the institutions are glorious! and the poorest British peasant has more independence than a prince in many other countries.[34]

Kayat, before long, was to lose his soul to England. Nevertheless, he did have some negative comments to make:

> Woe to him who has neither friends nor a full purse in gigantic London. . . . Here, as in the East, they often had two prices; and this I discovered by changing my dress and going out at night in a European garb. Then I offered a price much lower than

> what I had been asked the day when in the company of the Princes, and it was accepted; but in some shops they had only one high price. . . . The English seemed to me grave and melancholy. Every one appeared absorbed in the endeavour to amass wealth, as the means of subsistence. I was amazed at once hearing a gentleman say, that the great luxury of London consisted in not knowing one's next door neighbour; but to me this artificial mode of life appeared a great interruption to their happiness. These observations apply more especially to the middle classes, for their nobles live like kings, and their rich persons like princes. The ladies are very beautiful and highly accomplished; and although it struck me as most extraordinary that they should be so much in society, and possess so much influence, yet a few months' residence convinced me, that it was quite a mercy for Englishmen to have such superior wives, otherwise I believe many would go mad. . . . The higher and lower classes are in nothing more different than in their mode of speech; unlike the people of the East, where a peasant or a Bedouin speaks as correctly as a grandee. . . . An Englishman will be more troubled to entertain a guest for a single night, than a Syrian would to receive ten people. In England, the arrival of a guest interferes with all the ordinary arrangements of the house. . . . One is in the constant apprehension of hearing, "Why does he not go to the inn?" I certainly did not in all respects like the style of their dinners. It disgusted me to see a man of refinement eat game, the very odour of which took away all my appetite, and the little ugly worms in cheese, and strangled animals with blood, which are held in abomination by Jews and Mohammedans as well as by Eastern Christians. This perplexes Orientals of all sects, and causes them to abstain from eating at English tables. I cannot tell how the Europeans can overlook the commands of God, both in the Old and New Testament; and I never heard the subject satisfactorily explained by any divine.[35]

It was apparently while Kayat was touring England with the Persian princes that he became concerned with "forming a decision as to [his] future career."[36] He began, he says, to "long to work for the good of [his] own people"[37]; more likely, his mind was set on observing opportunities for his own personal advancement as a native of Syria enjoying the advantage of developing connections with England. It was probably with this in view that Kayat developed his idea of what he called "native agency"—a Syrian Christian intermediary by means of which European missionary activity (and presumably other interests) in the Muslim world could best be served. No doubt, Kayat saw himself as the man ideally suited to take charge of such "native agency," but he also maintained that other Syrian Christians could also be involved in the project, if properly trained. The idea, as it was ultimately to take form in his mind, was as follows:

> A plan might be formed to build up the Eastern Church, by instructing its young clergy, by establishing schools, and promoting female education . . . by these means, under the blessing of God, Syria might become a light to lighten the nations; its geographic position being so central, that, from it, communication would be easy to any part of Asia or Africa. The natives of Syria being accustomed to the heat of their own climate, can travel without inconvenience through the deserts, and to all parts of the East; and, as they speak the Arabic language, which is common to above 160 millions of people, they can converse with most Asiatic

> and African nations. All the followers of Mohammad speak Arabic, and revere it as the language of heaven; while it is so difficult and copious, that it would take a foreigner at least ten years to learn it, and even then he would not be able to address his hearers in the peculiar idioms and parables used in the East. Again, an European would require double the amount to support him, compared to what would be requisite for a native, even if he survived the heat of the climate.[38]

As a businessman, Kayat was careful to point out the commercial benefits which would accrue to industrial Europe through the missionary and educational work which his concept of "native agency" involved:

> In England, the merchant and manufacturer well knows that his interest is promoted by the consumption of his goods, or an exchange with other countries, and by extended intercourse and enterprise; an Indian, Syrian, or Egyptian will there find a market for his corn, cotton, oil, fruit, silk, &c., as well as in France or Germany, from whence he may import the useful and beautiful Manchester, Birmingham, Sheffield, Glasgow, or colonial goods, as well as the beautiful manufactures of Lyons, Leipsic, and Trieste; and thus mutual interest will promote mutual intercourse and friendship; and then the natives and residents will naturally turn their attention to facilitate the means of transit, which can only be affected by making good roads, carriages, &c. But it may be asked, how is this intercourse to be initiated? By the Eastern learning the European languages; by his becoming acquainted with commercial houses in London, Liverpool, Manchester, Marseilles, Trieste, Hamburgh, &c., and forming connexions there; by his visiting these places in person. . . . The rapid steam communication of our day is so favourable to immediate superintendence by those who embark their capital in such enterprises, that very little opportunity is afforded for acts of dishonesty. . . . This intercourse of natives with other countries will, I fear, provoke the bitterest feelings of some of that class of individuals who had, before the introduction of steam, located themselves in different places; for they ignorantly and selfishly fancy that their whole interest depends upon the natives remaining in a state of ignorance. . . . Nevertheless, the spirit of the age, I believe, is conquering all these prejudices, bigotry and shortsightedness.[39]

Back in Beirut from his first visit to England, Kayat resigned his post as first dragoman to Consul-General Farren, announcing to him his intention of "giving up [his] fortune, and changing a life of ease and pleasure for one of poverty and the cross."[40] Judging by his activities in the years that followed, when he was devoting himself (as he claimed) to the "welfare of Syria," it does not appear that Kayat gave up much. After traveling through Syria to satisfy himself "that a great thirst for knowledge exists everywhere"[41] (one suspects that he satisfied himself to other things besides, including some profitable commercial transactions), he resolved to cross the desert to "visit Bagdad and Babylon."[42] His visit, he frankly admits, was "profitable in the way of business"—among other things, he made "profitable purchases" of "turquoise and pearls" from Persians coming to Iraq to visit the Shīʿite holy places.[43] It also appears that the journey was undertaken under official British auspices, and that Kayat left the British consular services only to be employed by Consul-General Farren more discreetly as a free-lance agent:

> I was providentially directed to seek the assistance of Jaad, one of the chiefs of the powerful Bedouin tribe Aanazee [ᶜAnaza], who agreed to escort me through the Desert. . . . The journey we made was the quickest ever performed, for I had a great object in view—I wished to ascertain the possibility of this route becoming the highway to India and central Asia, and I can see no reason why it should not. Wells might be dug for water, and two thousand regular troops, with four castles on the road, and some artillery, would suffice. An agreement might be made with the Aanazee tribe, and a certain annual sum paid to them would keep them quiet. In short, a line of easy communication might be established, to go from Beyrout to Bassara on the Persian Gulf, in fifteen days, and if by rails, in half the time, provided it was under the auspices of some great and wealthy European power, and entrusted to the management of enlightened natives well acquainted with that part of the East.[44]

It was, significantly, the same ᶜAnaza chief Jaad (or Jaed)—Kayat's guide on his journey to Iraq—who was engaged by Farren "to convey the mail to Bagdad by dromedaries"[45], as already indicated.

Consul-General Farren was recalled from his post in Damascus in 1838, shortly before the troubles which were to end with the expulsion of Ibrāhīm Paşa from Syria broke out. Kayat received the news upon his return to Damascus from Baghdad.[46] It is not made clear whether or not Farren's recall had anything to do with Kayat's own decision to leave Syria and proceed right away on a second visit to Britain. By April 1839, however, he was back in London, having undertaken the journey there apparently at his own expense:

> All who surrounded me [in London] were engaged in commercial pursuits, endeavouring to make money; while I was spending what I had earned in my younger days as a provision for old age. Still I felt I had entered upon a holy cause. . . . In the meantime, hearing that her Majesty Queen Victoria was soon to be crowned at Westminster Abbey, and that all the grandees of Europe were to be present, I thought this would prove a favourable opportunity for disposing of the jewels and fine pearls I had procured at Damascus and Bagdad, so as to cover my expenses. We should be miserable without hope.[47]

Although the better proportion of the jewels which Kayat carried were deftly removed from his possession by a sleek London pickpocket whom he "took to be a gentleman,"[48] the profitable sale of what remained was apparently enough to keep him going, as he went around establishing contacts to press his idea for the organization of a Syrian "native agency" under his personal charge. A letter of introduction from Consul-General Farren, which commended his "fidelity, zeal, and intelligence," his "urbanity of . . . manners," and his "integrity of purpose,"[49] recommended him to the attention of a number of influential individuals and agencies interested in missionary and philanthropic work in the East. A certain Miss Hope was so impressed by him that she readily agreed to have "the honour of originating the Society for the Promotion of Female Education in the East."[50] A friend of Miss Hope's, Miss Braithwaite, introduced him to "many members of the Society of Friends, called Quakers, who, with the greatest simplicity of life, yet enjoy all its true comforts."[51] A special letter of introduction from Farren recommended him to the attention of a certain Mr.

Coates, who was a prominent member of the Church Missionary Society. Kayat was invited to attend the May meetings of that society and address its members in a plenary session. He was subsequently introduced also to the British and Foreign Bible Society, the Religious Tract Society, the Society for the Home Missions, and the Temperance Society.[52] Wherever he was asked to make an address, he spoke of Syria and of the "Eastern or Greek Church," urging that the object of missionary work in the East should be the revitalization of that old-established and truly Christian communion rather than the creation of "schisms" within it. Who better than an educated, skilled and modernized Eastern Christian of Syria, trained in the learned professions, and exposed to the best in the European tradition, could serve as the means to win Asia and Africa over to the modern world?

It was by the efforts of Mr. Coates that a special meeting of the Church Missionary Society was convened, under the chairmanship of Lord Bexley, to discuss Kayat's proposal for the establishment of his "native agency." There was an embarrassing moment in the meeting when one of the more skeptical of the members of the society present "objected" to the fact that Kayat had brought over with him "valuable jewels" to sell in England. Not a man to take any browbeating, Kayat promptly retorted that "it was strange that an Englishman should look with contempt on commercial enterprise," and that it was clearly "more honorable [for a man] to live and carry out [his] plans on [his] own means, than to solicit the aid of others."[53] His argument was apparently well received, for "the other noblemen and gentlemen, having well considered the subject, resolved themselves into a committee" to raise funds for Kayat's scheme.[54] Satisfied with the progress, Kayat left London and proceeded "to read something of medicine, mathematics, and divinity" at Cambridge for the remainder of the year.[55] His studies there were interrupted when the news of his father's death resolved him to return home "to console [his] beloved aged mother, and to begin to put [his] plan in practice."[56]

Kayat, however, did not leave England right away. Back in London, he spent some time receiving training in St. George's Hospital and at the Chelsea Dispensary, where he learnt "bleeding, vaccinating, tooth-drawing, and the treatment of agues and fevers peculiar to hot climates." Armed with this rapidly acquired medical knowledge, he was finally ready for departure. The committee formed by the Church Missionary Society to promote his scheme presented him with a list of instructions to follow in his missionary work. He was to improve the "moral and spiritual condition" of his own Church, not by creating "any schism" in it, but by recalling its members "to the full knowledge of the Gospel, and to the practice of the first Christians, under the guidance of the inspired Apostles"—a task for which Kayat appears to have been clearly unsuited. He had to spend nine months of the year in Beirut, translating "religious and useful books" (which he never did), and attending "to the instructions of a few promising youths" who were to be taught English language and literature, and led in daily prayers and Scripture readings. The remaining months of the year were to be spent in travel and the distribution of "the Scriptures and other useful books or tracts'' to ''priests and other teachers throughout the country.'' He was to endeavor to have Bible schools established in ''every town or village,'' and to ''speak of Christ'' to any ''Christians or Mohammedans'' who would listen. His knowledge of medicine he had to make use of gratuitously, ''both at Beyrout and elsewhere.'' Because he was ''young and not experienced in Missionary work,'' he was to accept a ''general superintendence'' over his ''proceedings'' by the local representatives of the Church Missionary Society.[57]

This was not exactly what Kayat had come to England to bargain for, at least, so one is led to surmise. What the man had in mind, in essence, was to become the established local agent and manager of British missionary work in Syria, with all the prestige and opportunities for personal advancement that such a position would involve. Instead, he received appointment as a native missionary who was to work according to a carefully defined schedule in subordination to his British associates. For his services, he was to receive a salary of ''£200 per annum, including travelling expenses.'' Little wonder that he was dissatisfied with the arrangement, which he considered a ''humiliation'':

> The money I had spent in coming to England, and in a two years' residence there, independently of the sacrifice of my office and business and losses, would, if invested in the public funds, have brought me a larger income. Still, God supported and comforted me, and the soul's enemy could not triumph, though he tried to overcome my patience. I endeavoured to submit cheerfully, and called to mind that the sacrifice was made for the truth,—for the cause of Syria, my beloved country. To murmur, I felt, was only to vex myself,—to recover what I had lost was impossible.[58]

Kayat seems to have believed that it was the intrigues of ''an English merchant named K———'' against him with the Church Missionary Society which had spoiled things for him at the last moment. This K——— had sent word to the Society, through a London associate called Mr. M———, accusing Kayat of commercial malpractice, and Kayat was called upon to answer the accusation—which he did. ''The English, as a nation, are just,'' he says, ''and of course my side of the story was inquired into. . . . So the truth was victorious, and that mortifying accusation turned to my honor in the sight of my friends and the committee.''[59] The affair, however, left Kayat feeling bitter:

> The whole of this annoyance originated in the envy of some of the foreign petty merchants in Syria, who hate the idea of any improvement among the poor natives, lest they should take the trade with Europe out of their hands, which is not at all unlikely. . . . It is the fear of this that makes them envy any enlightened native. . . .[60]

Although the personal character of Kayat, judging by his own account of his activities, was certainly not above question, his cutting remark on the attitude of European residents in Syria toward the ''enlightened natives'' had a great deal of truth in it, and is well borne out by the missionary literature of the period.

Two months after the return of Kayat to Beirut, the ''horrid war'' of 1840 broke out in Syria, the missionaries and ''all Europeans'' left the land, and ''all prospect of doing anything towards education seemed at an end."[61] Kayat, as already pointed out, had no idea what the real issue—at the external or at the internal level—was all about. Why Britain and her allies intervened in the war to expel Ibrāhīm Paşa from Syria, and Bashīr II from Mount Lebanon, was beyond his comprehension:

> It is absurd to say that the Druses and Christians cannot agree, and are frequently at war. The Druses and Christians in Lebanon have lived as brethren for hundreds of years. All they want is their ancient mountain government [*sic*]; those who could rule Lebanon well formerly, could rule it now, if placed in power.[62]

When three British warships, under Commodore Sir Charles Napier, arrived outside Beirut, to be joined shortly after by other British, Austrian, and Turkish warships, the "Christians and Jews" of Beirut, along with some Muslims, fled to the mountains, and Kayat and his family were among the fugitives.[63] "I did long to be among the English," he says, "to give them a correct account of the actual state of the country, for I believe it was the want of true information that produced these disasterous consequences; but this was beyond my power, for the state of those around me was such, that if I had left them many would have been lost, and many would have starved."[64] From the mountain heights, the fugitives watched the bombardment of their city by the allied fleet. Kayat took up residence in the Greek-Orthodox convent of Dayr al-Ḥarf, in the Maṭn district—"so as to be in a central place within reach of visiting the scattered Syrians in different villages," he explains.[65] It was there, under the dire circumstances prevailing, that he was "joined in holy matrimony" to Martha Giamal (Martā al-Jammāl)—a young lady to whom he had become betrothed shortly before he left on his first visit to England:

> That very day, the day of my marriage, I was obliged to go, for the relief of a suffering family, to a neighbouring village. I often wished I had with me some of my English friends, that they might see what service a native might render to the cause of religion by charity and kindness, and above all by understanding the use of medicine.[66]

Back in Beirut after the hostilities were over, Kayat hastened to introduce himself to the British naval officers who now had their headquarters in the city, and to renew his acquaintance with Colonel Hugh Rose, an officer he had already met in Malta who was to become British consul in Beirut during the crucial years that followed. "My intimacy with these gallant officers," he says, "unfortunately excited fresh envy against me . . . chiefly among some resident Europeans, who thought I was making immense profit out of these friends."[67]

The war being over, Kayat was left with no excuse not to proceed with the missionary work with which he was entrusted. His heart, however, was clearly elsewhere, and the offhand manner in which he performed his missionary duties produced unimpressive results. He began by establishing a school which was attended by "twenty-five boys, and seven girls . . . among them . . . a little Druze princess, and some Mohammedan boys."[68] As a step toward the emancipation of women, he invited his married friends, with their wives, to meet his bride unveiled (so he proudly reports), whereupon some of his guests ordered their wives to remove their veils, and "the great wall of ages was pulled down."[69] Kayat shortly after took two pupils from Beirut, and two others from Damascus, into his own house for private tutoring, and engaged in some preaching and Bible reading among members of his community. To promote his image with his British sponsors, he intimated that a number of Greek Orthodox schools which were sprouting in Beirut, Damascus, and elsewhere at the time were established under his influence.[70] More likely, their establishment followed the general trend of the time. Six young men chosen by Kayat (at least one of them was a close relative) were sent to study in England at the expense of the sponsoring committee of the Church Missionary Society. Before long, however, the committee began to have second thoughts about the whole scheme:

> I wished much for funds to extend my operations; but, instead of receiving money from England for the establishment of schools and the support of young students, the exact reverse took place. I received many kind letters from my friends in England, but those that treated of money-matters were very gloomy.[71]

Meanwhile, Kayat began to lapse again into his favorite "commercial enterprise," this time to trade with an Armenian friend in Baghdad in Persian *tombac*—the tobacco smoked in water pipes.[72] His business soon became more diversified. "I set to work in earnest," he explains, "to labour for my bread, for the support of my school and other charities that have claims upon me. God having at all times prospered me in business, I got on very well . . ."[73] There was no lack of "petty English merchants" in Beirut to report home on the clearly nonmissionary activities which were now absorbing most of Kayat's time. Finally, in 1842, the sponsoring committee of the "native agency" summoned Kayat to England, ostensibly to see "what was to be done with the Syrian youths, &c." Where the committee was concerned, the "native agency" had proved a complete failure in practice, and the time had come to liquidate it. Kayat thereupon let his house in Beirut to "Monsieur de Weldenbourgh, the newly appointed consul-general of Prussia," and departed for the third time to London, this time with wife and child, on 28 October of that year.[74]

> On arriving in London, I waited on my committee. I was glad to see them, and they were glad to see me; but house or quarters for the reception of myself and family were not even mentioned.[75]

The honeymoon between Kayat and the missionaries was at last over, but appearances were properly kept up by both sides. As during his previous visit, Kayat went around England delivering lectures about Syria, the Eastern Church, and the project of "native agency" (which, to his mind, had not yet been properly understood, much less applied). The lectures were applauded, and at the end of each lecture a collection to finance the continued education of the Syrian youths already in England was made. Meanwhile, Kayat seized the opportunity of his prolonged stay in the country to complete his medical training at St.

George's Hospital, a training which continued for four years.[76] Finally, on 27 July 1846, he had "the honour of being admitted a member of the Royal College of Surgeons of England," and obtained his diploma "from that high authority."[77] It was at this high point in his curious career that the autobiography of Assaad Y. Kayat comes to an end with a flourish in praise of Britain and the British queen:

> The Victorian age is indeed the pride of Great Britain. The nation may justly glory in its Government. May the Lord God almighty bless the Queen and her Ministers, and the nation at large; and may peace, happiness, and prosperity, with true religion, fill the land and all the earth![78]

To meet the expenses of his long residence in England, Kayat—at last freed from the strict vigilance of his missionary friends—indulged freely in business. "I left no honourable means unemployed," he says, "I sent home for Eastern articles which would have a good sale, and a great many I imported from Syria, and sold at a considerable profit. I also sent out English goods, which sold well at home."[79] In addition to carrying out this commerce, he wrote a book of "English and Arabic dialogues" called *The Eastern Traveller's Interpreter, or Arabic without a Teacher,* which was published in London by Madden & Co. in 1843, and "was the first of its kind, and did well."[80]

Meanwhile, Kayat used his time profitably to remain in touch with influential Englishmen he already knew and to establish new contacts. The lists given in his autobiography of the British notables he came to know at various times read like pages from the *Court Guide,* a publication of which he admits having made full use in tracking down people he wanted to meet.[81] Among the most prominent men he came to know was Lord Palmerston, with whom he first became acquainted at the Foreign Office in 1835, while he was on his first visit to England with the Persian princes.[82] It was by such valuable contacts with powerful individuals that Kayat managed to gain admission to one of the finest centers of medical training in England, at a time when the missionaries were losing interest in him; it was also probably by such contacts that he managed to obtain for himself British nationality in 1846, shortly before or shortly after his medical studies were completed.[83]

While Kayat's prolonged flirtations with the various British missionary circles ended, ultimately, in a polite separation, leaving no more than feelings of suppressed bitterness behind, his connections with the British foreign service, which were probably never broken, were eminently more successful. Unlike the missionaries, the representatives of the British Crown in Syria, and the Foreign Office in London, were not concerned about how Kayat made his money, and had no reason to frown on his "commercial enterprise" which, in general, seems to have been indeed "honourable" (as he was always careful to maintain). What was important about the man was that he was intelligent, articulate, affable, well traveled and connected, alert, observant, discreet, fond of Britain and things British, and—most important—genuinely loyal. Hence, it is not surprising that Kayat, once he had become a British subject, became a candidate to be considered by Palmerston for the British consular service in Syria. Thus the man who came to England in 1842 to explain the failure of the missionary work he was entrusted with before the Church Mission Society returned to Syria in 1847, or shortly after, with an official appointment as British consul in Jaffa, a position he continued to hold until he died in 1865 at the early age of fifty-four.[84] After his death, two of his sons, Ḥabīb and William, were appointed to serve in the same post, although their claim to be British nationals by birth was never officially recognized.[85]

Kayat was in fact the first British consul to be appointed to Jaffa. The post was formally established by Palmerston in 1847 as part of a general expansion of the British consular service in Ottoman Syria. Its functions were "almost exclusively commercial,"[86] and it was subordinate to the British consulate-general which was now based in Beirut. After Kayat's death, the Jaffa consulate was made subordinate to the consulate in Jerusalem, whose functions from the beginning were political.[87]

As British consul in Jaffa, Kayat was remarkably active—a fact which was noted by Western travelers in Palestine at the time:

> He wrote a few despatches. Most of them were very short, and always in a hand which was virtually unreadable. Palmerston himself complained of the difficulty of deciphering Kayat's hand, but without any tangible results. Kayat was at his best when he wrote about business matters; his few ventures into the political field are not very impressive. . . . Kayat was from the beginning a member of the Jerusalem Literary Society,[88] and it was largely due to his initiative that experiments with planting cotton seeds were started . . . [in] the villages round Jaffa. . . . Kayat was obviously very happy with the result. Writing to Earl Russell on the subject, he says "This is the month of sowing cotton seeds in the country, and I never saw such excitement and eagerness shown by the natives of nearly all if not all the villages of this district as on the present of obtaining cotton seeds for sowing."[89]

The American explorer W. F. Lynch had nothing but praise for what he saw of Kayat's work in coastal Palestine:

> Dr. K. has just claims to be considered a benefactor to this section of the country. He has encouraged the culture of the vine; has introduced that of the mulberry and of the Irish potatoe; and by word and example is endeavouring to prevail on the people of the adjacent plain to cultivate the sweet potatoe. . . . In the court-yard we observed an English plough of an improved construction, imported by the consul.[90]

Herman Melville, who visited Palestine in 1857, lent a keen ear to the gossip circulating about "Dr. Kayat" among the local European and American residents, and spoke of him somewhat uncharitably:

> This gentleman, born in the Levant, was some years in England. He awakened great interest there in behalf of the Jews [*sic*], and came to Joppa [*sic*] at last to start some missionary project, and was not unprovided with funds contributed by the pious in England. Long since he gave up the whole project, engaged in trade, is now a flourishing man, & English Consul. At any hints in reference to Missions, he

> betrays aversion to converse. It is whispered that he was someway trickish with the funds.[91]

To the historian of nineteenth-century Syria, what is especially interesting about Assaad Y. Kayat is the outlook he represents rather than his career as a businessman, missionary-teacher, physician, or British consular agent. Here was a man who knew exactly what he was and what he wanted to be. He was an Eastern Christian, born into an Ottoman society in which non-Moslems had normally to content themselves with limited ambitions unless they attached themselves to some European power. He wanted to be a man of special consequence, and boldly set out to attain that end by making the best possible use of his native intelligence and of available opportunities. Unable to achieve the eminence he aspired to as a Syrian operating from Beirut, he went to England, acquired British citizenship, and returned to his native land as a consular representative of the leading European power of the day.

Kayat was supremely conscious of the fact that he was a man of the East, living in an age when the economic and political success of the West was rapidly reducing his Eastern world to subservience. Confident of his personal abilities, which were no doubt exceptional, he firmly believed that he could prove himself the equal of any Westerner in "enlightenment" and "enterprise." He was also determined to prove that his "beloved Syria," given the opportunity, could claim for itself a respectable place in the modern world. The civilization of Europe, as he saw it, did not come about by accident, or because the Europeans were a superior people. It was rather, to his mind, the result of a long process of historical development: it "came by degrees, with the increase of light and knowledge; and the same means employed in behalf of Syria might in time produce the same results."[92] In Kayat's view, to share in the heritage of progress in its developed European form did not involve a betrayal of Eastern values, because progress was the birthright of the whole human race, not of Europeans alone. There was a time, he maintained, when the East "contributed to the welfare of mankind, both in religion and learning",[93] and the West gained much then by profiting from the Eastern example. Now the time had come for the East to profit by the Western example, and the East could only gain by the process.

To Kayat, the abandonment of archaic ways in favor of advancement appeared as an imperative which no traditional society seeking to survive in a competitive modern world could afford to neglect. It was, indeed, this special awareness of the imperative of modernization that sets Kayat apart from the Beirut school of nineteenth-century Christian intellectuals who dabbled with modern ideas from a safe academic distance, without coming to grips with concrete realities. At the level of social thinking, these intellectuals were mainly concerned with devising a workable formula to accommodate the Arab Christian of Ottoman Syria to his predominantly Muslim environment. This formula was found in the emphasis of the Arab ethnic and cultural identity as a bond between Arabs which could transcend religious differences.

Kayat, who was no hairsplitting intellectual, paid hardly any heed to questions regarding his ethnic and cultural identity as a Syrian Christian. He was certainly conscious of the unpleasant discrimination which Christians in his society frequently experienced at the hands of their Muslim compatriots. What bothered him more, however, was the petty bigotry exhibited by European traders—and even by well-meaning Christian missionaries—with regards to all the people of the East, Muslims and Christians alike. The Eastern Christian, he was convinced, could always manage to win the confidence of the Muslim if he tried, because he could speak his language and understand his mentality. With some moral support from Christian Europe, with its amply demonstrated power, his position in the Muslim world would be fully secure. What was really important for Kayat was the development of a positive awareness among Eastern Christians of the special role they could play as intermediaries between the West and the East, since they belonged, in a way, to both worlds. As enlightened entrepreneurs, he maintained, the Christians of Syria were ideally suited to lead their society along the paths of modernization, and shield it at the same time from the indiscriminate voracity of direct Western exploitation. To him, the real enemy of the enlightened native—Christian or Muslim—was not so much the native bigot, who was ultimately teachable, as the Western exploiter who had a vested interest in the continued backwardness of the East.

The main problem with Kayat was that he conceived his ideas mainly in terms of himself and of his own personal advancement. This, however, does not make the ideas any less valid or forceful. It would be easy to agree with Herman Melville and dismiss Kayat as being no more than an exceptionally crafty Levantine who lived by his wits. In *A Voice from Lebanon,* Kayat gave clear articulation to the Levantine's world view, which is a powerful and intelligent one. Some of his reflections remain as relevant today as when they were first written one hundred and thirty years ago. This cannot be said as truly of much of the ''reformist'' Arabic literature produced in Kayat's century. In the final analysis, there may well be more pertinence in the intellectual quintessence of pure Levantinism than one is normally prepared to admit.

Notes

1. A. L. Tibawi, *British Interests in Palestine, 1800–1900,* London, 1961, pp. 142–146.
2. A. Y. Kayat, *A Voice from Lebanon,* London, 1847, p. 1.
3. Ibid., p. 18.
4. Ibid.
5. Ibid., pp. 12, 35.

6. Ibid., p. 31.
7. Ibid., pp. 27–29.
8. Ibid., p. 44.
9. Ibid., p. 45.
10. Ibid., p. 47.
11. Ibid., p. 48.
12. Ibid., p. 31.
13. Ibid., p. 35.
14. Ibid.
15. Ibid., p. 39.
16. Ibid., p. 42.
17. Ibid., pp. 42–43.
18. Ibid., p. 43.
19. Ibid., p. 50.
20. Ibid., pp. 51–53.
21. Ibid., p. 53.
22. Ibid., pp. 53–55.
23. Ibid.
24. The reference here is to the "Greek Catholics," who separated from the main body of the Melkite ("Greek Orthodox") church, starting in 1683, to enter into communion with Rome as Uniate Melkites. Also see in this book chapter 3 by Robert Haddad.
25. Kayat (cited n. 2), pp. 69–70.
26. Ibid., p. 74.
27. Ibid., p. 71.
28. Ibid., p. 85.
29. Ibid., pp. 263–265.
30. Ibid., pp. 40, 72, 89, 96, 97, 98, 99.
31. Ibid., p. 72.
32. Ibid., pp. 74–75.
33. Ibid., p. 111.
34. Ibid., pp. 122–124, 127, 129, 130–131.
35. Ibid., pp. 118, 126, 124–125, 129–130, 128.
36. Ibid., p. 131.
37. Ibid.
38. Ibid., pp. 202–203.
39. Ibid., pp. 411–413.
40. Ibid., p. 143.
41. Ibid., p. 157.
42. Ibid., p. 160.
43. Ibid., p. 168.
44. Ibid., pp. 160, 164.
45. Ibid., p. 97.
46. Ibid., p. 177.
47. Ibid., pp. 180–181.
48. Ibid., p. 212.

49. Ibid., p. 207.

50. Ibid., p. 182.

51. Ibid., p. 183.

52. Ibid., pp. 194–199.

53. Ibid., p. 209.

54. Ibid.

55. Ibid., p. 228.

56. Ibid., p. 231.

57. Ibid., pp. 239–241.

58. Ibid., pp. 237–238.

59. Ibid., pp. 235–236.

60. Ibid., pp. 236–237.

61. Ibid., p. 262.

62. Ibid., p. 275.

63. Ibid., p. 268.

64. Ibid., p. 270.

65. Ibid., p. 272.

66. Ibid.

67. Ibid., p. 277.

68. Ibid.

69. Ibid., p. 281.

70. Ibid., pp. 283–284.

71. Ibid., p. 290.

72. Ibid., pp. 282–283.

73. Ibid., p. 291.

74. Ibid., p. 296–297.

75. Ibid., p. 300.

76. Ibid., p. 352.

77. Ibid., p. 434.

78. Ibid., p. 436.

79. Ibid., p. 356.

80. Ibid., pp. 355–356.

81. Ibid., p. 118.

82. Ibid.

83. Tibawi (cited n. 1), p. 142.

84. Ibid., pp. 142–143.

85. Ibid., pp. 145–146.

86. Ibid., p. 143.

87. Ibid., p. 145.

88. This society, which was almost exclusively Protestant, was founded in 1849 by J. Finn, the British consul in Jerusalem, "for the literary and scientific investigation of all subjects connected with the Holy Land." Ibid., pp. 124–125.

89. Ibid., p. 144.

90. W. F. Lynch, *Narrative of the United States Expedition to the River Jordan and the Dead Sea,* Philadelphia, 1849, pp. 450–451.

91. H. Melville, *Journal of a Visit to Europe and the Levant, October 11, 1856–May 6, 1857*, ed. H. C. Horsford, Princeton, 1955, pp. 159–160. My attention was called to the last two passages by my colleague Dr. Marwan Boheiry of the American University of Beirut.

92. Kayat (cited n. 2), p. 131.

93. Ibid., p. 324.

7

Non-Muslim Communities in Arab Cities

Dominique Chevallier

Distinctions between religious communities have always existed in Islamic cities, but at what levels did they exist? In the Arab East during the Ottoman period what did they signify for the Muslim, Christian, or Jewish communities, which, despite their religious differences, did, after all, participate in the life of the same human milieu?

Communal groupings, with their self-perpetuating differences, were structured and interacted in a manner which was characteristic of Arab societies, a manner which was heir—but how?—to a pre-Islamic, "oriental," or "Semitic" past.[1]

Islam established a legal distinction between believers and *dhimmīs*, a distinction among those who follow the three great monotheistic religions which were revealed and issued from the same source. Thus the communities were institutionalized and hierarchically defined by a legal inequality which nonetheless did grant privileges, for it offered a legal guarantee that the conquest which subjected them to Muslim jurisdiction also granted them Muslim protection. These protected peoples, who became minorities well before the Ottoman period,[2] thus occupied a recognized position in Islamic civilization.

By forming closed groups the communities preserved their distinctive rituals, which were, more or less, linked to the religion by which they identified themselves. Religion gave legal and moral justification for distinctiveness even as it gave that sense of belonging to humanity which derives from the universal. This last comment expresses an essential transcendence. It allows one to understand how a culture can be both distinctive and shared, i.e., divided among different communities which in turn are subdivided by tribe and family, at the same time remaining the fundamental and unspoken basis of a civilization whose legitimacy and focus derives from the exclusive affirmation of the One.

In the urban setting whose development reached the millennium of the *hijra* under the Ottomans[3] how did religious minorities set themselves apart? The quarter which could be closed off by gates like all the other quarters of the city often brought together inhabitants of the same religion. This arrangement, however, was not the general rule. In Aleppo, for example, a Christian suburb endowed with churches and beautiful homes developed to the northwest, but Christian families also lived in quarters dominated by Muslims either because they were clients of powerful Muslim families or because of their trades. The differences between the communities might be reinforced by an ethnic division of labor. However the division of labor between Muslim and non-Muslim varied from region to region.[4] Finally, while dress was visually significant, it could also indicate social class or region as well as community.

In this arrangement, which the Ottomans inherited and maintained, the religious communities assumed particular characteristics and experienced differences in both profound and everyday ways, for their dogmas and religious practices, their legal circumstances, their customs and their economic roles functioned as boundaries which closed each one in his religious group. None of these groups offered the same responsibilities. None comprised the same social classes and divisions. None imposed the same restraints. None provided the same supports.

> ". . . celui qui s'est levé avant le jour pour curer les fontaines, et c'est la fin des grandes épidémies . . ."
>
> Saint-John Perse, *Exil,* IV.

The epidemics and the social, economic, religious, and political crises of the mid-nineteenth century underscored the contrasts which transformation from the outside heightened in the Levant, contrasts in the hopes and fears which were aroused in the communities and which exacerbated mutual hostility. New methods were accepted and adopted in different ways by different communities and thus had a different impact on each one.

Let us briefly consider some facts concerning the reactions and behavior of the communities in the face of the cholera epidemics which struck Syria. In addition to local evidence (still barely examined) there is the documentation, tinged with alarm, which European governments, fearing the spread of epidemic, gathered as a measure of information and protection.

Here is a case of a cholera epidemic which broke out in Aleppo in July and August of 1848. The population of the city was approximately 80,000: 78 percent Muslims, 17 percent Christians, 5 percent Jews.[5] In two months about 4,900 people died of cholera, some 6 percent of the total population. By community, however, the figures were 7 percent among Muslims, 3.5 percent among Christians and 6 percent among Jews.[6]

Death struck the communities unequally. Christians and Jews took better precautions against epidemic. Their sick were quarantined and even abandoned. The well-to-do, notably among the Christians, left the city for refuge in the villages.[7] Generally the disease decimated the poorest households, the least hygenic and the most undernourished.[8]

Another example which I have discussed elsewhere was Beirut whose rising population was supported by an increase of economic activity. Cholera epidemics struck in September 1848, July 1865, and July 1875. In each instance a large proportion of those who fled to the mountains escaped the disease while those who remained behind suffered death. "Who escapes? The Christians who join their families still in the village. Who dies? The Muslim lower classes whose social horizon was limited to the city. Thanks to a mountain refuge, health and disease were also related to religion."[9]

The behavior of the communities in the face of epidemics depended on standard of living, possibility of flight or quarantine, solidarity of action, customs (including cycle of religious holidays), diet, and sanitation. In the face of death the cleavages between the communities were accentuated. Death emphasized the social and economic disparities as well as the differences of religious and moral traditions which felt the new confrontation between East and West. All this was experienced through religion. All this added to the world view which the communal groups gained through their interaction with each other.

During a period when the Ottoman Empire was affected by Europe as both an industrial intruder and a constitutional model this situation sharpened both the demand of the *dhimmīs* for equality under law and the hostility of the Muslims toward those who, acting as middlemen, grew wealthy through and dependent upon the foreigners.

One must not forget the resurgence of old hatreds and rivalries which not only divided the minorities from the Muslims but also set Christians against Jews. In Damascus in February 1840, the mutilated bodies of the superior of the Spanish monastery and his servant were found in the Jewish quarter. Following these murders Christian opinion revived the ancient blood libel against the Jews and some wealthy Jewish merchants were arrested and tortured.[10]

Even more significant were the riots which broke out in Aleppo in 1850 and in Damascus in 1860. Each still requires detailed research. Although a great deal has been written about Damascus, the accounts too often are filled with emotion, prejudice, and misinformation. Muslim society felt beleaguered and weakened by the Ottoman reforms at a time when it saw the Christians profiting from the wealth and power of Europe. Both of these riots reveal that the Muslim uprising against the Christians came at a time when the lower classes suffered an economic crisis, the result of European expansion and fluctuations in the Western economy.[11]

The epidemics attested to the inequalities which divided the communities.[12] The revolts, by underscoring these divisions, consciously articulated the inequalities. Within each community, of course, there existed differences of wealth, economic activity, power, behavior, and intellectual outlook,[13] but the feeling of an internal communal solidarity, which guided its destiny, was the closest to the surface. During this period of change, communal instincts continued to inspire the crowd to action. The communities held their own. How did they manage?

Ties of family and clientage, which structure groups and define their relations within Arab society, were a source of strength for the community. The Ottoman administration knew to use these ties in order to impose its authority. Thus in

Damascus in 1860 it punished not only those who were indeed guilty but also the innocent chiefs of the leading families, whose clients were the rioters.

Another source was the awareness that ultimately the community provided each believer with a rationale for his place in the community and in the universe. This perception protected the *millet* system in the real world.

Syrian Muslims saw that their legal, administrative, governmental, and moral preeminence was being attacked while they were experiencing worsening social and economic conditions. This awareness at every level, supported by the solidarity of the group against external danger, was reinforced by the nature of the reforms, the economic disorder, and the social discontent. As for the Christians, significantly, those who sought to guarantee their wealth or their prospects for wealth by escaping Muslim jurisdiction often became protégés of a European power which benefited from the capitulations. It might be necessary to change *millet*s, but not to change communalism itself which in the nineteenth century was, in a large way, sustained by Western expansion. Communal emotions were exacerbated and reinforced by these ordeals, for they expressed moral, political, social, and economic demands and they were blooded with confrontations. However did not their compulsive character stem from a social culture that was common to all? Did the social tensions which became apparent in communal conflict imply fundamental differences on the level of social culture?

* * *

This question brings us back to a fundamental problem of this paper—the Arab city of Syria in the mid-nineteenth century, developed over more than a millennium of Islamic civilization. Did the non-Muslim communities merely submit to it or did they creatively adopt its norm?

Yes, the norm was common to all the inhabitants. Work which I intend to present in the future will substantiate this point further.[14] Here I will limit myself to some brief remarks.

The houses enclosing a courtyard and placed side-by-side, the quarters with a layout of twists and turns and placed side-by-side, both were found in all the communities. Ira M. Lapidus has shown how the *dhimmīs*, as a result of their large scale conversion to Islam during the tenth and eleventh centuries, helped reinforce a social organization specific to Islamic civilization.[15] By way of comparison over time and space one can also refer to the fine example described by S. D. Goitein in Fustat in the twelfth century.[16] The houses which Muslims, Christians, and Jews inhabited shared a common plan. They sheltered townsmen of the three religions alike and these townsmen were each others' neighbors. Moreover, can we not place the inhabitants, whatever their community, in one human milieu whose social culture and language they shared?

Let us return to Aleppo. The land-use ratio was the same in all house lots of the city, wealthy or modest, large or small, Muslim, Christian, or Jewish. The ratio was as follows: one-third, interior courtyard, two-thirds, building.[17] Moreover the large majority of masons were Christians and these were the ones who employed and transmitted this standard.

The creation and disposition of such space—the social space of the Arab city—can only be achieved in a social culture which was developed and sustained in the shelter of Islamic civilization.

The distinctions among communities were built into the formation of groups in the Arab East. Although each community, as a function of its distinctive legal and social-economic status, had its own ways of life, of self-defense, and of self-assertion, these differences did not reflect a difference in human nature. On the contrary, they were the expression of a common social culture, of the structures by which this culture was constructed. They were the reflection of a social organization common to all, whatever their religion.

The very delicate question of unity and disunity in the Arab-Islamic world is hereby laid to rest.

I would like to mention that the topic of this book invites taking refuge in the past—the middle of the nineteenth century. The problem of community conflict continues with the major transformation of our time, the old ways overthrown by urbanization and industrialization.

Notes

1. This question has frequently arisen in my work and in the work of others, notably those raising the problem of the "oriental city" (Eugen Wirth), the differentiation of social groups, the social role played by Islam, the organization of production, and the anthropology of nomadism.

2. The bulk of the indigenous population did not convert to Islam until quite late, the tenth and eleventh centuries, at a time when they wished to conform to the dominant and well-established standard. However, by converting en masse they were able to impose their style of life, customs, and especially characteristic groupings in the very heart of Islamic civilization. This pressure was all the more effective at a point when the Abbasid caliphate was weak and when de facto administrative autonomy favored the development of cities responsive to the structure and original needs of society. About this time, the schools of law in Sunni Islam adapted to these social realities, particularly to the ties of neighborhood which stemmed from "tribal" groups and from the necessity to bring these groups together in one unit. It was by this adaptation that they took and reinforced their aspect of distinct religious communities *(ta'ifa)* which represents an even tighter fit in the human milieu. The Shiite movements followed the same path. See Ira M. Lapidus, "The Early Evolution of Muslim Urban Society," *Comparative Studies in Society and History,* 15 (1973), pp. 21–50.

3. See Dominique Chevallier and others, *L'espace social de la ville arabe,* Paris, 1979.

4. This is not to claim that there were no occupations in which non-Muslims were more involved than others; rather one should be wary of excessive generalization. Among others see Robert Brunschvig, "Métiers vils en Islam," *Studia Islamica,* 16 (1962), 95–120.

5. Archives du Ministere des Affaires Etrangères (hereafter referred to as AE), Correspondance commerciale, Alep, 31, fol. 149; H. Guys, *Statistiques du Pachalik d'Alep,* Marseilles, 1853, p. 50.

6. Correspondance commerciale, Alep, 31, fols. 148–164.

7. The diary of a schoolteacher, Naum Bakhash, whose manuscript has been preserved in the Bibliothèque orientale of the Université Saint-Joseph, Beirut, describes the impact of this epidemic. Excerpts were published by Ferdinand Taoutel, ed., *Wathā'iq ta'rīkhīya ᶜan Ḥalab,* Beirut, 1962, vol. 3, 118–127.

8. By way of comparison, P. Verrollot, *Du choléra-morbus en 1845, 1846 et 1847, avec une carte indiquant sa marche pendant ces trois anneés,* Constantinople, 1848, pp. 281–296. This doctor from the French Hospital in Constantinople noted that in that city in 1848 cholera was responsible for the following death rates, per 1,000: 2.7 Muslims, 5.7 Catholics, 8.1 Jews. He said that the epidemic had a predilection for the dirtiest and most unhealthy quarters.

9. Dominique Chevallier, *La société du Mont Liban a l'époque de la révolution industrielle en Europe,* Paris, 1971, p. 45.

10. On this affair: Achille Laurent, *Relation historique des affaires de Syrie,* Paris, 1846, vol. 2; A. Ubicini, *Lettres sur la Turquie,* Paris, 1854, vol. 2, pp. 359–361; Salomon Reinach, *Cultes, Mythes et Religions,* Paris, 1923, vol. 2, pp. 462–463; and chapter 4 by Moshe Maᶜoz in this volume. Also: Archivio di Stato, Florence, Esteri 2529, 1840, correspondence, February to July 1840; Archives du Consulat Général de France à Beyrouth, 1840, cartons 25 et 26.

Count de Ratti-Menton, the French consul in Damascus who played an active role against the Jews in this affair, wrote on 21 March 1840 to his colleague in Beirut: "In this situation, I had to accept the spontaneous offers of a resident of the country, a Catholic Christian, M. Chubli, whose arrival in Damascus was of great help. Indeed, it is he who has just discovered the murder of Father Thomas's servant."

Jewish circles in Paris, London, and Vienna alerted opinion and as a result of the stir they created, Muḥammad ᶜAli stopped the prosecution and freed the accused.

Following Palm Sunday 1847 the Maronites of Dayr al-Qamar also accused the Jews of having slaughtered a Christian child for ritual purposes; Public Record Office, F. O. 78/712, Rose to Palmerston, Beirut, 2 April 1847.

(Like other minority communities, the Jewish community had the potential to become a base of operations for the Great Powers in the Levant. Here too, the powers kept an eye on each other. For example, after the withdrawal of Egyptian troops from Syria in 1840, the French representative in Beirut wrote: "Jerusalem is in the hands of the Osmanlis. With this, one is guaranteed that the British seriously have in mind taking advantage of the situation by creating a religious protectorate to re-establish the Israelite nation in Judea." AE, Correspondance commerciale, Beirut, 3, fol. 47, dispatch of Des Méloizes, 20 November 1840.)

11. For these questions see Chevallier (cited n. 9), especially, pp. 201–202, 269, 280–281. See also: Moshe Maᶜoz, *Ottoman Reform in Syria and Palestine,* 1840–1861, Oxford, 1968, pp. 103–107, and 231–240; Kamal Salibi, "The 1860 Upheaval in Damascus as Seen by al-Sayyid Muhammad Abu'l-Suᶜud al-Hasibi, Notable and later *Naqib al-Ashraf* of the city," in William R. Polk and Richard L. Chambers, *Beginnings of Modernization in the Middle East,* Chicago, 1968, pp. 185–202.

12. In the crucial area of demography historical rhythms also varied according to religious community. It is a vast subject worth developing. See Chevallier (cited n. 9), book II.

13. In examining statistics one should beware of certain generalizations that conceal differences of human and geographic origin. For example among the Jews of Syria there were both a native community of old stock and families who came from Spain via Italy and Constantinople.

14. For further details on these ideas see Chevallier and others (cited n. 3) and especially, in the order in which they appear, my own contribution and that of R. Berardi. See also Dominique Chevallier, "Signes de Beyrouth en 1834," *Bulletin d'études orientales,* 25 (1972) (actually published 1973), pp. 216–228; and Dominique Chevallier, "Les villes arabes depuis le XIXe siècle: structures, visions, transformations," *Revue des Travaux de l'Académie des Sciences morales et politiques,* 1972 (first semester), pp. 117–128.

15. See Lapidus (cited n. 2).

16. S. D. Goitein, "A Mansion in Fustat: A Twelfth-Century Description of a Domestic Compound in the Ancient Capital of Egypt," in Harry A. Miskimin, David Herlihy, A. D. Udovitch, *The Medieval City,* New Haven, 1977, pp. 163–178.

17. Jean-Claude David, "Alep, dégradation et tentatives actuelles de réadaptation des structures urbaines traditionnelles," *Bulletin d'études orientales,* 28 (1975) (actually published 1977), p. 47.

8

Image and Self-Image of the Syrians in Egypt: From the Early Eighteenth Century to the Reign of Muhammad ᶜAlī

THOMAS PHILIPP

Among Egyptian nationalist thinkers it has been a common notion that one of the typical traits of the Egyptian nation was—and still is—its ability throughout history to absorb all waves of foreign immigrants and eventually make them part of the Egyptian national entity.[1] This claim conveniently counters—though in somewhat mythical form—any doubts as to the impact of the frequent influx of foreigners into Egypt—be it as refugees, merchants, or political masters—upon the "Egyptianness" of the society and upon the historical continuity of the Egyptian national identity and culture.

European observers such as Lord Cromer were inclined to dismiss the whole notion of an Egyptian nation, looking only at the bewildering number and variety of religious, ethnic, and linguistic minority groups prominent in nineteenth-century Egypt.[2]

The intention of this chapter is to investigate the history of one of these minorities in Egypt in modern times, by examining the forces that encouraged the integration of the immigrant group and the factors that determined the limits of any possible dissolution of the minority within the majority society.

The Syrian immigrants shared several features which distinguished them clearly from other minority groups arriving in Egypt during modern times, and which, potentially at least, made a successful integration into Egyptian society more likely. Close commercial, cultural, and political links between Syria[3] and Egypt reach back into antiquity. In more recent times it was the Ottoman conquest of the Arab lands that provided the framework for such links. Of all the minorities immigrating to Egypt in modern times the Syrians were the first to come in great numbers and to play a significant role in the life of Egyptian society.

The issue of relations between the Syrian immigrants and Egyptian society encompasses many aspects. For reasons of space we cannot deal with all of them equally here. The following discussion will focus on issues of identity and self perception. The problem must be stated in twofold fashion: (a) Did the Syrians see themselves at all as one group coherent within and separate from their social environment? and (b) Did the Egyptians perceive of the Syrians as one distinct, non-Egyptian group?

These questions gain a certain complexity in the case of the Syrians, because common origin did not coincide with common religion. The Maghribis in Egypt, for instance, distinguished themselves by common origin only from Egyptians but shared with them the same language and religion. The Greeks, on the other hand, distinguished themselves by common origin, language, and religion. The Syrians were not only divided into Muslims and Christians, but the latter group itself was again subdivided into various communities, though all shared the same language with the Egyptians. In addition, the largest of the Christian communities, the Greek Catholic, was just then going through the process of establishing itself as an independent community; in other words, the Greek Catholic emigrants in Egypt had not only to work out their relations with the overall society but were at the same time concerned, as they were in Syria, with establishing their coherence as an autonomous group.

Trade and learning seem to have been the traditional reasons for Syrians to come to Ottoman Egypt. Al-Maqrīzi mentions a concentration of Syrian merchants in Khan Manṣur.[4] The Mamlūk Sultan Qā'itbay (1468–1495) is credited with establishing *riwāq al-shuwām,* the quarters for Syrian students at al-Azhar, and providing for them through endowments.[5] Though we are not informed about the details of its establishment we nevertheless can safely conclude that the Syrian students in al-Azhar were numerous and important enough to warrant the establishment of a *riwāq* of their own. Usually, however, students came to Egypt for a few years only. Rarely did one stay in Egypt after terminating his studies. The merchants too, were usually in Egypt on a semipermanent basis only. Their families frequently remained in Syria. Altogether the Syrians were a small group, almost exclusively Muslim, too temporary to organize itself or have any noticeable impact upon Egyptian society. At the same time it was distinctly perceived as a non-Egyptian group with its own parochial characteristics.[6]

The first changes in this situation can be observed after 1724 when a comparatively large number of Syrian Christians arrived in Egypt. The year 1724 witnessed the open break between the Greek Orthodox community in Syria and those of its members who had turned to the Roman Catholic Church and who henceforth were called Greek Catholic. The split resulted from more than a hundred years of Roman Catholic missionary activity and increasing European, especially French, commercial penetration in the area. These developments had been the first signs of a new Europe continuously expanding its economic and political power over the rest of the globe. In Syria the European commercial activities brought numbers of local Christians into contact with Europeans. This group benefited economically from European trade relations. Increasing European political influence in the Ottoman Empire eventually also provided some informal protection to this economically rising group of local Christians. But the changes in the socioeconomic status of this group did not yet reflect themselves in the adoption of any new secular ideology or political program. Rather, the traditional means of religious identity was used. Conversion to Catholicism was not only the obvious choice because of the work of Catholic missionaries. Being a member of the Catholic Church also ensured close and safe commercial relations with the French and the Italians. Eventually some political benefits could also be reaped from such a step, thanks to France's assertion that she was the protector of all European—and, by extension, all local—Catholics in the Ottoman Empire.

The Greek Orthodox community, enjoying Ottoman recognition and protection could, however, still exert considerable pressure upon its "schismatic", i.e., with Rome-united, members. Not recognized as a *millet* the Greek Catholics found themselves in a precarious situation. Many left Aleppo and Damascus for the Mt. Lebanon region, the coastal towns and Egypt, where the authority of the Ottoman government was weaker and that of the Greek Orthodox clergy often nonexistent. These were also areas which often offered better occasions for trade with Europe. The skilled and the wealthy in particular went to Egypt.[7] Their commercial contacts with the Italian cities and France soon established the Catholics from Syria as a flourishing community in Egypt.

Catholicism and commerce were the dominant causes for emigration to Egypt and it was only to be expected that the new arrivals should join the existing European Catholic community which was served by the Franciscan order in Cairo. In fact, it was the only possibility open to the Greek Catholics since their own community in Syria was only then beginning to organize its own institutional church and clergy. Greek Catholic priests were not yet available for the community in Egypt. In addition, the community was not recognized as an independent *millet*. Participating in church services held by the Franciscans was, however, also problematic. Legally the Greek Catholics remained subjects of the Ottoman sultan and could not claim the same status as the European Catholics in the Ottoman Empire. The Greek Orthodox Patriarch tried to prevent any contact between the renegade members of his community and the European Catholics. He procured in 1752 an imperial order forbidding Christian subjects of the sultan to attend European churches. The Mamlūk Ibrāhīm Katkhodā exploited this as a pretext to arrest four European priests in Cairo who let Greek Catholics attend their services.[8] Yet in the end it was not government interference that prevented the Greek Catholics from using European churches. It was rather the increasing wealth and numbers which intensified the community's self-assertiveness as it tried to emancipate itself from Franciscan tutelage.

Anṭūn Farᶜūn, a member of one of the most prosperous Greek Catholic families in Egypt, was able to buy a large piece of land in Old Cairo. Here he built his own residence together with a church which was independent from the

Franciscans and the Greek-Orthodox clergy. It recognized only the authority of the Greek Catholic Patriarch of Antioch. The Pope's official recognition of this link in 1772 consolidated the autonomy of the Greek Catholic community as a whole and strengthened the links between its members in Egypt and the patriarchate in Syria.[9]

In the same year the community in Cairo began to keep its own registers for baptism, marriages, etc.,[10] information which until then had been recorded in the registers of the Franciscans.

This newly acquired spiritual autonomy reflected also the community's rise to economic power. It reached its peak during the reign of ᶜAlī Bey al-Kabīr, when he put Greek Catholic Syrians instead of Jews in charge of the customhouses. These positions went only to people with considerable financial means and gave to their holders additional control over trade and opportunities to enrich themselves.[11] Precisely in 1772 Mikha'īl Fakhr, a Greek Catholic from Damietta and already director of customs in Alexandria, tried to unify and control all the Egyptian customhouses in Damietta, Bulaq, and Alexandria.[12] Mikhā'il Fakhr was soon exiled. But the Greek Catholic community was able to hold on to these lucrative and influential positions until the French invasion. Between 1774–1784 three brothers of the Farᶜūn family, Anṭūn, Francis, and Yūsuf, controlled the customhouses of Old Cairo, Bulaq, and Damietta, while a cousin, Ilyās, was head of customs in Alexandria.[13]

Syrian Christians, practically all of whom were Greek Catholics at the time, succeeded not only in ousting the Jews from their dominant position in trade but also in relegating their Muslim compatriots from Syria to an insignificant position in the important Egyptian-Syrian trade. The major market for Syrian merchants in Cairo during the eighteenth century was Khān al-Ḥamzāwī. At the beginning of the century the Syrian merchants there were almost exclusively Muslim. By the end of the same century the Christians had nearly monopolized that trade.[14] A similar shift of power can be observed in Damietta, where in 1769 the merchant al-Ḥajj ᶜUmar b. ᶜAbd al-Wahhāb from Tripoli lost an argument with Christian merchants. The case was brought to court in Cairo but through pressure exerted by Christian (Copt as well as Greek Catholic) secretaries and functionaries ᶜUmar b. ᶜAbd al-Wahhāb lost his case. His property was confiscated and he and his family were sent back to Syria. Only fifteen years later was he permitted to return to Damietta, where he died soon after his arrival, a sick and destitute man.[15]

The last quarter of the eighteenth century saw the apex of Greek Catholic economic power in Egypt. The Syrian Christians in general remained throughout the following century a very wealthy community, but never again did they obtain such a dominant and almost monopolist position in Egyptian trade and economy.

A sense of community made itself felt in Egypt among all Catholics from Syria (we are dealing here mainly with the Maronites and the Greek Catholics, since the Chaldaeans and Armenian Catholics were numerically and organizationally still quite insignificant). This sense of community expressed itself on the one hand in an attempt to disengage themselves from Franciscan control and, on the other hand in a close, though by no means always harmonious, cooperation between the various Catholic communities. At the same time each community strove to build up its own communal structure and religious hierarchy.

Syrian immigrants arrived in Egypt as individuals or as families, but were lacking any communal organization. For a long time, as we have stated, the Franciscans provided the religious guidance and organization. In Syria the Maronites could already look back on two centuries of close contact with Rome and a long conscious effort to reorganize and revitalize the community and the clergy, while the Greek Catholics were at the time barely beginning to lay down the organizational foundation for their own community.

Though numerically far inferior to the Greek Catholics in Egypt, the Maronites were the first who attempted to establish their own clergy there. In 1745 the Maronite Lebanese Order sent its first member, Father Mūsā Hailāna, to Damietta to organize the community there. Apparently this action was in response to a demand by the local Catholic communities in Damietta, who wanted "the spiritual functions to be fulfilled by *Eastern* (Catholic) priests, even if they were not of the same rite."[16] This "popular demand" was not necessarily a pious Maronite fiction to justify the setting up of a branch of the order in Damietta, a town which could barely call a handful of Maronites its own. The far more numerous Greek Catholics might have made this demand, since they did not yet dare to use their own clergy in Egypt due to its "illegality" and due to Greek Orthodox pressures. Father Mūsā Hailāna succeeded soon after his arrival in renting a building in Damietta to serve as a church for all Catholics. The financing of this project reflected the respective positions of the Maronites and Greek Catholics in Egypt: part of the money was raised by the local Greek Catholic merchants, the other part came from the Maronite order in Lebanon.

For the next forty years this arrangement seems to have worked very well: the Maronite Aleppine Order[17] provided the clergy from Lebanon for a community which was Greek Catholic. The arrangement was thrown into disarray, however, after the appointment of the Maronite Father Buṭrus Zikre (1784–1788) as priest for all Catholics in Damietta. The crisis was twofold: soon after Father Buṭrus's appointment a Franciscan sent from Jerusalem, Brother Pancracius, arrived in Damietta, to take care of the spiritual needs of Catholic sailors and merchants from Europe. Seeing that his own Latin community was too small to provide a living for him Pancracius proceeded to usurp functions in the local community which the Maronite clergy traditionally fulfilled.[18] Sharp protests by the Catholic Syrians in Damietta and Lebanon to Rome were the result. The Franciscans were ordered to withdraw their emissary from Damietta. Pancracius, however, refused and stayed until he died around 1791. In 1787 Father Buṭrus was faced with a second crisis. He clashed with part of the Greek Catholic community over the marriage of a Greek Catholic girl. We do not know the details, or if Buṭrus had truly given grounds for complaint, or whether the issue was not, rather, a means for the Greek Catholics to express a more general dissatisfaction with the way the Maronite priest was conducting business and the way his position was weakened by the presence of the Franciscan. Probably the clash also reflected in a general fashion the more self-assertive mood of the Greek Catholics after their recent rise to wealth and influence in the affairs of Egypt. As a result of this clash the Greek Catholics demanded and were granted by their patriarch in Syria the right to have only Greek Catholic clergy attending to their spiritual needs. The increased autonomy of the Greek Catholic community did not, however, lead to a permanent split with the Maronites. In 1789 an agreement was signed between the Maronite and the Greek Catholic priests under the auspices of the French consul arranging for cooperation between the two sides in Damietta. In the agreement all functions, revenues, and expenditures were to be equally divided between the two clergies, as was the use of the church.[19] The cooperation between the Catholic communities proved itself in the crisis of 1797 when Murād Bey tried to have the church closed and extorted high ransom for some priests and merchants whom he arrested.[20]

The close relations between the Catholic communities were also reflected in the issue of intermarriage, which occurred with some frequency. A well-known case was the marriage of the Italian merchant and consul Carlo Rossetti and the widow of the Greek Catholic Yūsuf Baytār. In 1797 the Greek Catholic and the Maronite patriarchs in Syria issued an edict making a patriarchal written permission a requirement for intermarriage. Because of the difficulties of communications with Syria this made intermarriage in Egypt practically impossible. In response some Maronite dignitaries from Damietta sent a letter pleading with their patriarch to revoke this ruling because the Maronites in Damietta had a surplus of young men and "because the habits in Egypt are different from those in Lebanon."[21]

The awareness that Egypt presented different conditions from those in Lebanon and that one found oneself in the "House of Islam," strengthened the ties with other Christians, not necessarily Syrian. In the case of al-Ḥajj ᶜUmar b. ᶜAbd al-Wahhab, the Syrian merchant in Damietta, Copts and Christian Syrians successfully worked together to have him removed from Damietta. But here, too, a special relation seems to have existed among Catholics. When in 1816 Muᶜallim Ghālī, a Catholic Copt, was removed from his position as *ra'īs al-kuttāb* and thrown into prison for embezzlement,[22] the Maronite Father Anṭūn Mārūn bewailed his fall from power as a disaster for all Catholic communities which he befriended. According to him, Muᶜallim Ghālī was most active in promoting the cause of the Catholic Copts. He applied to Rome for the appointment of a Catholic Copt bishop, supposedly obtained from the *ᶜulamā'*, a *fatwa* that all Coptic Church property should be evenly split between Catholic Copts and Monophysite Copts, and caused the conversion of many Copts to Catholicism. His activities provoked both the wrath of the established Coptic leadership who proceeded to denounce him to Muḥammad ᶜAlī for embezzlement and a recurring accusation against local Catholics in the Ottoman Empire, of espionage and collaboration with foreign powers. The Monophysite Copts succeeded in their strategem and one of their coreligionists replaced Muᶜallim Ghālī as *ra'īs al-kuttāb*.[23] The fall of Muᶜallim Ghālī did not, however, imply a general deteriorization of the Catholic position in Egypt. Muḥammad ᶜAlī's preoccupation with the modernization of Egypt as a basis for his own power prevented him from perceiving religious affiliations as a disqualification for persons whose services and skills he needed. Christians in general and many Maronites, Greek Catholics, and Armenians from Syria in particular were employed in various administrative and economic positions. The Christian Syrians flourished sufficiently to work further on the consolidation of their communities.

In 1824 Anṭūn Marūn had a dispute with the Franciscans which resulted in the exclusion of the Maronites and Armenian Catholics from the use of the Franciscan graveyard. Two years later the Maronites in Cairo acquired their own graveyard, and in 1837 their own church was erected. The Greek Catholics had already gained a decisive victory in this direction in 1797 when the confiscation of the church in Damietta eventually led to its first formal recognition by the authorities as a church under the control of the Maronite and Greek Catholic orders. With the elimination of the Franciscans from the Syrian communities the Maronite and Greek Catholic clergies were also granted by their respective patriarchs more and more authority to execute religious and organizational functions, e.g., the sacrament of confirmation and the keeping of the registers.

Regarding Christian communities, whose heads resided outside Egypt, the Egyptian authorities must have welcomed the establishment of local clerical hierarchies with their own autonomy. The local community authorities could be controlled and dealt with more easily. Any increase in their authority reduced interference by outside forces. When, for instance, the Greek Orthodox community in Alexandria decided to appoint its own patriarch, independent of the wishes of the Greek-Orthodox patriarch in Istanbul, Muḥammad ᶜAlī interceded actively with the Porte on behalf of the community in Alexandria. On the other hand, the Catholic Copts who had shown a vigorous desire for communal autonomy in 1816 had to wait until the end of the nineteenth century before they were recognized as an independent community. In their case the Egyptian government had nothing to gain in terms of a reduced outside interference in return for increased local autonomy.

The trend toward the consolidation of each of the various Catholic communities came to a first conclusion in the 1830s when the Ottoman government recognized in swift succession each of them as an independent *millet* with its respective patriarch as the officially accredited leader. These *firmans*, which referred to the whole Ottoman Empire, also provided the Catholic Christians in Egypt with a firm legal status of independence in all communal affairs and confirmed all previous developments in this direction.

While there is comparatively much information available concerning the development of the Christian Syrian communities in Egypt, the same cannot be said with regard to the Muslim Syrians in Egypt. During the whole period under discussion religious affiliation remained the main principle of identity. For the very same reason that we can find the Christian Syrians establishing their own distinct organizations, hierarchies, and records, the Muslim Syrians blended easily into the local Muslim environment.[24] The Muslim Syrians were a distinct enough group to merit a *riwāq* in al-Azhar, similar to that of the Maghribi,

Turkish, and Hijazi students. Syrian Muslim merchants in Cairo clearly gravitated to specific markets, the Khān Manṣūr in the fifteenth century and Khān Ḥamzāwī, the Jamāliyya quarter in the seventeenth and eighteenth century.[25] But it remains open to question whether this concentration occurred primarily because of a common origin or because of the specific merchandise the Syrians dealt in, for instance, textiles in Khān Ḥamzāwī.

The merchants or the students would each occasionally act to defend their interests, as any professional group would.[26] Beyond that we have very little evidence of an identity or loyalty of all Muslim Syrians which would have given them coherence as a group. The earlier mentioned merchant al-Ḥajj ᶜUmar b. ᶜAbd al-Wahhāb from Damietta every year invited many of the Syrian al-Azhar students to pass the month of Ramaḍān at his residence.[27] Syrian students' unrest at al-Azhar was also reflected occasionally in shop closings. Whether such action included merchants in general or was a specific sign of solidarity of the Syrian merchants remains open to speculation.[28]

Even more spurious is any evidence for a sentiment of community between Christian and Muslim Syrians. The only hint we can possibly find is in the fact that the Christian Syrian merchants did business in the same markets where the Muslim Syrians traded. But again it must be asked whether common origin or similarity of merchandise drew the Syrians together. Since at the same time other markets existed where textiles were traded, such as Khān Khalīlī, one is inclined to see the common origin as a factor bringing Muslim and Christian Syrians together. Commercial cooperation between the two might have made proximity in the market desirable.[29]

The last question which demands investigation is the relationship between the Syrians and the Egyptian society. The Egyptians called the Syrians *shuwām* (sing. *shāmī*), people from *al-Shām,* which could either mean Syria in general or Damascus in particular. In similar fashion people were called Maghribi or Hijazi, designating their place of origin. But the term *shāmī* itself does not help us much beyond pointing out a general awareness of geographical differences of origin which might lead to some special commercial ties or an organization of students at al-Azhar. The term *shāmī* is used for everybody from Syria and only from the context does it become evident whether Christian Syrians, Muslim Syrians, specifically people from Damascus or Syrians in general are meant.[30] Despite the use of the same term, the attitude of the Egyptians toward the Syrians depended profoundly on the latter's religious affiliation, just as society on the whole then conceived of itself first in religious terms. We rarely hear of actual differences between Muslim Syrians and Egyptians. One such occasion arose when the Ḥanafī Shaykh ᶜAbd al-Raḥman al-ᶜArīshī tried to become Shaykh al-Azhar in the autumn of 1779. An opposition group from the Shāfiᶜī School complained that (a) the Shaykh al-Azhar had never been a Ḥanafī and (b) especially nobody from far away *(afaqī),* who was not Cairene *(min ahl al-balda)* was ever made Shaykh al-Azhar. Al-Jabartī notes that al-ᶜArīshī was supported in his struggle by the Syrian community *(tā'ifat al-shuwām),* which included obviously more than just students, "because of their origin" *(jinsīyya).*[31]

But much more typical in Egypt was the situation in which Muslims from everywhere sided together, and Christians were seen as belonging to a separate group. Al-Jabartī's *ʿAjā'ib* provides many examples of how Copts, Christians from Syria, Greek Orthodox, and European Christians were all lumped together in one category. Al-Jabartī never specifies, when talking about Christian Syrians, whether he is speaking about Maronites, Greek Catholics, or Christians of other denominations, just as he was not aware of an internal struggle in the Coptic community between Catholic and Orthodox factions.[32] Perhaps the most dramatic description of this deep split between Muslim and *dhimmī* can be found in al-Jabartī's account of the feverish preparations of the Cairenes to defend themselves against the approaching French. Collections of food, money, and weapons are made and "at that moment nobody held back anything of what he owned." Some people "equipped groups of Maghribis and Syrians *(shuwām)*, with weapons, food, etc." Feelings of solidarity also embraced, at that moment of emergency, all the non-Egyptian Muslims. On the other hand "people searched the houses of the Syrian *(shuwām)*, Coptic, and Greek-Orthodox Christians, the churches and the monasteries for weapons. The masses would have been content only with killing the Christians and the Jews. But the authorities prevented them from doing so."[33] All Christians, whether indigenous or from abroad, were equally suspect, while Muslims from everywhere cooperated to defend the city. This was admittedly a time of great crisis, engineered by nonbelievers, and might, therefore, have aroused particularly intense feelings of Muslim solidarity. But even in less heroic times the relations between Egyptian and Syrian Muslims seem to have been by and large quite close and regular.

The relation of the Christian Syrians to the Egyptian society and government was quite different and changed frequently. During the period discussed the Christian Syrians became, as we saw, more numerous, wealthier, and better organized in their communities. But this trend did not reflect itself equally in greater power, improved personal security, or legal status, not to mention greater integration within the overall society.

The Greek Catholics did not suffer in Egypt from the severe persecution which they had experienced at the hands of the Greek Orthodox in Syria. In Egypt the Greek Orthodox community was small and disorganized.[34] Until 1846 the Greek Orthodox Patriarch of Alexandria resided in Istanbul and from there could exert very little influence on the Egyptian situation. On the other hand, as we have seen, the Greek Catholics and all the other Uniate communities were "illegal," i.e., not recognized by the Ottoman government as independent *millet*s until the 1830s. For instance, until then the Greek Catholics paid annual tributes to the Greek Orthodox Patriarch of Alexandria. By recognizing his authority at least formally they could, most of the time, avoid his open hostility.[35] The Maronites, who enjoyed traditional recognition of their autonomy in Mt. Lebanon, found themselves in a legally far more precarious position in Egypt, a situation similar to that of the Greek Catholics. The security of the Christian Syrians depended on the efficacy of their French connection and on the goodwill of the Egyptian authorities. Ibrāhīm Katkhodā and Murād Bey harrassed the Catholic communities on the grounds of their illegal organization and their conducting of church services. Clearly, the lack of even *dhimmī* status made the Catholics from Syria an easy target; their wealth made them a temptation. In the case of Murād Bey's closure of the church in Damietta it was only through French pressure at the court of Sultan Selim III that the church could be reopened.[36] In any case, a heavy ransom had to be paid. Under ᶜAlī Bey al-Kabīr the fortunes of the Greek Catholics improved. But his policy was not determined by any particular tolerance toward non-Muslims or, specifically, Syrian Christians. Nor was this step a serious attempt on his part to improve trade relations with Europe. The reports of the French merchants show that their lot did not improve in any way during his reign.[37] The obvious reason for ᶜAlī Bey al-Kabīr's promotion of the Christian Syrians was his need for money. After having squeezed the Jews dry, the Syrians constituted the wealthiest and therefore, for him, most attractive community. The fact that he filled many high offices, especially in the customs, with Greek Catholics did not mean that the community or even the individual officeholders enjoyed greater security. In fact they were, like Coptic or Jewish officeholders, easily replaceable.[38] ᶜAlī Bey al-Kabīr made use of this policy, as did Ibrāhīm Bey, who, in 1790, had his head of customs, Yūsuf Kasāb, drowned for an alleged conspiracy with Murād Bey and Ibrāhīm Bey.[39] Yūsuf Kasāb was a cousin of Anṭūn and Yusuf Farᶜun. Both served earlier in the customs office and enriched themselves considerably. The death of Yūsuf Kasāb and the expulsion of his brother appears to have frightened them sufficiently to leave abruptly for Livorno.[40]

This feeling of personal insecurity was, of course, not limited to the Christian Syrians. Coptic functionaries were equally exposed to sudden falls from power and confication of their property.[41] The measures taken by the authorities against individual officeholders, though, should not be mistaken for an expression of a general hostile policy toward one or the other community. Rather, they were attempts to extract money from individuals who usually had enriched themselves enormously while serving the government. Indeed, fallen functionaries were usually replaced by members of their own community. But neither should this latter phenomenon be understood as a preferential attitude by the government toward one or the other community. High functionaries would usually try to fill as many other positions as possible with their coreligionists. Rather than indicating specific governmental policies toward minorities the fact that certain offices were held again and again by members of the same community shows the strenuous effort of these communities to keep lucrative and influential offices in their own control.

The relations between the Christian Syrians and Egyptian society were determined by the overall relations between Muslims and Christians in Egypt at the time. Government policy regarding sumptuary laws, housing regulations, or police protection and popular sentiments, such as distrust, rioting, and looting, were usually directed toward all *dhimmī*s, and did not differentiate between indigenous and immigrant Christians, or between various Christian denominations.

We have already had occasion to observe how, in the moment of crisis, suspicion of the *dhimmī* was all-pervasive. During the riots of the Cairene population against the French occupation in 1798, Khān Malayat and the Jawaniyya quarter, mainly inhabited by Greek Orthodox and Syrian Christians, were ransacked.[42] On the day the French left Cairo for the first time, the anger of the population, a result of two years of accumulated frustrations and humiliation, found an outlet in the form of extensive mob action against all Christians.[43]

But if the Muslim population was hostile against the Christians, it seems that the latter justified such feelings, that is to say they shared with the Muslim a world view which determined loyalties and identity through religious affiliation. The Christians in Cairo saw in the French occupiers their natural protectors, identified with their cause,[44] collaborated with them frequently, and exploited the weak position of the Muslims.[45] A local Greek, a certain Bartholemew was made chief of police by the French. From the lowest class of the population, "he paraded with his retinue . . . on his head a headgear, of coloured silk, dressed in a fur . . . in front of him servants with silverplated spears. . . ." A sight which outraged even such a sober observer as al-Jabartī.[46] The French, themselves, must have sensed the inappropriateness of such behavior, especially at a time when they were still trying to win the sympathies of the local Muslim dignitaries. The Christians were forced to return to their traditional clothing, wearing black or blue turbans rather than their recently acquired white turbans and colorful cashmere shawls.[47]

Some Maronites had actually come together with the French forces, being hired in Rome to serve as translators for the French.[48] Other Syrian Christians joined the French as translators in Cairo.[49]

The position of the French in Egypt soon became precarious. After a first evacuation agreement failed, the French, under General Kleber, reestablished themselves in Cairo. Short of manpower, and finding themselves now in an extremely hostile surrounding, they did not hesitate to employ local Christians in their army. There seems to have been no difficulty in attracting Christians. A certain Copt, Yaᶜqūb Ṣaᶜīdī recruited an auxiliary corps of some eight hundred Copts who were put into French uniforms. The small Greek contingent already built up earlier under the command of Bartholemew was now expanded to some fifteen hundred to two thousand troops under their commanders Nicolas and Yanni. Finally, a troop of some one hundred Christian Syrians was organized under the leadership of Yūsuf Ḥamāwī. Most of the latter group came to Egypt in the French retreat from Syria.[50] Greeks from abroad had served—after converting to Islam—in small numbers under Murād Bey in the artillery corps and the marines. But it was a clear sign of the overturn of the old order to see *dhimmī*s in large numbers serving as regular soldiers.[51]

By taking up arms and joining the occupational forces, the *dhimmī*s completely committed themselves to the French cause. Little wonder then, that all the commanders of the auxiliary troops, their associates, and many other local Christians left Egypt together with the final French withdrawal in July 1801.[52]

Popular sentiment against the *dhimmī* took severe forms during the French occupation, when at least twice the mob of Cairo took over, plundering the houses of Christians and killing many of them. Already long before the French occupation, resentments against the Christians could be sensed. Al-Jabartī deplored the fact that "the Christians' position has risen. . . ." Hasan Paşa, the Ottoman admiral, upon his takeover of Cairo in August 1786 issued regulations forbidding Christians to ride, to have Muslim slaves, and to wear other than their traditional garb. This was not only an attempt to reestablish the traditional law and order but also, most likely, a response to public sentiments.

But it was only as a reflection of the extremely critical and confused situation that attacks against *dhimmī*s occurred in serious form during the French occupation. Muslim rulers might have considered it their privilege to extort great sums of money from *dhimmī* merchants and functionaries. This was a step directed not so much against the community as against rich individuals, often, by the way, Muslim merchants as well. Never did such an attitude, however, induce the rulers to condone mob action against the *dhimmī*s. Such popular action might easily have become uncontrollable "Law and order" meant not only that the *dhimmī* should submit to the rules and regulations restricting his life but also that his security be guaranteed. Certainly the populace could not be permitted to take the law in its own hands. Ḥasan Paşa combined his restrictive measures against the Christians with a declaration that they should not be molested.[53] On the eve of the French occupation of Cairo the authorities prevented the population from attacking the *dhimmī*s. During the second uprising in Cairo, ᶜUthmān, the representative of the Ottoman government, denounced all action against the Christian subjects of the sultan as crimes and sent troops to all Christian quarters to guard them.[54] When the Ottomans reentered Cairo after the final departure of the French, one of the first orders issued was a prohibition against harming any *dhimmī*s "whether they are Copts, Greek Orthodox or Christian Syrians, since they are subjects of the Sultan." At the same time the Christians were ordered to wear only their traditional blue and black attire.[55]

Muhammad ᶜAlī followed, in many ways, the existing patterns in his relation with the *dhimmī*s. He frequently employed them in high administrative and economic positions, yet did not hesitate to imprison some of the very rich and confiscate their vast fortunes. Public opinion might have resented the new ascendancy of the Christians, but the people had no way to vent their resentment once Muhammad ᶜAlī was firmly in power.[56] Bent on radical reform, Muhammad ᶜAlī was in dire need of people with modern skills and knowledge. This need could often only be fulfilled by employing Europeans or Christians from other parts of the Ottoman Empire. Muhammad ᶜAlī was too pragmatic to let religious considerations interfere with the execution of his plans. The legal status of the Greek Catholics and other Uniate Christians from Syria changed only with formal recognition of their communities as *millet*s in the 1830s. But, already before that, they had acquired unprecedented freedom and security in the Egypt of Muhammad ᶜAlī. They were permitted to build new churches, felt free to buy houses in Cairo wherever they pleased, and the restrictive regulations concerning their appearance in public had fallen into permanent disuse.

Conclusion

The Christians in Syria were exposed to contact with Europe earlier than other parts of society in the Middle East. The contact was established in the sixteenth century through missionary activities directed from Rome and, increasingly also, through commercial ties with Italian and French merchants in the Levant. These relations eventually lead to the formation of the Uniate communities, a development that itself caused the first massive migration of Christian Syrians to Egypt. The majority of the Syrian immigrants in Egypt in the eighteenth century were Greek Catholic. The Maronites were the numerically smaller but better organized group. Egyptian society and rulers of the time tended to consider all Christians as one group, putting native and immigrant, Orthodox and Catholic Christians into the same category of *dhimmī*. Religious identities prevented any actual ties between Muslim and Christian Syrians in Egypt with the possible exception of some commercial cooperation. Since the middle of the eighteenth century Christian Syrians increased in numbers and wealth and were able to capture a number of influential positions in the administration and the economy. This rise of the Christians was observed and lamented by al-Jabartī. Another indication of this development is the frequently issued orders of the government trying to enforce the regulations restricting the appearance of Christians in public. Such orders obviously implied that the traditional rules were not observed any more. Not only were Christians rich enough to build lofty houses and wear expensive clothes, but they also apparently felt secure enough to disregard the traditional rules and to display their new economic status in public. The frequency of the orders shows that they were not implemented or, at least, were soon again disregarded. The orders were usually addressed to *dhimmī*s in general, but the evidence shows that often the Christian Syrians were specifically the cause for them.[57]

The traditional relationship between Muslim and *dhimmī* in Egyptian society was upset during the eighteenth century. The major factor in this change was the immigration of Uniate Christians from Syria, in itself the result of Europe's expanding role in the Middle East since the sixteenth century. The contact with modern Europe strengthened the economic position of Syrian Christians who went to Egypt. To a limited degree it also resulted in political protection through European pressure exerted on the Ottoman government. But this contact had not yet led to a new self-perception or world view amongst the Syrian Christians. Without doubt, the conversion to Catholicism reflected a shift in orientation away from the Greek Orthodox and Ottoman authorities to Europe. But the shift still occurred in terms of religious identity. The development of a group identity of the Christian Syrians and the organization of their communities depended, therefore, mainly on religious identity. The Muslim held view, that all Christians belonged to the same group found little echo amongst the Catholic Syrians. Their relations with the Coptic and the Greek Orthodox communities in Egypt were minimal and, with the latter, often hostile. Catholic communities, on the other hand, had close social and religious ties and cooperated frequently. At the same time, each of these communities insisted on the development of its own organizational and spiritual autonomy. This occasionally led to tensions between the Maronites and Greek Catholics, usually reflecting parallel tensions in Syria. In Egypt, however, the communities were aware of the need for close cooperation vis-à-vis the whole society. The one remarkable departure from the pattern of identity by religion was the consistent effort of the Catholics from Syria to emancipate themselves from the tutelage of the Franciscans, i.e., the European Catholics.

Conversion to Catholicism reflected, as we have observed, a new orientation toward Europe, but it did not imply that the Uniates now considered themselves Europeans. The autonomy of the autocephalic churches within Roman Catholicism recognized geographic differences of origin. In this context we hear for the first time of such nonreligious differences as "Eastern" versus European; differences which described the clash between the Franciscans on the one side and the Maronites and Greek Catholics on the other side. But it should be immediately added that during the period discussed such territorial concepts did not yet provide a basis for a new nonreligious identity. "Eastern" consciousness did not lead to the breakdown of organizational barriers even between the Greek Catholics and the Maronites, not to mention any rapprochement between Muslims and Christians of Syrian origin in particular or in Egyptian society in general.

The Christian Syrian immigrants in Egypt worked since the middle of the eighteenth century toward the consolidation of their respective communities. This development came to its first conclusion during the time of Muhammad ᶜAlī. Under his reign the restrictive laws concerning the *dhimmī* population were finally abandoned. It was only natural that the Christians who had risen in their socioeconomic status strove to eliminate all regulations restricting their movement and appearance in public. At the same time, however, the Uniates insisted on their religious identity and demanded formal recognition as *millet*s. When the Ottoman government granted such recognition it also provided the Uniates in Egypt with a secure legal status. Ironically, however, it was this legal recognition which also confirmed the separateness of the Christian Syrians from the rest of the Egyptian society. At the very time when processes of secularization began to change Egyptian society in response to a new and much more intensive impact of Europe, religion was emphasized as a principle of communal organization and group identity with regard to the Christian Syrians. Recognition as *millet*s granted the Uniates the fulfillment of their original aspirations but also brought their intellectual and social development to a standstill in Egypt. As recognized religious minorities they remained outside the mainstream of the development of Egyptian society. Integration into the rest of society became less likely than ever.[58]

Secularizing tendencies appeared within the Christian Syrian communities in Egypt only during the second half of the nineteenth century. Only then did it become possible to search for a new secular basis for integration either into general Egyptian society or into a common Syrian community comprising Christians of various denominations as well as Muslims.

Notes

1. Husain Fawzi, *Sindibād misri,* Cairo 1969, pp. 144–145.

2. Earl of Cromer, *Modern Egypt,* London, 1911, pp. 558–559. He does not hesitate, however, to speak immediately afterward about "the Egyptian character," "the Egyptian mind"—usually when making negative generalizations about the population.

3. By this term we mean the geographical entity comprising the modern states of Syria, Jordan, Israel, and Lebanon.

4. Al-Maqrīzī, *Ighāthat al-umma bikashf al-ghumma,* Cairo, 1940, vol. 2, p. 92; E.W. Lane, *Arabian Nights Entertainment,* London, 1841, vol. 2, p. 421. Both quoted in A. Raymond, *Artisans et commerçants au Caire,* Damascus 1973, vol. 2, p. 480.

5. Muḥammad ᶜAbdallah ᶜInān, *Ta'rīkh al-jāmiᶜa al-azhar,* Cairo, 1958, p. 302. Surprisingly little information about the origin and history of the *riwāq* system is available. Al-Maqrīzī mentions *riwāq*s in general. Ibn Iyās is given as a source for Qā'ītbay's activities, but in his lengthy treatment of Qā'ītbay, which includes a list of the endowments the latter founded, no mentioning of the *riwāq al-shuwām* occurs. See Ibn Iyās, *Kitab Ta'rikh Misr. al-mashhūr bi-badā'ᶜi al-zuhūr fī waqā'iᶜ al-duhūr,* Cairo, 1311/1874, vol. 2, pp. 90–303.

6. Yūsuf al-Shirbīnī, *Ḥazz al-quhūf fi sharḥ qasīd abī sharūf,* 1963, p. 55 reports that the Egyptians are less educated and less refined than the Syrians. I am indebted to Prof. G. Baer for this reference.

7. Qustantīn Bāshā, *Muḥādara fi ta'rīkh tā'ifat al-Rūm al-kāthūlīk fi Miṣr,* Beirut, 1930, p. 11.

8. ᶜAbd al-Raḥman, al-Jabartī, *ᶜAja'ib al-athār fī'al-tarājim wa-al-akhbār,* Cairo, 1297/1880, vol. 1, p. 188 concludes his description of the episode with the somewhat resigned observation that the whole affair might very well have been a ruse of Ibrāhīm Katkhodā to get money. But even if the imperial order was not presented, he still could act on the assumption of the illegality of such visits to European churches.

9. Qustantīn, Bāshā, *Ta'rīkh usrat āl Farᶜūn,* Beirut, 1932, p. 82; Buṭrus Khūrī, *Ta'rīkh al-risala al-mārūnīyya fī al-qatar al-misrī,* Cairo, 1927, p. 40.

10. All the registers are today located in the Greek Catholic patriarchal archives in Faggala, Cairo.

11. For a discussion of the transfer of these positions from Jewish to Greek Catholic hands see J.W. Livingstone, "Ali Bey al-Kabir and the Jews," *Middle Eastern Studies,* 7 (1971), pp. 221–228.

12. Livingstone (cited n. 11), p. 225.

13. Bāshā (cited n. 7), pp. 79–80.

14. Raymond (cited n. 4), vol. 2, p. 455.

15. Al-Jabartī, vol. 2 (cited n. 8), pp. 90–91 does not mention whether the *dhimmī* merchants with whom ᶜUmar b. ᶜAbd al-Wahhab had an argument were Syrians or Copts. It is most likely, though, that they were Christian Syrians, since they, not the Copts, engaged in trade in Damietta. The fact that it was the Copt Muᶜallim al-Riza who engineered the exile of ᶜUmar b. ᶜAbd al-Wahhāb is indicative of the former's powerful position, which he used to protect the Christians in general. When the Greek Catholic functionaries Mikhā'īl al-Jamal and Yūsuf Bayṭār later specifically opposed the return of ᶜUmar b. ᶜAbd al-Wahhāb to Damietta, it seems they were protecting the interests of the Greek Catholics there.

16. Emphasis mine. Khūrī (cited n. 9), p. 13; letter of Father Anṭūn Yūnān to head of Franciscans in Rome June 12, 1789, published in Būlus Qar'ali, *Al-Sūriyūn fī Miṣr,* Beirut, 1933, vol. 2, p. 10.

17. The Maronite Order of St. Antun split in 1770 into two orders called the Lebanese Aleppine and the Lebanese Baladi Orders. It was the former which continued to work in Egypt. Khurī (cited n. 9), p. 18 n. 1; Isidor Silbernagl, *Verfassung der Kirchen des Orients,* Landshut, 1865, p. 328.

18. Khūrī (cited n. 9), pp. 20ff. Letter of Cardinal Antonelli to the head of the Lebanese

Aleppine Order Dec. 6, 1787 published in Qar'ali (cited n. 16), vol. 2, p. 7ff; *Arādu an yadaᶜa yadahu ᶜala' al-tujjār al-kathūlīkiyyīn al-sharqīyyīn.*

19. For a copy of this agreement see Khūrī (cited n. 9), pp. 21–22, Raymond (cited n. 4), vol. 2, pp. 36–37.

20. In a report by the Maronite priest of Damietta, Yūsuf al-Samᶜānī (1788–1808) to his patriarch, Yūsuf al-Tiyān, on December 23, 1797, he emphasized the role of the Greek Catholic community supporting their own and the Maronite clergy during this crisis. He mentioned the appreciation the Greek Catholic merchants had for him, al-Samᶜānī, and finally pointed out that Damietta is in the House of Islam, implying that such close cooperation amongst all Catholics is indeed needed. The letter is revealing also with regard to another point. Apparently the patriarch was highly dissatisfied with the fact that, after the crisis with Murād Bey blew over, the church was formally registered as property of the Greek Catholic San Salvadore Order and the Maronite Aleppine Order. The patriarch resented not only the fact that the Greek Catholics now shared officially in the property, but also that it was registered in the name of the Maronite order rather than the Maronite community, i.e. the Maronite patriarch. In fact the patriarch threatened to dissolve the Order as the "Pope had dissolved the Jesuits." We find here the first indication of a clash which would occupy the communities much more than a century later: the question of authority over the community in Egypt, in other words whether patriarchal clergy or the order were entitled to hold control. A new dimension is also added by the demands of the local community itself usually represented by its secular leaders and interests. For the letter by al-Samᶜānī see Khūrī (cited n. 9), p. 39.

21. Khūrī (cited n. 9), p. 38. Statistical information on marriages in the Greek Catholic community in Cairo are only available since 1837. Between that date and 1900, 195 out of 776 registered marriages were with women from outside the Greek Catholic community (the woman as a rule followed the rites of her husband). One hundred fifty-one women came from other Catholic communities, 42 from Orthodox communities, i.e., Armenian, Coptic, and Greek Orthodox; one woman was Jewish, one Protestant. The total annual number of marriages increases toward the end of the century, but the percentage of intermarriages remains erratic and does not indicate a trend. It varies from one or no incident per year, as in 1853 one of eight, 1881 one of eleven, to more than fifty percent as in 1844 eight of fourteen, 1858 four of eight, 1887 eleven of twenty and 1891 ten of twenty-five. If any conclusion can be drawn from this for an earlier time it would be that intermarriages occurred perhaps even more frequently than the above average of 27 percent since the absolute size of the communities was smaller and therefore the need to find suitable partners outside their own community greater. Intermarriage with other Catholics is roughly three times as frequent as with members of the Orthodox churches.

22. He held this position with intermissions for ten years. Al-Jabartī, vol. 3, p. 341; vol. 4, p. 122.

23. Letter from Anṭūn Mārūn to the Patriarch Yuhannah al-Ḥilū, Khūrī (cited n. 9), pp. 86–89. Al-Jabartī (cited n. 8), vol. 4, p. 242 gives a slightly different account of the incident. According to him the first initiative for the arrest of Muᶜallim Ghālī came from the authorities themselves. A group of Copts, *ṭā'ifa min al-aqbāt,* then exploited the situation, accusing him of additional embezzlement. Al-Jabartī is completely unaware of the sectarian dimension of this affair.

24. The same holds true to a large degree for the Greek Orthodox Syrians who were made part of the local Greek Orthodox community. They are therefore much more difficult to trace. It seems, however, that until the time of Khedive Ismāᶜīl the number of Greek Orthodox Syrians remained negligible in Egypt.

25. Raymond (cited n. 4), vol. 2, p. 480.

26. Al-Jabartī (cited n. 8), vol. 2, p. 51; vol. 4, p. 164.

27. Ibid., vol. 2, p. 90.

28. Ibid., vol. 2, p. 163.

29. Especially the transportation of merchandise belonging to Muslim merchants on ships owned by Greek Catholic merchants at a time when Maltese pirates attacked ships of "infidels"; a term that

comprised all non-Catholics. See R. M. Haddad, *Syrian Christians in Muslim Society*, Princeton, 1970, p. 44.

30. Qar'alī (cited n. 16), vol. 2, p. 106 and Bāshā (cited n. 9), p. 76 err when they claim that the term *shāmī* was only applied to all Syrians after a substantial immigration of Greek Catholics from Damascus in the 1750s. See for instance Ibn Iyas (cited n. 5), vol. 2, p. 264 for the use of the term *riwāq al-shuwam* which most likely goes back to the fifteenth century.

31. Al-Jabartī (cited n. 8), vol. 2, p. 53–54. Al-ᶜArīshī lost out in the end, because he antagonized the (Turkish) authorities when he covered up for Syrian students who attacked students from the *riwāq al-atrāk*. Again al-Jabartī explains the siding of the authorities with the Turkish students by their sentiment of *jinsiyya*.

32. Compare al-Jabartī (cited n. 8), vol. 2, p. 90; vol. 3, p. 190; vol. 4, p. 280; etc.

33. Al-Jabartī (cited n. 8), vol. 3, p. 7.

34. Clot Bey, *Aperçu general sur l'Egypte*, Brussels, 1840, vol. 1, p. 135 estimates their number to be around 8,500.

35. Ibid., p. 134; Khūrī (cited n. 9), p. 86.

36. Khūrī (cited n. 9), p. 26.

37. R. Clement, *Les Français d'Egypte*, Cairo, 1960, pp. 210 ff.

38. Livingstone (cited n. 11), p. 225.

39. Al-Jabartī (cited n. 8), vol. 2, p. 188.

40. Bāshā (cited n. 9), p. 90, Bāshā, ibid., pp. 161–162 also gives another version, according to which the two brothers *Anṭūn* and Yūsuf already left Egypt in 1884, fleeing from Murād Bey. This obviously demands further clarification. In either version, however, it seems to have been a flight from pressure and insecurity.

41. E.g., Muᶜallim Ibrāhīm al-Jawharī, al-Jabartī (cited n. 8), vol. 2, p. 120, 262; or Muᶜallim Ghālī, al-Jabartī (cited n. 8), vol. 4, p. 242.

42. N. Turc, *Chronique d'Egypte*, ed. and trans. by G. Wiet, Cairo, 1950, p. 42. Al-Jabartī (cited n. 8), vol. 3, p. 25 tries to deemphasize the religious connotation of this mob action, by making only the riffraff *(zuᶜr,)* of the city responsible and by pointing out that houses of Muslims were also plundered. But it seems that these houses were plundered rather incidentally because they were neighboring the Christian quarter. the original direction of the rioting clearly pointed toward the Christian quarters.

43. Measures were also taken against individual Muslim collaborators. See Turc (cited n. 42), p. 101ff. Al-Jabartī does not mention these events directly but records the order of the Ottoman authorities prohibiting all excesses against Christians and Jews. In addition soldiers were posted at all Christian quarters. See Turc, p. 102.

44. Al-Jabartī (cited n. 8), vol. 3, p. 27.

45. Ibid.

46. Ibid., vol. 3, pp. 11–12.

47. Ibid., vol. 3, p. 45.

48. Qar'alī (cited n. 16), vol. 2, p. 89 lists three names: Ilyās Fatḥalla, Yūsuf Musābikī, Shāmī Mashḥara.

49. The Greek Catholic Father Anṭūn Rufā'īl Zākhūr, for instance, Jamāl al-Dīn al-Shayyāl, *Ta'rīkh al-tarjama wa-al-ḥaraka al-thaqāfiyya fī ᶜaṣr Muḥammad ᶜAlī*, Cairo, 1951, p. 74.

50. Turc (cited n. 42), pp. 111–114, 134; al-Jabartī (cited n. 8), vol. 3, p. 115 gives two thousand Copt recruits. See also ibid., p. 187; A.G. Politis, *L'hellenisme et l'Egypte moderne*, Paris, 1929, vol. 1, pp. 133–137.

51. Politis (cited n. 50), vol. 2, pp. 89–91. Bartholemew and Nicolas both served under Murād Bey, Nicolas as the commander of the Greek marines. Both transferred their loyalties very easily to the French, ibid. pp. 116–120, 125–129. After the withdrawal of the French, many Greek soldiers

seem to have had little trouble regaining Ottoman employ; "the strangest thing was that some Greek Orthodox Christians who had served in the French army, now put on Ottoman uniforms and equipped themselves with weapons and *yaqṭānāt*; (slingshots?); became part of them (Ottomans) acted haughtily; offended Muslims in the streets with beatings and insults in Turkish, and in their insults called the Muslim 'French infidel'. Only the very astute observer could have discerned them (to be Greek Orthodox and not Ottomans) be it then that he knew them from before," al-Jabartī (cited n. 8), vol. 3, p. 190.

52. Turc (cited n. 42), p. 134; al-Jabartī, vol. 3, p. 187. Qar'alī (cited n. 16), vol. 2, p. 92, estimates the number alone of the Greek Catholics who left to have been around five hundred. Most of those settled later in Marseilles.

53. Al-Jabartī (cited n. 8), vol. 2, p. 115.

54. Turc (cited n. 42), pp. 101–102.

55. Al-Jabartī (cited n. 8), vol. 3, pp. 190–191.

56. Ibid., vol. 4, p. 254: "The Armenians are the confidants of the government now" and their houses are therefore protected: In 1820 al-Jabartī, vol. 4, p. 315, observed: ". . . especially the enemies of religion: they constitute now the nobility; they take over positions; they dress like great lords . . . they live in high and splendid houses, which they buy for the highest prices . . . obtaining unprecedented rank they humiliate the Muslims . . . men of high status and commoners stand humiliated before the infidel."

57. Such orders were issued at various times: (a) July 3, 1787 by Ḥasan Paşa the Ottoman admiral, after taking Cairo from Murād Bey and Ibrāhīm Bey, ibid., vol. 2, p. 115. (b) December 14, 1787 by ᶜĀbdī Paşa who revoked his order to destroy Christian houses only after he was paid by the Christians 35,000 rial, more than half of which was paid by the Syrians, ibid., vol. 2, p. 155. (c) February 13, 1799 by the French, who explicitly asked the Christians from Syria to return to their traditional attire, ibid., vol. 3, p. 45. (d) July 26, 1801 by the Ottoman commander upon taking Cairo from the French, ibid., vol. 3, p. 190. (e) August 2, 1803, the issue of attire was brought up again with the arrival of a French consul in Cairo. Many Christians came to see him. Especially Christians from Syria considered themselves now under direct protection of the French and again wore colorful rich clothes. But all those who could not produce an official *baret* were ordered by the authorities to again wear traditional attire, ibid., vol. 3, p. 260, Turc (cited n. 42), pp. 184–187. (f) August 12, 1816. The new energetic *muḥtasib,* Mustafa Kashīf Kurd, who was appointed by Muḥammad ᶜAlī to bring the markets under control and eliminate corruption and profiteering, took his task very seriously and, amongst other things, also issued an order that Armenians, Greek Orthodox and Christian Syrians should evacuate their houses in Old Cairo, which they built there and embellished, that they should not employ Muslims, and should, again, wear their traditional costumes. This time, however, the Christians complained to the Pasha "who made allowances for them since they had become the confidants of the government, the companions of his Highness, and (his) intimate friends" al-Jabartī (cited n. 8), vol. 4, p. 280.

58. Bey (cited n. 34), p. 134: "Les Syriens—catholique du rit grec—s'allient ordinairement entre eux et perpetuent, avec leur race, leurs moers et leurs usages."

9

The Political Situation of the Copts, 1798–1923

DORIS BEHRENS-ABOUSEIF

Introduction

Salāmā Mūsā once said, "I am a Christian by religion and a Muslim by fatherland." This ambivalent identity is practically the only one possible for a Christian nationalist in Islamic society, but at the same time it has taken many successive adjustments for the Copts to reach this rather sophisticated point of view.

We will examine the problems arising during the time that the modern Egyptian state, Islamic in religion, was gradually absorbing the *milla* society. We will also look at the conflict the Copts experienced during their transition from the separateness in which they had lived for centuries to their integration into a political community with a Muslim majority, remembering that the majority itself was torn between an Islamic past and European modernism.

It is important to note the difference between Coptic-Muslim relations on the one hand and Christian-Muslim relations in general on the other. Since the fifth century the Egyptian struggle against the Byzantines was a national religious struggle. The Monophysite Church of Alexandria fought the Byzantine Orthodox Church on a political level. Ever since it has rejected dogmatic compromise with foreign churches. Thus it defended itself strictly throughout the centuries against protection by or affiliation with foreign powers, a fact which irritated foreign churches and the political powers behind them, since they considered the Copts no less heretical than the Muslims. The Copts, in addition, did not form a separate class. Like their Muslim countrymen they were mostly peasants—and since they hardly played any role as merchants, they did not come to enjoy foreign consular and religious protection and thereby enter into contact with foreign cultures and ideas. Not being merchants and therefore not mobile, they had no opportunity either to become, in the fashion of other Oriental Christians, mediators between East and West, or to represent advanced causes in a changing society.

On the contrary, the modernizing reforms introduced into Egypt under Muḥammad ᶜAlī were initiated by a Muslim ruler who employed foreigners and other more mobile Christian immigrants such as the Syrians and Armenians. Educational reform, printing, journalism, parliamentary institutions, and benevolent societies were adopted by the Copts only after they were already introduced into Egypt by the rulers. Following this pattern, the Copts became involved only later in national problems.

The Copts in the Eighteenth Century

When the French expedition was sent to Egypt at the turn of the nineteenth century, the French scholar Jomard, writing about Christian minorities in Egypt, tried to correct the ideas prevailing in Europe which did not correspond to the actual situation. In fact, he stated, Christians did not live in walled quarters and they were free to move as they wished.[1]

The French estimated the number of Copts as being ten thousand, making up one-thirtieth of the total population; half a century later, Lane gives the same number, but finds it to be one-fourteenth.[2] This same one-fourteenth is given in the 1910, 1927, and 1937 census statistics.[3] This proportion must have been reached under the Mamluks during the fourteenth century, when their number was greatly reduced after massive conversions to Islam.[4]

The Copts, already in Lane's time, were proportionally more numerous in cities than in rural areas, especially in Upper Egypt, where Copts made up 21.5 percent of the population of Asyūṭ. However, the bulk of the Copts, like their fellow countrymen, were and are *fallāḥīn,* with customs and life-styles no different from Muslim *fallāḥīn*. In villages differences between Copts and Muslims were not very prominent, and the traditional Islamic restrictions on the *dhimmī* not to ride horses or wear white turbans as well as not to carry weapons, were much less respected in villages than in cities.[5] As observed by a longtime resident European in Egypt, a Coptic peasant has much less in common with a Copt from the city than he has with a Muslim peasant.[6]

Within the cities the Copts, unlike the Jews and the Syrians, hardly played any role as merchants. They were craftsmen or clerks, mainly involved in government finance and taxation. As artisans, they were known to be specialists in certain crafts. Thus they were jewelers, where they formed a majority, woodworkers, masons, tailors, and weavers. Their financial importance as craftsmen seems to have been quite minor during the seventeenth and eighteenth centuries, but connected with their specialization in dealing with precious metals, they also dealt widely in moneylending.[7] The majority of Copts were employed in the civil service, where Muslim authorities never successfully managed to do without them or to break their monopoly. This situation persisted, in spite of several attempts during the Middle Ages to dismiss them with the argument that the employment of Christians in government service was contrary to Islamic law.[8]

Since only in a few exceptional cases were certain crafts or trades exclusively practiced by certain religious groups, guilds were generally interconfessional, but with Muslim heads. During the French occupation Coptic names were mentioned as guild heads, but this may be, as Raymond notes, an innovation of the French. Thus the places of work of Copts in Cairo were dispersed all over the city, indicating no religious segregation.[9] Nonetheless, the Copts in Cairo were concentrated in four quarters: north of Azbakiyya, west of al-Qanṭara al-Jadīda, near the Mu'ayyad mosque, and Bayn al-Ṣūrayn, all indicated by Jomard, who also mentions that the palace of the Copt Muᶜallim Jawharī, a high finance official, was at Birkat al-Fīl, alongside the residences of the Muslim dignitaries of the country.[10]

The autonomous *milla* headed by the patriarch and the clergy was also represented by some high ranking laymen who took part in making important decisions concerning community life. Like all the *ṭawā'if* in the Ottoman Empire, the Copts had their *ra'īs,* a person responsible for the *ṭā'ifa,* to be called on when the government needed funds from the community or other special tasks.[11] This *ra'īs al-Aqbāt* was usually the *Sarraf Başı,* the head of the finance clerks, since the *ṣarrāfīn* were the most important professional group among the Copts, who, in turn, had a virtual monopoly in this activity. On the other hand, the *ra'īs al-Aqbāṭ* could, on occasion, use his influence on official authorities to obtain special favors or exemptions for his community. Historical examples are a *fatwā* allowing the Copts to make their pilgrimage to Jerusalem,[12] a special *firman* for the erection of a new church, a dispensation for clergy from paying the *jizya,*[13] and other material advantages.

The effective declaration of the independence of Egypt from Ottoman rule in 1769 under ᶜAlī Bey al-Kabīr, was the first opportunity offered the Copts for a long time to play a prominent role in the Egyptian administration. It was during this Mamluk upheaval that the Copt Muᶜallim Rizq became chief of the mint and principal adviser to ᶜAlī Bey in financial matters. Along with the Syrians other Copts were allowed to replace the Jews in the customs administration after an anti-Jewish campaign led by ᶜAlī Bey.[14] Among the Copts of this period who had successful careers and accumulated large fortunes under the protection of powerful Mamluks were the brothers Ibrāhīm and Jirjis al-Jawharī, who also were *ra'īs al-Aqbāṭ* and supported their community in different respects. While Ottoman power reached the crumbling stage, the Copts remained a constant indispensable factor in running the administration and ascended in its hierarchy. Such an accumulation of wealth combined with an ever-growing influence gave the Copts, who had been a silent minority since the Middle Ages, a new consciousness which took concrete forms when they considered that the moment was propitious.

The French Expedition

The French occupation (1798–1801) brought the first direct confrontation between Egypt and the West since the Crusades. The Crusaders were as hostile toward the Copts as the Muslims since they considered the Copts heretics. When the French came, they declared themselves as sympathetic to Islam. Nonetheless, the Coptic community somehow saw an opportunity in the situation, and their leadership reacted to the coming of the French which was so deeply to affect the modern history of Egypt. Muᶜallim Jirjis al-Jawharī, *ra'īs al-Aqbāṭ,* wrote an appeal to Napoleon, as a disciple of the French Revolution, to change practices unfavorable to the Copts and to grant them full equality with their fellow countrymen.[15] Bonaparte's initial response was positive, and legal restrictions and discriminations against Christian minorities were in fact abolished under the French. In a commission of twelve members instituted for local justice, six were Muslim, while the other six were Copts. A Copt as well was the head of the commission, Muᶜallim Malaṭī.[16] Bonaparte himself, however, did not have a very high opinion of the Copts whom he accused of being dishonest and disloyal.[17] He is reported to have ordered his officers not to grant the Copts any special treatment since they would, in any case, support the French.[18] But meanwhile, the Copts became more indispensable. Since so many Turks fled with the arrival of the French, the Copts were able to take over the vacant bureaucratic posts left by them. In this way Jirjis al-Jawharī was appointed to a key position in control of taxation.

Under Bonaparte's successors a Coptic Legion under General Yaᶜqūb was formed. The role of General Yaᶜqūb under the French has been the subject of several studies,[19] his career being considered, quite romantically, as "a prelude to an independent Egypt neither French nor Turkish." A look at his background will tell us something about Coptic political development during the nineteenth century. Muᶜallim Yaᶜqūb Ḥannā was in the service of Amīr Sulaymān Bey. In charge of the security of the province of Asyūṭ he was able to acquire military training under Mamluk tutelage. He even fought in several inter-Mamluk battles. Under the French his knowledge of the situation of Egyptian roads and means of communication made his services of paramount value. Bonaparte appointed him as his adjutant while Desaix was occupied in Upper Egypt. Yaᶜqūb fought bravely and efficiently against the Mamluks, and it was his collaboration which made it possible for the French to subdue the whole of Upper Egypt. He also showed marked ability in organizing the postal service for the French army. After the battle of Heliopolis the French authorities approved his plan for a Coptic Legion to consist of two thousand recruits, mainly from Upper Egypt. But this plan met with a great deal of resistance from the patriarch[20] as well as the Coptic community at large, who argued that the families of the recruits would be deprived of their source of income.[21] The Coptic troops were trained by professional officers and Kléber appointed Yaᶜqūb as their commander with the rank of colonel, promoting him in March 1801 to general. When the French decided to leave Egypt they permitted the Egyptians who wished to depart with them to do so. Accordingly, Yaᶜqūb decided to leave with his family and some friends. He died shortly afterwards in August, 1801. Before dying, Yaᶜqūb asked Laskaris, a knight of the Order of Malta who was traveling with him, to transmit a message to the British government in the name of the Egyptian people, pleading for Egyptian independence. The message was delivered and later similar messages were submitted by other members of the Egyptian delegation to Bonaparte as first consul and to Talleyrand, his foreign secretary. The Coptic community of Cairo was to suffer a great deal from the Turks as well as from their Muslim countrymen for their collaboration with the French. Several Copts were put to death. Muᶜallim Malaṭī, the head of the Legal Commission, was beheaded. Coptic property was confiscated and special taxes levied on the community. Riots took place during which Coptic quarters were attacked and houses burnt and plundered. The traditional distrust of Copts took physical form. The reigning patriarch during the French expedition was Mark VIII. In the Coptic record of his patriarchate is the following report:

> During his bishopric there were many afflictions and many adversities; chiefly in that two years after his coming to the Chair a multitude from the Frank country, called the French, came and took possession of Egypt. The inhabitants of Cairo rose against them, and there was war between them for three days. . . . The people suffered very much at the hands of the French: many places were laid to waste, and many of the churches made desolate. The Patriarch also suffered many adversities, for which cause he left Ḥārat al-Rūm and came to Azbakiyya, where he built a large precinct and a large church in the name of Saint Mark the Evangelist.[22]

The Reign of Muḥammad ᶜAlī

Previous events, however, did not halt the progressive development that Coptic society had been undergoing for a certain time, and under Muḥammad ᶜAlī's religious tolerance, the Copts were able to consolidate their position. The restrictions on dress and riding were renewed once again, for the last time, in 1817 after the French abolished them. Jabartī, who reports this and complains that Copts and Greeks have exaggerated in demonstrating pomp and carrying weapons, expresses his pessimism as to the practicability of these measures which he, as a pious Muslim, supported.[23]

During Muḥammad ᶜAlī's reign, Christians were allowed for the first time to ring their church bells as well as to carry the cross in public. The Copts in particular seem to have enjoyed less favor under him than other Christians. Among the students he sent to study in Europe there were several Christians from Egypt, as well as Greeks, Syrians, Ethiopians, and Armenians, but no Copts.[24] In financial matters, however, the Copts kept their monopoly. Muḥammad ᶜAlī's chief treasurer was Muᶜallim Ghālī, but for a reason about which the sources are not explicit, he was murdered by order of the paşa himself.[25] Under Muḥammad ᶜAlī some Copts rose to the rank of bey[26] and some were allowed to belong to the class of important landowners.[27] They had to pay the same taxes as the Muslims plus the *jizya* which at that time seems to have had only a symbolic value.[28]

Mark's successor and a contemporary of Muḥammad ᶜAlī was Peter VII (1809–1852). He was not prone to involvement with foreign powers and politely declined an offer by the Russian Czar for financial support to the Coptic Church.

Muḥammad ᶜAlī was grateful for this attitude and honored it by paying a personal visit to the patriarch.[29] Peter VII shared in the fruits of the conquest of Sudan in 1823 and was permitted to consecrate a Coptic bishop there.

The Reforms of Cyril IV

The next important event in the modern history of Coptic society was the Patriarchate of Cyril IV, called Abū al-Iṣlāḥ or "Father of Reforms."[30] Dāwūd, his name before investiture, was born in 1806 in the province of Jirjā. He had a brilliant career in the Church hierarchy and after some argument between conservative members of the clergy and the reform partisans among the laymen, he was elected in 1854 as patriarch. Cyril's reforms, particularly in the field of education, had a great impact on Coptic life. His reforms essentially prepared Copts for the post of the average civil servant or secretary, with a good knowledge of foreign languages, able to work and deal with Europeans. Cyril built new schools, one of them at Ḥārat al-Saqqāyīn, the first school for girls established by Egyptians. In order to encourage new pupils to attend his schools, he selected his choir from among the graduates. He reorganized the administration of the patriarchate, creating a new diwan for clerical affairs and a register for church property. He established a special school for the education of the clergy and set salaries for priests under the condition that they have knowledge of the Coptic language. He also imported an Arabic printing press from Europe, the first one in Egypt after the one in Būlāq,[31] and asked the Khedive Saᶜīd to allow four Copts to learn printing in the Būlāq press. The arrival of the press at the Cairo railway station was celebrated by the patriarch and his clergy with a solemn procession.

Cyril IV was not only a progressive patriarch but also an enlightened leader with ambitions for his community. Considering the delicate political situation of Egypt during the reign of Saᶜīd (1854–1863), a conflict between the two leaders was almost inevitable. After Muḥammad ᶜAlī had, for the first time in modern Egyptian history, recruited *fallāḥīn* as soldiers in his wars against Syria, Saᶜīd continued the policy of Egyptianizing the army. Consequently, he saw the necessity of drafting Copts as well as Muslims in his Egyptian army. A few years earlier the draft of an Ottoman law provided for compulsory military service for Christian subjects, while at the same time exempting them from the *jizya*.[32] Analogous to the Ottoman law two important decrees were to introduce a distinct change into the status of the Coptic *milla* in Egypt. In December 1855 the *jizya* was officially abolished. One month later compulsory military service for Copts was introduced.[33] One year earlier, Saᶜīd had already renounced his claim on the sum of fifteen thousand Egyptian pounds of *jizya* due from the Copts.[34] This new compulsory draft was of course met by extremely negative feelings since the Copts were previously envied by their Muslim countrymen for not having to serve in the army in exchange for a minimal sum paid as *jizya*.[35]

Although some European authors report that Copts refused to serve in the military because of ill treatment, Coptic sources do not mention discrimination in this context.[36] The aversion of the Copts to military service has already been demonstrated in their opposition to General Yaᶜqūb, and therefore does not need too much of a political interpretation. The Copts, moreover, were not the only group in Egypt to protest against compulsory draft. Saᶜīd also had to use force to make the sons of the *shuyūkh* as well as the bedouins bear arms.[37] The Coptic community accused Cyril of using his new schools as recruiting centers for Coptic troops; the cases which were delivered to the schools were said to contain arms instead of books.[38] Cyril's attitude in this matter is not quite clear to us. From one side it is reported that he appealed to the British consul to put pressure on the viceroy to withdraw his decree,[39] while yet another Coptic source reports that Cyril vehemently defended himself, denying ever being such a coward as to request the exemption of the Copts from their "patriotic duty."[40]

Whatever the case, foreign intervention took place for the Coptic cause. The French consul offered Cyril his help if the patriarch would intervene with the negus of Ethiopia to allow the Jesuits to establish their order there.[41] Cyril refused this offer, but the British seem to have been more successful since it is said that Saᶜīd had to revoke his decree and the Copts were freed from military service. This was not the first time a foreign power was involved in Coptic affairs during Cyril IV's reign. When Cyril was a candidate for election in 1853–1854 the British put pressure on the paşa, at that time ᶜAbbās (reigned 1848–1854), who opposed the election because he accused the future patriarch of being involved in a conspiratory relationship with the negus of Ethiopia while Cyril was still a monk.[42] After Cyril was elected in spite of the paşa's opposition ᶜAbbās retaliated by dismissing a great number of Copts from the civil service. Saᶜīd's reaction was similar after the conflict over military service. Cyril's request for equality of treatment for Copts and Muslims in hiring practices for leading positions, as well as admission practices to engineering and medical schools, met with a negative response.

Another political crisis between the Copts and the viceroy occurred when Cyril IV was sent to Ethiopia to settle disputes concerning the borders between Sudan and Ethiopia.[43] Shārūbīm reports that Cyril was instructed to convince the negus to replace his British military advisors with Egyptian ones. The British, who heard of this, denounced the patriarch to Saᶜīd, accusing him of plotting against Egyptian interests. In the meantime, relations between Saᶜīd and Cyril were not at their best, and it was not hard to convince the viceroy of the patriarch's disloyalty. On the Ethiopian side, things developed in an equally unfavorable way for Cyril, who was arrested, and only through his mother's intervention did he escape execution. The British were accused of having instigated the Ethiopians against the patriarch. Upon his return to Egypt, Cyril IV was received by his community with a great public celebration, again giving Saᶜīd occasion to summon the patriarch and ask him for an explanation as to why the cross was carried in public. Cyril answered that this was already permitted under Muḥammad ᶜAlī. The next conflict was due to Cyril's dreams of pan-Orthodoxy. While he was conferring in Būsh with the Greek Orthodox and Armenian patriarchs on matters of church unity Saᶜīd Paşa summoned him. He arrived, after several summons, in poor health so Saᶜīd sent him his own physician. The patriarch died shortly afterwards in January 1861. It is said that Saᶜīd poisoned him.[44] Shārūbīm accused the British of having again set up a plot against the Coptic Patriarch by accusing him of attempting to put the Coptic Church under Russian protection.[45] Later Saᶜīd advised Cyril's successor, Demetrius II, "Do not behave like your predecessor! Whenever you have any request, come and tell me about it, and I will help you."[46]

The election of an enlightened patriarch like Cyril IV demonstrates that the Coptic community in the middle of the nineteenth century was not inclined to remain passive while Egyptian society was moving toward the modern age. Cyril's educational reforms reveal Coptic ambitions to consolidate their position as an indispensable group in Egyptian administration. In fact, the generation of Copts who attended his new schools managed to almost monopolize all government institutions during the second half of the nineteenth century. With their abilities in foreign languages acquired in these as well as in the missionary schools, they also proved to be useful to the large number of Europeans who settled in Egypt during the reign of Ismāᶜīl.

Coptic emancipation attempts since the adventures of General Yaᶜqūb were always connected with foreign involvement. The Muslim rulers, for their part, had looked with a suspicious eye upon Coptic contacts with foreign powers since the time of the Crusades. Even broad-minded rulers like Muḥammad ᶜAlī and Saᶜīd who gave ample evidence of their religious tolerance during their reigns, do not seem to have trusted the Copts, whom they did not readily include in their policy of liberalism toward Christians.

Khedive Ismāᶜīl

It was not until the reign of Khedive Ismāᶜīl that the political situation was such that the *milla* could become less and less definite as a social reality. Ismāᶜīl wished to regard Egypt as a part of Europe. This policy coincided well with Coptic ambitions, and the Copts were to consider the era of Ismāᶜīl as their golden age.[47] The growing importance of capital gave them ample opportunity and cause to invest their large fortunes. A new generation of Coptic businessmen and pashas came into being. No obstacles were present to prevent their ascendancy in the hierarchy of the civil service. The government recognized their diplomas so graduates of Coptic schools had the same chance of employment as graduates of government schools.

In 1866 the foundation of the first parliamentary assembly *(majlis shūrā al-buwwāb)* marked a new era for Egyptians in general, but for Copts in particular. The election law *(lā'iḥa asāsiyya)* did not connect religion with the right to vote or to be elected. In fact, one decade after abolishing the *jizya* Copts were already being elected, even in districts where they did not form the majority of the population,[48] and Coptic troops were fighting beside their Muslim countrymen in Crete, the Balkans, and in Sudan.[49] The new liberal atmosphere, as well as a growing interest in politics, prompted the Copt Mīkhā'īl ᶜAbd al-Sayyid, to start a newspaper called *al-Waṭan* in 1877, one year after the founding of *al-Ahrām*. As the name indicates its aims were political and not restricted to community affairs. The term *al-waṭan* was used for the first time in Egypt in its modern patriotic meaning as the title of a book by ᶜAbd-Allāh al-Nadīm, who later became ᶜUrābī's partner and spokesman.

The war in 1877–1878 between Turkey and Russia aroused great interest in the entire Egyptian press which published detailed reports daily of the events of the war. But now the situation was different than twenty years before when the Crimean War divided public opinion in the Ottoman Empire along religious lines; in Egypt as well tension had been felt between pro-Russian Copts and pro-Turk Muslims.[50]

The Nationalist Movement

It is not an easy task to analyze the role of the Copts in the nationalist movement which took shape as Ismāᶜīl's policies were leading Egypt toward bankruptcy. Since no Coptic names are mentioned in connection with the Egyptian intelligentsia of that period and the national movement it created, a glance at the various elements included in this movement may help us to speculate on the position of the Copts.

Muḥammad ᶜAbduh's program offered a reformed humanistic understanding of Islam. He himself admitted that he was speaking only in the name of the Muslims since non-Muslims were only a minority.[51] His ideal was the golden age of Islam under the democracy of ᶜUmar although he did not plead for pan-Islamic solidarity. Common historical experience should be the basis of nationalism in spite of religious differences. Besides nationality or *damm wa jins* (blood and race), religion should be an essential criterion for the leadership of state, at least as important as race, if not more so.[52] For Muḥammad ᶜAbduh the leader of Egypt had to be a Muslim.[53] The group of intellectuals around Muḥammad ᶜAbduh was quite heterogenous, including Syrian Christians and Jews who based their statements on humanitarian and liberal rather than specific religious ideas.[54] He, however, spoke in terms of an Islamic society to which the Copts, and here lies an important difference between the political conception of the Syrian Christians and the Copts, did not feel that they belonged since they saw themselves as the true Egyptians undermined by Arab domination.

Aḥmad ᶜUrābī incarnates the rebellion of the Egyptian army, first against the Turkish element and later against European interference in Egyptian political and financial affairs. In April 1879 a group of nationalists signed a manifesto demanding the formation of a completely Egyptian cabinet without foreigners. The petitioners were composed of religious leaders, parliament members, businessmen, civil servants, and army officers. They called themselves the *ḥizb waṭanī* or *jamᶜiyya waṭaniyya*. Among the religious leaders who signed was the Coptic Patriarch.[55] Three years later, after ᶜUrābī prepared his army to rebel against the British, Cyril V with some other Coptic dignitaries signed another petition condemning the dismissal of ᶜUrābī by the Khedive Tawfīq.[56] This kind of solidarity with ᶜUrābī's actions may have been more than a simple formality since ᶜUrābī guaranteed the Copts political and legal equality with the Muslims. He also seems to have obtained some material support from the Coptic population.[57] Although European sources tend to identify later xenophobic excesses which his rebellion resorted to as fanatic persecution of Christians,[58] there is no evidence that Copts were singled out during the 1882 riots, although they may well have had fears in this respect. Shārūbīm mentions the persecution of the *naṣāra,* but specifies that they were Syrian, Greek, and British.[59] Also, Butcher mentions only that possible harm could have come to the Copts if the British had not interfered at the right time by occupying Egypt. In fact there was no real antagonism between the Copts and ᶜUrābī. Even Cromer did not automatically exclude the Copts as possible allies of ᶜUrābī as he did the Syrians and Armenians. But after considering the *fallāḥīn,* the *shuyūkh,* the Copts, and the *ᶜumad* he comes to the conclusion that only the *shuyūkh* could have cooperated under a ᶜUrābī government, if it had been successful. Cromer eliminates the Copts not only because of their lack of political power but also because of religion.[60] The political abstinence of the Copts at that time can also be observed in the fact that they were not active in the constitutional liberal wing of the nationalist movement which developed under the modernistic influence of Syrian Christian immigrants to Egypt. Still this tendency would seem to have appealed to Coptic opinion as expressed by the newspaper *al-Waṭan* and the Coptic historian Shārūbīm, as it was the least difficult of the possibilities offered for Coptic political integration.

Contacts between Syrians and Copts were restricted to rapprochement efforts between the two churches. An intellectual or political affinity between the communities does not seem to have existed. An article in the Syrian paper *Mir'āt al-Sharq* gives a negative picture of the Copts who are described as being decadent and backward.[61] During the reign of Ismāᶜīl European control was established over Egyptian financial affairs. The first British head of the accounts department, Gerald Fitzgerald, and his successors started to reform the archaic Coptic system of keeping state accounts by replacing a number of Copts with Syrians. The Coptic newspaper *al-Waṭan* led a campaign for years against the prejudicial treatment of the "educated sons of the fatherland."[62] During the British occupation the Coptic monopoly as clerks was to be gradually broken. According to Coptic reckoning Copts made up 90 percent of the civil servants in Egypt.[63]

The British Occupation

Like the French before, Lord Cromer, the British high commissioner, had no intention of favoring the Copts, of whom he had no higher opinion than of their Muslim countrymen.[64] He did not trust their collaboration and regarded them as opportunists who knew how to direct their sympathies according to circumstances. He preferred to support the Syrians, whom he considered as modern, emancipated, and closer in mentality to Europeans. They and the

Armenians were the elite of the Orient, in his opinion. He encouraged these groups to start newspapers. The Copts at the same time as they were losing hold of their traditional field, the civil service, quickly learned to adapt themselves to the new situation the British occupation created.

> Thanks to the freedom, the justice, and the rapid improvement the Nile valley was experiencing under British rule, Coptic dignitaries and their families were able to develop their abilities for work and finance, and concentrate almost exclusively their zeal in accumulating fortunes in land, stocks and bonds, companies, etc. . . . As if the government policy of preventing them from holding high positions in government, had urged them to deploy their energy in order to open up new zones of power, enabling them to hold on to their position in the country.

This is a statement made by a Copt at the beginning of the century.[65] The Copts also came to enjoy the protection of foreign consulates. In Upper and Lower Egypt they were the consular agents for European countries and enjoyed the same immunities as foreigners.

The next phase in the nationalist movement discouraged the Copts, their resentment against the British notwithstanding, from supporting the nationalists. In 1889 Shaykh ᶜAlī Yūsuf, a disciple of Jamāl al-Dīn al-Afghānī, started the newspaper *al-Mu'ayyad* to plead for the unity of Islam all over the world. Another more militant paper, *al-Miqyās,* founded by the same editor, openly called for a struggle against unbelievers.[66] These pan-Islamic and anti-Christian tendencies, even if they were directed primarily against the British and other Europeans, confirmed the Copts in their feelings of political isolation. For them the British remained the lesser evil.

The National Party started by Muṣṭafā Kāmil appealed for Muslim solidarity through its newspaper *al-Liwā'*. But Muṣṭafā Kāmil's understanding of Islamic solidarity was political rather than religious. He was impressed by European nationalism, which he thought to be connected with faith, and he referred to Bismarck's words that love of the fatherland could not be separated from faith.[67] Islam was for him not only a religious bond but a cultural, social, and political one as well which could all the same include non-Muslims. Muṣṭafā Kāmil meant to appeal to the Copts, when he referred to all Egyptians as sons of the pharaohs, since the majority of the original population of Egypt had converted to Islam.[68] He seriously tried to find a formula which would win them over. "Copts and Muslims are one people, linked through nationality, traditions, character, and mentality";[69] "we as Egyptians, Copts and Muslims, we talk about religion only in the church or in the mosque."[70] Thus his policy did not imply just tolerance but solidarity of an oriental community against European imperialism.

But now the Copts found themselves in a no-man's land: the ancient autonomous community was given up for an Islamic identity which they never thought of adopting. A conflict between the Nationalists and the Copts could not be avoided. "The Copts are the true Egyptians," wrote *al-Waṭan.*[71] "They are the real masters of the country. All those who have set their foot on Egyptian soil, be they Arabs, Turks, French, or British, are nothing but invaders. The originators of this nation are the Copts. . . . Whoever calls this country an Islamic country means to disregard the rights of the Copts and to abuse them in their own fatherland. Not one of them would accept such a thing.'' Beside *al-Waṭan,* another Coptic newspaper *Miṣr* (founded in 1895) joined the campaign against the National Party under Muṣṭafā Kāmil as a ''party of destruction and evil.'' Both papers rejected the project for a new parliament planned by the General Assembly which till then had only an advisory function. *Miṣr* organized a petition signed by several Coptic dignitaries to protest against any change in the political situation which would introduce more freedoms. The Egyptians, it stated, would not be able to handle any further liberty since the press was already being used as ''a sword in the hand of a child.''[72] This petition was opposed by another group of Copts, but *al-Waṭan* estimated that 90 percent of the Copts and 10 percent of the Muslims preferred to remain under British rule.[73]

Proposals were made for the foundation of a Coptic political party, but secular tendencies prevailed and instead the ''Coptic Reform Society'' was set up by the Protestant lawyer and journalist, Akhnūkh Fānūs, for the defense of Coptic interests. Its members were, according to *al-Liwā'*,[74] mainly railway employees and teachers in Anglican schools. Their main objective was equality with Muslims for employment in the civil service. While the British high commissioner refused to consider such claims, the Nationalists as well refused to consider any separate Coptic problem, all difficulties being part of the Egyptian struggle against the British. Any political split between Copts and Muslims would only be to the advantage of the occupation regime and would delay Egyptian independence. Meanwhile, the National Party was able to convince a few Copts that Muṣṭafā Kāmil's nationalism was not incompatible with Coptic identity.

Wīṣā Wāṣif is better known for his role in the later Wafd Party than for his role in the National Party. He was the first Copt active in the nationalist movement. Tādrus, in his biography of famous Copts of the twentieth century, does not mention him. Wīṣā Wāṣif opposed the idea of a Coptic political party as well as Coptic organizations for Coptic interests. He was a member of the Head Committee of the National Party and tried, after Muṣṭafā Kāmil's death, to promote an understanding between Copts and the Nationalists, urging his coreligionists to take an interest in political affairs and to join parties to contribute to the struggle for Egyptian independence. But Wīṣā Wāṣif's appeals were not to be successful for quite a while. *Al-Waṭan* called him Judas Iscariot.[75]

Coptic-Muslim Conflict

A violent crisis arose between Copts and Muslims soon after Muṣṭafā Kāmil's death. As a reaction to an article in *al-Waṭan,* in which the Islamic conquest of Egypt was called oppressive,[76] the chief editor of *al-Liwā'* wrote a highly insulting and derogatory article against the Copts under the title ''Islam, a stranger in its own country.''[77] For the next two years Coptic-Muslim relations were poisoned and a kind of journalistic civil war broke out within the press. The author of the anti-Coptic article being a Tunisian, the Copts saw themselves confirmed in their traditional animosity toward pan-Islam. Muṣṭafā Kāmil's and Wīṣā Wāṣif's attempts to integrate the Copts in their movement suffered an important setback.

Buṭrus Ghālī was surely not the right Copt to become prime minister, particularly at that time. He was born in 1846 and educated in Cyril's school at Ḥārat al-Saqqāyīn. He learned several languages and was employed as a teacher, translator, secretary, and then chief secretary. He became vice-secretary in the Commission de la Dette Publique and then secretary of state in the Ministry of Justice. Under ᶜUrābī he was secretary of the cabinet and was accorded the title of *mīr mīrān* after the battle of al-Tall al-Kabīr between the British and ᶜUrābī where he mediated between ᶜUrābī and the khedive. Under the British, he became consecutively minister of justice, finance, foreign affairs, and finally in November 1908, prime minister and minister of foreign affairs at the same time. Buṭrus Ghālī disappointed the Copts by not using his influence in government to meet their demands. Neither did he support the reform partisans in their quarrel with the patriarch and the clergy.[78] The Nationalists, too, had a list of accusations against him: his role in the Treaty of Sudan in 1899; in the Dinshuwāy trial,[79] in the revival of press censorship, as well as the renewal of the Suez Canal concessions.

Blunt considers Buṭrus Ghālī as a capable but not independent enough man, an Anglophile, ready to do anything he was asked as long as he could keep his position and his three thousand Egyptian pounds of annual salary.[80] Upon his appointment as prime minister *al-Liwā'* noted that Buṭrus Ghālī was the only member of the cabinet without a high degree.[81] Qalīnī Fahmī Paşa, a Coptic member of the National Party, remarked that Buṭrus Ghālī was appointed prime minister only because he was a Copt.[82] In February 1910 a young Nationalist and partisan of the National Party, Ibrāhīm al-Wardānī, murdered the Coptic prime minister after a session in the Legislative Assembly concerning the Suez Canal concessions. The Copts blamed the fanaticism of the National party and thus Buṭrus Ghālī became a martyr.

In Asyūṭ, the capital of the Copts as it was called, leading personalities of the Coptic community decided to hold a congress in order to emphasize their claims. The government feared trouble in Asyūṭ because of the great number of Copts living there and so asked Patriarch Cyril V to intervene and to propose Cairo as a meeting place. But neither the government nor the patriarch, who himself was not on the best of terms with his community, managed to convince the Copts. They held their spectacular congress in Asyūṭ in March of 1910, including 1,158 delegates from all the provinces of Egypt. They demanded Sunday as holiday for the Copts and a change in the election law to include one of two possible provisions. The first of these would be to have representation in proportion to the percentage of Copts in the total population. The second would be to combine all Coptic votes, gathered from all over the country, so that they would have a majority in some districts. The latter possibility was modelled on Belgian electoral practice. The reason for this proposal was that the Copts were under-represented; they had only ten (instead of sixteen) members out of two hundred and thirty-three delegates in representational bodies. In his report for 1911,[83] British High Commissioner Eldon Gorst heavily criticized the Copts and their congress, which he said was organized by a few rich landowners who did not make up more than twelve thousand of the total Coptic population of seven hundred thousand. He emphasized the great economic power of the Copts which was comparatively greater than that of their Muslim countrymen. He considered this due to their exploitation of the common man and particularly the poor peasants who were made to suffer enormously at the hands of the Coptic moneylenders. More Coptic influence in local administration, as was demanded, would only make the Copts more unpopular. He accused the Copts of interpreting the impartial treatment of Copts and Muslims by the British as prejudicial to the Copts.

In retaliation, an ''Egyptian Congress'' was held by the government to object to the activity of religious lobbies as well as the use of terms like *umma qibṭiyya* (Coptic people or nation) by the Copts. The National Party and Muḥammad Farīd repudiated the Egyptian Congress as having been organized by the British to divide the Egyptian people.[84] In Muḥammad Farīd's view non-Muslims of the Middle East share the same fate as their Muslim neighbors in their relationship to European colonialism which he regarded as a ''continuation of the Crusades,'' against Eastern peoples, be they Muslims or not.[85]

Public opinion in general was against the Copts; the khedive and the prime minister, who till then kept ourselves out of the Coptic-Muslim conflict and above reproach for religious fanaticism, supported the Egyptian Congress. The Syrian and Egyptian press showed no sympathy for Coptic protests, even including, to the great disappointment of the Coptic press, the liberal *al-Jarīda,* the newspaper published by Aḥmad Luṭfī al-Sayyid.[86] The image of the Copts, then, in the first decade of the twentieth century was that of either unpopular wealthy moneylenders or of a class of clerks privileged enough to hold 69 percent of the posts in the Ministry of Interior, 44 percent in the Ministry of Finance, 48 percent in the Ministry of Posts and Railways, 30 percent in the Ministry of Justice and 6.14 percent in the Ministry of Culture.[87] According to Coptic estimates they made up 30 percent of educated Egyptians and controlled 19 percent of the economy[88] while they composed 7 percent of the population. They demanded proportional representation in elected governing bodies, at the same time asking that the government ignore proportions and consider only ability wherever employment was concerned.[89] Some thought it appropriate that they should be represented according to the taxes they paid and not according to their percentage in the population.[90]

On the Muslim side, the Copts' support of the British and the success of Protestant missionary activity during the British occupation gave them even more reason for mistrusting the Copts. Although British official policy did not favor the Copts the missions created a common ground between British and Copts, encouraging the latter in anti-Islamic tendencies. This foreign element also played an important role in the conflict between laymen and clergy over Church affairs and policymaking. The patriarch and his partisans saw foreign influence as the reason for this division in the community. They were backed in their opinion by the government as well as the nationalists while the British sympathized with the reform movement.[91]

The isolation of the Copts at that stage and their discouragement with the situation they were trapped in, on one side excluded from the nationalist movement, on the other abandoned by the British, their church and community divided by the missions, made a change of attitude necessary. The Coptic press with bitterness and resignation adopted an anti-British attitude accompanied by a nostalgia for the lost Egyptian past: "What has weakened us if not the murder of the Egyptian soul and the destruction of the Egyptian personality and character?"[92] "We speak a language which is not ours; our religion has been adulterated by foreign teachings which have brought us only hate and discord."[93] This nostalgia for ancient Egypt as an expression of present humiliation became the leitmotif of a very pathetic kind of poetry written by Copts and published in Coptic newspapers.[94] But this nostalgia contained at the same time the nucleus of secular thinking and secular nationalism.

Secular nationalist tendencies were crystalizing around the newspaper *al-Jarīda,* founded by the father of Egyptian liberalism, Aḥmad Luṭfī as-Sayyid, in 1908. He promoted modernistic liberal ideas and a nationalism based on Egyptian solidarity rather than on pan-Islamic, Pan-Ottoman, or pan-Arab lines. His newspaper attracted a group of rational liberal intellectuals from the *haute bourgeoisie*. The Umma Party, which grew up around *al-Jarīda* and which influenced the later Wafd Party, attracted many Copts and became the link between the Copts and the nationalist movement. Other Copts joined the National Free Party which was formed around the pro-British Syrian newspaper al-Muqaṭṭam, and the Copt Akhnūkh Fānūs founded the Party of Independent Egyptians[95] with a liberal and secular platform. As Blunt observed in 1911 the new generation of Copts was becoming more politically minded.[96]

The outbreak of World War I and the declaration of Egypt's status as a British protectorate led the Egyptian nationalist movement into a new active phase. A new economic situation during the war changed the social structure of the country. The old system of classes divided according to ethnic, religious, and social groups was replaced by a system based on economic level. By the time of the 1919 revolution Copts and Muslims were celebrating national unity. A cross within a crescent was the emblem of the revolution. Unlike other minorities in the Middle East the Copts did not collaborate with foreign powers during the war. Three Copts, including Wīṣā Wāṣif, were a part of the *wafd* (delegation) which was sent to the Peace Conference in Paris in 1919 under the leadership of Saᶜd Zaghlūl to press for Egypt's right to independence. During the boycott of the Milner Commission in the same year a Copt, Yūsuf Wahbā, became prime minister. A Coptic rally at the St. Mark's Cathedral condemned him for accepting this office and thus breaking the boycott.[97]

One last discussion concerning the legal status of Copts took place on the eve of the signing of the new Egyptian constitution in 1923. When the declaration of

Egyptian independence was made in 1922, the British reserved for themselves the right to protect minorities. They suggested that the Copts be granted the constitutional right to be represented in parliament in proportion to their number in the population. In the 1913 constitution the British guaranteed the Copts four of the seventeen appointed seats in the Legislative Assembly.[98] A lively debate on representation took place in the entire Egyptian press, the Copts themselves being of divided opinion. Tawfīq Daws, as well as other Coptic dignitaries who organized the Coptic Congress, supported the proposal for a defined proportional representation of the Copts in parliament since the new constitution would declare Islam as the state religion. Most intellectuals and politicians rejected the idea of a religious minority treated as a political party with a separate political platform within the parliament. Ṭāhā Ḥusayn feared that a separate status for minorities within governing bodies would result in a kind of "state within a state."[99] Sa^c^d Zaghlūl saw nothing wrong with material and social interests of minorities being separately treated, but within parliament only political ideas should count.[100] Salāma Mūsā, the first Arab socialist and a Copt, saw no special advantage for the Copts in forming a separate faction in parliament, since it could still, after all, be outvoted by the Muslim majority.[101] A number of Copts gathered at the St. Mark's Cathedral under the leadership of the lawyer Salāma Mīkhā'īl, to present a paper to the Constitutional Commission, which included five Copts among its thirty members. In the paper special treatment of the Copts was rejected as incompatible with the sovereignty of state, and Copts should not have separate interests from the rest of their countrymen.[102]

The results of the first parliamentary elections proved better than the proposed law, since the number of elected Coptic deputies was higher than a special status would have allowed.[103] Independent Egypt's first cabinet, under the leadership of Sa^c^d Zaghlūl, included as ministers two Copts and one Jew. The head of the Chamber of Deputies was Wīṣā Wāṣif.

One could say that when the Copts voted against what Ṭaha Ḥusayn called a "state within a state" the *millet* status was definitely given up, not only formally but consciously. The dissolution of the *millet* structure had been, as demonstrated, a gradual, complex, and somehow painful process for the Copts. Medieval society had granted them autonomy in that it allowed them to preserve their traditions at the price of being *dhimmī,* i.e. not sharing the same privileges and duties of their Muslim neighbors. They could accept this arrangement or convert to Islam. The Copts, those who had preserved their religion through the centuries, sometimes at great sacrifice, considered themselves the genuine Egyptians, the real masters of the country, who had long had to live under foreign domination.

When in the second half of the nineteenth century Egypt started to adopt the structures of a modern state, the Copts saw themselves threatened with the possibility of becoming a minority of individual non-Muslim citizens living with a majority of Muslims instead of being part of an autonomous community with its own identity. They would now have to give up their autonomy and share the same duties and rights as their Muslim neighbors within the framework of a national identity defined by the Muslim majority.

The national movement which followed, inspired by an Islamic past and by the cultural glory of the Arabs, was seen by the Copts as yet another subjugation under Muslim Arab domination. However, this time there was the added disadvantage that they give up what they had maintained for centuries: a separate identity based on a pre-Arab past and a religion that was not Islam.

The factor of a common language and a common history motivated the Syrian Christians of Egypt "to identify themselves imaginatively with the past as embodied in the language they used, even if that past had been molded by a religion other than theirs and if their fathers would have regarded it as in some sense alien. [This] reinterpretation of the Islamic past, not as a religion but as a human culture,"[104] was too far from Coptic thinking at that phase of their history. The Copts did not have the same mercantile, mobile background the Syrians had or the close contacts with European culture which gave the Syrians the intellectual equipment to shape their identity in terms of modern nationalism. They were the isolated "modern sons of the pharaohs" as they were called by a British traveler.[105] The Copts did not have al-Azhar or an equivalent institution, nor did they possess as did the Syrians, the knowledge of the politics, science, and technology of Western Europe, to qualify them in the eyes of the British. During the Coptic-Muslim conflict *al-Waṭan* published an article in which it protested against the project of the government to publish some works of classical Arabic literature with the argument that Arabic literature was of minor value and characterized by religious fanaticism.[106]

The educational reforms of Cyril IV, along with the missionary schools, enabled Copts to consolidate their position as the indispensable civil servant. Tādrus, in his book, warns the Copts that if they are not careful, the Muslims will soon reach their level of education.[107] They felt that by all means they had to keep their lead in education, but this did not cultivate any tradition or shape intellectuals. Among the Copts who became journalists or historians were Ibrāhīm al-Jundī of *al-Waṭan,* al-Manqabādī of *Miṣr,* Shārūbīm and Rufayla. The last two, both authors of historical works, were originally civil servants who later started writing. Correspondingly Coptic ideals concentrated for a long time on keeping their domination unbroken in the civil service. It was not until Makram ᶜUbayd with his nationalism based on Arab culture and language attacked the Coptic clerk caste and urged his coreligionists to look for other professions that the Coptic preference for civil service came to an end. In 1937 only 9.1 percent of government employees were Copts.[108]

As long as the Copts did not feel culturally and historically involved with Muslim Egyptians, religion remained the main identification factor, and the relations between Copts and Europeans were considered with suspicion by the Muslims. However, the Crusaders did not regard the Copts as any better than Muslims; the French preferred the cooperation of a majority of Muslims to a minority of Christians; the British, combining both attitudes, gave the Copts once and for all the feeling of being part of Muslim society and culture.

To compare again with the Syrian community of Egypt, the line between Christians and Muslims was "not sharply drawn" as Hourani notes. Both shared the same fate of being immigrants in Egypt, but "in some ways their view of the world was different." The Syrian Christians tended more toward collaboration with the Europeans, first the French and later the British, while it was the Syrian Muslims of al-Azhar who planned Kléber's murder. Later Syrian Muslims stuck to the principles of Islam in their political thinking while the Christians moved toward wholly secular political thought.

The Copts, once they found their way to nationalism, whether based on Egyptian or Arab solidarity, found no alternative to the obvious path of secularism. The Muslims, for their part, saw no conflict in abolishing all the barriers which would lead to a "state within a state." However, as of today, Muslims have still not moved to a completely secular society. The Copts in Egypt are a minority of Christian citizens within a majority of Muslim citizens in a Muslim state.

Notes

1. M. Jomard, "Description de la ville et de la citadelle du Caire," in *Description de l'Egypte*, second edition, Paris, 1824, p. 327.

2. Edward W. Lane, *An Account of the Manners and Customs of Modern Egyptians*, London, 1954, p. 535.

3. *Majmūᶜat aᶜmāl al-mu'tamar al-misrī al-awwal*, Heliopolis, 1911, p. 193; M. Clerget, *Le Caire*, Cairo, 1932, vol. 1, pp. 212ff.; Gabriel Baer, *Population and Society in the Arab East*, London, 1964, p. 50.

4. F. Wüstenfeld, trans., *Macrizi: Geschichte der Copten*, Göttingen, 1846, pp. 29ff.

5. Lane (cited n. 2), p. 535; Charles Watson, *The American Mission in Egypt*, Pittsburgh, 1904, p. 54.

6. P. van Bemelen (pseudonym: Boutros), *L'Egypte et l'Europe*, Leiden, 1881, vol. 1, p. 86.

7. André Raymond, *Artisans et commerçants au Caire au XVIIIe siècle*, Damascus, 1974, vol. 1, p. 282.

8. See Donald Richards, "The Coptic Bureaucracy under the Mamluks," in *Colloque internationale sur l'histoire du Caire*, Cairo, 1969; Ibn al-Naqqāsh, "Fetoua relatif à la condition juridique des dhimmis," *Journal Asiatique*, 18 (1851), pp. 417ff. and 19 (1852), pp. 97ff.

9. Raymond (cited n. 7), pp. 457ff.

10. Jomard (cited n. 1), p. 333.

11. Raymond (cited n. 7), pp. 458ff.

12. ᶜAbd al-Raḥmān Jabartī, *ᶜAjā'ib al-athār fī al-tarājim wa-al-akhbār*, Cairo, 1297/1880, vol. 1, p. 195.

13. Ibid., vol. 4, p. 232.

14. Stanford J. Shaw, *The Financial and Administrative Organization of Ottoman Egypt, 1507–1798*, Princeton, 1962, p. 103.

15. A. S. Atiya, *A History of Eastern Christianity*, London, 1968, p. 101.

16. Tawfīq Iskārūs, *Mawābigh al-aqbāṭ wa-mashāhīruhum fī al-qarn al-tāsiᶜ ᶜashar*, Cairo, 1910, vol. 2, p. 313ff.

17. Napoleon Bonaparte, *Campagne d'Egypte et de Syrie,* Paris, 1847, vol. 1, p. 119.

18. Jacques Tājir, *Aqbāṭ wa-muslimūn mundhu al-fatḥ al-ᶜarabī ilā ᶜāmm 1922,* Cairo, 1950, p. 213.

19. See bibliography in Atiya (cited n. 15), pp. 101ff.

20. Rudolf Strothmann, *Die koptische Kirche in der Neuzeit,* Tübingen, 1932, p. 19.

21. Jabartī (cited n. 12), vol. 3, p. 196.

22. E. L. Butcher, *The Story of the Church of Egypt,* London, 1897, vol. 2, p. 356.

23. Jabartī (cited n. 12), vol. 4, p. 309.

24. *Mu'tamar Miṣrī* (cited n. 3), pp. 83ff.

25. Butcher (cited n. 22), vol. 2, p. 367.

26. Lane (cited n. 2), p. 548.

27. Baer, *A History of Landownership in Modern Egypt,* London, 1960, pp. 63ff.

28. J. Bowring, *Report on Egypt and Candia,* London, 1840, pp. 44ff.

29. Ramzī Tādrus, *Al-aqbaṭ fī al-qarn al-ᶜishrīn,* Cairo, 1910–1911, vol. 2, pp. 48ff.

30. Yaᶜqūb Nakhla Rufayla, *Ta'rīkh al-umma al-qibṭiyya,* Cairo, 1898, pp. 305ff.; Manassā (Qummus), *Ta'rīkh al-kanīsa al-qibṭiyya,* Cairo, 1924, 660ff.; Iskārūs (cited n. 16), vol. 2, pp. 59ff.; B. Evetts, "Un prélat reformateur, le patriaque Cyril IV (1854–1861)," *Revue de l'Orient Chrétien,* 17 (1912), pp. 3ff; Strothmann (cited n. 20), pp. 24ff.

31. Muḥammad ᶜAlī had sent the Syrian Nīqūlā Masabjī to study printing in Italy in order to direct the Būlāq press. Albert Hourani, "The Syrians in Egypt in the Eighteenth and Nineteenth Centuries," in *Colloque internationale sur l'histoire du Caire,* Cairo, 1969, p. 225.

32. H. A. R. Gibb and H. Bowen, *Islamic Society and the West,* London, 1957, vol. 1, part 2, p. 252 notes.

33. Tājir (cited n. 18), p. 238.

34. Ibid., p. 255.

35. Lane (cited n. 2), p. 548.

36. Butcher (cited n. 22), vol. 2, pp. 379ff.; Tājir (cited n. 18), p. 236; Strothmann (cited n. 20), p. 28.

37. Paul Merruau, *L'Egypte contemporaine, de Mehmet Ali à Said Pacha,* Paris, 1858, p. 27.

38. Mīkhā'īl Shārūbīm, *Al-kāfī fī ta'rīkh miṣr al-qadīm wa-al-ḥadīth,* Cairo, 1900, vol. 4, pp. 130ff.

39. Manassā (cited n. 30), p. 717; Butcher (cited n. 22), vol. 2, p. 380.

40. Rufayla (cited n. 30), pp. 320ff.

41. Butcher (cited n. 22), vol. 2, p. 380ff.

42. Shārūbīm (cited n. 38), vol. 4, pp. 129ff.

43. Ibid., pp. 119ff.

44. W. Fowler, *Christian Egypt: Past, Present and Future,* London, 1901, pp. 132ff.

45. Shārūbīm (cited n. 38), vol. 4, pp. 119ff.

46. Strothmann (cited n. 20), p. 32.

47. Tādrus (cited n. 29), vol. 1, p. 171, vol. 2, pp. 52ff.; *Mu'tamar Qibṭī,* p. 2ff.; Fahmī Qalīnī, *Mudhākkirāt,* Cairo, 1932, p. 32.

48. Tājir (cited n. 18), pp. 242ff.

49. *Al-Waṭan,* March 22, 1879.

50. Charles Watson, *The American Mission in Egypt,* Pittsburgh, 1904, pp. 104ff.

51. Muḥammad Rashīd Riḍā, *Tar'ikh al-ustādh al-imām Muḥammad ᶜAbduh,* Cairo, 1908, vol. 2, p. 390.

52. Ibid., pp. 298ff.

53. Wilfred Scawen Blunt, *My Diaries: 1888–1914,* New York, 1921, p. 624.

54. Elie Kedourie, *Afghani and Abduh,* London, 1966, pp. 18ff.

55. ʿAbd al-Raḥmān al-Rāfiʿi, *ʿAṣr Ismāʿīl,* second edition, Cairo, 1948, vol. 2, p. 171.

56. ʿAbd al-Raḥmān al-Rāfiʿī, *Thawrat 1919,* Cairo, 1946, vol. 1, pp. 439ff.

57. Blunt, *Secret History of the English Occupation of Egypt,* 2d edition, London, 1907, pp. 153, 164, 169, 204, 327, 352.

58. Butcher (cited no. 22), vol. 2, pp. 390–391.

59. Shārūbīm (cited n. 38), vol. 4, p. 325.

60. Cromer, *Modern Egypt,* vol. 2, p. 324.

61. *Mir'āt al-Sharq,* No. 6.

62. *Al-Waṭan,* November 30, 1878.

63. Tādrus (cited n. 29), vol. 1, p. 181.

64. Lord Cromer, *Modern Egypt,* London, 1908, vol. 2, pp. 202ff.

65. Tādrus (cited n. 29), vol. 1, p. 173.

66. Ibrāhīm ʿAbduh, *Taṭawwur al-ṣaḥāfa al-miṣriyya: 1798–1951,* 2d edition, Cairo, 1951, pp. 151ff., 191.

67. Nadav Safran, *Egypt in Search of Political Community,* Cambridge, 1961, p. 87.

68. Fritz Steppat, "Nationalismus und Islam bei Mustafa Kamil," *Die Welt des Islam,* 4 (1956), p. 256.

69. Tājir (cited no. 18), p. 250.

70. Steppat (cited n. 68), p. 267.

71. *Al-Waṭan,* May 22, 1908.

72. Ibid., March 19, 1907, May 20, 1907; and *Al-Ahrām,* March 20, 1907.

73. *Al-Waṭan,* December 16, 1907.

74. *Al-Liwā',* June 2 and 4, 1908.

75. *Al-Waṭan,* June 5, 1908.

76. Ibid., June 15, 1908.

77. *Al-Liwā',* June 17, 1908.

78. *Al-Waṭan,* September 3, 1908.

79. The Dinshuwāy trial, in which the British punished an entire village—including several death penalties—for the death of a British soldier, was followed by an anti-British campaign led by the National Party. This campaign eventually resulted in Cromer's resignation.

80. Blunt (cited n. 53), p. 706.

81. *Al-Liwā',* November 17, 1908.

82. *Al-Waṭan,* June 1, 1910.

83. Kyriakos Michail, *Copts and Moslems under British Control,* London, 1911, pp. 36ff.

84. ʿAbd al-Raḥmān al-Rāfiʿī, *Muḥammad Farīd ramz al-ikhlāṣ wa-al-taḍḥiyya,* second edition, Cairo, 1948, p. 244.

85. Ibid., p. 253.

86. *Al-Waṭan,* June 27, 1911; *Miṣr,* February 28, 1911.

87. See report in *Mu'tamar Miṣrī* (cited n. 3).

88. *Al-Waṭan,* October 7, 1910.

89. *Mu'tamar Miṣrī* (cited n. 3).

90. Michail (cited n. 83), p. 73.

91. Cromer (cited n. 64), vol. 2, pp. 212ff.; *Al-Waṭan,* February 8, 1893, Murqus Simayka, "By a Coptic Layman," *Contemporary Review* 71 (1897), p. 741.

92. *Al-Waṭan,* February 7, 1908.

93. Muḥammad Sayyid Kaylānī, *Al-adab al-qibṭi qadīman wa-ḥadīthan,* Cairo, 1962, pp. 51ff.

94. Ibid., passim.

95. Jacob M. Landau, *Parliaments and Parties in Egypt,* Tel-Aviv, 1953, pp. 143ff.

96. Blunt (cited n. 53), p. 762.

97. Rāfi^{c}ī (cited n. 84), vol. 2, pp. 81ff.

98. Gerry Kampffmeyer, "Die agyptische Verfassung vom April 1923," *Westasiatische Studien,* Abteilung II, 16–27, Berlin, 1924, p. 17.

99. *Miṣr,* May 24, 1922.

100. *Al-Waṭan,* October 12, 1920.

101. Kaylānī (cited n. 93), p. 169.

102. Virginia Vacca, "Le minoranze religiose ed il projetto della nuova costituzione egitiana," *Oriente Moderno,* 2 (1922), p. 44.

103. ^{c}Abd al-Raḥmān al-Rāfi^{c}ī, *Fī a^{c}qāb al-thawra al-miṣriyya,* 2d edition, Cairo, 1957, vol. 1, p. 23.

104. Hourani (cited n. 31), p. 230.

105. See S. H. Leeder, *Modern Sons of the Pharaohs,* London, 1918.

106. *Al-Waṭan,* December 15, 1910.

107. Tādrus (cited no. 29), vol. 1, pp. 30ff.

108. Baer (cited n. 3), p. 97.

Bibliography

I. Medieval Islamic Background

Ahmad, Barakat, *Muhammad and the Jews,* New Delhi, 1979.

Anawati, Georges C., "Factors and Effects of Arabization and Islamization in Medieval Egypt and Syria," in S. Vryonis, ed. *Islam and Cultural Change in the Middle Ages,* Wiesbaden, 1975.

Cahen, Claude, *"Dhimma," EI²,* vol. 2, pp. 227–231.

———, *"Djizya," EI²,* vol. 2, pp. 554–567.

———, *Turcobyzantina et Oriens Christianus,* London, 1974.

Chehata, Chafik, *"Dhimma," EI²,* vol. 2, p. 231.

Dennett, Daniel C., *Conversion and the Poll Tax in Early Islam,* Cambridge, 1950.

Fattal, Antoine, *Le statut légal des non-Musulmanes en pays d'Islam,* Beirut, 1958.

Gabrieli, Francesco, "La tolleranza nell' Islam," in *Arabeschi e studi Islamici,* Naples, 1973, pp. 25–36.

Goitein, S. D., *A Mediterranean Society,* 3v., Los Angeles, 1967–

———, *Letters of Medieval Jewish Traders,* Princeton, 1973.

———, *Jews and Arabs: Their Contact through the Ages,* New York, 1974.

Meyendorff, John, "Byzantine Views of Islam," *Dumbarton Oaks Papers,* vol. 18 (1964), pp. 115–132.

Nagel, Tilman, et al., *Studien zum Minderheitenproblem in Islam,* vol. 1, Bonn, 1973.

Paret, Rudi, "Toleranz und Intoleranz in Islam," *Saeculum,* vol. 21 (1970), pp. 344–365.

Rosenthal, Erwin I. J., *Judaism and Islam,* London, 1961.

Stillman, Norman A., *The Jews of Arab Lands: A History and Source Book,* Philadelphia, 1979.

Strauss (Ashtor), Eli, "The Social Isolation of Ahl adh-Dhimma," *Essais orientales . . . à la mémoire du P. Hirschler,* Budapest, 1950, pp. 73–94.

Tritton, Arthur Stanley, *The Caliphs and their Non-Muslim Subjects,* London, 1970.

Vajda, Georges, *"Ahl al-Kitāb," EI²,* vol. 1, pp. 264–266.

von Grunebaum, Gustav E., "Eastern Jewry under Islam," *Viator,* vol. 2 (1971), pp. 365–371.

Zaydān, ᶜAbd al-Karīm, *Aḥkām al-Dhimmiyyīn wa al-Musta'minīn fī Dār al-Islām,* Baghdad, 1963.

II. Ottoman Relations with Christians and Jews

Barkan, Omer Lutfi, "Les deportations comme méthode de peuplement et de colonisation dans L'Empire ottoman," *IFM* (French version) vol. 11 (1949–1950), pp. 67–131.

Beldiceanu, Nicoara, *Le Monde Ottoman des Balkans (1402–1566),* London, 1976.

Binswanger, Karl, *Untersuchungen zum Status de Nicht-Muslime im osmanischen Reich des 16. Jahrhunderts, mit einer Neudefinition des Begriffes "Dimma",* Munich, 1977.

Cağatay, Neşet, "Osmanlı Imparatorluğunda Reayadan Alınan Vergi ve Resimler," *Ankara Üniversitesi, Dil, Tarih, Coğrafya Fakültesi Dergisi,* vol. 5 (1947), pp. 483–511.

Carleton, Alford, "The Millet System," Ph.D. Thesis, Hartford Seminary Foundation, Kennedy School of Missions, 1937.

Cohen, Amnon and Bernard Lewis, *Population and Revenue in the Towns of Palestine in the Sixteenth Century,* Princeton, 1978.

Davison, Roderic H., *Reform in the Ottoman Empire, 1856–1876,* Princeton, 1963.

———, "Turkish Attitudes Concerning Christian-Muslim Equality in the Nineteenth Century," *AHR,* vol. 59 (1953–1954), pp. 844–864.

Duda, Herbert W., *Balkantürkische Studien,* Vienna, 1949.

Evliya Çelebi, *Travels of Evliya Effendi,* tr., Joseph von Hammer-Purgstall, London, 1846.

Galabov, Galab D., and Herbert W. Duda, *Die Protokollbücher des Kadiamtes Sofia,* Munich, 1960.

Gibb, Hamilton A. R. and Harold Bowen, *Islamic Society and the West,* vol. 1, parts 1 and 2, London, 1962–1963.

Grignaschi, Mario, "La valeur du temoinage des sujets non-musulmans *(dhimmi),*" *Recueils de la Société Jean Bodin,* Brussels, 1963, pp. 211–323.

Haddad, William W. and William Ochsenwald, ed., *Nationalism in a Non-National State: The Dissolution of the Ottoman Empire,* Columbus, 1977.

Heyd, Uriel, *Ottoman Documents on Palestine, 1552–1615: A Study of the Firman According to the Mühimme Defteri,* Oxford, 1960.

Hurewitz, J. C., *The Middle East and North Africa in World Politics: A Documentary Record,* vol. 1, New Haven, 1975.

Inalcik, Halil, "Osmanlılarda Raiyyet Rüsumu," *Belleten,* vol. 23 (1959), pp. 575–610.

———, *The Ottoman Empire, the Classical Age 1300–1600,* London, 1973.

Jennings, Ronald C., "Women in Early 17th Century Ottoman Judicial Records—The Sharia Court of Anatolian Kaysari," *JESHO,* vol. 18 (1975), pp. 53–114.

Kabrda, Josef, "Les anciens registres des Cades de Sofia et de Vidin et leur importance pour l'histoire de la Bulgarie,'' *Archiv Orientalni,* vol. 19 (1951), pp. 329–392, 642–643.

Kunt, Metin Ibrahim, ''Ethnic-Regional *(Cins)* Solidarity in the Seventeenth-Century Ottoman Establishment,'' *IJMES,* vol. 5 (1974), pp. 233–239.

Lewis, Bernard, *Notes and Documents from the Turkish Archives,* Jerusalem, 1952.

Mantran, Robert, *Istanbul dans la seconde moitie du XVII siècle,* Paris, 1962.

———, and Jean Sauvaget, ed. and tr., *Les reglements fiscaux ottomans: les provinces syriennes,* Paris, 1951.

Ma^{c}oz, Moshe, *Ottoman Reform in Syria and Palestine,* Oxford, 1968.

Menage, V. L., ''Devshirme,'' EI^2, vol. 2, pp. 210–213.

Nedkov, Boris Khristov, *Die Gizya (Kopfsteuer) im osmanischer Reich. Mit besonderer Beruecksichtigung von Bulgarien,* Leipzig, 1942.

Shopova, Dushanka, *Makedonija vo XVI, XVII Vek Dokumenti od Carigradskite Arhivi,* Skopje, 1955.

Stavrianos, Leften S., *The Balkans since 1453,* New York, 1963.

Sugar, Peter F., *Southeastern Europe under Ottoman Rule, 1354–1804,* Seattle, 1977.

Todorov, Nikolai, *La Ville Balkanique sous les Ottomans (XVe–XIXe s.),* London, 1977.

Ubicini, J. H. Abodolnyme, and Paret de Courteille, *État présent de l'Empire ottoman: statistique, gouvernement, administration, finances, armée, communautes non-musulmanes. . . ,* Paris, 1876.

———, *La Turquie actuelle,* Paris, 1855.

———, Letters on Turkey: *An Account of the Religious, Political, Social and Commercial Conditions of the Ottoman Empire,* tr. Lady Easthope, 2v., London, 1856.

Wittek, Paul, ''Devshirme and Shari^{c}a'', *BSOAS,* vol. 17(1955).

Young, George, *Corps de droit ottoman,* 7v., Oxford, 1905, esp. vol. 2.

III. The Orthodox

Argenti, Philip P., *Diplomatic Archive of Chios 1577–1841,* 2v., Cambridge, England, 1954.

Arnakis, Georgiades, ''The Greek Church of Constantinople and the Ottoman Empire,'' *Journal of Modern History,* vol. 24 (1952), pp. 235–250.

Baggally, John Wortley, *The Klephtic Ballads in Relation to Greek History (1715–1821),* Oxford, 1936.

Baker, D., ed., *The Orthodox Churches and the West,* Oxford, 1976.

Birnbaum, Henri and Speros Vryonis, Jr., *Aspects of the Balkans: Continuity and Change,* The Hague, 1972.

Blancard, Théodore, *Les Mavroyeni: Histoire d'Orient (de 1700 à nos jours),* 2 v., Paris, 1909.

Bryer, A. A. M., *The Empire of Trebizond and the Pontos,* London, 1980.

Candea, Virgil, ''Les intellectuels du sud-est-europeen au XVIIe siècles,'' *Revue des études sud-est-europeen,* vol. 8 (1970), pp. 181–230, 623–668.

Chaconas, Stephen, *Adamantios Korais; a Study in Greek Nationalism,* New York, 1942.

Chassiotis, G., *L'Instruction publique chez les Grecs depuis la prise de Constantinople par les turcs jusqu'a nos jours,* Paris, 1881.

Clogg, Richard, ed., *Balkan Society in the Age of Greek Independence,* London, 1974.

———, tr., ''The Dhidaskalia Patriki (1798): An Orthodox Reaction to French Revolutionary Propaganda,'' *Middle Eastern Studies,* vol. 5 (1969), pp. 102–108.

———, ed., *The Movement for Greek Independence,* London, 1976.

Cobham, Claude D., *The Patriarchs of Constantinople,* Cambridge, 1911.

Crusius, Martin, *Turcograecia,* Basle, 1584.

Dakin, Douglas, *The Greek Struggle for Independence, 1832–1833,* London, 1973.

Dawkins, Richard M., *Modern Greek in Asia Minor,* Cambridge, England, 1916.

———, ''The Crypto-Christians of Turkey,'' *Byzantion,* vol. 8 (1933), pp. 247–275.

Doukas, *Decline and Fall of Byzantium to the Ottoman Turks,* tr. Harry J. Magoulias, Detroit, 1975.

Embiricos, Alexandre, *Vie et institutions du peuple grec sous la domination ottomane,* Paris, 1975.

Eyice, Semavi, ''Anadolu'da Karamanlica Kitabeler,'' *Belleten,* vol. 39 (1975), pp. 25–48.

Finlay, George, *The History of Greece Under Ottoman and Venetian Domination,* Edinburgh, 1856.

Gelzer, Heinrich, *Geistliches und Weltliches aus dem türkisch-griechischen Orient,* Leipzig, 1900.

Gennadios Scholarios, *Oeuvres complètes,* L. Petit, X. A. Sideris, M. Jugie, ed., 8v., Paris, 1928–1936.

Giese, Friedrich, ''Die geschichtlichen Grundlagen für die stellung der christlichen Untertanen im osmanischen Reich,'' *Der Islam,* vol. 19 (1931), pp. 264–277.

Gottwald, Joseph, ''Phanariotische Studien,'' *Leipziger Vierteljahrsschrift für Sudosteuropa,* vol. 5 (1941), pp. 1–58.

Hadjiantoniou, George A., *Protestant Patriarch: The Life of Cyril Lucaris 1572–1638, Patriarch of Constantinople,* Richmond, Va., 1961.

Hadjimichali, A., ''Aspects de l'organisation économique des grecs dans l'empire ottoman,'' *Le cinq-centieme Anniversaire de la Prise de Constantinople, 1453–1953, L'Hellénisme Contemporaine,* Athens, 1953, pp. 261–278.

Hadrovics, Laszlo, *Le peuple serbe et son église sous la domination turque,* Paris, 1947.

Hasluck, Frederick William, *Athos and Its Monasteries,* London, 1924.

Hellenism and the First Greek War of Liberation (1821–1830): Continuity and Change, Nikiferos P. Diamandouros, John P. Anton, John A. Petropulos, Peter Topping, ed. Salonica, 1976.

Henderson, G. P., *The Revival of Greek Thought, 1620–1830,* Edinburgh, 1971.

Hering, Gunnar, *Ökumenisches Patriarchat und europäische Politik, 1620–1638,* Wiesbaden, 1968.

———, "Das islamische Recht und die Investitur des Gennadios Scholarios, 1454," *Balkan Studies,* vol. 2 (1961), pp. 231–256.

Hill, George, *A History of Cyprus, IV: The Ottoman Province. The British Colony, 1571–1948,* Cambridge, England, 1952.

Inalcik, Halil, "The Policy of Mehmet II toward the Greek Population of Istanbul and the Byzantine Buildings of the City," *Dumbarton Oaks Papers,* vol. 23 (1970), pp. 213–249.

———, "Stefan Dušan'dan Osmanlı imparatorluğunda XV asırda Rumeli'de hıristiyan sipahiler ve menşeleri," *Fuad Köprulü Armağani,* Istanbul, 1953, pp. 207–248.

Jelavich, Charles and Barbara, ed., *The Balkans in Transition: Essays on the Development of Balkan Life and Politics since the Eighteenth Century,* Berkeley and Los Angeles, 1963.

Kabrda, Joseph, "Sur les bérats des métropolites orthodoxes dans l'ancien Empire ottoman au XVIIIe s.," *Izvestiia na bulg. Istorichesko pruzhestvo,* vols. 16–17 (1939), pp. 259–268.

———, "Les documents turcs relatifs aux impots ecclésiastiques prélevés sur la population bulgare au XVIIe s.," *Archiv Orientalni,* vol. 23 (1953), pp. 136–177.

———, *Le Systeme fiscal de l'Eglise orthodoxe dans l'Empire ottoman (d'après les documents turcs).* Brno, 1969.

Kritovoulos, *History of Mehmed the Conquerer,* tr. Charles T. Riggs, Princeton, 1954.

Layton, Evro, "Nikodemos Metaxas, the first Greek Printer in the Eastern World," *Harvard Library Bulletin,* vol. 15 (1967), pp. 140–167.

———, "The Modern Greek Collection in the Harvard College Library," *Harvard Library Bulletin,* vol. 19 (1971), pp. 221–243.

Leo, Michel, *La Bulgarie et son peuple sous la domination ottomane, tels que les ont vues les voyageurs anglo-saxons (1586–1878),* Sofia, 1949.

Llewellyn-Smith, M., *Ionian Vision. Greece in Asia Minor, 1919–1922,* London, 1973.

Markova, Zina and Vasil Gjuzelev, "Les racines historiques de la lutte des Bulgares pour une Eglise indépendant," *Bulgarian Historical Review,* vol. 2 (1974), pp. 28–39.

Mendelssohn-Bartholoy, Karl, *Geschichte Griechenlands von der Eroberung Konstantinopls durch die Türken im jahre 1453 bis auf unsere tage,* 2v., Leipzig, 1870–74.

Meyer, F., *Die Haupturkünden für die Geschichte der Athosklöster,* Leipzig, 1894.

Miklosich, Franz and Joseph Muller, ed., *Acta et diplomata graeca medii aevi sacra et profana,* 10v., Vienna, 1860–1890.

Neophytus Monk of Cyprus, *Annals of Palestine 1821–1841,* ed. S. N. Spyridon, Jerusalem, 1939.

Ostrogrosky, George, *History of the Byzantine State,* tr. Joan Hussey, New Brunswick, 1957.

Pallis, Alexandros A., *Greece's Anatolian Venture and After,* London, 1937.

Pantazopoulos, N. J., *Church and Law in the Balkan Pennisula during the Ottoman Rule,* Salonica, 1967.

Papadopoullos, Theodore, *Studies and Documents relating to the History of the Greek Church and People under Turkish Domination,* Brussels, 1952.

Papadopoulos, G., *Les Privilèges du Patriarcat oecuménique (communauté grecque orthodoxe) dans l'empire ottoman,* Paris, 1924.

Papadopoulos, Stelios, ed. *The Greek Merchant Marine, 1453–1850,* Athens, 1972.

Papoulia, Basilike, *Ursprung und Wesen der "Knabenlese" im osmanischen Reiche,* Munich, 1963.

Patrinelis, C., "Mehmed II the Conqueror and his Presumed Knowledge of Greek and Latin." *Viator, Medieval and Renaissance Studies,* vol. 2 (1971), pp. 349–354.

———, "The exact time of the first attempt of the Turks to seize the Churches and convert the Christian people of Constantinople to Islam," *Actes du Congres international des études balkaniques et sud-est-européenes,* vol. 3, pp. 567–572, Sofia, 1969.

Paul of Aleppo, *The Travels of Macarius, Patriarch of Antioch,* tr. Francis C. Belfour, 2v. London, 1836; Arabic original and French tr., Basile Radu, Paris, 1930.

Pernot, Hubert, ed. and tr., *Chansons populaires grecques des XV et XVI siècles,* Paris, 1931.

Petit, L., "Reglements generaux de l'église orthodoxe en Turquie," *Revue de l'Orient Chrétien,* vol. 3 (1898), pp. 405–424; vol. 4 (1899), pp. 227–246.

Pentzopoulos, Dimitri, *The Balkan Exchange of Minorities and its Impact upon Greece,* Paris, 1962.

Petropulos, John A., "The Compulsory Exchange of Populations: Greek-Turkish Peacemaking, 1922–1930," *Byzantine and Modern Greek Studies,* vol. 2 (1976), pp. 135–160.

Politis, A. G., *L'Hellénisme et l'Egypte Moderne,* 2v., Paris, 1929–1930.

Politis, Linos N., *A History of Modern Greek Literature,* Oxford, 1973.

Pollis, Adamantia K., "The Megali Idea: A Study of Greek Nationalism," Ph.D. thesis, Johns Hopkins University, 1958.

Rizos, P., ed., *Memoires du Prince Nicolas Soutzo, Grand-Logothète de Moldavie 1798–1871,* Vienna, 1899.

Rizos Neroulos, Iakōbos, *Histoire moderne de la Grèce depuis la chute de l'empire d'Orient,* Geneva, 1828.

Roberts, R., "The Greek Press at Constantinople in 1627 and its Antecedents," *The Library,* vol. 22 (1967), pp. 13–43.

Rozemond, Keetje, ed., *Cyrille Lucar Sermons, 1598–1602,* Leiden, 1974.

Runciman, Steven, *The Fall of Constantinople, 1453,* Cambridge, England, 1965.

———, *The Great Church in Captivity,* Cambridge, England, 1968.

Salaville, Sévérien and Eugène Dalleggio, *Karamanlidika, Bibliographie analytique d'ouvrages en langue turque imprimé en caractères grecs,* 3v, Athens, 1958–1974.

Sathas, Constantine N., ed., *Documents Inédits Rélatifs à l'histoire de la Grèce au moyen age,* 9v, Paris, 1880–1890.

Scheel, H., *Die staatsrechliche Stellung de okumenischen kirchen fursten in der altern Turkei. Ein Beitrag zur geschichte der Turkischen Verfassung und Verwaltung,* Berlin, 1943.

Simonescu, Dan, "Impression des livres arabes et karamanlis en Valachie et Moldavie au XVIIIe siècle," *Studia et Alta Orientalia,* vols. 5–6 (1967), pp. 48–75.

Stamatiadis, Epaminondas I., *Biographiai ton Ellenon Megalon Diermeneon tou Othomanikou Kratous,* Athens, 1865.

Stoianovich, Traian, "The Conquering Balkan Orthodox Merchant," *Journal of Economic History,* vol. 20 (1960), pp. 234–313.

Stourdza, Alexandre A. C., *L'Europe orientale et le role historique des Maurocordato, 1660–1830,* Paris, 1913.

Svoronos, N. G., *Le commerce de Salonique au xviiie siècle,* Paris, 1956.

Synvet, A., *Les Grecs de l'empire ottoman. Etude statistique et ethnographique,* 2nd rev. ed., Constantinople, 1878.

Tekindağ, Şahabettin, "Osmanli Idaresine Patrik ve Patrikhane," *Belgelerle Türk Tarih Dergisi,* vol. 1 (1967), pp. 52–55.

Topping, Peter, *Studies on Latin Greece A.D. 1205–1715,* London, 1977.

Ursul, George Richard, "The Greek Church in the English Travel Literature of the Nineteenth Century," Ph.D. thesis, Harvard University, 1966.

Vacalopoulos, Apostolos R., *The Greek Nation, 1453–1669: The Cultural and Economic Background of Modern Greek Society,* tr. Ian and Phania Moles, New Brunswick, 1976.

———, *A History of Thessaloniki,* tr. T.F. Carney, Salonica, 1963.

———, *History of Macedonia,* 1354–1833, tr. Peter Megann, Salonica, 1973.

———, *Origins of the Greek Nation: The Byzantine Period, 1204–1461,* tr. Ian Moles, New Brunswick, 1970.

Visvisis, J., "L'administration communales des Grecs pendant la domination turque," in *Le cinq-centieme anniversaire de la prise de Constantinople, 1453–1953. L'Hellénisme contemporain,* Athens, 1953, pp. 217–238.

Vryonis, Speros, Jr., *The Decline of Medieval Hellenism and the Process of Islamization from the Eleventh through the Fifteenth Century,* Berkeley, 1971.

———, "Religious Change and Continuity in the Balkans and Anatolia from the Fourteenth through the Sixteenth Century," in *Islam and Cultural Change in the Middle Ages,* Wiesbaden, 1975, pp. 127–140.

———, *Byzantium: Its Internal History and Relations with the Muslim World: Collected Studies,* London, 1971.

———, ed., *The "Past" in Medieval and Modern Greek Culture,* Malibu, Ca., 1978.

Vucinich, Wayne S., Stanford J. Shaw and Traian Stoianovich, "Discussion: The Nature of Balkan Society under Ottoman Rule . . ." *Slavic Review,* vol. 21 (1962), pp. 597–638.

Ware, Timothy, *Eustrathius Argenti: A Study of the Greek Church under Turkish Rule,* Oxford, 1964.

Zakythinos, Dionysius A., *The Making of Modern Greece,* Oxford, 1976.

Zallony, Marc-Philippe, *Essai sur les Fanariotes,* Marseille, 1824.

IV. Armenians

Arlen, Michael, *Passage to Ararat,* New York, 1975.

Arpee, Leon, *A Century of Armenian Protestantism, 1846–1946,* New York, 1946.

———, *A History of Armenian Christianity,* New York, 1946.

———, *The Armenian Awakening: History of the Armenian Church 1820–1860,* Chicago, 1909.

Artinian, Vartan, "A Study of the Historical Development of the Armenian Constitutional System in the Ottoman Empire, 1839–1863," Ph.D. thesis, Brandeis University, 1970.

Aslan, Kevork, *Armenian and the Armenians,* tr. Pierre Crabites, New York, 1926.

Bagün, Necla, *Türk Ermeni İlişkileri Abdülhamid'in cülusundan zamanımıza kadar,* Ankara, 1970.

Baliozlan, Ara, ed., *Armenia Observed,* New York, 1979.

Bardakjian, Kevork, *The Mekhitarist Contributions to Armenian Culture and Scholarship,* n.d., n.p., [Cambridge, 1976].

Basmadjian, K.J., *Histoire moderne des Arméniens, 1375–1916,* Paris, 1917.

Boutros,-Ghali, Anna Naguib, *Les Dadian,* Cairo, 1965.

Çark, Y.G., *Türk devleti hizmetinde Ermeniler 1453–1953* Istanbul, 1953.

Carzou, Jean Marie, *Un Genocide exemplaire; Armenie 1915,* Paris, 1975.

Chamchian, Michael, *History of Armenia,* tr. Johannes Avdall, 2v., Calcutta, 1827.

Cheraz, M., "L'Église arménienne, son histoire, ses croyances," *Le Museon,* vol. 16 (1897), pp. 232–242, 324–329.

Contenson, Ludovic Guy Marie du Bessey de, *Les Reformes en Turquie d'Asie; la question arménienne, la question syrienne,* 2nd ed., Paris, 1913.

Dadian, Prince Mek.-B. *La société arménienne contemporaine; les Arméniens de l'empire Ottoman,* Paris, 1867.

Daniel, R.L., "The Armenian Question and American-Turkish Relations, 1914–1927," *Mississippi Valley Historical Review,* vol. 46 (1959), pp. 252–275.

Davison, Roderic H., "The Armenian Crisis, 1912–1914," *AHR,* vol. 53 (1947–48), pp. 481–505.

Deliorman, Altan, *Turklere karşı Ermeni Komitecileri,* Istanbul, 1973.

Des Coursons, R. Vicomte, *La rébellion arménienne,* Paris, 1895.

De Serpos, Giovanni, *Compendio storico di memorie cronologiche concernenti la religione e la morale della nazione armena suddita dell'Impero ottomano,* Venice, 1786.

Dwights, H.G.O., *Christianity in Turkey: A Narrative of the Protestant Reformation in the Armenian Church,* London, 1854.

Dyer, Gwynne, "Turkish 'Falsifiers' and Armenian 'Deceivers': Historiography and the Armenian Massacres," *Middle Eastern Studies,* vol. 12 (1976), pp. 99–107.

Eroğlu, Veysel, *Ermeni mezâlimi,* Istanbul, 1973.

Etmekjian, James, *The French Influence on the Western Armenian Renaissance, 1843–1915,* New York, 1964.

Ferrier, R.W., "The Armenians and the East India Company in Persia in the Seventeenth and Early Eighteenth Centuries," *Economic History Review,* vol. 26 (1973), pp. 38–62.

———, "The Agreement of the East India Company with the Armenian Nation, 22nd June, 1688," *Revue des études arméniennes,* vol. 7 (1970), pp. 427–443.

Gidney, James, B., *A Mandate for Armenia,* [Kent, Ohio, 1967].

Great Britain, Foreign Office, *The Treatment of Armenians in the Ottoman Empire, 1915–1916: Documents Presented to Viscount Grey of Fallodon, Secretary of State for Foreign Affairs by Viscount Bryce,* ed., Arnold J. Toynbee, London 1916.

Gregorian, Vartan, "The Armenian Community of Isfahan, 1587–1722," *Iranian Studies*, 7(1974).

Grousset, Rene, *Histoire de l'Arménie,* Paris, 1947.

Hartunian, Abraham H., *Neither to Laugh nor to Weep: A Memoir of the Armenian Genocide,* Boston, 1968.

Hepworth, George Hughes, *Through Armenia on Horseback,* London, 1898.

Hornus, J.M., "Le Protestantisme au Proche-Orient: l'American Board en Turquie et le développement du protestantisme Arménien," *Proche Orient Chrétien,* vol. 8 (1958), pp. 37–68, 149–167.

Housepian, Marjorie, *Smyrna 1922: The Destruction of a City,* London, 1972.

Hovannisian, Richard G., *Armenia on the Road to Independence, 1918,* London, 1967.

Ivanescu, R.C., "Une épisode de l'histoire des Arméniens de Moldovie au XVIe siècle," *Studia et Acta Orientalia,* vol. 7 (1968), pp. 215–232.
Kerr, Stanley, E., *The Lions of Marash,* Albany, 1973.
Kinnier, MacDonald, *Journey through Asia Minor, Armenia, and Kurdistan,* London, 1818.
Koças, Sadi, *Tarih Boyunca Ermeniler ve Turk-Ermeni İlişkileri,* Ankara, 1967.
Kolandjian, "Les Arméniens en Transylvanie Xe-XVIIIe siècle," *Revue des études arméniennes,* vol. 4 (1967), pp. 355–376.
Kömürcüyan, Eremya Çelebi, *Eremya Çelebi Kömürcüyan, İstanbul Tarihi XVII. Asırda,* tr., Hrand Anreasyan, Istanbul, 1952.
———, *Eremya Chelebi Kömürjian's Armeno-Turkish Poem "The Jewish Bride,"* ed., Avedis K. Sanjian and Andreas Tietze, Weisbaden, 1981.
Korganoff, G., *La participation des Arméniens à la guerre mondiale sur le front du Caucase: 1914–1918,* Paris, 1927.
Krikorian, Mesrob K., *Armenians in the Service of the Ottoman Empire 1860–1908,* London, 1977.
Lang, David M., *Armenia Cradle of Civilization,* London, 1978.
Langlois, Victor, *Voyage dans la Cilicie et dans les montagnes du Taurus, exécuté pendant les années 1852–1853,* Paris, 1861.
Laurent, Joseph, *Etudes d'histoire arménienne,* Louvain, 1971.
Leart, Marcel, *La Question arménienne à la lumiere des documents,* Paris, 1913.
Lepsius, Johannes, *Le rapport secret du Dr. Johannes Lepsius president de la deutsche Orient-Mission et de la Société Germano-Arménienne sur les massacres d'Armenie,* Paris, 1918.
Lynch, H.F.B., Armenia: *Travels and Studies,* 2v., London, 1901.
MacFarlane, Charles, *The Armenians. A Tale of Constantinople,* 3v., London, 1830.
Macler, Frédéric, *Autour de l'Armenie,* Paris, 1917.
———, *Les Arméniens en Syrie et en Palestine,* Marseille, 1919.
Mécérian, J., *Histoire et institutions de l'Eglise arménienne,* Beirut, 1965.
———, "Un tableau de la diaspora arménienne—La situation des Arméniens de l'Empire Ottoman à la veille de la première guerre mondiale," *Proche Orient Chrétien,* vol. 8 (1958), pp. 340–366.
Mehmed-Zāde Mirzā Balā, *Ermeniler ve Iran,* Istanbul, 1927.
Mikirtitchian, L. "Was there an Armenian Renaissance?" *Caucasian Review,* vol. 5 (1957), pp. 26–33.
Morgan, Jacques de, *The History of the Armenian People,* tr. Ernest F. Barry, Boston, 1965.
Muyldermans, J., "Méchitar de Sébaste et le Méchitharistes," *Le Muséon,* vol. 43 (1930), pp. 117–132.
Nalbandian, Louise, *The Armenian Revolutionary Movement,* Berkeley, 1963.
Nersessian, Vrej, *An Index of Articles on Armenian Studies,* London, 1976.
———, *Catalogue of Early Armenian Books, 1512–1850,* London, 1980.
Ormanian, Maghak'ia, *The Church of Armenia,* tr. G. Marcar Gregory, ed.

Terenig Poladian, London, 1955.
Oscanyan, C., *The Sultan and his People,* New York, 1857.
Pastrmajian, H., *Histoire de l'Arménie depuis les origines jusqu'a traité de Lausanne,* Paris, 1949.
Premrou, Miroslav, ''Jermenska kolonija u Beogradu; istoriska skica spokumentima,'' *Srbska akademija nauka i umetnosti, Beograd, spomenik,* vol. 66, 2d. cl. book 52 (1926), pp. 213–224.
Rolin-Jaequemyns, Gustave, *Armenia, the Armenians and the Treaties,* London, 1891.
Rooy, S. Van, ''Armenian Merchants' Habits as Mirrored in 17–18th Century Amsterdam Documents,'' *Revue des études arméniennes,* vol. 3 (1966), pp. 327–357.
Sanjian, Avedis, ''Armenian Works on Historic and Modern Communities,'' in *Report on Current Research on the Middle East, 1958,* Washington, 1958, pp. 47–54.
———, *The Armenian Communities under Ottoman Dominion,* Cambridge, 1965.
———, ed. and tr., *Colophons of Armenian Manuscripts, 1301–1480,* Cambridge, 1969.
Sarkiss, Harry Jewell, ''The Armenian Renaissance, 1500–1863,'' *Journal of Modern History,* vol. 9 (1937), pp. 433–448.
Sarkissian, A.O., *History of the Armenian Question to 1885,* Urbana, 1938.
Siruni, D.H., ''Le spathaire Nicolae Milescu et son rôle dans les relations des Arméniens avec Pierre le Grand,'' *Studia et Acta Orientalia,* vol. 2 (1954), pp. 207–216.
———, ''Le role des Arméniens de l'Inde dans le mouvement d'émancipation du peuple arménien,'' *Studia et Acta Orientalia,* vols. 5–6 (1967), pp. 297–336.
Sonyel, Salahi R., ''Yeni Belgelerin Isıgı Altında Ermeni Tehcirleri - Armenian Deportations: A Re-appraisal in the Light of New Documents,'' *Belleten,* vol. 36, no. 141 (1972), pp. 31–64.
Ternon, Yves, *Les Armeniens: Histoire d'un Genocide,* Paris, 1977.
Torossian, Hrant, *Histoire de la Litterature arménienne des origins jusqu'a nos jours,* Paris, 1951.
Tozer, Henry F., *Turkish Armenia and Eastern Asia Minor,* London, 1881.
Tutundjian, Télémaque, *Du pacte politique entre l'État Ottoman et les nations non musulmanes de la Turquie; avec un exposé de la constitution arménienne de 1863,* Lausanne, 1904.
Uras, Esat, *Tarihte Ermeniler ve Ermeni Meselesi,* Ankara, 1950.
Vartoogian, Jack Lewis, ''The Image of Armenia in European Travel Accounts of the Seventeenth Century,'' Columbia, Ph.D., 1974.
Walker, Christopher, *Armenia, the Survival of a Nation,* London, 1980.
Zouche, Robert Curzon, *Armenia: A Year at Erzeroom, and on the Frontiers of Russia, Turkey and Persia,* New York, 1854.

V. Jews

Ankori, Zvi, "From *Zudecha* to *Yahudi Mahallesi:* The Jewish Quarter of Candia in the Seventeenth Century," *Baron Jubilee Volume,* vol. 1, Jerusalem, 1975, pp. 63–127.

———, "Jewish Life in Crete Under Muslim Rule as Reflected in the Ottoman Sicillāt," *Proceedings of the Twenty-Sixth International Congress of Orientalists, New Delhi, January 4–10, 1964,* Poona, India, 1970, vol. 4, pp. 193–198.

Annuaire des Juifs d'Égypte et du Proche Orient, Cairo, 1942.

Babinger, Franz, "Ja'qub Pascha, ein Leibartz Mehemeds II," *Rivista degli Studi Orientali,* vol. 26 (1951), pp. 87–113.

Bar-Asher, Shalom, Jacob Barnai, and Joseph Tobi, *History of the Jews in the Lands of Islam during Modern Times,* (in Hebrew) ed., Shmuel Ettinger, Jerusalem, 1981.

Baron, Salo, W., *A Social and Religious History of the Jews,* New York, 1937-present.

———, *The Jewish Community,* 3v., Philadelphia, 1942.

———, "The Jews and the Syrian Massacres of 1860," *Proceedings of the American Academy for Jewish Research,* vol. 4 (1932–1933), pp. 3–31.

Ben-Zvi, Itzhak, "Eretz Yisrael under Ottoman Rule, 1517–1917" in Louis Finkelstein, ed., *The Jews: their history, culture and religion,* New York, 1960, 3rd ed., vol. 1, pp. 602–689; also in L. Finkelstein, ed., *The Jews: Their History,* 4th ed., pp. 399–486.

———, *The Exiled and the Redeemed,* Philadelphia, 1957.

Berlin, Charles, "A Sixteenth Century Hebrew Chronicle of the Ottoman Empire: The *Seder Eliyahu Zuta* of Elijah Capsali and its Message," in Charles Berlin, ed., *Studies in Jewish Bibliography, History, and Literature in Honor of I. Edward Kiev,* New York, 1971, pp. 21–44.

Birnbaum, Eliezer, "Hekim Yaᶜqūb, Physician to Sultan Mehemmed the Conqueror," *The Hebrew Medical Journal,* vol. 1 (1961), pp. 222–250.

Cohen, Hayyim J., *The Jews of the Middle East,* 1860–1972, New York, 1973.

Danon, Abraham, "La communauté juive de salonique au XVIᵉ siècle," *REJ,* vol. 40 (1900), pp. 206–230; vol. 41 (1900), pp. 98–117, 250–265.

———, "Étude historique sur les impots directs et indirects des communautés Israélites en Turquie," *Revue des études juives,* vol. 31 (1895), pp. 52–61.

———, "Karaites in European Turkey," *JQR,* vol. 15 (1924–25), pp. 285–360; 17(1926–27), pp. 165–198, 239–322.

Emmanuel, Isaac Samuel, *Histoire de l'industrie des tissus des Israélites de Salonique,* Paris, 1935.

———, *Histoire des Israélites de Saloniques,* 2v. Paris, 1936.

Epstein, Mark Alan, *The Ottoman Jewish Communities and their Role in the Fifteenth and Sixteenth Centuries,* Freiburg im Breisgau, 1980.

Fargeon, Maurice, *Les Juifs en Egypte depuis les Origines jusqu'à ce Jour,* Cairo, 1938.

Franco, Moïse, *Essai sur l'histoire des Israélites de l'empire ottoman depuis les origines jusqu'à nos jours,* Paris, 1897.

Galanté, Abraham, *Documents officiels turcs concernant les Juifs de Turquie,* Istanbul, 1931.

———, *Don Joseph Nassi,* Istanbul, 1913.

———, *Don Salomon Aben Yaèche,* Istanbul, 1936.

———, *Esther Kyra,* Istanbul, 1926.

———, *Fatih Sultan Mehmed zamanında İstanbul yahudileri, Les juifs d'istanbul sous le sultan mehmed le conquerant,* Istanbul, 1953.

———, *Histoire des Juifs d'Anatolie,* 2v., Istanbul, 1937–1939.

———, *Histoire des Juifs d'Istanbul,* 2v., Istanbul, 1941–1942.

———, *Histoire des Juifs de Rhodes,* Chios, Cos. Istanbul, 1935.

———, *Hommes et choses Juifs Portugais en orient,* Istanbul, 1927.

———, *Médecins Juifs au service de la Turquie,* Istanbul, 1938.

———, *Turcs et Juifs,* Istanbul, 1932.

———, *Türkler ve Yahudiler,* Istanbul, 1947.

———, *Türkler ve Yahudiler eserlerime ek, appendice á mes ouvrages turcs et juifs,* Istanbul, 1954.

Gaon, Moshe David, *Yehudey Ha-mizraḥ Be-eretz Yisrael,* 2v., Jerusalem, 1928–1938.

Goldman, Israel M., *The Life and Times of Rabbi David Ibn Abi Zimra,* New York, 1970.

Goodblatt, Morris, S., *Jewish Life in Turkey in the XVIth Century as Reflected in the Legal Writings of Samuel de Medina,* New York, 1952.

Graetz, Heinrich, *History of the Jews,* vol. 4, Philadelphia, 1897, esp. pp. 593–630.

———, *Sefer Divrey Yemey Yisrael,* ed. S.P. Rabinovitz, vol. 6, Warsaw, 1898.

Grunebaum-Ballin, P., *Joseph Naci, duc de Naxos,* Paris, 1968.

Heyd, Uriel, "The Jewish Communities of Istanbul in the Seventeenth Century," *Oriens,* vol. 6 (1953), pp. 299–314.

———, "Moses Hamon, Chief Physician to Sultan Süleymān," *Oriens,* vol. 16 (1963), pp. 152–170.

Hyamson, A.M., *The British Consulate in Jerusalem (in relation to the Jews of Palestine, 1838–1915),* 2v., London, 1939–1942.

Landau, Jacob M., *Jews in Nineteenth Century Egypt,* New York, 1969.

Leveen, Jacob, "An Eye-witness account of the Expedition of the Florentines Against Chios in 1599," *BSOAS,* vol. 12 (1948), p. 553.

Lewis, Bernard, "The Privilege Granted by Mehmed II to His Physician," *BSOAS,* vol. 14 (1952), pp. 550–563.

Livingstone, John W., "Ali Bey al-Kabir and the Jews," *Middle Eastern Studies,* vol. 7, pp. 221–228.

Lowy, A., *The Jews of Constantinople: A Study of their Communal and Educational Status,* London, 1890.

Mann, Jacob, *Texts and Studies in Jewish History and Literature,* 2v, New York, 1972.
Mendelssohn, Sidney, *The Jews of Asia, Especially in the Sixteenth and Seventeenth Centuries,* London-New York, 1920.
Milano, Attilio, *Storia degli ebrei Italiani nel Levante,* Florence, 1949.
Nehama, Joseph, *Histoire des Israélites de Salonique,* 7v., Salonica, 1935–1977.
Rozanes, Salomon Abraham, *Divrey Yemey Yisrael Bitogarmah 'al-pi Meqorot Rishonim,* 6v. Vol. 1, Tel Aviv, 1930; vol. 2, Sofia, 1937–1938; vol. 3, Sofia, 1938; vol. 4, Sofia, 1934–1935; vol. 5, Sofia, 1937–1938; vol. 6, Jerusalem, 1945. Vols. 2–6 are entitled *Qorot Hayehudim Beturqiyah Veartsot Haqedem.* Vols. 2–5 include French title page, *Histoire des Israélites de Turquie (Turquie, Hongrie, Serbie, Bulgarie, Bosnie, Albanie et Grèce) et de l'Orient (Syrie, Palestine, Egypte, etc.).*
Sassoon, David S., *A History of the Jews in Baghdad,* Letchworth, 1949.
Scholem, Gershom, *Sabbatai Ṣevi,* Princeton, 1973.
Schwarzfuchs, Simon, "La Décadence de la Galilee juive du XVI siècle et la crise du textile du Proche-Orient," *Revue des études juives,* vol. 121 (1962), pp. 169–179.
———, "Les marchands juifs dans la méditerranée orientale au XVI siècle," *Annales,* vol. 12 (1957), pp. 112–118.
Tadić, Jorjo, *Jevreji u Dubrovniku du Polovine XVII Stolveća,* Sarajevo, 1937.
Taragan, Bension, *Les Communautés Israélites d'Alexandrie,* Alexandria, 1932.
Werblowsky, R.J.Z., *Joseph Karo: Lawyer and Mystic,* Oxford, 1962.

VI. Christians in Arabic-Speaking Lands, Roman Catholics, and General Works

Arberry, A.J., ed., *Religion in the Middle East,* 2v., Cambridge, England, 1976.
Argenti, Philip P., *The Religious Minorities of Chios: Jews and Roman Catholics,* Cambridge, England, 1970.
Atiya, Aziz S., *A History of Eastern Christianity,* London, 1968.
Attwater, Donald, *The Christian Churches of the East,* 2v., Milwaukee, 1948.
al-Bāshā, Qustantīn, *Muḥadāra fī Ta'rīkh Ṭā'ifat al Rum al-Kāthūlīk fī Miṣr,* Beirut, 1930.
———, *Ta'rīkh Ṭā'ifat al-Rūm al-Malakiyyan,* 2v, Sidon, 1938.
Behrens-Abouseif, Doris, Die Kopten in der agyptischen Gesellschaft von der Mitte des 19. Jahrhunderts, bis 1923, Freiburg im Breisgau, 1972.
Beth, Karl, *Die orientalische Christenheit der Mittelmelerländer. Reisestudien zur Statistik und Symbolik der griechischen, armenischen und koptischen Kirche,* Berlin, 1902.
Betts, Robert B., *Christians in the Arab East,* Atlanta, 1978.
Bliss, F.J., *The Religions of Modern Syria and Palestine,* New York, 1912.

Blunt, J. Elijah, *The People of Turkey: Twenty Years' Residence among Bulgarians, Albanians, Turks and Armenians,* London, 1878.

Boutros, Morcos, *Die westlichen Missionen in ihrer Begegnung mit der koptischen Kirche,* Hamburg, 1961.

Carayon, Auguste, *Relations inédites de la Compagnie de Jésus à Constantinople et dans le Levant au XVIIe s.*, Poitiers, 1864.

Catholic Church, Congregatio pro ecclesia orientali, *Oriente Cattolico: Cenni storici e statistiche,* Vatican City, 1962.

Denton, William, *Christianity in Turkey,* London, 1863.

Duker, Ivan, *Il cattolicesimo in Bulgaria nel sec. XVII secondo i processi informativi sulla nomina dei vescori cattolici,* Rome, 1937.

Evetts, B., "Un prélat réformateur, le patriarque Copte Cyrill IV (1854–1861)," *Revue de l'Orient chrétien,* vol. 17 (1912), pp. 3–15.

Famin, Cesar, *Histoire de la Rivalité et du Protectorat des Eglises chrétiennes en Orient,* Paris, 1853.

Farley, James Lewis, *Turks and Christians: A Solution of the Eastern Question,* London, 1876.

Fekete, L., "Turk devrinde Budin'de Latinler," *VI Türk Tarih Kongresi,* Ankara, 1967, pp. 274–280.

Fowler, M., *Christian Egypt: Past, Present, and Future,* London, 1901.

Haddad, Robert M., *Syrian Christians in Muslim Society,* Princeton, 1970.

Harik, Iliya, *Politics and Change in a Traditional Society, Lebanon, 1711–1845,* Princeton, 1968.

Hasluck, Frederick William, *Christianity and Islam under the Sultans,* 2v., Oxford, 1929.

———, *Letters on Religion and Folklore,* London, 1926.

Hasluck, Margaret, *The Unwritten Law in Albania,* ed. J. H. Hutton, Cambridge, England, 1954.

Heyworth-Dunne, J., "Education in Egypt and the Copts", *Bulletin de la société archeologique copte,* vol. 6 (1940).

Hilaire de Barenton, *La France catholique en Orient durant les trois derniers siècles d'aprés des documents inédits,* Paris, 1902.

Homsy, B., *Les capitulations et la protection des chrétiens au Proche-Orient aux XVIe XVIIe ss.,* Paris, 1956.

Hourani, Albert, *Minorities in the Arab World,* London, 1947.

———, "The Syrians in Egypt in the Eighteenth and Nineteenth Centuries," in *Collque international sur l'histoire du Caire,* Cairo, 1969.

Iskārūs, Tawfīq, *Nawābigh al-Aqbāṭ wa Mashāhiruhum fi al-Qarn al-Tāsi^c 'Ashar,* 2v., Cairo, 1910.

Jessup, H.H., *Fifty-Three Years in Syria,* 2v., New York, 1910.

Joseph, John, *Nestorians and Their Muslim Neighbors,* Princeton, 1961.

Khūri, Butrus, *Ta'rīkh al-risāla al-māruniȳya fī al-qaṭar al-maṣrī,* Cairo.

Kyriakos, Diomedes, A., *Geschichte der Orientalischen Kirchen von 1453–1898,* Erwin Rausch, tr. Leipzig, 1902.

La Croix, Sieur de, *État present des nations et églises Grecque, Arménienne et Maronite en Turquie,* Paris, 1695.

Leeder, S.H., *Modern Sons of the Pharoahs,* London, 1918.

Manassā (Qummus), *Ta'rīkh al-Kanīsa al-Qibṭiyya,* Cairo, 1924.

Ma^c^oz, M., ed., *Studies on Palestine during the Ottoman Period,* Jerusalem, 1973.

Michail, Kyriacos, *Copts and Moslems under British Control,* London, 1911.

Minqaryūs, Yūsuf, *Al-Qawl al-Yaqīn fī Mas'alat al-Aqbāṭ al-Orthūdhuksiyyīn,* Cairo, 1893.

Mordtmann, Andreas, *Anatolien, Skizzen und Reisebriefe aus Kleinasien (1850–1859).* Hanover, 1925.

———, *Stambul und das moderne Turkenthum,* 2v., Leipzig, 1877.

Na^c^ūm, Ephraem Isidor, *Al-Kharīda al-Nafīsa fī Ta'rīkh al-Kānisa,* 2v., Cairo, 1923.

Nešev, G., "La propagande catholique dans les terres bulgares au XVIIe siècle et le développement historique du Sud-Est européen," *Bulgarian Historical Review,* vol. 3, no. 3, pp. 43–52.

Pelikan, Jaroslav, *The Christian Tradition,* vol. 2: *The Spirit of Eastern Christendom (600–1700),* Chicago, 1974.

Rabbath, Antoine, ed., *Documents inédits pour servir à l'histoire du christianisme en orient,* Paris, 1905–1921.

Richards, Donald, "The Coptic Bureaucracy under the Mamlūks," *Colloque International sur l'histoire du Caire,* Cairo, 1969, pp. 373–381.

Rondot, Pierre, *Les Chrétiens d'Orient,* Paris, 1955.

———, "L'évolution historique des coptes d'Egypte," *Cahiers d'orient contemporain,* vol. 22 (1950).

Rufayla, Ya'qūb Nakhla, *Ta'rīkh al-Umma al-Qibṭiyya,* Cairo, 1898.

Rycaut, Paul, *The Present State of the Greek and Armenian Churches,* London, 1679.

Schopoff, A., *Les Réformes et la protection des Chrétiens en Turquie 1673–1904,* Paris, 1904.

Shaykhū, L. (Cheikho) "Aftimiyus Ṣayfī, Muṭrān Ṣaydā, Munshi al-Rahbāniyyat al-Mukhallisiyyat," *Al-Machriq,* vol. 14 (1911), pp. 647–648.

Sidarouss, Sésostris, *Des patriarcats. Les Patriarcats dans l'Empire ottoman et spécialement en Egypte,* Paris, 1906.

Silbernagl, Isidor, *Verkassung und Gegenwartiger Bestand sämtlicher Kirchen des Orients. Eine kanonstisch-statische Abhandlung,* 2nd ed., rev. by Joseph Schnitzer, Regensburg, 1904.

Skendi, Stavro, *Balkan Cultural Studies,* New York, 1980.

Slaars, Bonaventure F., *Étude sur Smyrne,* Paris, 1868.

Steen de Jehay, F., *De la situation légale des sujets ottomans non-musulmans,* Brussels, 1906.

Strothmann, Rudolf, *Die koptische Kirche in der Neuzeit,* Tubingen, 1932.

Tādrus, Ramzi, *Al-Aqbāṭ fī al-Qarn al* ᶜIshrīn, 4v., Cairo, 1910–1911.

Tājir, Jacques, *Aqbāṭ wa Muslimūn mundhu al-Fatḥ al-*ᶜArabī ilā ᶜAmm 1922, Cairo, 1951.

Touma, Toufic, *Paysans et Instiutions féodales chez les Druses et les Maronites du Liban du XVII*ᵉ *siècle à 1914,* Beirut, 1971.

Wakin, E., *A Lonely Minority,* New York, 1963.

Wittek, Paul, "Yazijioghlu 'Ali on the Christian Turks of the Dobrujua," *BSOAS,* vol. 14 (1962), pp. 639–688.

Wright, Arnold, *Twentieth Century Impressions of Egypt,* London, 1909.

Index